Re

A Primer

Joseph P. Martino

Also by Joseph P. Martino
The Justice Cooperative

In Memory of Patrick Henry

Table of Contents

Preface

According to Freedom Houses (www.freedomhouse.org), of 194 nations in the world, 47 nations, with a population of 2.3 billion people, are "not free." Residents of Those countries (one hesitates to call them "citizens") lack political freedom and civil rights. The oppressive governments in some or all of those countries deserve to be overthrown; peacefully if possible, by force if necessary.

If you live in such a country, and you're reading this book, I assume you're already thinking about the possibility of armed resistance to an oppressive government. This book is intended as a primer, not as a handbook or an encyclopedia. A handbook tells you what you realized you didn't know. It answers questions you knew enough to ask. This book is a primer. It's intended to introduce you to what you might not realize you don't know, and therefore wouldn't think to ask. It provides a basic introduction to each topic, then identifies resources which can provide you with additional information.

Most of the material will be presented in terms of general principles. To make the application of the principles more concrete, specific illustrations will be used. Many of these specific illustrations will be drawn from past revolutions. However, readers will need to adapt them to conditions in their own countries, or to their own circumstances. Readers must not allow the illustrations to mislead them into thinking the principles would apply only to the specific cases used as illustration. The principles apply everywhere; the application must take concrete circumstances into account.

As will become apparent to the reader, there is an enormous amount of information available on various aspects of armed resistance. Even the References at the ends of the chapters only scratch the surface. While this book is intended for information purposes only, information should eventually lead to action when action is justified. Readers must not allow themselves to be trapped in an information-gathering mode, seeking to learn ever more about ever-finer aspects of the topic. If armed resistance is justified, there comes a time when one must close the book and act.

i

Chapter 1

Why Armed Resistance?

The Biggest Killer

War was not the Twentieth Century's biggest killer. Tyranny was. The contest wasn't even close. Hard to believe? Look at the numbers.

Comparing the death toll

Professor Rudolph J. Rummel, of the Political Science Department, University of Hawaii, has made an extensive study of both wartime and peacetime deaths by government action during the Twentieth Century. His findings are summarized in the following table.

Persons Killed In The Twentieth Century, By Cause		
Cause	Total (Millions)	Average per 100,000 Population
Government Non-War (all)	119.4	349
Communist	95.2	477
Other non-free	20.3	495
Partially free	3.1	48
Free	.8	22
War (all)	35.7	22
International	29.7	17
Civil	6.0	26

"Government" killings include those persons killed by government officials, or with government acquiescence in the killing by others. Those categorized as government killings in the table specifically *exclude* execution for criminal acts (murder, rape, spying, treason, kidnapping, etc.). The government killings counted in the table also do not include those killed by police in riots or other conflict events, nor those killed in bombing of urban targets or through enemy siege or embargo. That is, those counted as government killings include only official terror, pogroms, genocide, and similar actions.

War deaths include those killed in any international or civil conflict (guerrilla war, rebellion, revolution, or terrorist campaign) that brought about more than 1000 deaths (thus excluding minor riots).

Professor Rummel's data are complete only up to 1990. The figures quoted in the table do not include war deaths in the former Yugoslavia, in Afghanistan and Iraq. Nor do they include the non-war but government-inspired massacres in Rwanda and in certain of the successor states of the former Soviet Union. Adding these numbers in, however, would not change the overall picture significantly.

While the figures in the table cannot be precise, especially for peacetime deaths in totalitarian countries, the results are so clear-cut that any likely errors do not change the overall picture.[1] Deaths at the hands of governments, in peacetime, totaled over three times as many as all war deaths in the same period. Moreover, the peacetime deaths presented in the table may be underestimates. For instance, Professor Rummel utilized the best figures available in the 1980s regarding deaths through government terror in Communist China, which came to about 60 million. More recent information indicates the toll may have been as many as 80 million. Hence the disparity between deaths through war and deaths through peacetime government action may be even greater than it appears from the table.

---

[1] The governments involved do not publish figures for these deaths. Rummel and other observers such as Cortois used multiple sources to make their estimates as good as possible. However, even if their estimates were off be as much as 50%, the main point is still valid. Tyranny caused far more deaths than did war.

Moreover, the contrast between free and unfree governments is also striking. The total for "free" governments includes at least 36,000 Algerians massacred by the French, and nearly 800,000 Soviet citizens, Prisoners Of War, and Russian exiles forcibly repatriated to the Soviet Union by US and British forces after World War II, and then executed by the Soviet government. Professor Rummel argues that these deaths should be charged against the free nations that acquiesced in the executions by carrying out the repatriations, rather than to the tyrannical government that actually carried out the executions. If these figures are excluded, the total for peacetime killings by free governments drops to nearly zero. The story told by the numbers, then, is that tyranny is far and away the biggest killer of the century. War is a distant second.

Gun Control and Genocide

But how were tyrannical governments able to carry out such massive killings? After all, government officials are always a tiny minority of the population. How were these officials able to kill many times their own number? Jay Simkin, Aaron Zelman and Alan M. Rice, writing for Jews for the Preservation of Firearms Ownership, offer a very simple answer: the victims were disarmed first. In their study, Mr. Simkin and his fellow researchers have specifically investigated the most significant cases of genocide since 1900, and determined the then-existing laws regarding ownership of firearms. A brief summary of their findings is as follows.

Turkey

The Turkish massacre of Armenians from 1915 - 1917, which resulted in some 1,150,000 deaths, was preceded by a gun control law imposed in 1911. That law completely banned the ownership, sale, or manufacture of guns, gunpowder, and explosive materials, except for those with government permission. Needless to say, the Armenians did not receive permission to own firearms and ammunition. Thus when mass deportations of Armenians were ordered by the Turkish government in 1915, the Armenians had no means of resisting.[2] Even the Armenians serving in the Turkish army were "disarmed, demobilized, and grouped into labor battalions." Moreover, each Armenian community was not only disarmed but also required to produce a specified number of weapons. If the community did not turn in the specified number, its leaders were arrested for secretly hoarding arms. If they did turn in the specified number, the leaders were arrested for conspiring against the government. The result was to remove the leadership of the Armenian communities, further reducing the possibility of resistance.

Soviet Union

The Bolsheviks imposed their first gun control laws in 1918, during the civil war. In August of 1918, a law was passed requiring registration of all firearms, ammunition, and sabers. Of course, gun registration is always followed by gun confiscation. The only reason for a government to register the firearms of honest people is to know where they are, so they can be confiscated later. The other shoe fell in October 1918, when the registration certificates were revoked and ownership of firearms banned. In 1922 the various gun control laws of the civil war era were incorporated into the Criminal Code. Unauthorized possession of a firearm was punishable by hard labor. By 1929, when Stalin began his various genocidal campaigns, the population was completely disarmed. Only the police and the army had any weapons. According to Professor Rummel, over fifty million people were killed in the resulting genocide. This number doesn't include those deported from the nations of Eastern Europe to Siberia after the Soviet occupation of those countries. At least 1.2 million Poles, and about 127,000 in total from Lithuania, Latvia, and Estonia were deported. Of these, a third to a half died on the way or in the labor camps. The total killings by the Soviets in Eastern Europe significantly exceeded those of the Nazis when they occupied the same territories.

---

[2] It must be recognized that the Turkish action against the Armenians was not totally unprovoked. Some Armenians did side with the Russians in their invasion of Turkey. However, this does not justify the massacre that followed.

4

Perhaps the most poignant statement of the situation of the unarmed people of the Soviet Union is that by Alexander Solzhenitsyn:

"How we burned in the prison camps later thinking: What would things have been like if every [Soviet] police operative, when he went out at night to make an arrest, had been uncertain whether he would return alive? . . . [I]f during periods of mass arrests people had not simply sat there in their lairs [apartments], paling with terror at every bang of the downstairs door and at every step on the staircase, but had understood they had nothing to lose and had boldly set up in the downstairs hall an ambush of half a dozen people with axes, hammers, pokers, or whatever else was at hand? . . . [T]he organs[3] would very quickly have suffered a shortage of officers . . . and notwithstanding all of Stalin's thirst, the cursed [Communist government] machine would have ground to a halt."

Solzhenitsyn's point is a good one. Had the Russian people been willing to resist, even with household tools, things might have been different. But wouldn't firearms have been better than axes, hammers and pokers? And wouldn't resistance have been more likely if the disparity in weapons between the people and the "organs" had been smaller?

Germany

The Weimar Republic, in 1919, confiscated all firearms. In 1928, the firearms ban was relaxed. A law was passed licensing firearms dealers, and establishing a system of permits to purchase firearms and ammunition. As a result of this law, the police had lists of everyone legally owning firearms (of course, criminals, Nazis and Communists didn't register their firearms). When Hitler came to power, these lists were used to disarm all opposition to the government, particularly Jews. The Nazi gun law of 1938 essentially banned all private ownership of firearms. However, it

---

[3] "Organs of state security," the former Soviet term for its secret police.

specifically exempted from its ban police and military units, the SA (Stormtroopers) and the SS (Blackshirts). That is, government officials and Nazi thugs were allowed weapons; no one else was. All possible opposition to the Nazis was disarmed.[4] Despite a significant degree of opposition to the Nazis among Germans[5], there was no effective resistance because of the lack of arms.

After World War II broke out, there was organized resistance to the Nazis in several occupied countries. Resistance forces included the Maquis in France, the Chetniks and Partisans in Yugoslavia, the Home Army in Poland and the ELAS in Greece, as well as smaller forces in Denmark and Norway. These resistance movements used arms retained from prior to the occupation or captured from the occupying Nazi forces, as well as arms supplied by British and U.S. airdrops. However, in the main they suffered from lack of arms. One British officer, air-dropped to a Maquis unit in France, reported:

> "The thirty men in the camp were disciplined, well fed and happy. Divided into groups of five each commanded by an NCO, all the armament they possessed between them consisted of one Sten gun with a hundred rounds, three French rifles with five rounds each and ten revolvers with ten rounds each; there were no grenades at all. The available arms were used by all in turn for instructional purposes, drill, weapon-stripping and field craft exercises by night. Lack of ammunition prevented target practice. (Marshall, quoted in Asprey (1975), p. 477).

---

[4] Those now possessing weapons and ammunition are at once to turn them over to the local police authority. Firearms and ammunition found in a Jew's possession will be forfeited to the government without compensation. ... Whoever willfully or negligently violates the provisions ... will be punished with imprisonment and a fine. In especially severe cases of deliberate violations, the punishment is imprisonment in a penitentiary for up to five years. -- German Minister of the Interior, Regulations Against Jews' Possession of Weapons", 11 November 1938
[5] For details see the book by Thomsett.

For all practical purposes, the nations occupied by the Nazis had already precluded effective resistance by disarming their own people.

A particularly significant instance of armed resistance to Nazi genocide took place in the Warsaw Ghetto in 1943, precisely because the Jews there had obtained a relative handful of weapons. For several weeks, the residents of the Ghetto held off a Nazi division, utilizing their initial supply of weapons, augmented by those captured during the fighting. Think how much better they could have done had they not been disarmed to start with.

Overall, some fifteen million people were killed by the Nazis because they had no means to resist.

Communist China

After their takeover in 1949, the Chinese Communists imposed a gun control law in 1957 that prohibited the unauthorized manufacture, purchase, or possession of firearms or ammunition. When the Red Guards began their government-sponsored campaign of terror in the 1960s, the people had no weapons with which to oppose them. The death toll was (as noted above) possibly as high as eighty million. Clearly if any significant fraction of those eighty million had been armed, most of them would have survived. The terror might not even have begun, if the Chinese government had recognized it faced an armed populace.

Uganda

In 1955, the British had passed a gun control law restricting firearms ownership. After Uganda achieved its independence, a slightly modified version of that law was passed in 1970. This law required a government license to purchase or possess firearms or ammunition. It also authorized the "chief licensing officer" of each district to deny or cancel licenses without cause and without appeal. Idi Amin seized power in 1971. He first purged the army of the followers of ousted President Obote. An army numbering no more than 25,000 men, supplemented by a secret police numbering 3,000, then killed some 300,000 Ugandans and oppressed a population of thirteen million. This was possible, despite the disparity in numbers, only because the population was disarmed. Clearly, if the 300,000

7

victims had been armed, they would have been able to defend themselves against an army only one-twelfth their numbers. If the population at large had been armed, they would have been able to defend themselves against the tyrants.

Cambodia

Cambodia holds the record for genocide as a fraction of the nation's population. More than a third of Cambodia's 7 million people were killed by the Khmer Rouge between 1975 and 1979. Gun control in Cambodia dated back to a 1938 Royal Order, which remained in effect after Cambodia achieved independence in 1953. The Khmer Rouge won the civil war that started in 1970, and seized power. After that, the Khmer Rouge administrators and troops would enter a village, and tell the villagers that they didn't need firearms any longer, since the troops were there to protect them. [6] When the few people who had licensed arms, and whatever number had unlicensed arms, surrendered their weapons, the Khmer Rouge then herded the villagers out of their homes into the "killing fields." A relative handful of Khmer Rouge troops found they could easily massacre large numbers of unarmed victims. If the Cambodians had been armed, the massacre would never have started, let alone reached the astonishing total it did.

Afghanistan

If gun control is the prelude to genocide, is an armed citizenry proof against genocide? Afghanistan provides one example to answer that question. Afghanistan is the genocide that didn't happen. The Afghan Penal Code of 1976 had only one article regarding firearms. That prohibited the knowing supply of firearms to criminals. Other than that, the possession of firearms and ammunition was completely unrestricted.

The Soviet invasion of Afghanistan, in 1979, could have resulted in the same kind of genocide that had been visited on Eastern Europe after it was occupied by the Soviets. It didn't, because the Afghans were armed to the teeth. No, they didn't have

---

[6] The Cambodian version of "I'm from the government, and I'm here to help you."

tanks, cannons, and missiles, but they had rifles. These were enough. The rifles allowed the Afghans to hold out until the U.S. and its allies, shamed by the Afghan resistance, finally supplied them with weapons capable of dealing with tanks and helicopters. Not only was genocide prevented, the Afghans maintained their independence from the Soviet Union.

The evidence is clear. Genocide is impossible when the victims are armed and able to resist. Disarming the population is always the first step to genocide. Gun registration is always the first step to gun confiscation. Moreover, the experience of Germany and Cambodia shows that the government that does the disarming may not be the government that commits the genocide. Once a "decent" government has disarmed the people, on whatever pretext, the way is open for a tyrannical government to oppress them. The Hitlers and the Pol Pots succeed only because the people have previously been disarmed.

The emphasis on genocide should not be allowed to obscure an important point, however. While tyranny is history's biggest killer, that's not the only mark against it. Even if you survive under tyranny, you lose your freedom. Freedom is ultimately the most important thing. No matter what your personal or political objectives are, from animal rights to vegetarianism, you can't accomplish them if you lose your freedom. Freedom is the prerequisite for any other economic, political or social activity, from rearing your children to holding a job to providing for your own spiritual welfare.

As Joseph Story wrote, "One of the ordinary modes, by which tyrants accomplish their purposes without resistance, is by disarming the people, and making it an offense to keep arms." History bears him out.

Even though loss of freedom is the most important long-term consideration, nevertheless, tyranny's threat to life is the most immediate concern. As Augustine, Bishop of Hippo, wrote in the Fifth Century about the *Pax Romana*: "Peace and war had a contest in cruelty and peace won the prize." He might well have been

9

writing about the Twentieth Century. What, then, should you do when faced with a tyrannical government?

America's Founding Fathers On Armed Resistance

The people who founded the American Republic had very definite views on how to deal with a tyrannical government. Thomas Jefferson was very blunt about it:

> The strongest reason for the people to retain the right to keep and bear arms is, as a last resort, to protect themselves against tyranny in government.

Alexander Hamilton, although one of the firmest advocates of a strong central government among the founding fathers, still said: "The best we can hope for concerning the people at large is that they be properly armed."

Hamilton also said:

> "If the representatives of the people betray their constituents, there is then no resource left but in the exertion of that original right of self-defense which is paramount to all positive forms of government."
> (Federalist No. 28)

Thomas Jefferson also said:

> The Constitution of most of our states (and of the United States) asserts that all power is inherent in the people; that they may exercise it by themselves; that it is their right and duty to be at all times armed; that they are entitled to freedom of person, freedom of religion, freedom of property and freedom of the press."

That is, Jefferson is saying that governmental power originates in the people, not in the government. When it comes to the people versus the government, it is the government that must give way, and the people not only may but must be armed in order to keep the government under control. Moreover, note that Jefferson ranks the right to keep and bear arms right up there with freedom of religion, freedom of the press, and the right to own property.

George Washington, who certainly understood how to prevent tyranny, said:

> "Firearms stand next to the constitution itself. They are the American people's liberty teeth and keystone under independence. To ensure peace, security, and happiness, the rifle and pistol are equally indispensable. The very atmosphere of firearms everywhere restrains evil interference -- they deserve a place of honor with all that is good."

What did these men see as the proper role of government? The best answer is to be found in the Declaration of Independence:

> "We hold these truths to be self-evident, that all men are created equal, that they are endowed by their Creator with certain unalienable Rights, that among these are Life, Liberty and the pursuit of Happiness. -- *That to secure these rights, Governments are instituted among Men, deriving their just powers from the consent of the governed.*" (Emphasis added)

That is, governments are established by the people, not people by governments. Governments are not to run people's lives for them, but instead are to protect the people in the peaceful conduct of their lives.

This idea is not unique to the American Founders. C. S. Lewis, the famous British writer, observed that:

> "The State exists simply to promote and to protect the ordinary happiness of human beings in this life. A husband and wife chatting over a fire, a couple of friends having a game of darts in a pub, a man reading a book in his own room or digging in his own garden -- that is what the State is there for. And unless they are helping to increase and prolong and protect such moments, all the laws, parliaments,

armies, courts, police, economics, etc., are simply a waste of time." (Lewis p. 169)

St. Augustine looked at the issue from the reverse standpoint, not of what a government is for, but how to regard it when it fails in its duties. In the *City of God*, he tells of a pirate who was brought before Alexander the Great and asked how he dared rob ships. The pirate replied that he stole from a small area, and was called a pirate; Alexander looted the whole world and was called Emperor. Augustine went on to say that without justice, a government is nothing but a band of robbers.

What, then, when the State fails to carry out its duty to protect the daily lives and activities of its citizens, or worse yet, actively hinders or opposes those activities and becomes a band of robbers? The Declaration of Independence goes on to say:

> "That whenever any Form of Government becomes destructive of these ends, it is the Right of the People to alter or to abolish it, and to institute new Government, laying its foundation on such principles and organizing its powers in such form, as to them shall seem most likely to effect their Safety and Happiness."

This idea was not something limited to the founding generation of Americans. Abraham Lincoln offered a similar view:

> "This country, with its institutions, belongs to the people who inhabit it. Whenever they shall grow weary of the existing government they can exercise their constitutional right of amending it, or their revolutionary right to dismember or overthrow it."

This view didn't end with Lincoln. In 1912, Woodrow Wilson wrote:

> "Liberty has never come from the government. Liberty has always come from the subjects of it. The history of liberty is a history of resistance."

The late Senator Hubert Humphrey, a liberal Democrat, had this to say about armed citizens:

> "Certainly one of the chief guarantees of freedom under any government, no matter how popular and respected, is the right of the citizens to keep and bear arms. This is not to say that firearms should not be carefully used and that definite safety rules of precaution should not be taught and enforced. *But the right of the citizens to bear arms is just one guarantee against arbitrary government and one more safeguard against a tyranny which now appears remote in America, but which historically has proved to be always possible.*" (Emphasis added)

The view of a long line of Americans, then, is that government exists solely to protect the ordinary lives of its citizens. It does not exist for reasons of its own. When it fails to protect the ordinary lives of its citizens they have the right to get rid of it and establish one that will protect them.

But, it might be asked, what have these American views to do with the rest of the world? What about the victims or potential victims of tyranny in other countries? What about your country? The point is a simple one. These Americans were not basing their remarks on something unique to America. They took it for granted that the rights and freedoms they wished for Americans were the natural endowments of people everywhere. As Benjamin Franklin said, "[I]t is a common observation here that our cause is the cause of all mankind, and that we are fighting for their liberty in defending our own."

In declaring American independence of England, Jefferson and Washington were not demanding some kind of special treatment. Their argument was precisely that England had violated rights which pre-existed all governments, and "came with the territory" of being human. Thus their arguments do not depend on anything peculiar to American history. Their arguments were intended to apply to America a general principle that they believed was true for all peoples in all places. As John Adams, second President of the United States put it,

> "You have rights antecedent to all earthly governments; rights that cannot be repealed or restrained by human laws; rights derived from the great Legislator of the Universe."

In Adams's view, these rights weren't something possessed only by Americans, but by all people everywhere.

Indeed, the ideas expressed by America's founders have a long and honorable history. Aristotle voiced the same sentiments as Jefferson and Washington when he wrote: "Both Oligarch and tyrant mistrust the people, and therefore deprive them of their arms." (*Politics*, Chapter 10, para. 4)

John Locke wrote, "Whenever the legislators endeavor to take away and destroy the property of the people, or to reduce them to slavery under arbitrary power, they put themselves into a state of war with the people, who are thereupon absolved from any further obedience."

As if to make the point indelibly clear, the Shogun Toyotomi Hideyoshi (1536-1598) issued this edict on the eighth day of the seventh month, Tensho 16: "The people of the various provinces are strictly forbidden to have in their possession any swords, short swords, bows, spears, firearms, or other types of arms. *The possession of unnecessary implements makes difficult the collection of taxes and tends to foment rebellion.*" (emphasis added) (Quoted in Suprynowicz, p. 327-328) One could hardly ask for a more definitive statement of why governments want their subjects to be disarmed.

In more recent times, M. K. Ghandi wrote:

"Among the many misdeeds of the British rule in India, history will look upon the act of depriving a whole nation of arms, as the blackest." (p. 446)[7]

George Orwell also wrote on the importance of an armed citizenry:

> The totalitarian states can do great things, but there is one thing they cannot do: they cannot give the factory-worker a rifle and tell him to take it home and keep it in his bedroom. That rifle hanging on the wall of the working-class flat or labourer's (sic) cottage, is the symbol of democracy. It is our job to see that it stays there.[8]

The French have a witticism: *Cet animal est très méchant; quand on l'attaque, il se défend* (This animal is very wicked; when you attack it, it defends itself). From the standpoint of a tyrannical government, defending yourself against it is wicked. From the standpoint of the victim of tyranny, however, it is the tyranny itself that is wicked. You have every right to defend yourself against tyranny, up to and including armed resistance. This also implies you have a right to what Washington called "liberty's teeth," namely weapons.

But how is that right to defense against tyranny justified, and when can it be exercised? When is actual armed resistance moral?

---

[7] This quotation may shock those who look upon Ghandi as the "patron saint of pacifism." However, "passive resistance" was a very realistic position on Ghandi's part. Had he called for open revolt, the unarmed Indians would have been slaughtered. Ghandi's only hope was to call upon the good will of the English people. The quote can also be found at http://www.mahatma.org.in/books/showbook.jsp?id=384&link=bg&book=bg0001&lang=en

[8] By implication, any government that does not trust its citizens with firearms is already a tyranny, or is planning to become one.

The Morality Of Armed Resistance

Is there a moral justification for armed resistance? Are there any guidelines to help the victim of tyranny decide where to draw the line in the sand?

Over the last 15 centuries, the Western world's ethical thought on the legitimate use of force has been codified in what is known as the Just War Doctrine. Although this Doctrine has been developed for the most part by Christian religious thinkers, it in no way depends upon any specifically Christian foundation or revelation. Similar conclusions have been reached by commentators from Judaism and Islam, and even by natural-law scholars arguing from a completely non-theistic starting point. However, since most of the writing on Just War Doctrine has been by Christians in the West, this discussion will be based upon the Doctrine as it has been developed by Christian commentators.

The Just War Doctrine is customarily divided into two parts, the first dealing with when war itself is justified, the second dealing with what actions are justifiable in war. That is, would-be belligerents must first justify the war itself, then limit their conduct to just actions within the war.

According to the Just War Doctrine, recourse to war is permissible if the following requirements are met:

- Just cause;
- Comparative justice;
- Right intention;
- Last resort;
- Probability of success;
- Proportionality; and
- Competent authority.

To be permissible in war, conduct must satisfy the following requirements:

- Discrimination; and
- Proportionality (again).

These requirements are primarily intended to apply to wars between nations. However, since they represent the results of a great deal of thinking about the ethical issues involved in use of force, they can be used as a guide to armed resistance as well as to international war. Let's look at each in turn, to see how it applies to armed resistance.

Just Cause simply means that there must be some serious and morally justifiable reason for going to war. Traditionally, Just War scholars recognized three types of just cause: to repel an attack; to retake what has been unjustly taken; and to vindicate justice on behalf of a victim of unjust attack. Clearly the first of these is the most relevant with regard to armed resistance to one's own government. In international war, the "attack" being repelled must be an armed attack of some sort. However, governments have ways of attacking their own citizens which only indirectly depend on the government's coercive power, such as seizure or forfeiture of assets, conviction of "crime," assessment of fines for "violating regulations," harassment by tax collectors or environmental regulators, and withdrawal of a license to practice a profession or trade. Widespread use of such measures against opponents of the government could well be looked upon as an attack justifying armed resistance. As Thomas Jefferson put it in the Declaration of Independence,

> [W]hen a long train of abuses and usurpations, pursuing invariably the same object, evinces a design to reduce them under absolute despotism, it is their right, it is their duty, to throw off such government, and to provide new guards for their future security.

Hence victims of oppression need not wait for their government to initiate an armed attack against them. A just cause exists if the government is systematically using its legal apparatus, on a massive scale, to oppress them.

A statement by Patrick Henry is particularly apt here:

17

"Guard with jealous attention the public liberty. Suspect everyone who approaches that jewel. Unfortunately, nothing will preserve it but downright force. Whenever you give up that force, you are ruined."

Henry St. George Tucker gave the same warning when he wrote:

"The right of self-defense is the first law of nature; in most governments it has been the study of rulers to confine this right within the narrowest limits possible. Wherever standing armies are kept up, and when the right of the people to keep and bear arms is, under any color or pretext whatsoever, prohibited, liberty, if not already annihilated, is on the brink of destruction." (quoted in Blackstone's 1768 *Commentaries on the Laws of England.*)

The point here is that whenever a government attempts to disarm its citizens, a *prima facie* case exists that Just Cause is satisfied. The experience of genocide in the Twentieth Century, outlined above, is adequate justification for citizens faced with disarmament to ask, "Just what are you planning to do to us that you're so eager to disarm us first?" And remember, even if the government that disarms its citizens is a benign one, the examples of Adolph Hitler and Pol Pot should warn us that the next government might not be benign.

There may not be a government action as drastic as an "out of the blue" gun ban. The government may impose its totalitarian rule gradually. Henry May wrote, regarding the Nazi "tightening of the screws" in Germany:

Each act, each occasion, is worse than the last, but only a little worse. You wait for the next and the next. You wait for the one great shocking occasion, thinking that others, when such a shock comes, will join with you in resisting somehow. . . . In between come all the hundreds of little steps, some of them imperceptible, each of them preparing you not to be shocked by the next. . . . And one day, too late, your principles, if you were ever sensible of them, all rush in upon you. The burden of self deception has grown too heavy. (quoted in Taylor)

Thus you may find that "drawing the line" becomes very difficult. The government's most recent step is too small a step beyond the previous one to get excited about. This process must be recognized early on, as "Just Cause."

Comparative Justice means that the party considering the use of force must be comparatively more just than the party against which force is to be used. If it's merely a case of one set of thugs trying to replace another set of thugs, the Comparative Justice criterion isn't satisfied. Robbers or murderers cannot justly claim they are "repelling an attack" when the police of even a tyrannical government go after them. Even a tyrannical government has the right and duty to suppress genuine crime. As applied to armed resistance, then, Comparative Justice means that pirates or brigands, or those who merely want to replace the current oppressive government with their own brand of oppression, fail this criterion. This criterion can be satisfied only by honest citizens whose rights are being violated by their government, and who intend to restore or establish a government which will respect those rights.

Right intention means the would-be belligerent must be seeking a just peace, not revenge or loot. In particular, the intentions of the would-be belligerent must not go beyond achieving the just cause that provides the reason for the resistance. Anything that would create bitterness or sow the seeds of further conflict must be excluded from the would-be resister's intention. This doesn't mean that such things can't happen, but they must not be intended. In the case of armed resistance, right intention might include restoration of a constitution, or returning to power a legitimate ruler who was unjustly deposed. Vengeance or "settling scores" must not be part of the resister's intention. Note, however, this does not rule out an intention to give fair trials to those agents of the government who are accused of specific acts of oppression.

Unfortunately, meeting this requirement in armed resistance is difficult. Liddel Hart says of the guerilla warfare instituted by the Allies in World War II:

> The material damage that the guerillas produced directly, and indirectly in the course of reprisals, caused much suffering among their own people and ultimately became a handicap to recovery after the liberation.

> But the heaviest handicap of all, and the most lasting one, was of a moral kind. The armed resistance movement attracted many 'bad hats.' It gave them license to indulge their vices and work off their grudges under the cloak of patriotism. . . Worse still was its wider effect on the younger generation as a whole. It taught them to defy authority and break the rules of civic morality in the fight against the occupying forces. This left a disrespect for 'law and order' that inevitably continued after the invaders had gone.

In the same vein, Archbishop Jean-Louis Tauran, Vatican Secretary for Relations with States (equivalent to Foreign Minister), stated "Whenever men are forced to take up arms in order to defend their rights, the logic of violence takes over, and that is always dangerous for mankind." (Interview with Guenois)

As Simon Weil said:

> It is not the cause for which men took up arms that makes a victory more just or less, it is the order that is established when arms have been laid down.

A just victory, then, must result in setting up a just order, or at least one more just than the one against which the Resistance fought.

This consideration puts an immense burden on the leaders of the armed resistance. They must try to assure that their fight is *not* providing a cover for brigandage or private vengeance. It is crucial that the leaders instill and maintain discipline among their subordinate forces. More will be said about this in Chapter 20 on justifying the armed resistance to the public at large.

Last Resort means that all reasonable peaceful means must be exhausted before the would-be belligerent is justified in resorting to force. In the case of wars between nations, peaceful means might include seeking mediation through a third party, appealing to the United Nations, or taking the case to the World Court. Such means must have been exhausted before a resort to force is justified. In the case of armed resistance in a democratic country this criterion would mean that election campaigns, lawsuits, petitioning, lobbying, protest marches, strikes, and other recognized forms of legitimate protest must have been tried without success, or have been made illegal by the government, before armed resistance is justified. However, this doesn't mean that the victims of oppression must go through the motions of trying to unseat locked-in incumbents in fraudulent elections, appealing to corrupt judges, or lobbying legislators who pay them no attention, all the while the government is taking away their means of armed resistance. If the means of armed resistance are being taken away, then the time of "last resort" has arrived. In the case of countries with authoritarian or totalitarian governments, the range of "peaceful means" might be much more limited. Even resort to a strike might bring almost as much retaliation from the government as would armed resistance itself. In such cases, because the government has limited the peaceful options of the population, this criterion is much easier to satisfy. In any case, once a government has effectively begun war against its citizens, "last resort" has been satisfied.

Probability of Success means the would-be belligerent must have some reasonable hope of winning, i.e., of achieving the Just Cause that provides the reason for resistance. In war there are no absolute guarantees. Everyone who takes up arms thinks he has a chance of winning, otherwise he'd try something else instead. This criterion simply means that the persons contemplating armed resistance must have some objective reason to believe that they can prevail. Certainty isn't required, but a "good chance" is. Otherwise they are spilling blood in vain, which would be immoral. If an opponent initiates an armed attack, however, this criterion is satisfied no matter how poor the chances of success. Resistance against overwhelming odds can still be a "witness" to a Just Cause. No one, for instance, argues that the defenders of the Alamo should have surrendered simply because they couldn't win. The same applies to the victims of oppression even when the odds are against them. The Jews in the Warsaw Ghetto were justified in resisting the Nazis in 1943, even though they were unlikely to win, because they knew they'd be sent to a death camp anyway.

Proportionality, in considering whether to initiate use of force, means that the would-be belligerent must compare the unavoidable damage that will be done by the war with the damage that will result if no resistance is offered. The harm done by the war must not outweigh the good to be achieved and the harm averted by the war, i.e., it must be proportional. In comparing the damage to be done with the good achieved and damage averted, however, the would-be belligerent must look beyond merely physical damage. Protection of human rights, preservation of liberty, and restoration of justice are sufficient to offset a great deal of physical damage and human suffering, because the violation of rights in the long run will itself cause an enormous amount of suffering. In the case of armed resistance, the would-be resisters must evaluate whether their Just Cause is worth the damage and suffering which will inevitably follow that resistance. In making that evaluation, they just give proper weight to the harm done by the existence of an oppressive government, and the warping of human existence brought about by lack of freedom.

Competent authority, in the case of international war, means that war must be declared by some public authority with the legal or constitutional power to do so. Just War scholars would condemn as unjust a war in which the ruler violated his own government's constitutional processes in order to go to war. In the case of armed resistance, however, Just War scholars have not given much helpful guidance. Who has the authority to call the people to revolt? Obviously no one can have such a legal or constitutional power. In a nation with a federal system of government, the governor of an individual state might reasonably be held to have the power to call the people to arms to resist an unjust act by the central government.[9] Even in nations without a federal system, or even if a state governor fails to call for resistance to oppression by the central government, the people themselves retain the right to overthrow an oppressive government. Armed resistance is justified by the belief that lawful power originates in the people, not in the government, and the people have a right to resist a government that exceeds its lawful authority.

Jonathan Mayhew, in *Discourse Concerning Unlimited Submission and Non-Resistance to the Higher Powers*, wrote

> To say that subjects in general are not proper judges of when their governors oppress them and play the tyrant, and when they defend their rights, administer justice impartially, and promote the public welfare, is as great a treason as man ever uttered . . . The people know for what end they set up and maintain their governors. (quoted in Churchill, p. 31.)

Thomas Jefferson, in the Declaration of Independence, wrote

> That whenever any Form of Government becomes destructive of these ends, it is the Right of the People to alter or abolish it, and to institute new Government in such form, as to them shall seem most likely to effect their Safety and Happiness. (quoted in Churchill, p. 173)

In short, the people themselves are their own "competent authority" to judge when Resistance is justified.

Ultimately, individuals may have to "draw a line in the sand" for themselves, and resist when the government crosses that line. Such individuals may set an example for others to follow, or may actually take a leadership role in organizing resistance, attracting followers, and elaborating the "just cause" rationale for the

---

[9] In 1932, the governor of the state of Sao Paulo in Brazil unsuccessfully attempted to declare independence from Brazil, after Getulio Vargas seized the national government in a *coup*. The argument of the residents of Sao Paolo was that they were resisting a violation of the Brazilian constitution.

resistance. To the extent that they are successful in attracting followers, the "competent authority" criterion is satisfied.

Alexander Hamilton, in *The Federalist No 28*, wrote:

> If the representatives of the people betray their constituents, there is then no resource left but in the exertion of that original right of self-defence (sic) which is paramount to all positive forms of government. (quoted in Churchill p. 47)

Rysard Kapuscinski wrote in *The Shah of Shahs*:

> All books about all revolutions begin with a chapter that describes the decay of tottering authority or the misery and sufferings of the people. They should begin with a psychological chapter, one that shows how a harassed, terrified man suddenly breaks his terror, stops being afraid. This unusual process, sometimes accomplished in an instant like a shock or a lustration, demands illuminating. Man gets rid of fear and feels free. Without that there would be no revolution. (Quoted in the *Wall Street Journal*, 7/2/2009, p. A13)

That is, when a citizen reaches the point where resistance appears better than continued oppression, when fear of the government no longer outweighs the determination to throw off the shackles, the spark of revolution is struck. Whether the spark dies out, or instead starts a flame, depends on other circumstances. But the citizen who has been pushed to the limit, whose "line in the sand" has been crossed, can satisfy competent authority if others follow him.

If all these requirements are met, then armed resistance is justified. However, even within a justified war, it is not true that "all's fair." The two requirements for war conduct must also be met.

Discrimination means that attacks must be directed only at those who are responsible for the evils that justify the war. In a war between nations, enemy soldiers and enemy leaders are legitimate targets. Citizens of the enemy country who are simply going about their normal peacetime activities are not legitimate targets. In the case of armed resistance to an oppressive government, legitimate targets certainly include officers of that government, such as legislators, judges, and officials of government agencies that enforce oppressive laws and regulations, including the police. Depending upon circumstances, legitimate targets might also include physical installations that provide support to the government, such as radio and TV stations and newspapers that transmit government propaganda, munitions plants, and power stations that supply power to government facilities. In attacking these legitimate targets, the principle of discrimination means that the attack must be aimed accurately and sized to the target, rather than being overkill. In armed resistance, this criterion rules out "terrorist" activities, such as car bombs in shopping malls, while allowing direct attacks on persons and places responsible for the oppression that justifies the resistance.[10] Having a sniper kill an unjust judge would be legitimate; blowing up the judge's house, including his wife and children and possibly his neighbors, would not be justified.

Proportionality, within a just war, means that each action must still be proportional: the good achieved by that specific action in helping to bring the war to a successful conclusion must not be outweighed by the harm done to innocents by that action. This criterion is based on the recognition that even a discriminating attack may inadvertently kill some innocent bystanders, or may result in destruction of the property of someone who has no part in the acts that provided the just cause for the war. This criterion then says that such "spillover" must be kept to a minimum, and that it may not exceed the good achieved by the action. In particular, disproportionate acts may create bitterness among the "innocent" members of the enemy population that makes it more difficult to achieve a just peace. This criterion applies to armed resistance even

---

[10] In 1997 the African National Congress claimed that its "terror" during the fight against Apartheid was "just," in retaliation for government terror, but still issued an apology for deaths and injuries to civilians (Beresford).

more so than to international war. It is crucial that the resistance forces not create bitterness among their fellow citizens by actions that are seen as "excessive" or that bring unnecessary suffering to those who had no part in the government's oppressive activities. In particular, terrorist activities intended simply to "make the country ungovernable" would violate this criterion.

If resistance forces limit themselves to discriminating and proportionate actions, they increase the risk to their own forces. However, it is this very willingness to assume risk upon themselves in order to avoid unnecessary harm to their fellow countrymen that shows that their actions are discriminating and proportionate. How much risk should the resistance forces be willing to accept in order to avoid unnecessary harm to innocent bystanders? That depends upon how much risk their fellow countrymen are willing to take in supporting the resistance. If the population at large sits passively by, allowing others to take the risks associated with freeing them, but refusing to take such risks themselves, the resistance forces likewise need accept little risk. Actions that injure bystanders become more acceptable. If the population accepts risks by actively supporting the resistance forces, the resistance forces must reciprocate by accepting a higher level of risk in order to avoid "spillover" damage to the population.

While Just War scholars have historically been concerned primarily with wars between nations, the prevalence of civil wars and wars of liberation in recent times has caused more attention to be given to these issues. For instance, the *Catechism of the Catholic Church* has the following to say about the legitimacy of armed revolt.

Armed *resistance* to oppression by political authority is not legitimate, unless all the following conditions are met:

1) There is certain, grave, and prolonged violation of fundamental rights;

2) All other means of redress have been exhausted;

3) Such resistance will not provoke worse disorders;

4) There is well-founded hope of success; and

5) It is impossible reasonably to foresee any better solution. (#2243) (emphasis in original)

Note that these conditions are equivalent to the Just War doctrine criteria for going to war, with the exception that the "proper authority" criterion is not included. As noted above, the Just War doctrine was intended to apply to war between nations; it is impossible to prescribe a "proper authority" to call for a revolt. Only the people, who retain the right to govern themselves, can undertake revolt when the proper conditions are met.

Neither the Just War criteria as outlined above, nor the more specific criteria given in the *Catechism*, can be applied mechanically. The criteria represent guidelines, not measuring rods. Prudence and judgment are still required, to determine whether the proper conditions are met in a specific instance.

Moreover, the Just War criteria cannot be applied with micrometric precision. War, especially armed resistance, is a bloody and messy business. One need only look at the places recently in the headlines, such as Darfur, to see this. Initiating armed resistance, which may lead to horrors like Darfur, is a step not to be taken lightly. It must always be remembered that, as Pope John-Paul II said during the first Gulf War, "war is an adventure from which there is no return." (quoted in Guenois) However, failing to initiate armed resistance against a potentially tyrannical government can lead to horrors like the Gulag, Hitler's death camps, or the Cambodian killing fields.

The criteria of the Just War Doctrine, even if not absolutely precise, still provide helpful guidelines in determining when armed resistance is justified. The victims of government oppression can use these guidelines to help determine the timing and scope of armed resistance, and to justify it to their fellow citizens and the rest of the world.

Summary

In summary, then, tyranny is the reason for armed resistance. Tyranny is deadlier than war, because it consists of an armed government making war on its own unarmed citizens. People don't have to submit to tyranny. On the contrary, they have a moral obligation to resist.[11] There are guidelines that people can use to help determine when tyranny has reached the point at which resistance is justified. The most important consideration, however, is that tyranny must be stopped early, even at a high price, because if allowed to continue it will exact an even higher price. In particular, tyranny must be stopped while the means to stop it are still available to the population. To wait until a government removes the means of resistance is in effect to surrender to that tyranny.

Additional Reading

Asprey, Robert B., *War in the Shadows*, New York, Doubleday & Co., 1975.

Asprey, Robert B., *War in the Shadows* (revised), New York, William Morrow & Co., 1994.

Beresford, Duane, "ANC says its terror was just," *Dayton Daily News*, May 13, 1997, p. 1.

Ghandi, Mohandas K., *Ghandi: An Autobiography*.

Guenois, Jean-Marie, "Justice, Not Vengeance," *Catholic World Report*, November 2001, pp. 34 – 35.

Kapuscinski, Ryszard, *The Shah of Shahs*, New York, Random House, 1985, ISBN 0-679-73801-0.

Lewis, Clives Staples, *Mere Christianity*, New York, MacMillan, 1960.

---

[11] "There exists a law, not written down anywhere, but in our hearts…. I refer to the law which lays it down that, if our lives are endangered by plots, or violence, or armed robbers, or enemies, any and every method of protecting ourselves is morally right."—Cicero (106-43 BC)

Liddell Hart, B. H., *Strategy*, 2nd revised edition, London, England, Faber & Faber Ltd.

Marshall, Bruce, *The White Rabbit*, London, Evans Brothers, 1964.

Mayer, Milton, *They Thought They Were Free: The Germans, 1938-1945*, Chicago, University of Chicago Press, 1966.

Orwell, George (pseudonym for Eric Blair), "Don't Let Colonel Blimp Run the Home Guard," *Evening Standard*, January 8, 1941. (See http://www.orwelltoday.com/readerriflequote.shtml for the complete reference)

Paine, Thomas, *Common Sense*, Mineola, NY, Dover Publications, 1997 (originally published 1776).

Rummel, Rudolph J., *Lethal Politics*, New Brunswick, Transaction Publishers, 1990.

Simkin, Jay, Aaron Zelman and Alan M. Rice, *Lethal Laws*, Milwaukee, Jews for the Preservation of Firearms Ownership, 1994.

Suprynowicz, Vin, *Send In The Waco Killers*, Las Vegas, Mountain Media, 1999

Taylor, Jameson, "Tyranny and Television," *HLI Reports*, July/August 20023, pp. 40 – 41.

Thomsett, Michael C., *The German Opposition to Hitler*, Jefferson, NC, McFarland, 1997, ISBN 0-7864-0372-L

Chapter 2

Probability Of Success

Even if moral, is armed resistance futile? Is it impossible for an armed citizenry to overthrow an oppressive government? History shows that it is possible, but not always successful. In this chapter we will examine some successes and some failures, to identify some of the problems and possibilities.

Current historical trends have both favorable and unfavorable factors affecting armed resistance. A successful resistance movement will necessarily take as much advantage of the favorable factors as possible while minimizing the effects of the unfavorable factors.

One of the effects of the invention of gunpowder was to strengthen central governments against local governments and ordinary citizens. Cannon could knock down castle walls, and the king could afford more and bigger cannon than could the barons. Castles were replaced by far more expensive forts, and armies became professionalized. The result was to strengthen central governments in their struggles with local leaders and rebellious citizenry.

In the nineteenth century, however, two inventions started a train of events that has led to a shift in the balance between central governments and dissident groups. The first of these was the metallic cartridge. The second was smokeless powder.

Prior to the invention of the metallic cartridge, which incorporated primer, powder charge, and projectile in a single unit, loading a gun was a complicated operation. The gunner had to pour a measured charge of powder down the barrel, ram a bullet down on top of the powder, then arrange for a cap or a flint to ignite the powder. Most firearms were smoothbore muskets, because it was too difficult to ram a lead ball down a rifled barrel. The slow rate of fire of the individual firearm, in combination with the low accuracy from the smooth bore, meant that massed troops were necessary to fight a battle. A body of well-drilled troops, trained to hold their ground and fire in massed volleys, could defeat any undisciplined body of rebels in a fight on open ground.

The metallic cartridge changed part of that. It made the repeating rifle possible. Bolt-action and lever-action firearms could be operated rapidly by relatively untrained troops. Thus the rate of fire of the individual fighter was determined by the firearm itself, not by the skills of the gunner.[12] Ultimately this led to the semi-automatic rifle, which reloaded itself after each shot, and the machine gun, which fired continuously so long as the trigger was pulled.

However, black powder still presented a problem. It fouled the barrel quickly. After a few shots, the firearm became inaccurate. The invention of smokeless powder changed that. Hundreds of rounds could be fired before leading or other metallic fouling in the barrel caused accuracy to deteriorate.

Another virtue of smokeless powder was, literally, the absence of smoke. Each time a black powder weapon is fired, a thick cloud of smoke reveals the shooter's position. Smokeless powder made concealed firing possible. Sniping and ambushing became much more feasible. The ability to fire from concealment further shifted the balance away from regular troops and toward rebels.[13]

---

[12] Colonel John Mosby's Rangers, which operated behind Federal lines in Northern Virginia during the Civil War, were a cavalry unit. Mosby found that by arming his Rangers with revolvers, they could defeat Federal cavalry units of much larger size that were armed with sabers, the traditional cavalry weapon. It was the metallic cartridge that made the revolver practical.

[13] Another advantage of the metallic cartridge was ease of storage. Storing large quantities of black powder was hazardous. It was customary to store powder in a "powderhouse," specially designed to keep the powder dry and to resist fire. The individual could store at most a few pounds without serious risk. With the advent of the metallic cartridge, individuals could safely store hundreds or thousands of rounds. Central storage was no longer so important.

With the twentieth century came many more weapons that further strengthened rebels and dissidents:

- The trench mortar, which gave small units the equivalent of short-range artillery;
- The recoilless rifle, which provided even more firepower to small units;
- The bazooka, the Panzerfaust, the rocket-propelled grenade (RPG), and similar weapons which gave the individual the ability to defeat tanks and low-flying helicopters;
- The Redeye, the SA-7, and the Stinger, which gave the individual some protection against aircraft.

These twentieth-century weapons are all the products of industry. Rebels depending upon them need a source of supply, usually external to the country in which they are fighting. However, with such a source of supply, a substantial resistance operation can be conducted.

Without such a source of supply, a resistance force is limited to rifles and pistols.[14] However, ammunition for these is comparatively simple to manufacture, provided the consumables (primers, powder and bullets) can be obtained. The expended cartridge cases must be recovered so they can be reloaded, but this can be accomplished if resistance forces are not driven off the battlefield before they can salvage the brass.

In short, then, while the development of gunpowder initially had the effect of strengthening central governments against their citizens, more recent developments have shifted the balance back towards the citizens.

In the remainder of this chapter, we will briefly look at several resistance movements, and their success or failure.

---

[14] There are exceptions to this rule. The Engineering Department of the Irish Republican Army successfully produced "barracks buster" mortars. The Palestinian Liberation Organization successfully produced short-range rockets (which, however, were unguided and useful only as area weapons).

Successful Resistance Movements

Recent history has seen several successful Resistance movements. A few will be described briefly here, with the intent of bringing out some lessons.

The American War for Independence

The American War for Independence did not come about overnight. The first battles, Lexington and Concord, were the flashpoints for a struggle that had been building for almost a generation.[15] Taxes and commerce restrictions were the major sore points. Americans were British citizens. They demanded the same rights they would have had in England, particularly the right to have their own legislatures levy taxes. In addition, they demanded the right to trade with other nations besides England.

The actual trigger for the War of Independence was the British attempt to prevent war by disarming the Americans. After first confiscating all the privately-held guns in Boston, and confiscating all the gunpowder stored in Boston's powderhouses, the British attempted to seize guns, cannon and powder in the rural areas around Boston.[16] The troops sent to do this met with initial success, easily defeating the militia forces they encountered. However, the British attempt to make an orderly withdrawal to Boston turned into a disaster, as they had to fight almost every foot of the way.

The Americans then laid siege to Boston. They fortified Breeds and Bunker hills. The British, rather than make an amphibious landing behind the fortifications, instead made a series of frontal attacks. Each attack was beaten off until the Americans ran out of ammunition.

From one standpoint the battle was a victory for the British. They ultimately took and held the ground. However, from another standpoint, it was a defeat for the British. American casualties were

---

[15] See *Common Sense* by Thomas Paine. Paine lays out the case that had been building for a generation.

[16] Note that cannon were privately owned by American colonists.

about 150 dead and 300 wounded, out of 1500 in the battle, for a casualty rate of 30%. British casualties were 1150, with 250 killed, out of a total force of 2500 men, or nearly 50% casualties.[17] Stokesbury writes:

> In all seven years of actual fighting, and twenty more or less major battles, one eighth of British officer deaths, and one sixth of wounds, were sustained at Bunker Hill. There were valid grounds for arguing that the British Army, and especially Sir William Howe [commander of British forces], did not recover from that gory afternoon.

Totting up the strengths and weaknesses of the British and Americans would lead one to assume the British could have everything their way. They had a navy that eventually blockaded all American ports. They had what was possibly the best army in the world, with plenty of experience in combat and competent leaders. They had the resources of an empire behind them.

The Americans, by contrast, had little or no military background, although most were familiar with firearms. The Resistance forces were perennially short of food, clothing, medical supplies, and ammunition, and sometimes went months without pay. Enlistments were for a short time (often three months), which required General Washington to plan his battles around the terms of enlistment of his troops, who tended to disappear when their enlistments were up. Public opinion in America was, at first, badly split over the war. In the South, there were even Loyalist militias opposed to independence. Moreover, because of the number of Loyalists among the population, the British were always well informed of the dispositions of the American forces.

However, the British had many problems as well. They had an empire to run, and the war in America was to a certain extent a distraction. British merchants did a great deal of business with the

---

[17] This emphasizes the point that a Resistance force is les interested in "holding ground" than it is in inflicting casualties on the government forces, while keeping its own strength intact.

colonies, and the war hurt their business. The British government itself was divided, with some officials determined to bring the colonies to heel, but others willing to compromise in some way. Thus the British war effort was not as vigorous as it might have been.

One factor leading to the American victory was that the Patriot forces seized control of governmental bodies: local, colonial, and eventually national. In effect they had a "government in being." They thus became clothed with some degree of legitimacy, which the Loyalists lacked. A second important factor was the colonial shipping industry, which quickly turned to privateering, seizing British merchant ships at sea. This provided the American forces with cash and military supplies, as well as correspondence between the British government and its officials in America. This shipping industry also was important in importing military supplies, particularly Dutch-supplied gunpowder. A third important factor was the support of the French, clandestine at first, but later with ships and troops. France became an important source of supply for guns and uniforms.

Converting British subjects in America to American patriots was a necessary part of the American war effort. Some British miscues, such as hiring Hessian mercenaries, helped the American cause. However, an important part of this process was pro-American propaganda. Thomas Paine's pamphlet *Common Sense* sold half a million copies. The thrust of it was that the problem was the British government; Americans needed to throw it off and form their own government. The Declaration of Independence, essentially a legal brief for the American colonies, was finally published after more than a year of fighting. Paine's later pamphlet, *The Crisis* ("These are the times that try men's souls. . ."), rallied the flagging spirits of the Americans to continue the struggle.

It was crucial to the American cause to obtain allies in Europe. While most of the nations of Europe disliked the British, they could not afford to appear allied to the Americans while the success of the war was in doubt. Eventually France was the only European power willing to provide major support. The Dutch did allow use of their possessions in the Caribbean as bases for privateers, and for supplies. French support turned out to be a major factor in the ultimate success of the American cause.

A serious mistake the American forces made was conducting raids against settlements near Halifax, Nova Scotia, turning potential allies into Loyalists and losing the territory for the future United States. It cannot be said too often that Resistance forces must *not* antagonize the people they claim they are trying to free from tyranny.

The British made a similar mistake, in using their Indian allies to attack the colonies from the west. Scalping of women and burning of farms and towns was not the way to regain the loyalty of the Americans. To many Americans, the Indians were worse than the Hessians.

Ultimately, the single thing that made the American victory possible was that, despite everything, the American army didn't disintegrate. This was in no small measure due to the efforts of George Washington. Nevertheless, there were several developments during the course of the war. First, untrained militia learned to stand and fight. After that, officers learned to maneuver their forces effectively. Finally, the generals learned how to be generals, and those who couldn't learn were shoved aside. Almost any Resistance movement will likely have to go through a similar process. Keeping the force "in the field," learning while bleeding, will be difficult but necessary.

Once it was clear that the American forces could win battles, European powers, especially France, were willing to take sides openly. Working with allies is not the easiest thing to do, and there were many misunderstandings between the Americans and the French. Despite the fact the French were actually more interested in possessions in the Caribbean than in helping the Americans, ultimately the war was decided by the Battle of Yorktown. British General Cornwallis was bottled up there, with the French fleet holding the mouth of the Chesapeake Bay, and both French and American troops besieging the British. Even after the victory at

Yorktown, it took two more years for a peace treaty to be signed. Those were two years of raids and counter-raids, while General Washington struggled to keep his army together. But with a final peace treaty, America became a nation.

The Communist Revolution in China

The Communist victory in China came at the end of a set of very complex events: exploitation of China by European countries during the 19th century; the 1911 revolution against the Emperor; fragmentation of China by armed warlords; establishment of the Kuomintang, at first with support from communist Russia; union of Kuomintang and the Chinese communists; the invasion by the Japanese; split between Kuomintang and the communists; and finally civil war between Kuomintang and communists. Rather than try to untangle this history, the following discussion will be devoted to the factors that led to the communist victory.

It is common to say that the Nationalist government was corrupt. It undoubtedly was. Most governments are. But more important, it was weak. It was incapable to enforcing its own laws or implementing its own policies throughout China. To the average Chinese, the government was "them," not "us."

The communists did an excellent job of convincing the average Chinese that the communists were part of "us." There was a lot more coercion of the populace and elimination of "capitalists" than apologists for the communists are willing to admit. However, the communists did gain favor with the people by killing landlords, corrupt government officials, and moneylenders. They also recruited warlords to their cause, or failing that killed them and took over their armies. All of this not only eliminated some obstacles to their progress, but gained the support of the people who had been victimized by the communists' targets.

Mao Zedong was a brilliant leader, both military and political. He recognized that political leadership was at least as important as military leadership. He recognized the need for five components of his revolutionary movement.[18]

1. Mass support
2. Party organization
3. Military organization
4. Favorable terrain
5. Economic strength

Mass support was critical. Without that Mao's revolution would have failed. Hence his famous statement that the guerrillas are the fish, and the people are the sea in which they swim. Military organization is an obvious necessity. Less obvious, but at least as important, is party organization. This is what allows the guerrillas to replace the government in areas where the government is weak, or has been driven out by military force. People need a framework in which laws are enforced, criminals punished, and disputes adjudicated. In China, it was the lack of this framework that gave the communists their greatest opportunity. They provided this framework, even if their law enforcement was driven by Marxist ideology.

"Favorable terrain" becomes a bit tricky. What is "favorable" depends on the nature of the war. For Lawrence of Arabia, the desert was favorable terrain. For the Viet Cong, jungle was favorable terrain. For Hamas, cities are favorable terrain. Hence the would-be Resistance leader must determine, of the terrain available to him, which is favorable and which is not. There can be no general answer. The experience of the Norwegian Resistance against the Nazi invasion suggests that mountains are not necessarily favorable terrain. It was comparatively easy for the Nazis to cut off the Resistance fighters' access to food and other supplies. Likewise, prior to World War II, the French and Spanish were able to isolate the Rif guerrillas in the mountains of North Africa, bringing their revolt to a halt. In any case, Mao was able to make effective use of the terrain available to him. Other Resistance leaders must do the same.

---

[18] Thompson, p. 11.

The Japanese invasion turned out to be a benefit to the communists in two ways. First, the communists largely avoided fighting the Japanese. The Nationalists bore the brunt of the anti-Japanese battle, while the communists husbanded their strength for the post-war battle. Second, the Soviets invaded Manchuria at the end of World War II, accepted the surrender of the Japanese armies there, and turned over the captured Japanese weapons to the communists. The Soviets continued to supply weapons to the communist forces following the end of World War II. Thus the presence of a border with a friendly country was an important asset to the communists.

Even with supplies from the Soviets, the communists in China would have had a much harder time without their political and military organizations. These were critical to their victory. Other Resistance leaders should learn from this experience. Armed groups are little better than bandits unless they have the support of the people. That support can be gained only through a good political organization.

The Cuban Revolution under Fidel Castro

The Cuban revolution took place against a government that was both corrupt and inept. Fulgencio Batista had overthrown an elected President in 1952. The result was that most Cubans denied Batista's legitimacy as ruler.

Although Cuba was the fourth most prosperous country in Latin America at the time of Castro's revolution, it still had large numbers of poor peasants. Moreover, it had a middle class that was dissatisfied with Batista and his corruption.

On July 26, 1953, Cuban rebels attacked the Moncada Barracks. The attack was a disaster, with nearly half the attackers being killed, and the rest captured. Castro was imprisoned. He was released after two years, as part of a general amnesty. He then went to Mexico, where he formed the July 26th Movement among Cuban exiles. In 1956, Castro and 81 followers invaded Cuba by sea. The result was again a disaster, with most of the invaders being captured.

Castro and a handful of followers reached the Sierra Maestra Mountains, where they carried out a guerrilla war against the Batista government. Castro received considerable help from the people in the area, who were upset by the Batista government's curtailment of civil liberties.

However, Castro's group was not the only Resistance group. Other rebel groups were formed in other parts of Cuba. In a departure from Maoist doctrine, the Cuban revolution was largely a middle-class revolution rather than a peasant revolution. In the cities, strikes, riots and urban terrorism prevented the Cuban army from concentrating on Castro's forces. Most of the recruits to Castro's forces came from the cities, not from the countryside.

Castro's efforts gained little support outside Cuba until Herbert Matthews, a reporter for the *New York Times*, made his way to Castro's headquarters, and wrote glowing reports characterizing Castro as a "romantic hero," who was fighting for a "democratic Cuba."[19],[20] The US press then took up the cause of the revolution, pointing out how bad Batista was (but not saying a word about Castro's communist connections).

In the face of support for Castro in the US press, the US government stopped supporting Batista with arms and training. The Cuban armed forces themselves began to mutiny against Batista, and "moderate" forces in Cuban society, seeing no other alternative, joined forces with Castro. The end result was Castro's triumphant entry into Havana on January 8, 1959. After a failed attempt by others to form a government, Castro assumed complete control of Cuba.

One major disadvantage faced by Castro's rebels was the fact that Cuba is an island. Supplies could be brought in only by ship, and then they had to be transported inland to the rebel bases. In fact, most of Castro's weapons and other supplies had to be diverted from legal sources within Cuba, rather than be brought in directly.

---

[19] Thompson, p. 66

[20] This illustrates the importance of "getting the story out" to an international audience. This will be discussed in more detail in Chapter 20.

A major "advantage" of the Cuban rebels was the Batista government itself. Not only was it a dictatorship, but it was an incompetent one. Its denial of civil liberties turned the Cuban population against it, especially the middle class. Because of its corruption and incompetence, it was unable to deal effectively with the revolution. Even the armed forces were unreliable. One important key to the success of the revolution, however, was the lack of support for the Batista government from other governments, especially the US government. The Batista government was isolated, and unable to mount a successful counterattack to Castro or any of the other revolutionary groups that opposed it.

The VietMinh

The Vietnamese revolution against the French was, like the communist victory in China, a complex affair. A look at some of the factors behind the Viet Minh's success (as compared with the Viet Cong's later failure) is instructive.

Under the Yalta agreements at the end of World War II, with the surrender of Japan, Vietnam was to be occupied in the south by British forces, and in the north by Chinese forces, until French forces could re-establish the pre-war colonial government. The Chinese had no love for the French, so they were quite happy to allow the Viet Minh to form a government in the North. Later French attempts to oust the Viet Minh foundered on their failures to alleviate problems in the North. In particular, the Japanese had plundered the area of rice for several years. The Vietnamese were literally starving. The French made no attempt to deal with the food shortage. They occupied the cities, but left the Viet Minh in control of the countryside.

The Vietnamese had no reason to support the French. Ho Chi Minh put together a coalition of anti-French and nationalist groups, arguing that they could achieve independence. The Viet Minh also began what was essentially a terror campaign against the French and any Vietnamese who supported the French. Ultimately, rather than surrender to French demands, in December of 1946 the Viet Minh forces attacked French garrisons, and the war was on.

The Viet Minh were led politically by Ho Chi Minh, and militarily by Vo Nguyen Giap. While Ho organized a government in the areas under Viet Minh control, Giap succeeded in gaining control of territories adjacent to China. With the success of the communists in China in 1949, this meant that the Viet Minh had a border with a friendly country. They were able to obtain weapons and other support, including materiel trans-shipped from Russia through China.

Politically, the French were faced with an impossible situation. Vietnamese leaders, both communist and nationalist, wanted independence. This the French were unwilling to grant. They feared that if the Vietnamese received independence, the French possessions in North Africa would also demand independence. Various halfway measures, such as making Vietnam an independent state within the French Union, were unacceptable to the Vietnamese.

Ultimately, for better or worse,[21] the French were unable to gain the support of enough Vietnamese to overcome the Viet Minh. The end result was a partition of Vietnam, with the North under communist rule, and the South under a puppet emperor, and later under a dictator.

Israel

Most often the picture of Israel is as a state that demonstrated its military effectiveness after obtaining independence. However, it gained that independence through armed resistance.

There had been a Jewish presence in Palestine even after the destruction of the Judean state by the Romans about the year 70. However, that presence increased significantly after 1870, when Theodore Herzl organized a Zionist movement to bring Jews back to Palestine. Total numbers were about forty thousand by 1900, and eighty-five thousand by 1917. The important point here is that the Jewish "return" was not an invasion in the usual sense. Individual Jews bought land from individual Arabs, and settled on it.

---

[21] Following the French departure from North Vietnam, thousands of Vietnamese were driven south, and many thousands more died as the victorious communists eliminated any who opposed them.

42

Unfortunately, in some cases the immigrating Jews bought land from absentee Turkish and Arab landowners, displacing Arabs who had been tenants on that land for generations.

In 1917 Britain issued the Balfour Declaration, which promised the Zionists a homeland in Palestine. This was done largely to gain support for Britain among Jews worldwide.[22]

Following World War I, Britain was given a League of Nations mandate to govern Palestine. Large numbers of Jews migrated to Palestine, in part driven by anti-Semitism in Europe. Britain needed access to Middle Eastern oil, and tried to maintain peace between Arabs and Jews. If anything, British policy favored the Arabs rather than the Jews.

The Jewish population in Palestine grew to half a million by 1935. In 1936, the Arabs started an armed rebellion, which wasn't stamped out by the British until 1938. Although there had been Jewish militias in Palestine since 1905, the British attempted to discourage the Jews from organizing defensive units. However, with the Arab rebellion, the Jews saw the need to develop more effective armed groups. In 1941 the British allowed Haganah ("defense organization") to organize guerrilla groups to operate in Syria, a French Mandate from the League of Nations. Some thirty thousand Palestinian Jews fought in British Army units, gaining military experience. Although the Jewish Brigade Group was officially disbanded at the end of World War II, an underground Haganah group continued to exist. It consisted of not only guerrilla units but a ready reserve and territorial militias, all professionally commanded, as well as covert supporters.

In addition to Haganah, an essentially conventional military and guerrilla force, there were several Jewish terrorist organizations, particularly Irgun and the "Stern Gang." These latter attacked not only British officials but also "moderate" Jews.

Jewish "resistance" involved smuggling Jews from refugee camps in Europe into Palestine, and smuggling weapons into

---

[22] Note that Britain did not own Palestine, and had no right to give it to anyone.

Palestine. Both smuggling efforts were difficult, since the territory had no "friendly" border, and the British controlled the eastern end of the Mediterranean. The refugee ship *Exodus 1947*, carrying forty-five hundred Jews, was caught and forced to return to Hamburg, where the refugees were simply dumped on the dock.[23] However, considerable numbers of Jewish refugees, and weapons, were successfully smuggled into Palestine.

Britain, exhausted by World War II, no longer had the will to maintain peace between Jews and Arabs. After hanging a few terrorists, and suffering some retaliatory hangings in return, the British announced they would give up their mandate effective May 15, 1948. This left the UN partition plan, dividing Palestine between Jews and Arabs, as the internationally accepted outcome. As history was to show, this was only a temporary result, but it did mean that a Jewish state would come into existence.

Three things need to be noted here. First, Jewish armed resistance against Arab attacks was important to the ultimate establishment of the state of Israel. Second, terrorism by Irgun and the Stern Gang had an unfavorable impact on public opinion in nations important to Israel. Third, the military training received by large numbers of Jews during World War II served as the basis for Haganah and the later Jewish Army.

Algeria

The French invaded Algeria in 1830. As noted above, they were successful in isolating Rif guerrillas in mountainous terrain, and neutralizing them. Algeria effectively became part of metropolitan France. However, it was run in a feudal manner by French colonists and a small Muslim elite.

The nationalistic feelings of the Algerians came to a head on VE day, May 8, 1945, with Muslim riots in North African cities that led to the death of over 100 French colonists. French militias retaliated, killing some 20,000 Algerians.

---

[23] Leon Uris's book *Exodus*, based on this incident, was effective in gaining international sympathy for the Jews. This emphasizes the importance of "getting the story out."

Algerians who had served in the French Army in World War II, and later some who had been imprisoned by the Viet Minh and indoctrinated with anti-French nationalism, formed a guerrilla army, the *Organisation Secrete* (OS). The initial operations of the OS were unsuccessful, with the leader Ben Bella being captured and imprisoned.

Despite French attempts at reform in Algeria, it was too little and too late. In 1954 the OS, after spending several years in covert training and fund-raising, attacked thirty French military posts, and distributed propaganda leaflets demanding independence, while promising to respect European rights and maintain close contact with France.

The French response was repressive, which drove even moderate Algerians into the arms of the armed resistance. To complicate things further, France granted independence to Morocco and Tunisia. This gave Algeria two borders with friendly countries. The *Front de Liberation Nationale* (FLN) was able to use those borders to bring in weapons, and to escape from French forces. Despite building a "fence" along the border with Tunisia, the French were unable to stop infiltration. Announcing a "right of pursuit" into Tunisia further alienated the Tunisian government.

The FLN prematurely went to battalion-sized operations against the French. They were not yet ready to fight a regular army in the field, and suffered heavy casualties. Furthermore, the French made effective use of long-range patrols and helicopters to defeat the FLN forces. Defeated in the countryside, the FLN switched to terrorism in the cities. Ultimately, however, the success of the Algerian revolution came through the fall of the government in Paris, bringing General de Gaulle to power. He decided to "cut his losses," and agreed to negotiate independence for Algeria.

Again, the Algerian war for independence illustrates the importance of borders with countries sympathetic to the Resistance, and the importance of giving the populace a goal they can support and sympathize with. Independence was such a goal.

East Timor

The eastern half of the island of Timor was colonized by the Portuguese; the western half by the Dutch, as part of the "Dutch East Indies." The island was occupied by the Japanese during WW II. An anti-Japanese guerrilla movement was fostered by Australian commandos.

Following the Japanese defeat, the nation of Indonesia declared independence, including the western part of Timor as a province. Following a 1974 coup in Portugal, the Portuguese government freed all its former colonies. The Revolutionary Front for an Independent East Timor won a short civil war and declared East Timor's independence in 1975.

Indonesian military forces invaded East Timor shortly after the declaration of East Timor's independence. Lacking an army, the people of East Timor were not able to put up formal military resistance. However, they put up a successful guerrilla war for over three years. However, in January 1979, the Indonesian forces surrounded and wiped out the last guerrilla force still operating against them.

In 1980 a new guerrilla force was organized, using primarily captured Indonesian weapons.

Neither Portugal nor the United Nations recognized Indonesia's claim to East Timor. The East Timorese never accepted rule by Indonesia. However, their guerrilla effort was unable to dislodge the Indonesians. The population suffered enormously, from torture, massacres, and starvation. The Indonesian occupation is estimated to have cost the lives of 100,000 East Timorese, out of a population of approximately a million.

International pressure finally forced the Indonesian government to accept a referendum in East Timor, in 1999. The East Timorese overwhelmingly voted for independence. A transition administration from the UN lasted for two years, followed by establishment of a local government.

The primary lesson from the Resistance in East Timor is the importance to the Resistance of simply surviving and keeping up the fight. Allowing the Resistance forces to be surrounded and wiped out leaves the civilian population undefended. Another lesson is the importance of having the full support of the population. For over twenty years, the civilians in East Timor suffered tremendously, but never wavered in their desire for independence. Yet another lesson is that even without significant external support, a Resistance movement can survive and continue to fight using captured weapons and equipment.[24]

Unsuccessful Resistance Movements

Most Resistance movements are not successful. A few examples follow, to illustrate some of the reasons for lack of success.

Greek Civil War

The Germans had occupied Greece during World War II. They evacuated Greece in late 1944. Communist guerillas had already begun action against the Germans during the war.

With the arrival of British forces in October 1944, the communist forces began their attempt to take over Greece. They quickly established themselves in areas vacated by the Germans but not yet controlled by the British. Moreover, the incoming British forces were too small to effectively control the country.

Despite agreements to disarm, the communist forces were able to use Yugoslavia and Albania, both under communist control, as sanctuaries. By 1946, the communist forces were conducting raids on villages in Greece, and taking hostages to assure the cooperation of the local people. By 1947, the communist forces controlled large portions of Greece.

Unfortunately for the insurgents, they alienated the population instead of gaining its support. The guerrillas kidnapped

---

[24] More information about the Timorese Resistance can be found at http://en.wikipedia.org/wiki/East_Timor and in the article by Woodruff.

nearly thirty thousand Greek children and sent them to be raised in neighboring countries under communist control. They also committed random acts of terror, and murdered numerous government officials. All of this cost them the support of the Greek people.

On the government side, the Greek Army greatly improved its capabilities. At first it attempted sweeps and clearing operations. Eventually it shifted to protection of the population against guerrilla attacks. Once the guerrilla forces were cut off from the population, they were deprived of intelligence about the Greek Army, and were eventually defeated. Another factor in their defeat was the Yugoslav government's closing of the border, depriving the guerrillas of their sanctuaries.[25]

A lesson from this insurgency is the importance of *not* antagonizing the population on which the insurgents depend for support. Another is the importance of a friendly border. Yet another is the foolhardiness of lightly-armed guerrilla forces attempting to defeat a regular army in conventional battle.

Philippine Insurgency

During World War II the Japanese occupied the Philippines. Several resistance groups operated against the Japanese throughout the occupation. One of these was the "Hukbalahap," or "People's War to Fight the Japanese." With the surrender of Japan and re-establishment of American control over the Philippines, the Huks initially attempted to gain control by political means. However, the Philippine government denied seats in the legislature even to legally elected Huks.

The result was a return to guerrilla war by the Huks. They announced a "land to the landless" campaign, to gain support from the people. The initial government response by President Roxas was a conventional military one. Sweeps, massive attacks, heavy use of artillery, and much thrashing with little effect. This resulted in

---

[25] Asprey downplays the importance of the border closing, arguing that other factors were more important.

antagonism between the Army and the Philippine population. The Huks were ready to take advantage of this antagonism. They obtained food and intelligence from the local population.

However, the Huks overplayed their hand. Some of their members were criminals who used the insurgency for their own profit. Individual Huk commanders were jealous of their own authority and were reluctant to cooperate with each other. The Huks assassinated the popular widow of former President Quezon. All these things made the people wary of them.

In addition, the Huks controlled an area in central Luzon. They had no friendly border. They had little access to a seacoast. They were restricted to the supplies they could obtain from the local population, and the weapons they could capture from the Army. They simply did not have the logistical capability to mount a major campaign.

The turning point came with the appointment of Ramon Magsaysay as Minister of Defense. He believed that the role of government was to protect the population. He took measures to improve discipline in the Army, and to bring the Army to look on the population as its allies rather than its enemies. He also offered an amnesty program to defectors from the Huks. He also encouraged the Army to use small-unit tactics to surprise and ambush the guerrilla forces, rather than engage in sweeps.

These measures brought the Huk insurgency under control within eighteen months. However, Magsaysay was unable to convince the rest of the government to adopt the political reforms needed to undercut any future insurgency. He resigned from his post and ran for President. He was elected in 1953. He died in a plane crash in 1957, and attempts at reform died with him. The insurgency resumed after his death.

The Huk insurgency emphasizes the importance of gaining the cooperation of the local population. Intimidating them into cooperation works only until the government provides effective protection for them. Also, selecting the area of operations should take into account logistics as well as the ability to hide.

Malayan Insurgency

During World War II the Japanese occupied the British colony of Malaya. The British government fostered the growth of guerrilla units to fight the Japanese. With the surrender of Japan in 1945, the British returned to Malaya. However, it soon became apparent that the pre-War status could not be re-established.

Communist guerrillas, primarily ethnic Chinese, fought against restoration of British rule. In addition to guerrilla units, they developed a network of civilian supporters, the Min Yuen, to provide supplies and intelligence about British activities. Initially, the communists were very successful in intimidating the non-Chinese population and establishing "liberated areas."

The ultimate downfall of the communists came from the British recognition that, first, they had to promise independence to the people of Malaya, and second, they had to protect the population against the guerrillas. The British built new villages and moved large numbers of the rural population into them. The displaced population actually lived better than they had in their old villages. In addition, no one was moved into a new village until a police post was established and manned, to provide the villagers with protection against communist sympathizers in their midst.[26] The result was two-fold: denial of intelligence to the guerrillas, and increased intelligence available to the British.

Another important feature of the British response was devolution of operational responsibility down to platoons and squads. Instead of large-unit sweeps and use of artillery and aircraft, these small units were given the initiative to pursue guerrillas, based on locally-obtained intelligence.

---

[26] The British recognized that "the man with the knife," already inside the village, who murdered those who collaborated with the British, was viewed by the villagers as a greater threat than an attacking force.

The final result was the collapse of the communist insurgency. By 1955 the government could cease offensive operations, and by 1960 the war was over.

From the standpoint of the insurgents, one of their big problems was that the insurgency was based on an ethnic minority, the Chinese. They never succeeded in gaining the willing support of the Malay population. Once they could no longer terrorize the majority, their effectiveness dropped dramatically.

Another problem was the lack of a friendly border. The government of Thailand, the neighboring country, was not sympathetic with the communists. On the contrary, it was fighting its own battle against communists on the other side of the border.

Perhaps the most fundamental reason for the failure of the Chinese insurgents in Malaya was that they were not trying to overthrow a tyrannical government. On the contrary, they were trying to establish one. The British offer of independence, with majority Malayan rule, was something the communist insurgents could not match.

The Viet Cong and National Liberation Front
Following the defeat of the French, a 1954 Geneva Conference agreed to partition Vietnam at the 17th Parallel, pending elections to unify the country. Over 800,000 refugees moved from North Vietnam to South Vietnam. Although many Viet Minh fighters moved to the north, many cadres remained behind to serve as the focal point for later insurgency.

Initially, prospects looked good for a renewed insurgency in South Vietnam. The Diem government was corrupt and inept. An attempt at "land reform," providing land to the peasants, resulted in large tracts of land being claimed by Diem's relatives and supporters. Abandoned land had been claimed by the Viet Minh cadres and turned over to peasants, gaining their support. Attempts to move the rural population into fortified hamlets ("agrovilles") failed. The peasants were very reluctant to abandon the graveyards of their ancestors, and the government never provided adequate funding for the moves.[27]

American advisors tried to mold the Vietnamese Army into an American-style army, heavy on armor and artillery, and road-bound. The task of dealing with insurgents at the local level was left to inadequately-trained and poorly-equipped Civil Guards.

There were many nationalist groups in South Vietnam, all of which had their own reasons for opposing the Diem government. They soon allied themselves with the communists in the National Liberation Front. In September 1960 the North Vietnamese government officially recognized the existence of the NLF, and called for "liberation" of the South and reunification of the country.

The communists gradually gained control of the NLF and began following Mao's approach: consolidating the areas they already controlled, establishing base sanctuaries, and setting up a parallel government in areas still under control of the Government of Vietnam.[28] The successful Viet Minh organization was copied: main force regiments, effectively regular troops, and paramilitary forces that could defended their own villages against government forces, and could be called upon to supplement main force actions. The NLF also carried out a very successful propaganda campaign to gain support of the peasants. This was done mainly through individuals and small groups that would visit a village, listen to the villagers' grievances, and offer the possibility of a better life if the existing government were overthrown and its foreign supporters evicted.

In all of this, the Vietnamese Army, and the American forces that had started as advisors and later grew to combat forces, failed to understand the nature of the war they were fighting, the war the NLF was winning. The NLF was giving the peasant something worth

---

[27] The government built only a few agrovilles, for lack of money. Villagers to be moved had their homes destroyed, and were told to move their belongings to their new agroville by themselves.

[28] Asprey, p. 733.

fighting for, and the counterinsurgents weren't offering anything in competition.

The introduction of American combat troops escalated the war, but did not change its basic nature. Sweeps, attrition, and "search and destroy" missions failed to end NLF activity, and did nothing to stop the infiltration of the North Vietnamese army. The sweeps might uncover NLF supply dumps, but did nothing to protect the peasants against the NLF. The war dragged on, and the NLF had no trouble recruiting to replace its combat losses.

What went wrong? Ultimately the NLF overreached itself in the Tet Offensive of 1968. This consisted of attacks on major cities throughout South Vietnam. Contrary to the expectations of the NLF, there was no popular uprising in response to these attacks. Despite the NLF's efforts at propagandizing, they still depended too much on intimidation to gain the support of the people. When the people could not be intimidated, that support was withdrawn. The Tet offensive, instead of resulting in an uprising against the South Vietnamese government, resulted in the destruction of the NLF. For the rest of the war, the NLF was irrelevant. It was the North Vietnamese Army that marched into Saigon in 1975, after defeating the South Vietnamese Army in a series of conventional battles. The NLF played no role whatsoever in the subsequent unification of Vietnam.

The Maoist program of starting with a guerrilla campaign in rural districts, and growing to the point of developing a conventional army to conquer the cities, worked in China against a weak and inept government. It also worked for the Viet Minh in North Vietnam, especially once the French government lost the will to continue the war. However, it did not work in South Vietnam. Despite the numerous mistakes made by the American Army in Vietnam, the NLF could not defeat it in conventional battles.

The primary lesson from the failure of the NLF and the Viet Cong is that outwaiting a powerful army while bleeding it may be more effective than trying to defeat it in conventional battle.

John Brown

Brown's "adventure" is probably most instructive as a lesson in what not to do. It was botched from start to finish.

Brown had participated in the fighting between pro-slavery and anti-slavery forces in Kansas in 1856, and was an accused murderer and fugitive. He came up with the idea of fomenting a slave uprising. His plan was to attract slaves to a wilderness area in the Appalachian Mountains and conduct guerrilla warfare. Knowing that the slaves would not be familiar with firearms, he intended to arm them with pikes.

In 1859, Brown conducted a raid on the Federal arsenal at Harpers Ferry, in Virginia. In doing so, he violated almost every rule of warfare imaginable. In seizing the arsenal, he placed the Potomac River between himself and his base of supplies on a farm in Maryland. He failed to leave a force on the Maryland side of the Potomac to secure his line of communications. By failing to secure the heights over the arsenal, he and his men were vulnerable to the Federal sharpshooters who soon occupied those heights.

Worst of all, he had no thought-out plan for what to do after he seized the arsenal. Even had slaves been willing to rebel, most never heard of his raid, and would have had no means of traveling to join him if they had heard. In short, his tactics were poor and his strategy nonexistent. John Brown provides an excellent example of just about everything not to do.

The State Can Be Beaten

The following quotation is taken from the *Mises Memo* for Summer 2002:

> [I]n so many ways, the state is a fiction. It has no existence apart from the people's willingness to believe it and give it life with their money and obedience. It was 12 years ago that the immense and seemingly permanent apparatus of the Soviet world empire wasted away like Oz's wicked witch of the

west. Why? Because the willingness to believe had been withdrawn.

This is a key point. The object of any resistance movement is, ultimately, to cause people to quit believing in the existence of, and giving support to, the existing state. The focus of any resistance movement must be on the minds of the people. Armed resistance is simply a means of getting people to change their minds. The people must start looking at the state as "them," and the resistance movement as "us." History shows this can be done. When it is done, the task of the resistance movement is essentially finished, except for mopping up.

References

Asprey, Robert B., *War in the Shadows: The Guerrilla in History*, New York, Morrow, 1994.

Beilenson, Laurence W., *Power Through Subversion*, Washington, DC, Public Affairs Press, 1972

Bell, Y. Eric, "The Bielski Forest," *The New American*, July 20, 2009, pp. 32 – 38.

Chittum, Thomas W., *Civil War Two*, American Eagle Publications, Show Low, AZ, 1996.

Galvin, John R., *The Minute Men*, Washington, D.C., Brassey's, 1989.

Giap, Vo Nguyen, *Peoples War People's Army*, New York, Bantam Books, 1968.

Goodrich, Thomas, *Black Flag*, Bloomington, Indiana U. Press, 1995.

Griffith, Samuel B. (translator), *Mao Tse-tung on Guerrilla Warfare*, New York, Praeger, 1961.

Lande, D. A., *Resistance!*, Osceola, WI, MBI Publishing, 2000.

Ney, Virgil, *Notes on Guerrilla War*, Washington, DC, Command Publications, 1961.

Paine, Thomas, *Common Sense* (reprint), Mineola, NY, Dover Publications, 1997, ISBN 0-486-29602-4. (Originally published February 14, 1776.)

Stokesbury, James L., *A Short History of the American Revolution*, New York, William Morrow, 1991.

Sweig, Julia, *Inside the Cuban Revolution*, Cambridge, Harvard U. Press, 2002.

Thompson, Leroy, *Ragged War*, London, Arms and Armour Press, 1994.

Woodruff, Justin, "Your Friends Will Never Forget You," *Soldier of Fortune*, July 2006, pp. 32 – 39.

Chapter 3

Government Response

The government isn't going to ignore an incipient resistance movement or dissident group. The Nazi government of Germany suppressed dissent almost completely (but not quite; see below). The Soviet Union was particularly harsh on dissent. The mainland Chinese government has likewise been harsh on dissent. Nor is the crushing of dissent limited to outright totalitarian governments. For a description of actions taken against dissidents by the U.S. government in the 1960s, see the book by Glick. You need to anticipate government actions, and be ready for them. Here are some of the things you need to anticipate and prepare for.

Creating an atmosphere of crisis

"Necessity is ever the plea of tyrants."[29] One of the ways a government can "justify" repressive measures is by creating an atmosphere of crisis. Here are some of the ways in which this has been done in the past.

Crime Wave

One of the most important functions of government is to suppress crime. However, the government may deliberately fail to suppress crime, letting it fester instead, then use the crime level as justification for placing restrictions on ownership of weapons, disarming honest citizens, searching houses, seizing "crime-related" property, establishing data bases of all citizens, and requiring extensive controls on movement and travel. Beware when the government starts claiming the need for additional powers to "fight crime." Hitler gained power by this means. His Brown Shirts carried out beatings, set fires, and caused other kinds of trouble, while Hitler made speeches promising that he could end the crime wave if the German people would grant him extraordinary powers.

---

[29] William Pitt the Younger (paraphrased)

Illegal Aliens

One of the distinguishing features of a nation-state is that only citizens have a right to live in it. All non-citizens are there only with permission, not by right. This implies that effective control of the nation's borders is one of the functions of government. By deliberately failing in this function, the government can create a crisis.

If the government fails to stop illegal entrants at the borders, it can then use the massive presence of illegals as justification for identification cards, computerized registries, internal passports, travel and movement restrictions, and citizenship checks by employers and public institutions. When your government starts demanding these measures to deal with the problem of illegal aliens, it is a sign it has failed to control the borders. Start suspecting that the failure is deliberate, and the government's real objective is to control *you*, not the illegals.

Propaganda

Propaganda is another way of creating an apparent crisis. One current example is the techniques used by environmental extremists. Popularizers of an alleged environmental crisis have set the ground rules for discussing ecological problems so that people are led to think in abstract rather than concrete terms. For instance, instead of talking about a concrete issue such as deforestation, the envirofascists talk about "the environment." Since "the environment" literally takes in everything, by shaping the discussion in that way, they can advocate schemes of total control over individual behavior and government policy. Any attempt to talk about specific measures to deal with specific problems is brushed aside as not big enough to deal with the "whole environmental crisis."

Whatever the cause at issue, the government can use propaganda in the same way, to lead people to think in abstractions rather than in concrete terms. Once the people's thinking is directed to abstractions, to "the whole crisis," then extreme measures are easy to justify. (Note that a "war on crime," a "war on drugs," or a "war on terror," are all "wars" against abstract nouns, not against specific individuals, institutions or nations.)

Creation of an atmosphere of crisis is a very effective way for the government to justify its oppression. It's "necessary," it's "for the public good," and of course it's "just a temporary measure, until the crisis is over." But the people who decide when the crisis is over are the very people who gain power from the belief that a crisis exists. They will be very reluctant to give up that power. In the United States, for instance, a "state of emergency" was declared on March 9th, 1933. It has never been rescinded (Senate Report 93-549). On the contrary, it has been re-declared by every president since then, through World War II, the Cold War, and the "New World Order." Americans have lived under a continuously renewed "state of emergency" since the Great Depression.

Creeping Denial of Rights

Once the people have been convinced through sufficient propaganda that there is a crisis, they are more willing to see their rights taken away, one by one. At each step in the sequence, it seems like the next measure the government demands is not worth making a fuss over. It's just a slight increase in powers that already exist. The thing to keep in mind is that the end goal is to take away all rights, but do it slowly enough not to create a fuss (the classic "salami slice" technique).

One way in which a creeping denial of rights can be made palatable to the people is to claim that each measure is aimed at some small group, not the public at large. People will accept measures aimed at "racketeers" or "terrorists" or "drug kingpins," without recognizing that those measures will later be used against anyone.[30] By then it's too late.

People must beware of any encroachment on their rights, no matter how cleverly it is justified, or what dangers are conjured up

---

[30] The so-called USA Patriot Act, which gave the US government additional powers, was passed in the aftermath of the September 11, 2001 terrorist actions, allegedly as being necessary to protect the country against further terrorism. It has since been used primarily against common criminals.

to justify the encroachment. There is no tradeoff between individual rights and public safety.[31] A decrease in rights is simultaneously a decrease in safety. Rights exist as protections against power. Each decrease in rights means that much less protection against a government that is becoming oppressive.

Economic pressures

The government is not limited to the use of jack-booted thugs who will break down your door. "They have ways" to bring you to heel. Among these are economic pressures that attack you by impoverishing you. Some of these methods are:

Loss of your job

Does your employer do business with the government? Does your employer require a license from the government to operate? Perhaps someone from the government might give your employer a "word to the wise" about how your continued employment would jeopardize future contracts or bids, or renewal of a license.

Denial or withdrawal of license to do business

In your country, do you need a license or permit to conduct your normal business? In the U.S., there are some 700 professions or trades (e.g., accountant, barber, cab driver, doctor, engineer, etc.) that are licensed by state and local governments, or certified by professional groups. Thirty-five percent of all American workers are now regulated or licensed by government agencies.[32] Without your license, you can't work at your normal trade or profession. This makes you vulnerable. A threat to rescind your license, or not to renew it, is a threat to your livelihood.

False arrest

The U.S. government used this method against the Black Panthers. Panther members would be arrested on trumped-up charges. They would pay a bail bondsman to post bond. Then the

---

[31] If government control is a guarantee of safety, how come prisons are such dangerous places?
[32] Simon, Stephanie, "Texas Horse Dentists feel the Bite of State Regulatory Oversight," *The Wall Street Journal*, December 28, 2009, pp A1(4).

charges would be dropped. Of course they didn't get back their payments to the bondsman. This bled the savings of the Panther members, and the Panther treasury. It was an effective way of putting economic pressure on the group and its members.

Currency replacement

The government might call in existing currency and replace it with new currency. This is commonly done in countries that have a history of high levels of inflation. For instance, over the last several decades, Brazil has several times issued new currency that had the effect of simply chopping three zeroes off the face value of the old currency (one new bill for 1000 of the old). This eliminates the need for absurdly high denominations of bills for ordinary transactions. Another justification, currently being used by the U.S. government, is to provide currency that is more resistant to counterfeiting.

In December 2009, North Korea introduced a new currency, with 100 of the old *won* exchanged for one of the new *won*. Moreover, there was a limit on the amount of old *won* that could be exchanged. The reason for the limitation was to hamper the "unofficial" market that was outside government control. The result was to destroy the savings of people who had dealt in the unofficial market.

Yet another justification for outlawing the old currency is to "take the profit out of crime." Criminals are presumed to be reluctant to bring attention to themselves by turning in large quantities of the old currency.

Even if the government officially places no limits on the amount of currency that an individual may exchange, if you attempt to exchange a large amount of currency you may be accused of drug dealing, money laundering, or other criminal activity. If the old currency is outlawed after the exchange, a cache of currency will become worthless. This means that if a resistance movement plans to keep its transactions untraceable by using cash only, its members may frequently have to justify exchanging large amounts of cash. The fact of the exchange also means the government knows who is holding large amounts of cash. In short, currency replacement is a way of attacking the "underground economy" of untraceable cash transactions. It can also be an effective means of crippling a resistance movement's financial operations.

Dependency on Government

The methods mentioned above are all directed at specific individuals or at causing certain individuals to "stand out." More generally, however, government economic activities may give people an incentive not to resist. Today many people are dependent upon the government, either as employees, contractors, or recipients of income transfers of one kind or another (welfare, farm subsidy, nationalized medical care). It would be hard to get them to rebel against their paycheck, their pension check, or their welfare check. By creating huge classes of people dependent in one way or another on government money, governments have reduced the likelihood of popular resistance to their actions.

Bureaucratic Sanctions

Government bureaucracies also "have ways" of making you sorry you resisted. Here are some of them.

Illegal actions

A government agency may take some retaliatory action against an individual, knowing that even if the individual eventually prevails in court, the process will take years and lots of money. Moreover, even if the individual eventually prevails, the agency officials won't suffer any penalties.

Foulup of pension checks

This might be a foulup of a pension check for yourself or your relatives. There are many ways in which this can be done. There may be "someone else with the same name." Your records might be falsely marked "deceased." Some "error" might be discovered in the records, which will have to be reviewed, and this can take several months. Can your elderly mother survive for six months without her pension check while her records are being "straightened out?" Isn't it amazing how quickly the records can be "straightened out" if you agree to become a government informer?

Meritless claims of taxes owed.

The government may claim you owe back taxes. Even if the issue is eventually resolved in your favor, you have been put to a great deal of hassle. Your bank account may have been seized, and even if you get it all back, you've lost the interest that would have accrued. If fighting the meritless tax claim takes too long or becomes too expensive, they may offer you a "settlement," in which you lose only part of your money instead of all of it. You may decide that putting up with the government is better than going through that again.

Meritless citations for failure to comply with regulations

Almost anything you do can result in a claim that you violated some regulation. Even if you win the resulting fight, you're out a great deal of time and money. Moreover, they can keep coming back at you time and again. They can wear you down without ever actually putting you in jail or doing anything "harsh." Just think of all the regulations they can get you for violating: environment, wetlands, fire code, building code, zoning, endangered species, and on and on. They can run you ragged with one meritless charge after another.

Harassment over environmental regulations

Environmental regulations are a bureaucrat's dream come true. Since virtually anything you do has some effect on the "environment," you can be cited for just about anything. This can range from filling in a mudhole to cutting down a tree to putting up a building. Remember that the issue is not whether they can make the charge stick, but how thoroughly they can keep you tied up in fighting a meritless charge.

The problem with fighting a bureaucracy is that the government is an amorphous blob. If some bureaucrat goes after you, there is no single point you can attack. What's more, if you fight the bureaucracy in court, you'll run out of money before the bureaucracy does. And ultimately they don't have to win. All they have to do is harass you until you're broke, or until you decide that fighting is futile. Moreover, even if you win, the bureaucrat who hassled you won't suffer in the least. Any penalties the court awards you will come out of other people's taxes.

Medical Care

If your country has some form of socialized medicine, or government-paid medical care, there is another way "they" can get at you: denying medical care to you or to your loved ones. It might not be as blatant as an outright refusal. There may be paperwork problems, or eligibility problems, or lengthy delays. Government control of medical care, however, gives the government one more weapon to use against dissidents.

Where to counterattack?

Armed resistance against a bureaucracy seems hopeless. If a revenue agent hits you with a big fine that will bankrupt you if you pay it, and will result in a jail sentence if you don't, whom do you shoot? If a safety inspector hits you with a regulation that bankrupts your business, whom do you shoot? If an environmental protection agent denies you the use of your property on some excuse about an endangered species or a wetland, whom do you shoot? Governments have ways of oppressing you that a gun does not seem to be a ready answer for. Keep in mind, then, that the more rules the government has, the more ways it can tie you down. It is essential to get rid of a government with such powers. But the best target may not be the specific government agencies that are causing the problems. The resistance movement must go for the head, not the appendages of the "monster."

National ID System

This government response is plausible and highly effective. While a high-technology, computerized ID system is the most threatening, high technology is not necessary. Josef Stalin was referred to by his Bolshevik comrades as "Comrade Filecard." He didn't need high technology to control a population of millions. A typewriter, pen and ink system, if pervasive enough ("Your papers, please") can be fully effective in denying people movement, food, medical care, education, and jobs.

A computerized system can be even more effective, especially if the computerized ID card is used for a drivers license, voter registration, medical care, financial transactions, and other activities. It can be justified on the basis of simplifying your life. "Look, you don't need to carry all those cards. This one card does everything for you." Indeed it does. Since every use of the card is recorded in some central registry, the card allows the government to track your every action. Moreover, by "shutting down" your card, the government can stop you from withdrawing money from your bank account, getting on an airplane, obtaining medical care, buying a gun, and anything else the card is used for. The attempt to establish some form of national ID card, particularly a computerized one, is in itself sufficient reason to oppose a government.

Infiltration of the Resistance

The government will attempt to infiltrate any resistance group, or even any dissident group suspected of the potential for resistance. From the 1950s through the collapse of the Soviet Union, the Communist Party, USA, was thoroughly infiltrated by the FBI, even to the extent that some of the most trusted leaders were in fact FBI informers. Any resistance organization must expect that the government will attempt to infiltrate it.

If the resistance is organized in small cells of five to ten people who knew each other before the resistance was organized, it becomes very difficult for the government to infiltrate the resistance. Instead, the government will attempt to suborn members of the cells. Thus the reliability of cell members becomes very important. A cell cannot afford to destroy itself through paranoia that one or more of its members may have been suborned, but on the other hand it cannot be oblivious to the possibility.

The Militia of Montana has published the following warnings about infiltrators:

There are those among us who would have us build or procure illegal commodities. Follow M.O.M.'s check list and you'll stay out of trouble. The following suggestions have been discovered the hard way by people who continue to pay the price for learning.

1) Beware of all strangers. Historically, resistance to tyrants has taken the form of small autonomous groups (cells) whose members know and trust one another from long experience.

2) Beware of the man who is "too perfect". He says all the right things, needs little persuasion, plus, he supplies a substantial amount of money.

3) Beware of handling someone else's firearms, or, you may find your fingerprints showing up at a crime scene.[33]

4) Doubly beware of a stranger who proposes illegal activities. You will soon find him testifying against you in federal court.

5) Beware of those who draw checks from the enemy. They are likely to have divided loyalties.

6) Avoid drunks, drug users and any one of unstable character. Always choose quality over quantity.

7) Beware of someone whose intellect, education and background appear different from those with whom he attempts to associate. Most people inter-relate with others of similar interests and background.

8) Do a little investigation. To be sure, the federals can create a good cover. But they seldom bother because up to now resistance groups have almost never checked their associates' backgrounds.

9) Recognize the ruthlessness of the tyrants and act accordingly. A government that will mass murder innocent families, including women and children, is not going to play "fair" with you.

---

[33] There is yet another reason not to handle someone else's gun. If the gun is captured by government agents in a raid on the owner's house, or after a gunfight, presence of other fingerprints on it can lead to arrest of other Resistance members.

10) Beware of signing up for any official government militia organization or you could find yourself taking orders from F.E.M.A. as much of California and 23 other states are now finding out.

11) Recognize the news media's tactics. Do not react to buzz words: Religious separatists; White Supremacists; Tax Protesters; Cultists; Nazis and other words that the masses are conditioned to hate. After the media has demonized the target, as in Ruby Ridge and Waco, the government is free to murder as it chooses.

These rules were developed in an American context, and not all of them will apply in all situations. Nevertheless, they can be adapted to almost any situation. Take them as a starting point for your own situation.

Creating a fake resistance

The Communists in the Soviet Union successfully fooled anti-communist émigrés, as well as Western intelligence services, with "The Trust." This was a fake anti-communist organization established by and run from the top of state security. According to Daily and Parker,

> Through the Trust, the Soviets were able to identify, expose, and neutralize opponents within the USSR. Many were allowed to operate for several years, not knowing that their activities were completely controlled by state security. It became possible, through Trust channels, for the secret police to prevent the establishment of a genuine anti-Communist underground in the USSR. Outside the Soviet Union, state security was able to penetrate the White paramilitary groups, who were then used to funnel disinformation to unsuspecting Western intelligence services and governments. (p. 7). (See also Chapter 2, "The Trust," of Epstein; "The Trust," Wikipedia

; and the
entry "Trust, The" in Polmar and Allen.)

The success of the Soviets in establishing such a bogus
resistance organization should be a warning to genuine patriots that
what appears to be a resistance movement may in fact be as
government deception operation. A genuine resistance organization
may find that a government deception operation has more funds, is
more successful in recruiting dissidents, and appears to be immune
to police suppression. The bogus resistance organization may
attempt to infiltrate the genuine resistance by offers of alliance,
combined operations, funds and supplies. The genuine resistance
should beware of allowing itself to be "taken in" by such a
deception operation.

Decapitation of the Resistance

An obvious move on the part of a government faced with
armed resistance is to eliminate the leadership of the resistance, thus
decapitating the movement.

One example of this is the arrest of Armenian leaders by the
Ottoman Turkish government, on trumped-up charges, mentioned in
the first chapter.

The U.S. has practiced this method in the past. When the
U.S. invaded Haiti in 1915, the Haitians rebelled under the
leadership of a man named Perrault (pronounced, by coincidence,
the same as Ross "Perot"). The invading forces solved this problem
by infiltrating a small group of Marines into the Haitian rebels'
defensive perimeter and assassinating Perrault. The two Marines
who carried out the assassination received the Congressional Medal
of Honor (they undoubtedly earned it; theirs was a risky and difficult
mission; guilt for any wrongness involved lies with President
Wilson, not with them).

The Israeli Defense Force perfected the tactic of
assassinating Arab guerilla leaders by ambushing their cars from
helicopter gunships. For this to work, they needed to recognize the
car, to know when the leader is on the move, and the route of travel.
With this information, however, the method was very effective.

Elimination of Abimael Guzman of the "Shining Path" in Peru; of Abdullah Ocalan of the PKK in Turkey; and of Abu Musab al Zarqawi of Al Qaeda in Iraq, all deprived these movements of charismatic leaders. This led to confusion and disarray in the movements.

Decapitation doesn't always work. Virgil Ney notes several cases in the Philippines during World War II when the Japanese successfully killed the original leaders of anti-Japanese guerrilla bands, who were then replaced by even more effective leaders. More recently, Israeli commandos assassinated Abu Yusef, a leader of Black September and chief of the Fatah operations inside Israel. This brought Abu Jihad to a leadership position in the Palestine Liberation Organization. He proved to be a much more effective leader than had Abu Yusef.[34]

Nevertheless, decapitation works often enough, and government forces can be expected to attempt to decapitate the resistance. Two types of defense are available. The individual leaders must practice personal security measures. They must move about frequently, maintain secrecy about travel, and maintain hideouts where they can remain undetected. Use of "cutouts" and secure means of communication are required for them to continue to be leaders.[35],[36] The resistance groups themselves must develop leadership in depth. Loss of a charismatic leader can be devastating, unless it has been prepared for by letting the resistance members know this might happen, and that other people, whom they already know, are prepared to take over leadership of the resistance organization.

Roundup

Another government measure against dissidents is simply to round them up. They may be placed in detention camps or simply

---

[34] See the book by Katz, p. 308.
[35] The ability of Osama bin-Laden to escape capture is largely due to his use of these methods.
[36] The US used Predator drones in Pakistan to attack the Al Qaeda leadership. The Al Qaeda leadership adapted to these attacks by increasing operational security, and by killing anyone suspected of providing intelligence to the US.

held incommunicado. A good example of this tactic is the U.S. government's actions in rounding up over a thousand people of Middle Eastern background "suspected" of connections with the terrorists responsible for the September 11, 2001 aircraft hijackings and attacks on the World Trade Towers and the Pentagon. For a long time, no names of those held were released, nor were their locations identified. They had no legal representation, and were not accused of anything. They had simply been "disappeared."

An example on a larger scale is the U.S. Government's "relocation" of Japanese from the West Coast to "relocation camps" in the interior. Granted, these were not harsh camps; anyone who wanted to move yet farther from the West Coast was permitted to do so; and many of the camps' young men volunteered for U.S. Army service.[37] Nevertheless, the point is that large numbers of people can be "rounded up" on short notice once the decision is made.

If the government is going to round people up, it must have their names and addresses on a list somewhere.[38] It's best to stay off lists in any case (one more good reason to oppose gun registration). However, anyone contemplating the possibility of armed resistance should make every effort to stay off any government lists. Once you're on the list, though, you're not coming off. You might as well fight.

Isolation

Would-be resisters might argue that "they can't arrest us all; there aren't enough jails." Unfortunately, that's not true. They don't have to put individual resisters in jail. Governments have other means at their disposal.

---

[37] In fairness, it must be pointed out that the U.S. government had cracked the Japanese diplomatic code, and was aware of several hundred Japanese on the West Coast who were prepared to engage in espionage and sabotage. Jailing only these individuals would have revealed that the code had been broken. It was deemed simpler to relocate all the West Coast Japanese. In retrospect relocation seems to have been a bad solution to a genuine problem.

[38] Despite the fact that census data is supposed to be secret, the U.S. government utilized census data to identify residents of Japanese descent when rounding them up in 1942.

Perhaps the most egregious example of this is the way Stalin handled resistance to collective farming in Ukraine. He simply had the entire region cut off. All roads and railroads were closed. Only government officials and the military were allowed in and out. Government officials used the Red Army to confiscate all food supplies in the region. The people simply starved. Those who still had the strength to dig graves buried those who had already died. No one really knows the total number of people who died in this artificial famine, but the figure 10 million cannot be very far off the mark.[39] This shows it isn't necessary to create jails. Simply cutting off a section of the nation can become as effective as jailing the entire population of that district.

One "modern" way of carving a nation up into districts that can easily be isolated is construction of "superhighways" from border to border. If these are fenced, and there are few interchanges, it is easy to control passage from one district to another, or even to close off a district completely. This "closing off" may be disguised as "interchanges under repair," quarantine for some disease (animal or human), blocking the spread of some pest, or anything else their imaginations can conjure up. Be suspicious when such "superhighways" are proposed.

False claims of "tip-off"

The government may have obtained information about a Resistance leader through some means such as intercepting communications. It will then arrest the leader, and announce that the arrest resulted from a tip received from someone in the Resistance. The British were successful in seriously disrupting the organization of the Irish Republican Army in Northern Ireland by this means. The IRA "Provos" executed a number of suspected informers in their own organization as a result, most or all of whom were probably innocent. Security within the Resistance is important, but the Resistance must be on the alert for government attempts to induce paranoia.

---

[39] When a subsequent census showed a significant decline in the population of Ukraine from the previous census, Stalin had the census-takers shot, and bogus numbers published.

The 5-Step "Solution"

Here are the usual steps a government will take in suppressing resistance or dissidence. Check your situation against this list, to determine how far things have already gone, and what might be coming next. Only when you know these things can you prepare to neutralize government actions.[40]

1. Identify

The government will attempt to identify resisters, "troublemakers," and influential or motivational persons who might serve as focal points for organization of resistance. Without leadership, especially without widely recognized leadership, there are no "centers" around which resistance can coalesce. Even those individuals who might be ready to join a resistance movement will feel they are alone. Means the government may use to identify possible resistance groups or leaders include gun registration lists, computerized identification systems, and domestic intelligence gathering activities. Glick details examples of the latter, from American experience. Thomsett describes the measures Hitler used to identify possible focal points for resistance. During the Bill Clinton administration, the U.S. government compiled a list of anti-abortion leaders, on the grounds that they might commit violence against abortion mills. Your government may already be compiling lists of potential dissidents. Do your best to stay off them.

2. Marginalize

Once a group or individuals have been identified, the next stop is to marginalize them. The print, broadcast, and electronic media will proceed to present the identified group in unfavorable terms, to lead the public into viewing the group as "undesirable," "extremist," or simply on the fringes of society. Remember, the

---

[40] The Black Book of Communism gives a similar sequence as having been applied by Communists in various countries:
"The adversary is first labeled an enemy, and then declared a criminal, which leads to his exclusion from society. Exclusion very quickly turns into extermination...After a relatively short perioed, society passes from the logic of political struggle to the process of exclusion, then to the ideology of elimination, and finally to the extermination of impure elements. At the end of the line there are crimes against humanity."

Communists in the Soviet Union never killed any "people." Instead, they killed kulaks, capitalists, wreckers, saboteurs, enemies of the people, counter-revolutionaries, and similar "extremists." Likewise the Nazis never killed any Jewish "people." Instead they killed maggots, menaces to society, scum, parasites, bacilli, etc. By first marginalizing the people they wanted to destroy, these governments were able to get away with their murders. Note that in 1935, Joseph Goebbels, Nazi Propaganda Minister, organized "spontaneous" demonstrations against Jews. The purpose was to make the German people think anti-Jewish sentiment was much stronger than it really was. Those Germans who were not anti-Jewish were made to feel that they were in a minority.

In the U.S., this marginalization happened to the "militia movement" after the Oklahoma City bombing, even though there was no connection between the convicted bombers and any "militia" organization. During the government siege of the Branch Davidians at Waco, Texas, the Davidians were constantly referred to in the news media as a "cult" living in a "compound," not as a "religious group" living in a "community." This effectively marginalized them.

Once marginalization has been successful, the public is less likely to identify with or sympathize with the target group as the government campaign is stepped up.

3. Demonize or Label

Once the public has, in its mind, relegated the target group to fringe status, it is easier for the government to attack it. The public can be manipulated against the group. Public attitudes can be led from antipathy to open hatred. Hitler was very successful in using this against Jews, Gypsies, and other marginalized groups. During the spring and summer of 1935, the "spontaneous" public outbursts organized by Goebbels made it appear anti-Semitism was the norm in Germany. When the racist Nuremberg Laws were enacted in the fall of 1935, the public was already convinced that most Germans were anti-Semitic. Those who weren't anti-Semitic felt themselves to be a small and isolated minority.

4. Persecution

Once the target group has been pushed to the fringes of society and made out to be the "bad guys," violence against the group's members can be taken with impunity. Wholesale criminalization of the marginalized groups will lead to aggressive actions against them by law enforcement personnel. Thugs and goons who attack members of these marginalized groups will not be prosecuted. Anyone who attempts to oppose these actions on "civil rights" grounds will be regarded as some kind of freak.

5. Elimination

The last step is elimination of the target group. This need not go to such blatant extremes as Nazi Germany's "Final Solution," Stalin's anti-kulak campaigns or starvation of the Ukrainians, or the Chinese massacre at Tiananmen Square. Mass jailings, confiscation of property, loss of jobs, and various civil penalties may suffice to break the back of the resistance. However, once the target group is sufficiently demonized and persecution has begun, even such extreme steps as those taken by Hitler, Stalin, or the Chinese Communists will meet with little public opposition, especially if the government has created an atmosphere of crisis. Rounding up the members of the target groups will become a routine exercise in logistics and transportation.

Don't take it lying down

In the United States, marginalization of Constitutionalists and conservatives has already gone a long way. Moreover, the people are being softened up to accept limits on civil liberties in order to "fight crime" or wage the "war on drugs," or more recently, to "fight terrorism." According to a Tarrance poll taken in 1994, when asked if they were willing to give up rights to control crime, the overall responses were:

- Yes 46%
- Unsure 17%
- No 37%

74

Among various subgroups, the results were even more ominous:

- Self-described Liberals, 56% Yes
- Blacks, 59% yes
- Hispanics, 67% Yes

A more recent poll, reported in the McClatchy newspapers, found that 51% of Americans agreed that "it is necessary to give up some civil liberties in order to make the country safe from terrorism."[41]

These findings are frightening. They indicate that Americans have lost touch with their heritage. Benjamin Franklin said, "They that can give up essential liberty to obtain a little temporary safety deserve neither liberty nor safety." The US appears to be on the verge of giving up liberty for the illusion of safety.

The Declaration of Independence put it thus:

"[W]hen a long Train of Abuses and Usurpations, pursuing invariably the same Object, evinces a design to reduce [the People] under absolute Despotism, it is their Right, it is their duty, to throw off such Government, and to provide new guards for their future Security."

Government suppressive actions must be resisted, and they may even become the justification for increased resistance by the citizens. Watch for this in your own country.

After the shooting starts

Once armed resistance has broken out, the government has a further set of measures that can be taken. The following list is based on a list of "lessons learned" by the Soviet government in fighting Muslim guerrillas from the 1920s on, but which the Soviet

---

41 http://www.mcclatchydc.com/nation/v-print/story/82156.html

government failed to implement in Afghanistan.[42] They have been modified here to eliminate the specifically Soviet-Muslim content.

- Divide the adversary. There may be several factions in the resistance. The government will try to gain the adherence of one or more factions, setting them against the others.
- Win over crucial local groups. The Soviets focused on winning over specific tribal groups, but the same idea can be applied in almost any situation. The government may focus on winning over identifiable ethnic or social minorities or other discrete groups.
- Create a strong indigenous local Party apparatus. The Soviets fostered local Communist parties, but the idea can be applied almost anywhere. Within the area in which resistance is taking place, the government may try to foster an ideology and create a group adhering to that ideology that will then support the government. Essentially this will involve propaganda that can be used to unite some identifiable group against the remainder of those living in the contested area.
- Field a local army. The government will attempt to turn the fighting over to an army formed from people living in the area. This might involve mobilizing local Reserve forces, or an army may be developed from scratch. In either case, the idea is to conquer the resistance using local forces.
- Create a local government loyal to the national government. Once an ideological group has been formed, its members can be used to replace local government officials such as mayors, provincial or state governors, city council members, school board members, etc. The idea is to staff all local government offices with people known to be loyal to the national government.

One of the best books on counterinsurgency is that by Galula. The Resistance should use it in reverse, to anticipate actions of the government. The resistance must be aware of the measures the government can take against dissidents and against active

---

[42] Taken from Bennigsen, p. 4.

resistance, and be prepared to counter these measures. U.S. Army Field Manual 3-24 is another excellent source of information on possible government actions to counter an armed resistance.

References

Bennigsen, Alexandre, "The Soviet Union and Muslim Guerrilla Wars, 1920 – 1981," Santa Monica, Rand Corporation, N-1707/1 (available from online booksellers as well as from Rand)

Dailey, Brian D., & Patrick J. Parker, *Soviet Strategic Deception*, Lexington, MA, D.C. Heath, 1987.

Department of the Army, *Counterguerrilla Operations, FM 90-8*, August 1986.

Department of the Army, *Operations Against Irregular Forces, FM 31-15*, May 1961.

Department of the Army, *U.S. Army Counterterrorism Manual*, Mt. Ida, AR, Lancer Militaria, 1984.

Epstein, Edward Jay, *Deception*, New York, Simon & Schuster, 1989, ISBN 0-671-41543-3.

Galula, David, *Counterinsurgency Warfare*, Praeger Security, Westport, CT, 2006, ISBN 0-275-99303-5.

Glick, Brian, *War at Home*, Boston, South End Press, 1989, ISBN 0-89608-349-7.

Hammer, Carl (translator), *The Gestapo and SS Manual*, Boulder, CO, Paladin Press, 1996.

Katz, Samuel M., *The Night Raiders*, New York, Pocket Books, 1997, ISBN 0-671-00234-1.

Ney, Col. Virgil, *Notes on Guerrilla War: Principles and Practices*, Command Publications, Washington, D.C., 1961.

Polmar, Norman & Thomas B. Allen, *Spy Book*, New York, Random House, 1997, ISBN 0-679-42514-4

Security and Intelligence Foundation, "The Trust," Reprint Series, 1989.

Stove, Robert J., *The Unsleeping Eye*, San Francisco, Encounter Books, 2003. (A history of secret police operations.)

Thomsett, Michael C. & Jean, *The German Opposition to Hitler*, Jefferson, NC, McFarland & Company, 1997, ISBN 0-7864-0372-1

United States Senate Report 93-549, 93rd Congress, 1st Session.

U.S. Army & Marine Corps Counterinsurgency Field Manual (U. S. Army Field Manual No. 3-24), University of Chicago Press, ISBN 0-226-84151-0. Undoubtedly the finest manual ever written on the subject. It will almost certainly be used by tyrannical governments faced with freedom-oriented resistance forces, as well as by democratic governments faced with communist or fascist insurgencies. Resistance forces should study it carefully, to prepare for government counter-operations. (Also available as a download at http://www.fas.org/irp/doddir/army/fm3-24.pdf)

Chapter 4

Strategy And Tactics: And Why You Need Both

Karl von Clausewitz distinguished between tactics and strategy as follows: tactics is the art of winning battles; strategy is the art of selecting which battles should be fought (p. 62). "A strategy is not really a plan but the logic driving a plan." (Heidenrich) The resistance movement needs to consider both strategy and tactics.

Strategy

Strategy starts with a goal. What is the resistance movement attempting to achieve? Drive out a foreign occupying force? Restore a legitimate government? Overthrow a tyranny and replace it with a republican government? Or just what?

Once the goal is understood, a strategy is a roadmap for achieving that goal. What sequence of actions will lead to the goal? What alternatives are available? If the government successfully blocks one course of action, what alternatives will achieve the same goal? In those insurgencies inspired by Mao Zedong, the basic strategy is to conquer the rural areas first, and strangle the cities. Part of that strategy is to begin with guerrilla forces that can develop themselves to the point of operating as regular armies. As of this writing, this strategy is still being pursued by Marxist movements in South America. By contrast, the strategy of Hamas and Hezbollah in the Near East has been to place priority emphasis on the cities, largely ignoring the rural areas. Instead of trying to build up to regular armies, these organizations have focused on terrorist attacks against civilians in the cities.

The strategy adopted by a resistance movement will depend on the circumstances. As Clausewitz wrote, "the first, the greatest and the most decisive act of the judgment which a statesman and commander performs is that of correctly recognizing . . . the kind of war he is undertaking, not taking it for, or wishing to make it, something which by the nature of the circumstances it cannot be."

(p. 18) Strategy therefore involves both the goal of the resistance movement and the circumstances in which it must operate. Selecting a good strategy, which may include several options that depend on government responses, is the key to an effective resistance movement.

Perhaps the most important role of strategy is a negative one – to avoid anything, no matter how attractive it may seem at the time, that would hinder achieving the goal, or divert resources away from the goal. Every action taken by the resistance movement must be viewed in the light of the overall strategy. Does it further that strategy? Does it bring the goal nearer? Does it in any way create problems that will make achieving the goal more difficult (e.g., by antagonizing some important element of the population)?

In conventional warfare, the strategy is to bring the enemy's army to battle, with the intention of destroying it. However, Liddell Hart observes that "Guerilla action reverses the normal practice of warfare, strategically by seeking to avoid battle and tactically by evading any action where it is likely to suffer losses." (Liddell Hart, p. 365) German admiral von Tirpitz once observed that a battleship has three functions: "to stay afloat; to stay afloat; and to stay afloat." By the same token, the armed wing of a resistance movement has three functions: to survive, to survive, and to survive. So long as it exists in the field and can strike effectively, the government has not won. Thus the most important aspect of the strategy for a resistance movement is to assure that the armed wing is never put at such risk that it can be wiped out. Beyond that, the strategy must dictate only those battles that can be won. Ambushes, raids, strikes at isolated garrisons or posts, and sabotage become the battles that fit the strategy of a resistance movement.

The tactics to be employed in these actions will be discussed in later chapters. The emphasis here is on the need for a strategy to guide the choice of battles to be fought and actions to be taken.

Nonviolent Tactics

While this book is about armed resistance, there is a role for nonviolent tactics in any overall resistance movement. There are few historical examples of nonviolent resistance being successful in overturning a tyrannical government. Even the collapse of the Soviet Union involved a mutiny by portions of the Armed Forces that shelled government buildings. However, nonviolent tactics can be an effective complement to armed resistance.

Even the Nazis could be blocked by nonviolent tactics. In November 1936, the Nazi leader in the town of Cloppenberg decreed that crucifixes be removed from public schools. The Catholics in the area protested. Church bells were rung in protest, children went to school with crucifixes around their necks, and protest commissions demanded an end to the decree. The result was that the decree was rescinded. (Eggerz gives several more examples of nonviolent resistance to the Nazis.)

This interview with Shafeeq Ghabra regarding the resistance in Kuwait against the Iraqi invasion illustrates some of the roles nonviolent resistance can play.

Q. "You were part of the Kuwaiti resistance movement during the Iraqi occupation. Could you describe what the resistance movement did?"

A. "My wife and I and some faculty members from Kuwait University organized our own form of resistance. We resisted by cultural means, by political means and by passing on information to key people in Kuwait.

"My wife and I typed about seven or eight hours a day, giving people instructions on civil disobedience and medical instruction. We used a little Macintosh computer, a printer and photocopy machine. Then we met as Kuwaiti faculty to resist the attempt of the Iraqis to reopen the university under occupation.

"They started looking for us, and so we went into hiding. We opened cooperatives and supermarkets, distributed money and food, and organized boycotts of work and school. We boycotted everything. We shouted slogans from our roofs, calling for Kuwait's liberation. It brought our society together. And it went on through all the months of the occupation." (from the article in *The American Legion*)

During World War II the French Underground was able to use children to carry out nonviolent actions such as letting the air out of the tires of German vehicles, or soaping the windows of the vehicles (Breuer). At best these actions were only annoyances to the Germans, but they served two purposes. First, they let the Germans know just how unpopular they were. Second, they helped the French population realize that the Germans were not invincible. On the contrary, they could be made a laughing stock. A resistance movement can achieve both purposes for itself by carrying out these harassing and annoying tactics.

Some of the activities to be discussed in subsequent chapters, including propaganda and the development of an overt organization to complement the armed wing, can also be considered nonviolent tactics. As with the battles of the armed wing, these nonviolent actions must fit the strategy. They must be designed to bring the goal closer.

Considerations in Choosing a Strategy

The first consideration is of fundamental importance: what are you trying to achieve? What is the goal of your activities? It should be possible to state this goal in one declarative sentence (e.g., "Drive out the invader." "Restore the Constitution.") There are two reasons for this. First, it orders all your further choices toward that goal. Second, it serves the important purpose of providing a rallying point for your fellow citizens, and aids in gaining support from sympathetic foreigners. For both reasons, it is important that the goal statement not be vague or platitudinous, but that it describes a definite and potentially realizable outcome.

The second consideration is the government against which you are rebelling. What is the "center of gravity" of its strength? The armed forces? A specific ethnic group? A specific region of the country? A group united by an ideology? Or just what? Identifying the center of gravity of the government's strength tells you what you eventually have to destroy or neutralize (even if you don't attack it directly). In addition, what resources, both physical and moral, does the government have? The armed forces (size, composition, morale, willingness to fight for the government)? Control of the news media? Centralized control of the schools? Loyal supporters in local government? Some form of national ID system? Gun registration or outright ban? Apathetic acceptance by the citizenry? Government control of farming and food supply? Support from foreign governments that are either ideologically compatible or more interested in "stability" than in the justice of your cause? Or what?

The third consideration is your own resources. What do you have available and what can you obtain that will be useful in reaching your goal? Obviously your material resources will be scanty as compared with those of the government. The critical issue is not whether you can match the government's resources, but whether you have *enough* of what you need. Moral resources will weigh more heavily than material resources. Can you obtain the support of the people for whom you are allegedly fighting? Do the resistance members have sufficient dedication to the cause to spend a lifetime at it (Simon Bolivar (1783 – 1830) spent most of his adult life leading the revolt of South American countries against Spain)? Can you obtain the support of sympathetic foreign countries? If the moral support is available, the material support will follow.

The fourth consideration is the nature of the country. Is it mostly rural? Mostly urban? Desert? Mountainous? Forested? Plains?[43] Are there areas where government control is weak or anti-government sentiment is strong that you can use for a base area? Do you have access to the "outside" either through a seacoast or a border with a country that will not oppose your activities? Where will you have to do your fighting?

---

[43] T. E. Lawrence ("Lawrence of Arabia") recognized that one of his strategic assets was the Arabian desert itself. It was thinly populated by people who were either neutral or outright sympathetic to his cause. The occupying Turkish army held only the few cities and some isolated forts. The Turks depended on railroads to keep these isolated points supplied. Lawrence wrote that his forces moved like a gas, never giving the Turkish army something to attack. Instead, his forces, using horses, camels and (later) motorcars, could strike the Turks at any point without warning. Any resistance movement must ask, what kind of terrain is available, and how can it be used effectively?

A popular technique used by business corporations is called a SWOT analysis. That stands for Strengths, Weaknesses, Opportunities, and Threats. In determining your strategy, you must perform a SWOT analysis of the situation facing you. What are your strengths? What are your weaknesses? What opportunities present themselves or can be created? What threats do you face? The SWOT analysis, taken together with your stated goal, will help you define a strategy to achieve that goal.

There is no mechanical procedure for devising a strategy. It is not a mathematical process like proving a theorem. Nevertheless, it is subject to reason, and by thinking through your goal and the situation facing you, it is possible to devise a reasonable strategy for your resistance movement.

A partial analysis by an actual resistance group is given in the Appendix to this chapter. No implication is intended that this analysis is correct. It is, however, an example of the kind of analysis that a resistance group must make.

References

Breuer, William B., *Top Secret Tales of World War II*, New York, John Wiley, 2000.

Clausewitz, Karl von, *On War*, transl. O. J. Matthijs Jolles, Washington, D.C., Combat Forces Press, 1953 (more recent translations are available).

Eggerz, Solveig, "How a Small Band of Protesters Unmasked the Nazi Regime's Fear of Unrest," *The St. Croix Review*, vol. XXXVIII No. 6l, December 2005, pp. 24 – 37.

"Fighting Saddam With a Mac," *The American Legion Magazine*, August 2000, pp. 28-30.

Hanzhang, General Tao, *Sun Tzu's Art of War*, New York, Sterling Publishing, 1987.

Heidenrich, John G., *The State of Strategic Intelligence*, https://www.cia.gov/library/center-for-the-study-of-intelligence/csi-publications/csi-studies/studies/vol51no2/the-state-of-strategic-intelligence.html

Lawrence, Thomas E., *Seven Pillars of Wisdom*, New York, Anchor Books, 1991.

Liddell Hart, B. H., *Strategy*, 2nd revised edition, London, England, Faber & Faber Ltd.

Appendix to Chapter 4

Example of an analysis of regime strengths and weaknesses by a resistance group. (Taken from http://www.balochistanpeoplesfront.blogspot.com/ 3/4/2007 1:15:43 PM Balochistan People's Front)

Army power

1. The Iranian regime is more vulnerable than has been portrayed in international media.

2. The Iranian soldiers are less skilled than has been claimed.

3. The regime has less control on Iranian population than has been advertised.

4. The security forces and army are not dedicated to the Iranian regime as it has been claimed.

5. Military operations can be carried out almost everywhere in the country with full success.

6. The Iranian regime has more propaganda power than substance.

7. A small group of skilled fighters can generate a great impact on international and internal public opinion.

8. The Baluch fighters are using their own limited resources and if they have substantial support from a reliable source they can form a very strong force that can carry out huge operations, uprisings, civil campaigns, marches, protests and strikes in different parts of the country.

People's power

1. The people of Iran support a popular uprising if they are sure that the leaders of uprising are resolute in their decision and committed to success.

2. The people of Iran are prepared to join resistance movements as thousands of people have applied for membership of People's Resistance Movement of Iran.

3. The Iranian regime will collapse easily when the people realise (sic) that there is a reliable strong opposition group that can take the regime head on.

4. In spite of the government's claims the absolute majority people of Iran do not support this regime.

5. The regime has lost popularity.

6. The people have lost faith in the regime.

7. The people have realised (sic) that Islam has been used as a tool for seizing power and sustaining it.

Strategy power

1. The Iranian regime is not very competent in drawing and formulating effective strategies.

2. All the strategies that have been designed to trigger popularity among the masses have failed.

Proxy power

1. The Iranian regime has formed, trained, financed and equipped different militia to work in different provinces of Iran as well as in different countries.

2. These proxy groups in Baluchistan, Khuzistan, Kurdistan and other provinces have failed to live up to the expectations. These groups are not prepared to kill and get killed for the sake of the Iranian regime.

3. There are a lot of proxy groups in Baluchistan and regime expected them to work on their behalf for collecting information, participating in military operations and joining the army and security forces in their different operations. In practice, they have failed in the 90 percent of their objectives.

4. It seems that these groups are prepared to receive financial help to finance their families but they are not prepared to sacrifice their own selves or their families for the sake of regime they do not believe in anymore.

Religious power

1. The Iranian clerics have lost their religious influence on people.

2. The clerics have become so visibly corrupt that everybody can see their illegitimate activities.

3. Islam as a religion is losing its credibility among the Shia Muslim of Iran.

4. The clerics as a source of inspiration and guidance have lost their credibility and therefore they have become a source of discrimination and injustice.

5. Iranian people are not willing anymore to sacrifice their interests, beliefs, aspirations and objectives for the sake of the present regime.

Propaganda power

1. The Iranian regime is very strong in propaganda outside Iran.

2. Most of the success of the Iranian regime has been achieved through propaganda.

3. The Iranian regime has been successful in convincing its foreign enemies that it is too strong for them to take on.

4. The Iranian regime has been successful in convincing foreign countries that they have less power than Iran.

5. The Iranian regime has been successful in dividing international community through propaganda.

6. The Iranian regime is counting on the division among international community more than on its own power.

7. The Iranian regime has succeeded in convincing other countries that it can inflict heavy blows on them if they interfere in its affairs or its allies. But in practice it cannot do that.

Chapter 5

The Big picture

Armed resistance is only part of the entire Resistance effort. While important, it must be put in the context of that overall effort. This chapter is intended to provide a brief overview of that effort.

Revolutionary war is different from guerrilla or partisan war. Guerrilla war is intended to harass the enemy so the regular forces can more easily defeat them. Revolutionary war is intended to achieve decisive results on its own. This is true even if the strategy of the Resistance is to build up to the point where it can conduct conventional war. Ultimately, the goal of the Resistance is to replace the existing government, not simply harass it.

Thus the "big picture" must be the overall effort to *replace* the existing government. The dominance of policy applies to revolutionary war just as it does to conventional war. Fighting must be for the purpose of achieving the goals of the Resistance.

Clausewitzean friction applies to revolutionary war just as to regular war. Thus the Resistance must expect that things will not go smoothly. The overall strategy must allow for setbacks, losses, confusion, and the "fog of war." It has been said that the primary weapon in guerrilla war is not the guerrilla, but the organization. This holds true for revolutionary war as well. Despite Clauswitzean friction, the important thing is the survival of the Resistance organization.

The Armed Resistance

The armed wing of the Resistance is engaged in what has been called "deliberate political violence." This is the essence of armed resistance. The violence is not engaged in for its own sake, but for the sake of the political goals of the Resistance. This cannot be emphasized too strongly. It is crucial that the violent acts of the armed wing are subordinate to the overall strategy and policy of the Resistance.

A typical armed wing might be made up of three different elements:

- Rapid response units – "Minutemen" – who are prepared to respond on very short notice to achieve some objective: ambush an enemy unit, counter an enemy raid or "roundup," establish a roadblock or checkpoint, etc. They maintain normal lives, to the extent that this is possible.
- Regular militia. These are more heavily armed, and provide backup to rapid response militia. However, they are not subject to rapid response calls. On the contrary, their normal employment is in planned raids, attacks, and similar activities. They are normally "full time" fighters, although they may blend into the population where this is necessary.
- Militia auxiliaries. These do not ordinarily do any fighting. They provide safe houses and communications, and procure and store food, ammunition and supplies. They may also provide for long-term convalescence of wounded fighters.

Ordinarily, there will be many more people involved in the auxiliaries than in either the Minutemen or the regular militia. These auxiliaries really are the backbone of the armed wing. Without them, the armed wing will soon find itself incapable of operating. The strategy of the Resistance must provide for the recruiting and training of the auxiliaries.

The Government

The objective of the Resistance is to replace the existing government. The government's power rests on two pillars: its perceived legitimacy, and its ability to apply coercion. The Resistance must undermine both of these pillars. That need not mean attacking them directly, but they must be attacked in some way.

Attacks on the government's legitimacy will depend on the particular circumstances facing the Resistance. Was the government established through a coup? Through a fraudulent election? Through imposition by a foreign power? Has it lost legitimacy by engaging in unconstitutional activities? Has it violated widely-recognized human rights? Whatever the origin of the government, the Resistance must stress that the government either never had legitimacy, or has lost it through its own actions. When the people no longer concede legitimacy to the government, it must depend only on coercion.

Even legitimate governments ultimately depend on coercion. The tax collectors may start by sending a letter demanding payment of taxes, but ultimately an armed policeman will drag the recalcitrant tax resister off to jail. Part of the efforts of the Resistance must be directed at protecting the public from government coercion. This may range from activities such as juries refusing to convict those accused of opposing the government,[44] to assassinations of public officials who attempt to enforce unjust laws. Once the government has lost legitimacy in the eyes of the public; once it becomes "them" instead of "us;" the Resistance must find ways to shield the population from government coercion.

The Population

The population can be divided into two and possibly three different groups. The Resistance must address each of these groups.

Families of the Armed Wing

The families of the armed wing, especially the families of those in the Regular Militia, must be provided for. At the least, this means food, clothing, shelter, and the same level of medical care as the rest of the population. The Resistance may provide money, support in kind (food and clothing), real or fake ration cards and identity cards, and even jobs (real or make-work) with employers sympathetic with the Resistance.

In the extreme, families of the armed wing may have to be evacuated to areas controlled by the Resistance, or sent to neighboring countries as refugees. Whether as evacuees or refugees, they are still the responsibility of the Resistance. The fighters, especially those in the Regular Militia, must be confident that their

---

[44] Prior to the American Civil War, the Federal government passed "Fugitive Slave Acts," calling for punishment for people who aided runaway slaves. These laws were unenforceable because juries refused to convict the accused people.

families are being taken care of. Risking their lives is one thing; sacrificing the well-being of their families is something else entirely.

Regardless of whether the families remain in their usual location, become evacuees, or even refugees, they must be kept informed about the status of their absent family members. The amount of information given them must be limited to that which won't compromise the fighting forces. Nevertheless, the families must be reassured about the welfare of their absent members, and be reassured that the efforts of the armed wing are worthwhile.

The Population at Large

Tactical success of the Resistance will mean nothing if the people, who are the ultimate target of the Resistance's political activity, do not support the goals of the Resistance. The issue of getting the Resistance's story out to the general population will be discussed in Chapter 20. Here it will simply be noted that the general population must support the Resistance. Otherwise the efforts of the Resistance will ultimately be futile.

One way the Resistance can gain popular support is to organize neighborhoods to provide self-help and mutual aid. This would be the responsibility of the overt organization, to be described in Chapter 6, rather than that of the armed wing. This is simply one more reason why the Resistance must look to a much bigger picture than that of simply fighting the government's army and police.

Especially Threatened Minorities

Depending on the particular circumstances in a country, there may be minorities that are especially threatened by the government. The Resistance may need to hide members of the targeted minorities, or move them to safer areas. The Resistance may have to operate an "underground railroad" to evacuate people to safer areas. The evacuees may also include members of the Resistance targeted for capture. Measures to protect targeted minorities or members of the Resistance may involve bribing officials, faking documents, providing new or altered identities, or other measures as appropriate.

Measures to protect targeted minorities can be very effective. Evidence collected by various Jewish groups indicates that as many as half a million Gentile Europeans risked their own lives and the lives of their families to hide Jews from the Nazis, or to help them escape by providing false passports, visas, or other official papers. Many of these Gentiles were caught and died with their Jewish fugitives, especially in Poland. However, in Bulgaria, nearly ninety percent of Jews were saved; in Italy, some eighty-five percent of the Jews were saved, a total of nearly 40,000; in Finland almost all Finnish Jews were saved, a total of 3000.

If there are threatened minorities in the nation, the Resistance should make whatever efforts it can to protect them. At the very least, such minorities can be recruited into the Resistance. Even more, the Resistance may gain the sympathy and support of the larger population, and of foreign peoples.

Foreigners

It is almost impossible for a Resistance movement to succeed without some degree of support from outside the country. Supplies, weapons, ammunition, and medicines must be obtained, almost always from sources outside the country. The support of the Soviet Union and China for Communist revolutions was pointed out in Chapter 2. Likewise, support from France and Holland was crucial to the success of the American Revolution.

Even more important than material supplies is moral support. The support of the *New York Times* was crucial in providing credibility to Fidel Castro's revolution. Diplomatic support from France was important to the American Revolution.

More will be said about gaining foreign support in Chapter 20. At this point it will simply be noted that this is part of the big picture that the Resistance must take into account.

Summary

The armed wing of the Resistance may be likened to the spear point of the Resistance. However, there is a lot more to the spear than the point, and the spear without someone to use it is useless. While the fighting is what will win the war, that fighting is only a small part of a much bigger picture. It is crucial that the Resistance organization take that bigger picture into account.

References

Hagl, John A., *Learning to Eat Soup with a Knife*, Chicago, U. Chicago Press, 2002, ISBN 0-226-5677-2.

Hollander, Paul, *Political Will & Personal Belief,* New Haven, Yale University Press, 1999.

Mack, Jefferson, *Underground Railroad*, Boulder, CO, Paladin Press, 2000.

Sweig, Julia E., *Inside the Cuban Revolution*, Cambridge, Harvard U. Press, 2002.

Zedong, Mao, *Mao Tse-Tung on Guerrilla Warfare* (Samuel B. Griffith, Translator), New York, Frederick A. Praeger, 1961.

Chapter 6

Overt And Covert Resistance Groups

The resistance must have both overt and covert groups. The covert group is of course the "armed wing" of the resistance movement. Its membership must be secret from the government. The overt group is not armed, does not engage in combat, and is known to the government. It is crucial that the two groups appear to be distinct. There must be no trace of linkage between them. The overt group must be in the position of saying to the government, "If you don't negotiate with reasonable people like us, you'll have to fight those extremists who have taken up arms."

Examples of parallel groups include the following:[45]

Overt	Covert
Sinn Fein	Irish Republican Army
People for the Ethical Treatment of Animals[46]	Animal Liberation Front
Earth First!	Earth Liberation Front
Gay and Lesbian Anti-Defamation (GLAAD)	ACT-UP
African National Congress	"Burning Spear"
Palestinian Authority	Hamas
Min Yuen	Malaysian People's Liberation Army
Batasuna (Basque separatist party)	Euskadi ta Askatasuna (Homeland and Freedom)

The point here is simply that the idea of overt and covert organizations is not a new one, but is in fact fairly common among resistance organizations. The practice should be adopted by any serious resistance organization.

---

[45] Listing of these groups as "parallel" does not imply that they are in fact connected. I do not know this to be true. However, the activities of the covert groups listed do reinforce the messages and actions of the overt groups.

[46] PETA has given money to Animal Liberation Front, although spokepersons for PETA say it was not for terrorist activities.

In addition to presenting a posture of "reasonableness," the overt group must seek alliances. It must attempt to gain support from other groups in society who have grievances against the government. It must attempt to gain sympathy from other groups by presenting its case to them as "reasonable." It must deal with "friendly" politicians and government officials. These may be people who sympathize with the goals of the Resistance but cannot or will not join it, or they may simply be opportunists who see in the Resistance a way to achieve their own goals. The Resistance should use these latter where it is to its advantage, but must never trust them.

It is crucial, however, that the overt group never make promises on behalf of the covert group, such as "if you do this, they will end the fighting." Such a promise clearly admits the linkage between the two groups.

The difficulties that can arise from failing to maintain the apparent separation between the two groups are illustrated by the following quotation from *National Review*:

> President Clinton has decided to recognize Sinn Fein, the "political wing" of the terrorist IRA, and to authorize U.S. officials to hold talks with it. Vice President Gore informed Sinn Fein President Gerry Adams of this . . .Exactly what has Mr. Adams done to deserve such regard? He has promised that the IRA will stop murdering people for the time being. This promise implies that he has some power in these matters. If so, he is presumably responsible for at least some of the IRA's murders and maimings over the last 25 years. ("Broth of a Boy," *National Review*, October 24, 1994, p. 20)

In the case of Sinn Fein and the IRA, the connection had been apparent for years. Nevertheless, everyone involved kept up the fiction that they were not connected. It is much better, however, if the Resistance can maintain the "respectability" of the overt organization, and keep the connection secret.

Despite the apparent separation of the overt and covert groups, however, it is important that they actually work together. The resistance must be a single organization. There must be coordination between the two groups, even if it is carefully hidden, including being hidden from the majority of members of both organizations.

In addition to dealing with the government, the overt wing may engage in strikes, protests, marches, and similar actions. These cannot be random actions. They must be chosen to support the strategy of the Resistance. Each such action must be orchestrated to bring public attention to some aspect of the Resistance's strategy. Planning for a protest or march must include the following questions: Who is the intended audience? What do you want them to do? How does your "action" lead to that? The Ruckus Society's manual has good information on planning actions such as these. See the references for a URL.

One danger in maintaining the separation between overt and covert organizations is that the overt organization may at some time be tempted to betray the covert organization. If the overt organization leaders see, or think they see, their way to power through some offer of accommodation by the government, they may decide that they no longer need the covert organization.[47] They should remember that it was the guns of the covert organization that brought the government to the bargaining table. Once they betray

---

[47] A recent example of this possibility is hinted at in the following alleged quote from a Palestinian leader, published on the Internet on Feb. 5, 2002: "Al-Haj Abu-Ahmad, founder and leader of Al-Aqsa Martyrs Battalions,. . . warned against the dangers of the secret security and political talks, which some Palestinian Authority leaders are holding behind our backs, saying such talks are considered as circumventing our people's struggles and abandoning the sacrifices of their sons and the blood of their martyrs." See also the review of Gerry Adams's book by O'Sullivan, which cites instances of Adams' lying to the IRA's "armed wing," about measures he had taken to gain respectability. Yet another example comes from the *Wall Street Journal* for August 1, 2005 (p. A8). Gerry Adams announced that the IRA was giving up its armed struggle. One interpretation is that Adams has achieved "respectability" of a sort, and no longer needs the IRA. He is thus willing to abandon the goals the IRA fought for over a period of nearly 40 years, and the members of the "armed wing" themselves.

the bearers of those guns, they no longer have any influence with the government.

The Covert Resistance

The covert resistance is what people typically think of when the issue of "armed resistance" arises. It is the covert resistance that carries out "direct action" against the elements of the oppressive government. The covert resistance must be able to operate effectively despite the government's superiority in numbers and equipment, to survive government counteraction, and to work towards the strategic goals of the Resistance (see chapter 4).

Organizing the covert resistance

Since the covert Resistance will be doing the fighting, it is essential to recruit people who are willing to fight, to kill, and to risk being killed. They must be strongly motivated. Open recruiting, however, will usually not be possible, and government infiltrators must be guarded against.

Start at the bottom

In organizing the covert resistance, it is important to keep it simple. The organization should be built from the bottom up: individual cells of people who already know each other and can trust each other. Starting at the top is like trying to build a house starting with the shingles first.

The domestic US group Earth Liberation Front provides a good example of organizing from the bottom up. The following is taken from an article in the *New York Times* by Bruce Barcott:

> The E.L.F. is made up of a series of small cells that remain mostly unaware of one another's identities and plans. In "Igniting the Revolution: An Introduction to the Earth Liberation Front," a $10 video sold in Portland's counterculture bookshops, Craig Rosebraugh, then the E.L.F.'s spokesman, urges volunteers to start their own units rather than try to join one. "There's no realistic chance of becoming

active in an already existing cell," he says. "Take initiative; form your own cell."

Other groups, including the I.R.A., Al Qeda (sic) and right-wing patriot factions, were organized around this leaderless resistance model but never were truly leaderless. Their imagined world ultimately requires a hierarchy. The E.L.F., rooted in a philosophy of anarchist primitivism, dreams of peaceful leaderless tribes living in robust ecosystems. "In a tribe, you take care of each other," Critter [a tree-sitter being interviewed in jail by Barcott] says. "There's no need for Big Brother to take care of you."

This is the conundrum of the E.L.F., and the reason the group is so difficult to track or to stop: there is no membership; there are only acts. Anyone can join – tonight – by torching a science lab. Existing cells may applaud your crime but will not contact you. And so law enforcement agencies have found the group impossible to infiltrate. "They know each other and don't tolerate strangers," says Bob Holland, a Eugene, Ore., police detective who has been investigating eco-terror crimes since 1997. "It's not like infiltrating the Mafia, where you can go to Joe Bonanno and say, 'The goodfellas down the street recommended me.' These people are hanging with people they've known for years, and when they decide to do a direct action, they're the only ones talking about it."

The covert Resistance organization cannot be this totally leaderless. However, it must consist of cells that are made up of people who know and trust each other. Contact with other cells must be made only through the leadership of the Resistance, not directly. Even there, the cells must deal only with people whom they knew "before," and can trust.

This semi-leaderlessness has implications for the covert group's combat activities. The leadership of the armed wing of the Resistance cannot command these groups in detail. Individual cells may be given general assignments, but must be permitted to carry out those assignments as they think best. They are on the spot; they know their own capabilities; they *should* know the capabilities of the Government forces they are operating against (the issue of tactical intelligence will be taken up in Chapter 28).

The members of the covert resistance will in many cases have families. The resistance is only as strong as the preparedness of each individual family involved in it. The families need to ask themselves, if you can't eat it, wear it, or shoot it, do you really need it? What good are your guns and bullets if your stomach is empty and your feet are bloody or frozen? Preparation by the families of those in the covert resistance is therefore very important. Likewise, it is important that the Resistance take care of the families of those in the armed wing.

Recruiting

From a World War II French Resistance recruiting pamphlet:

Men who come to the maquis to fight live badly, in precarious fashion, with food hard to find; they will be absolutely cut off from their families for the duration; the enemy does not apply the rules of war to them; they cannot be assured of any pay; every effort will be made to help their families, but it is impossible to give any guarantee in this matter; all correspondence is forbidden. (Erlich, quoted in Asprey, p. 473)

Despite this off-putting recruiting information, the maquis was successful in obtaining the support of numerous Frenchmen. The Resistance must find means of attracting fighters in the numbers and quality required by the overall strategy.

How many recruits are needed? That depends on the size of the country, the available population, and the strength of the government. Nevertheless, historical Resistance movements have had surprisingly few members.

For instance, the Provisional IRA had only 150-200 members on active service, with about 50 running daily operations. It had about an additional 800 providing safe houses, intelligence, and supplies. It was organized into cells of 4 to 10 members. Only the leaders knew the leaders of other cells (DiGregorio, 1994). More will be said in a later chapter about logistics, but the proportions given above should be kept in mind. For every member actively engaged in fighting, at least four other members are required to provide support.

Leadership

The function of leadership is to *lead*. That is, to assure that the actions of the covert Resistance are directed toward the strategic goals of the Resistance, and that the tactics used do not unnecessarily endanger the Resistance forces. In addition, it is the duty of the leadership to see to the provision of supplies, training of recruits, distribution of intelligence, and care of wounded.

As the Resistance grows in numbers, the leaders must remember that all the fighters are volunteers. They will come from all walks of life, and bring varied life experiences to the Cause. Leaders must guard against letting their egos spoil their leadership. They should look upon their role as servants rather than rulers. Their job is to make it easier for the fighters to live, fight, and survive. They should study Sun Tzu's *The Art of War* until they are thoroughly familiar with it. They must understand that respect from their followers must be earned. It cannot be demanded.

Organizing the overt resistance

The overt Resistance requires a different form of organization from that of the covert Resistance. The overt Resistance has two functions: gathering public support for the strategic goals of the Resistance, and using that support to put pressure on the government to achieve those goals.

Gathering public support means communicating with the public. The overt Resistance must convey to the public what is wrong with the current situation, and what the situation should be (i.e., the strategic goals of the Resistance). Putting pressure on the government means encouraging the public to take *legal* actions to show opposition to the government. Those legal actions might include symbolic protests, civil disobedience, picketing, strikes, boycotts, demonstrations, "white sabotage" (working strictly to the rule book), voting against current government officials,[48] jurors refusing to convict opponents of the government ("jury nullification"),[49] and refusing to cooperate with government officials. Wikipedia has a fairly comprehensive article on nonviolent resistance. The books by Gene Sharp give numerous examples of nonviolent action taken in various nations. The exact nature of the actions to be taken by the public will depend on the situation.

It should be remembered that only in rare occasions has nonviolent action succeeded in overthrowing a dictatorship. It can be successful only when the leaders of the dictatorship have already lost confidence in their own cause, and are at best half-hearted in defending it. So long as the leaders of the dictatorship are willing to imprison or execute the nonviolent resisters, it is at best a supplement to armed resistance.[50] Nevertheless, the Resistance should make every attempt to encourage those nonviolent actions that will hinder the government but not lead to bloodshed among the general public.

Going Public

The overt Resistance must make its case to the public. How this will be done depends on the degree of control exerted by the government. If "letters to the editor" and petitions to government officials are possible, these should be used. If the news media are under strict government control, other avenues must be used:

---

[48] As in the Polish campaign against a Communist government: "cross out the single name." That is, where there is no opposition candidate, cross out the name of the government candidate.

[49] Prior to the American Civil War, the Federal government passed so-called "Fugitive Slave Acts," providing for punishment of people who aided slaves escaping from the South. These laws were almost impossible to enforce because Northern juries refused to convict, even when the accused was clearly guilty.

[50] Had Ghandi been dealing with Hitler or Stalin instead of the British, he would have ended up in an unmarked grave and no one would have ever heard of him.

leafleting, handbills, posters, graffiti, guerrilla theater,[51] "soapbox speeches," anti-government jokes, web sites and blogging. The important thing is to let people know that "they are not alone" in their opposition to the government.

Recruiting

The overt Resistance does not need formal members. On the contrary, membership rosters and membership cards are to be avoided, as they simply provide the government with lists of people to "round up," or to apply other sanctions to (see Chapter 3 for some possible government responses). In this case, "recruiting" means attracting people to the cause; bringing them to support the strategic goals of the Resistance, or if that is too big a step, to supporting some intermediate goals.[52] It means inspiring them to take some small risks by participating in the nonviolent actions that the Resistance will be promoting. Strikes, demonstrations, etc., are effective only if large numbers of people participate. People must be encouraged to participate in these actions, with some expectation that they will make things better, not worse. Note that if the government controls the news media, the overt Resistance must find other means to mobilize the large numbers of people needed for demonstrations, etc. One method that has been found successful in several nations is sending text messages to cell phones, asking the recipients to forward them to everyone on their address list. Handbills, posters, and graffiti are also possible methods of letting people know of a coming demonstration.

Leadership

The leaders of the overt Resistance serve primarily as spokesmen who promote the strategic goals of the Resistance. They

---

[51] The presentation of short propaganda plays or skits, usually on sociopolitical themes, as war or repression, often on the streets or in other nontheater locations. ("guerrilla theater." *Dictionary.com Unabridged (v 1.1)*. Random House, Inc. 26 Jul. 2008. <Dictionary.com http://dictionary.reference.com/browse/guerrilla theater>.)

[52] If the ultimate goal is to get rid of a tyrannical government, it may be counterproductive to announce this publicly. That gives the tyrannical government an excuse to "go after" the overt Resistance. An intermediate goal might be to allow opposition parties to run candidates in internationally supervised elections.

must be people who are willing to "stick their necks out," and publicly voice opposition to specific government policies. They must be people whom the public already knows, respects and will trust. Possible candidates for leadership include authors (e.g., Aleksander Solzhenitsyn), labor leaders (e.g., Lech Walesa), religious leaders (e.g., the Dalai Lama), or other popular figures (e.g., Mohandas K. Ghandi, Aung San Suu Kyi).

Part of the role of the leadership is negotiating with officials of the government. In this role popularity and charisma are not sufficient. Leaders must be hard-nosed negotiators who understand the strengths and weaknesses of the government as well as their own, and who will push for as much as they can get at any given time. So long as they do not put the government in a position from which it cannot back down, they can come back later for what they cannot get this time.

There may be politicians who, if not exactly friendly, are at least willing to support some of the goals of the Resistance. The leaders of the overt Resistance must negotiate with them, and attempt to use their influence to alter government policies. A price must be paid for this, of course. The Resistance leaders must in turn support the private goals of these officials. Hard-nosed negotiating is necessary here, too. In dealing with these officials, two things must be kept in mind. The Resistance must not compromise its strategic goals, and it must always remember that these officials cannot be trusted over the long term. If they are not playing a double game at the start, they may turn on the Resistance once their own goals have been achieved. However, the Resistance should not hesitate to make use of these officials where possible.

Summary

The Resistance needs both overt and covert wings. While the two must work together to achieve the strategic goals of the Resistance, they must appear to be separate. Moreover, they will be organized and operate differently. Coordinating their actions without revealing their links will be difficult, but is necessary.

References

Asprey, Robert B., *War in the Shadows*, New York, Doubleday & Co., 1975.

Cerami, Charles A., "Half a Million Schindlers," *America*, October 15, 1994, pp. 13 - 17.

Erlich, Blake, *The French Resistance*, London, Chapman & Hall, 1966.

DiGregorio, Michael, "From Both Sides Now," S.W.A.T., November 1994, pp. 41 - 49.

O'Sullivan, John, "Arms and the Man," *Wall Street Journal*, 3/17/04, p. D4, a review of Adams, Gerry, *A Farther Shore*, New York, Random House. (Adams's autobiography.)

Ruckus Society, The, *Action Planning Training Manual*, Oakland, CA. Can be downloaded at http://www.ruckus.org/downloads/RuckusActionPlanningManual.pdf

Sharp, Gene, *Politics of Nonviolent Action*, Parts 1, 2 and 3, Porter Sargent Publishers, 1973.

Wikipedia, http://en.wikipedia.org/wiki/Nonviolent_resistance

Chapter 7

Personal Weapons

As noted in an earlier chapter, there has been a significant shift in weaponry, toward increasing the firepower available to the individual soldier. Balor describes it as follows:

> *Personal weaponry* – arms and ammo you can carry and shoot – is being revolutionized. You yourself, Joe [Balor addresses the reader personally], can take out enemy armor, aircraft, bunkers, whole buildings containing, perhaps, whole roomfuls of officials. *Portable assault weapons are now being developed at a faster pace than are the defensive systems needed to repel them.*
>
> For the world, this is a mixed blessing: good news for rebels, a disaster for forces defending the established order. For you, Joe Merc, it means you've gotta stop thinking in terms of defending the status quo and get into attack systems. That's your natural role anyway. (pp. 116 – 117)(emphasis in original).

What Balor says about mercenary soldiers applies as well to the Resistance movement. Initially, anyway, the resistance will not have artillery, and it will probably never have aircraft. What the resistance needs, instead of these resource-guzzlers, are weapons that are light and portable, but which deliver enormous shock at close range. This means assault rifles[53], submachine guns, hand grenades, grenade launchers, light mortars, and anti-tank rockets (the latter useful against both armored vehicles and fortifications).

All but the first of these will probably require external supply of some sort. This may come from a foreign ally, or may simply be bought on the international arms market. They may also be obtained from government armories through raids, bribery, and

---

[53] True assault weapons, not the semi-automatic firearms misleadingly called "assault weapons" by U.S. newspapers and anti-gun politicians.

theft. Ultimately, the resistance may be able to manufacture these weapons, once it has developed sufficient resources and secure areas. More will be said about this in the chapter on Logistics.

Initially, however, the resistance fighter will likely be equipped with only a semi-automatic rifle and a pistol, either semi-auto or revolver. These weapons are the types that can most readily be obtained prior to the open initiation of armed resistance.

Government Sources of Arms

Historically, the initial phase of armed resistance has often involved raids on government armories and police stations, in order to obtain weapons. Raids will be discussed in a later chapter. Note that once a few raids on these sources of weapons have been carried out, the remaining targets will be more heavily guarded and made more secure. Thus it is important to strike quickly at many of these sources before they are "hardened."

Weapons can be obtained from government stockpiles by means other than raids. The Resistance should also consider bribery and theft. Tyrannical regimes, of the sort that justify armed resistance, are also rife with corruption. Low-level officials can often be bribed to supply weapons. A policeman can report "my gun fell out of my holster while I was chasing a suspect, and was lost." Police and military reserve forces can be infiltrated by the resistance. These sympathizers on the inside can steal weapons for the resistance. These more subtle means should be employed right from the outset, if at all possible, since they do not alert the government to the fact that the resistance is acquiring arms.

Interview with Shafeeq Ghabra

"Q. Could you describe what the resistance movement did?"

"A. There was also a militant aspect of the resistance movement. It started immediately after the invasion. Youth and former soldiers decided they could conduct a military resistance.

"They knew where the Kuwaiti Army's weapons facilities were. And they were able to get these arms before the Iraqi Army got there.

"Even though the Iraqis had control over the country, it took them several days to get to these weapons facilities, and by then, many Kuwaitis had weapons. The Iraqi security force focused a lot of its energies on breaking the back of the military resistance.

"There were many clashes, attacks, public executions. But they were able to hold on. There were acts of resistance going on until just days before Kuwait's liberation."

To some extent, the government of Kuwait hampered the development of an armed resistance by disarming its own people before the invasion. Thus the Resistance forces had to loot their own government's armories for weapons. If at all possible, the resistance should acquire as many weapons as possible through legal channels prior to the initiation of armed resistance.

Choice of weapons

As with everything else, the Resistance will have to make do with what weapons it can obtain.[54] Nevertheless, there are some things to consider.

One of the most important issues will be ammunition. Even if the Resistance develops its own arsenals for manufacturing ammunition, commonality of ammunition is important. To the extent possible, all members of the same Resistance unit should be armed with rifles of the same caliber.[55] This eases resupply and allows sharing of ammunition among unit members. To the extent

---

[54] This quote from George Washington is apposite here. "It is to be wished, that every Man could bring a good Musket and Bayonet into the field, but in times like the present, we must make the best shift we can, and I wou'd (sic) therefore advise you to exhort every Man to bring the best he has. A good fowling Piece will do execution in the hands of a Marksman." - George Washington to John D. Thompson, Head Qurs., Wilmington, Aug. 28, 1777.

[55] Exceptions may be made for snipers and other specialized troops.

possible, each Resistance unit should be standardized on the same caliber of rifle ammunition.

Resupply of ammunition will be a problem throughout the war. It is important, then, to standardize as much as possible on popular rifle ammunition calibers. Worldwide, Winchester .308 (7.62 x 51 mm NATO), .223 Remington (5.56 x 45 mm NATO), and Russian 7.62 x 39 mm are the most popular and are widely available. If the Resistance plans to use ammunition obtained from Government stocks, either by subterfuge or by capture on the battlefield, it must adopt as standard whatever the Government forces have standardized on.

Rifles capable of fully automatic fire are desirable but not absolutely necessary. When the Rhodesian Army ran low on ammunition, the rifles in the hands of troops were modified to be semi-automatic only, and effectiveness against guerrillas was about as good as before. Tactics turned out to be more important than the ability to fire full-auto. A Resistance force, which will be chronically short of ammunition, will probably be well advised to settle for semi-automatic rifles. Even if select-fire weapons are available (selectable between semi-auto or full auto, i.e., true assault rifles), Resistance forces would be well advised to use full-auto only in extreme circumstances.

Far more important than the issue of semi-auto or full-auto is the issue of reliability. Again, the Resistance will have to make do with what it can obtain. Nevertheless, where choices are available, rifle models should be chosen with reliability in mind. This means not only resistance to breakage, but resistance to jamming and fouling, and ability to continue to operate when wet or muddy.

Pistols are a close-range weapon. In conventional armies, higher-ranking officers are armed with pistols for self-defense, but do not carry rifles because they are not expected to engage in direct combat. Front-line infantry are typically not armed with pistols because they are not expected to fight at close range (that is, range too short to maneuver with a rifle).

Resistance forces will find more uses for pistols than do conventional armies. Assassinations, ambushes, and urban fighting are done at close enough range that pistols are reasonable choices for weapons. In addition, they are concealable, whereas rifles are not. Moreover, pistols are easier to obtain, and easier to make, than are rifles.

As with rifles, choice of pistols will be determined by the availability of ammunition. The most popular pistol calibers are 9 mm, .40 Smith & Wesson, and .45 ACP for semi-auto pistols, and .38 and .357 magnum for revolvers.[56] Glock has introduced the .45 GAP semi-auto pistol to take advantage of improvements in powder since the introduction of the .45 ACP, however, these are not yet as widely available as the .45 ACP. The Resistance should standardize on a caliber that is readily available.

The choice between revolvers or semi-auto pistols can be and has been argued for decades. From the standpoint of the Resistance, it will be necessary to accept what is available, not engage in esoteric arguments over which is best. Both are good. Revolvers are easier to use than are semi-auto pistols. They will take more abuse and neglect and keep operating. They are more reliable when wet or muddy. For people totally unfamiliar with firearms, revolvers are easier to learn to use than are semi-autos. Conversely, semi-auto pistols hold more ammunition, and are easier to shoot accurately because of their lighter trigger pull. Beyond that, preferences between the two are personal and highly subjective.

The book by Camper has descriptions of many weapons. Several of the other books listed in the References also provide good descriptions of weapons. The book by Ezell is especially good. These references should be helpful in making choices when there are alternatives firearms available.

---

[56] Some revolvers are chambered for .45 ACP, but must use special clips to hold the rounds in place in the cylinder.

Cleaning Equipment

Weapons must be cleaned and oiled regularly. Otherwise they will rust or become fouled with powder and lead or copper residue. Every fighter must be equipped with the tools necessary to clean his firearm(s). At a minimum, this includes cleaning rod, bronze or nylon brushes (steel brushes will damage the barrel), patches, cleaning solvent, and lubricant. Specific details vary with the weapon, but in general it is necessary to clean the barrel, and to clean and lubricate all moving surfaces such as slide rails and bolts. Cleaning the barrel means running a patch soaked with solvent through the barrel (from breech to muzzle, if at all possible, to avoid damage to the muzzle), followed up by using a brush, then alternating solvent-soaked and dry patches until a dry patch comes out clean. Surfaces that slide or bear against each other should be lubricated with oil or light grease. Excessive lubrication should be avoided, since it can collect dust in dry environments, and become hard in cold environments. Dry lubricants are available for desert or arctic conditions. However, these are not as effective in providing lubrication as are oil and light grease.

Optics

Optics on rifles have traditionally been associated with snipers. However, recent developments in optics have changed this. "Red dot sights," holographic sights, and similar devices are now becoming more popular. "The ACOG mounted on the M16 service rifle has proven to be the biggest improvement in lethality for the Marine infantryman since the introduction of the M1 Garand rifle in World War II." (Statement by Major General J. N. Mattis, former commander of the 1st Marine Division in Iraq, quoted in *Guns and Ammo* for April 2006, p. 36.)

The primary advantage of such sights is that they allow quicker alignment with the target than do the conventional iron sights. It is not necessary to align front and rear sights; simply place the dot or circle on the target. In addition, optics with low magnifications (2x or 3x) aid in hitting small targets such as a head peering around a corner. Moreover, these optical sights are easier to teach than are iron sights, for people who are not familiar with firearms.

As with anything else, there are downsides to these optical sights as well as advantages. Rough handling can knock them out of alignment or damage them. They may be vulnerable to internal or external fogging in humid or cold weather. They must be cleaned carefully so as not to scratch the lenses. A narrow field of view (inevitable with high magnification) makes it harder to track a moving target at close range.

Mounting these sights on a rifle can be difficult, if the rifle is not designed for such sights. Rifles with MIL-STD 1913 rails will accept these sights with no problems. Other rifles may require special mounts.

As usual, the Resistance will have to make do with what is available. Nevertheless, the advantages of these optical sights are sufficient that they should be used if at all possible.

Night Vision Devices

From initial beginnings with German forces in World War II, night vision devices (NVDs) have become widespread among not only regular armies but guerrilla forces, terrorist groups, and resistance forces.

The benefit of NVDs is that they allow a fighter to see potential targets at night without the targets knowing they are being observed and targeted. As Roberts notes, "our night vision capability was second to none, and gave us a giant advantage over troops not similarly equipped."

Basically, NVDs utilize light amplifiers of one kind or another. Faint starlight may be sufficient for the NVD to produce a useful image. Some NVDs are equipped with infrared illuminators, to supplement the natural light when it is not sufficient to give a good image. However, these illuminators betray their users if the other side is also equipped with NVDs. An illuminator will stand out like a searchlight in another NVD.

If at all possible, the Resistance should obtain NVDs for its forces. Being without them will allow government forces to utilize infrared illuminators with impunity, as well as being able to target Resistance fighters even in the dark.

The article by Fortier gives a good summary of NVDs as of the time the article was written. NVDs were until recently based on use of "microchannel plates;" plates with millions of channels through them that multiply the electrons given off by a photocathode, and direct them to a phosphor screen where they form an amplified version of the image focused on the photocathode. More recently, NVDs have utilized digital technology, with the photocathode replaced by a "charge coupled device" similar to the detector in a digital camera, and a "liquid crystal display" similar to the image display in a digital camera. These are not yet as effective as the earlier technology. However, they are less expensive and lighter, and have longer battery life.

The Resistance will have to use whatever NVDs are available, but should attempt to equip its troops with NVDs to counter Government forces.

References

Balor, Paul, *Manual of the Mercenary Soldier*, Boulder, CO, Paladin Press, 1988.

Camper, Frank, *Live to Spend It*, El Dorado, AR, Desert Publications, 1993.

Ezell, Edward Clinton, *Small Arms of the World*, New York, Barnes & Noble, 1983.

"Fighting Saddam With a Mac," *The American Legion Magazine*, August 2000, pp. 28-30.

Fortier, David M., "Night Vision Devices," *Shooting Times*, August 2004, pp. 76 – 79.

GunManuals.net http://gunmanuals.net/ (downloadable manuals for a wide range of firearms)

Hogg, Ian V., *The Greenhill Military Small Arms Data Book*, Mechanicsburg, PA, Stackpole Books.

Randall, J., *Personal Defense Weapons*, Port Townsend, WA, Loompanics, 1992. (Out of print. Try used book dealers.)

Roberts, Craig, "Marine Scout Sniper," *Soldier of Fortune*, August 2004, pp. 36 – 40, 75.

Savage, Cliff, *The Sling*, Port Townsend, WA, Loompanics, 1984. (Out of print. Try used book dealers.)

Truby, J. David and John Minnery, *Improvised Modified Firearms*, Boulder, CO, Paladin Press, 1992.

Chapter 8

Personal Equipment

The Resistance forces will obviously not be as well equipped as the government forces. Nevertheless, it is important that they have an adequate minimum of personal equipment, to enable them to fight effectively. The Resistance forces should not be like those of George Washington at Valley Forge, leaving bloody footprints in the snow because they had no boots.

In many cases, at least at the outset of open armed resistance, the Resistance members will have to bring their equipment with them, equipment they purchased with their own funds in anticipation of joining the Resistance. During World War II the French Resistance gave the following instructions to recruits regarding personal equipment to be brought with them.

> Bring two shirts, two underpants, two pair wool socks, a light sweater, a scarf, a heavy sweater, a wool blanket, an extra pair of shoes, shoe laces, needles, thread, buttons, safety pins, soap, canteen, knife and fork, flashlight, compass, a weapon if possible, and also if possible a sleeping bag. Wear a warm suit, a beret, a raincoat, a good pair of hobnailed boots.
>
> You will need a complete set of papers, even false, but in order, with a work card to pass you through road-blocks. It is essential to have food ration tickets. (Asprey, p. 315)

While this list may have been appropriate for France in the 1940s, it is not appropriate for all conditions. Jungle, desert, or arctic conditions would require changes in the list. Resistance leaders must take into account the climate, geography, and topography of the combat theater in defining the personal equipment needed by Resistance fighters. Total weight must also be taken into account. Burdening the fighter with too much equipment can be as bad as not

115

having enough of the right equipment. Extensive research has shown that forty pounds is about the maximum that a fighter can carry indefinitely.

The remainder of this chapter is concerned, not so much with what to require as personal equipment, but what to take into account in selecting and deciding on personal equipment.

Armies throughout the world have developed personal equipment for their troops. Some is good, some is not so good, and some gets thrown away immediately by the experienced soldier because it's worthless. Much of this equipment is available on the military surplus market. Resistance forces should take advantage of that availability *when the equipment is suited for their use.* Obtaining the wrong equipment is a waste of resources and a burden on the fighter. Where the right equipment exists but cannot readily be obtained, it might serve as a model for local manufacture.[57] This will be discussed in more detail in the chapter on Logistics.

In personal equipment as in everything else, Resistance forces must settle for what they can get, not what they would like. Nevertheless, where choices are available, the following considerations may be helpful.

Clothing

The international treaties regarding Laws of Land Warfare require that irregular forces wear recognizable uniforms, armbands, or similar means of identifying them as fighters rather than civilians. The Resistance leadership must decide what requirements this imposes on selection of clothing. It will not be discussed further here.

In addition, the clothing should allow the fighters to blend into the local landscape. More will be said about this in the chapter on Camouflage.

---

[57] Simon Bolivar's rebel forces in South America used an American military canteen as a model to be duplicated by local tinsmiths.

The three most important requirements for clothing are that it must be suited to the climate (warm clothing for cold weather, light clothing for warm weather), that it should be comfortable to wear, and that it should be durable. Extra padding at knees and elbows is desirable. It should also have lots of pockets. Liners, vests, jackets, leggings, and other "layers" allow the wearer to adjust to varying temperatures.

Gloves are a necessity in cold weather. They help prevent frostbite of the hands. If possible, the fighter should be provided with a thin leather glove or shell that will allow him to operate his rifle, and heavier gloves to be worn over the shell when shooting is not required.

Rain Gear

Ponchos are superior to raincoats for wet weather wear, because they allow circulation of air beneath them. In addition, military ponchos are designed to be used as shelter halves. Two ponchos snapped together form a pup tent. Alternatively, the edges may be snapped together to form a sleeping bag. The poncho should be hooded, to keep rain from running down the soldier's neck.

When necessary, additional warm clothing may be worn under a poncho. It is thus suitable even in winter rains. The key point is that it must be waterproof, but not too heavy. Moreover, it should shed water, not become waterlogged after long exposure to rain. It should be dull, not shiny. It should not make any noise when the soldier moves.

The chief drawback to a poncho is that it covers the user's arms, making it difficult to fire a rifle or operate other weapons such as machine guns or artillery. In such situations, a raincoat is necessary. Like the poncho, it should be lightweight, waterproof, silent, and dull.

If the Resistance forces will be operating on regions where rain is possible, these considerations should be taken into account in selecting raingear.

Footwear

Napoleon is reputed to have said that an army marches on its stomach. However, soldiers walk on their feet, and their boots must be suited to the task. There is no "one type fits all cases" solution to choice of boots.

Boots should be comfortable. Padded insoles should be considered a necessity. Spongy insoles, that circulate air around the feet, are even better. Boots for cold-weather wear should be insulated sufficiently to prevent frostbite.

Boots for use in rocky or mountainous country should have non-slip soles. However, boots intended for use in tropical areas should have soles that shed mud. Moreover, tropical boots should not have heels, as they make it harder to pull a boot out of the mud.

Boots are usually seen as intended to *keep* water out. However, boots to be worn in hot, humid climates should *let* water out. The wearer will perspire heavily, and the perspiration will accumulate in the boot. If there are no provisions for draining the boot (cloth upper, drain eyelets, etc.) the wearer will soon get "trench foot." In hot, humid climates, *keeping* water out is not nearly as important as *letting* water out. Even if the wearer has to wade a stream, draining the boot is more important than keeping the water out.

Drinking Water

Traditionally soldiers have carried water in canteens. In modern times these were made of metal, but primitive armies used leather or even animal stomachs as canteens. Currently, collapsible plastic canteens are available. They are lighter than metal canteens. Being collapsible, they don't slosh and give away the soldier's location when only partly filled. Another current technology is the "hydration system," consisting of a bladder worn under the soldier's backpack and connected to a tube held near the soldier's mouth. Instead of tipping up a canteen, the soldier simply sucks on the tube. These hydration systems are more expensive than canteens, but for selected troops such as snipers and sappers, they reduce exposure to enemy observation, since they can be used without the wearer raising his head to tip up a cup or canteen.

In a combat theater, readily available water is usually not safe to drink. It is likely to be contaminated with bacteria or *giardia*. Boiling water sufficiently long will always kill this kind of contamination. However, this requires that the fighter have some means for holding the water over a fire. A plastic container obviously will not do. During the Twentieth Century, soldiers in the armies of industrialized countries were provided with chemicals (iodine or chlorine compounds) that would, given time, kill any bacteria in the water. These were not always effective against the cysts causing *giardia*, however. The best current technology is micron-pore filters that are capable of removing essentially all bacteria and cysts. Water should be pre-filtered to remove mud and sediment before passing it through one of these filters, but they represent the best current approach to making water safe to drink. They are available as drinking straws, and as hand-pump devices for filling bottles and canteens.

If at all possible, the Resistance fighters should be equipped with these micron-pore filters. Failing that, they should be supplied with purification tablets to use in the field. In camp, they should drink boiled water.

Sleeping Gear

The type of sleeping gear needed will vary depending on the climate and local conditions. In cold weather, sleeping gear should provide warmth. In warm weather, sleeping gear should allow the user to remain cool while keeping out insects. In either case, the sleeping gear should protect against rain or snow. In some cases hammocks are suitable; in other cases a ground pad of some kind is more appropriate. If insects are a problem, hammocks should have a loose-hanging double bottom, to prevent insects from biting the user through the bottom. Whether the user is sleeping in a hammock or on the ground, some form of mosquito netting, to be draped several inches away from the sleeper, should be provided if insects are a problem.

Tents

In addition to hammocks or sleeping bags, tents are desirable. In cold weather they provide additional shelter against cold or snow. In rainy weather they give the fighter a chance to dry out his clothing and boots overnight.

Ponchos that are designed as shelter halves, so two fighters can snap them together to form a tent, have long been used by various armies. However, the shelter half does not protect the user against ground that is already wet or muddy. Ideally, a one-man or two-man tent should have a sewn-in floor so that the user does not need a separate ground cloth.

Once a tent is used in rainy weather, packing it up then presents a problem. If not given a chance to dry out, it will be much heavier than when dry, adding to the fighter's already heavy load, and if made of cotton or other natural fibers, it will soon rot. If at all possible, tents should be made of nylon or other synthetic materials. Such tents will dry more quickly than tents made of natural fibers, and are lighter to begin with.

Cooking & Rations

The reality is that the Resistance forces will most likely have to depend upon locally-obtained food supplies. They cannot afford the logistical tail involved in providing rations such as MREs (Meals Ready to Eat), freeze-dried camping rations, and similar items. This means that food will have to be cooked and meals prepared "from scratch."

In general, it is more efficient to centralize meal preparation. Even if there is no "mess hall" for the Resistance fighters to eat in, cooking the food is probably better done in a central location, even if this is nothing more than a lean-to or canopy. Stews and soups can be prepared in a single large pot. Meat and even vegetables can be grilled or barbecued directly over a fire.

When individual cooking is appropriate or necessary, the individual fighter must be supplied with some form of "mess kit" in which meals can be both cooked and eaten. There are numerous designs for mess kits in the various armies of the world. If "original" items cannot be obtained in quantity, samples can usually be copied by a tinsmith.

In addition, some form of portable stove must be provided. There are many types of folding stoves available to campers and to military forces. Some are designed to use hexamine or trioxane tablets. These are fine for armies that can afford a logistical tail. Resistance forces will almost always have to make do with individual cooking stoves that burn twigs and wood shavings. A folding stove is desirable because it is compact when not being used. However, some moderate degree of manufacturing capability is required to produce them. Workable stoves can be made from tin cans, but they don't fold and are more difficult to carry than are folding stoves. Of course, a stove can be dispensed with entirely if rocks are available to contain a fire and support a skillet or cooking pot. However, if folding stoves can be made available, they would be more desirable than rocks.

Maps, Compasses, etc.

The chapter on Land Navigation will describe use of maps, compasses, and other navigation equipment. The discussion here is primarily about the equipment itself.

Maps

Paper maps will disintegrate quickly under combat conditions. Maps for use by the Resistance should be coated with plastic or some material that will shed water and resist abrasion. Plastic-laminated maps are best, but they may not be available for the area of interest, and are somewhat bulky. In that case, clear plastic cases to hold paper maps are an acceptable solution.

Compasses

Compasses should have luminous dials and needles, allowing them to be used at night without shining a light on them. They should be rugged enough to withstand hard use. It is desirable that they protect the needle bearing against shocks: either a locking mechanism that lifts the needle off its bearing and holds it motionless when not in use, or else be fluid-filled. Some sighting device is desirable, to allow the user to "shoot a bearing." Another desirable feature is a built-in map scale.

A compass should have some adjustment to compensate for the magnetic declination that arises because the true north pole and the north magnetic pole do not coincide. In Siberia, for instance, the "north" end of the compass needle will actually point almost due east. By contrast, in Sweden the "north" end points almost due west. In Pakistan the "north" end points almost due north. Electronic compasses have built-in adjustments to compensate for magnetic declination (warning: they need batteries, which tend to die when they're needed most). Ordinary magnetic compasses may have some kind of rotating scale that will allow the user to compensate for declination.

Compasses should be waterproof. Even if they are not submerged, they tend to pick up moisture when the humidity is high. If waterproof compasses cannot be obtained, some form of waterproof and airtight container should be provided to protect the compass when it is not actually being used.

Global Positioning System (GPS)

The GPS utilizes signals from a constellation of satellites to "trilaterate" the user's position. The GPS receiver should be waterproof and dustproof. It should be rugged enough to survive the rigors of the battlefield. The display should be illuminated for use at night. The controls should be operable even if the user is wearing heavy gloves.

The biggest problem with GPS receivers is that they require batteries. Murphy's Law applies here: the batteries will go dead at the time the receiver is most needed. Thus the receivers should be selected to use readily-available batteries, and the batteries should be light enough that the user can carry at least one set of spares.

If the GPS system is available to the Resistance, it makes an excellent navigation tool. The user always knows his location, day or night, and many GPS receivers will compute bearing and distance to a specified destination from the user's known location. However, the GPS receiver alone will not provide directional information. The user needs a compass in addition to the GPS (note: some GPS receivers do have a built-in compass; these receivers are preferred if they are light-weight and portable).

Load-Bearing Equipment

Soldiers carry loads: weapon, ammunition, sleeping gear, mess kit, first aid pack, entrenching tool, and on and on. Resistance forces may be fortunate in one respect: they carry less than a typical soldier because they have less. Even so, Resistance forces will require some form of load-bearing equipment: backpack, Y or H suspenders, vest, or belt.

Load-bearing equipment should be sturdy enough to survive the rigors of field use. At the same time, it should be as light as possible. These are often contradictory requirements, but with careful design and choice of materials, they can both be met. Unfortunately, Resistance forces may not have the design or manufacturing capability to achieve a good compromise between durability and weight. Nevertheless, every effort should be made to provide Resistance forces with sturdy but light-weight backpacks, vests, and belts.

In addition to being sturdy and light-weight, load-bearing equipment should fit the wearer well. Loads should be carried as close to the body as possible (this is one of the big advantages of a load-bearing vest), and low enough to avoid making the wearer top-heavy. Packs should provide large, unobstructed interior space for things like sleeping bags and ponchos, but should also have multiple pockets or compartments where the user can stow things that need to be found in a hurry, without rummaging through a lot of other things. Packs should also have provisions for lashing items to the outside. For vests, D-rings serve the same purpose. If at all possible, load-bearing equipment should be made from synthetic materials like nylon instead of cotton. Frames or packboards should be made of fiberglass instead of wood or aluminum. Packs should be waterproof, and vests should have waterproof compartments.

Medical & Hygiene

The chapter on Survival will deal with the medical organization of the Resistance. The concern here will be the measures taken by the individual Resistance fighter. It will be necessary for the Resistance to establish hospitals and other facilities for surgery and for long-term treatment of wounds. However, the responsibility for the health of the individual Resistance fighter lies first and foremost with the fighter himself. The Resistance fighter must avoid injuries, especially those from environmental causes, and must provide his own first aid and treatment of minor injuries. The individual fighter must also provide immediate care for himself or for a comrade when a serious injury or wound occurs, prior to transportation to a medical facility.

Medical kits

The individual medical kit should contain those items likely to be needed for treatment of minor injuries and disease, and for the stop-gap treatment of major injuries or wounds. Suggested items would include:

- Adhesive bandages
- sterile gauze pads and tape
- pressure bandage for bleeding wounds
- disinfectant such as tincture of iodine (not recommended for tropical areas because it damages sweaty skin) or an antibiotic powder (preferred) or ointment (acceptable)
- water purification tablets
- antimalarial tablets (if the Resistance is operating in areas where malaria is a threat)
- sunscreen (if operations are in areas where sunburn is a threat)
- antiseptic wipes
- quick-clotting powder for arterial or venous bleeding (this, plus a pressure bandage, is a life-saving stop-gap treatment until the wounded fighter can reach a medical facility)
- snake-bite kit (if the Resistance is operating in an area where this might be needed)

- anti-fungal ointment (primarily important in jungle areas and in temperate areas during summer; over-the-counter medicines for athletes foot are acceptable)
- diarrhea medicine

Every Resistance fighter should be equipped with these items, if at all possible, and should know how to apply them to himself or to a comrade.

Personal Hygiene

This means more than just keeping oneself clean, although it definitely includes that. If the fighter's skin and clothing are clean, a wound or injury is much less likely to become infected.

Fighters must be trained to treat minor scratches and insect bites promptly with antibiotic ointment or powder, to prevent infection. This is especially important in tropical areas.

Fighters must keep their feet dry, if at all possible, and at the very least dry them at night when they take off their footwear. Fungal infections are common when the fighter's feet stay wet for an extended time. These infections must be treated promptly before they become major problems, since they can readily provide an avenue for bacteria such as streptococcus to create a more serious infection.

The individual fighter must take responsibility for removing ticks, leeches, and thorns as promptly as possible. Failure in this aspect of personal hygiene can lead to more serious problems in short order.

Protection against insects

In tropical and temperate areas, and in arctic areas during summer, insects can be a serious problem. At best, they are an annoyance. At worst, they carry very serious diseases such as malaria, dengue fever, typhus, and West Nile fever. The individual fighter needs to be protected against insects.

Exposed skin should be protected by an insect repellent such as DEET. Repellants other than DEET are also effective, but don't last as long as DEET. They must be applied more frequently. Whatever repellent the fighters are using, it must be applied often enough to remain effective.

Clothing should be sprayed or soaked with a repellent such as permethrin. Once properly treated, clothing will repel insects for up to two weeks. Re-treatment should be applied as necessary.

Mosquito netting can be hung from a broad-brimmed hat to protect the face and neck from insects. When properly used, this netting will still allow the fighter to fire a rifle or a crew-served weapon.

Cutting Tools

There are two purposes for cutting tools: cutting things, and fighting.

For clearing underbrush, for cutting tent pegs, for cutting branches to make a lean-to, or for cutting small branches for firewood, a machete is the best tool. A typical machete has a blade 18 to 24 inches long. Both back and edge are straight, except the blade is curved at the tip. The handle has a knob at the end, to help prevent the machete from slipping from the user's hand at the end of a swing. The blade should be made of a type of steel that will hold an edge for a considerable period without needing sharpening. However, it should not be so hard that it is prone to breaking. The machete requires a sheath. It should be made of material that doesn't rot, and any fasteners or hardware should be of rustproof material. Also, the lighter the better.

The machete actually makes a good fighting knife. However, in areas where a machete is not required for clearing brush or similar purposes, a lighter knife is more desirable. The blade should be five or six inches long. A guard between blade and grip is desirable. The grip should be of some non-slip material. As with the machete, holding an edge is desirable, but the material should not be so hard that there is danger of chipping or breaking. Since the fighter will use his knife for many more things than fighting (cutting tent pegs or firewood, digging small holes, probing for land mines, prying things open), the blade should be sturdy and the tang should extend all the way through the grip.

Regardless of whether the fighter carries a machete or a knife (or both), an essential part of his equipment is a sharpening stone. A small carborundum stone works nicely. If at all possible, the stone should have both coarse and fine grit. The coarse grit will speed the process of smoothing out nicks in the blade, while the fine grit hones the final edge.

Digging Tools

Resistance forces do not often occupy fixed positions. Their tactics are instead to "disappear" when confronted with a strong government force. Nevertheless, from time to time Resistance fighters will need digging tools: preparing a sniper's hide; preparing an ambush; preparing an overnight bivouac; burying things that would otherwise tip off government forces of their presence; digging a latrine. Some form of entrenching tool is needed for these purposes. It should be adjustable for use as either a shovel or a pick. The blade should be sturdy enough to cut through fairly thick roots. There should be no sharp or rough edges or corners where the user holds the tool. If the tool folds, it will be easier to carry. While sturdy enough to be functional, the entrenching tool and its cover should be as light as possible.

It should be noted that Russian "Spetsnaz" forces carry non-folding shovels with straight but fairly short handles. They have found these to be effective as digging tools, and with one edge of the blade sharpened like a knife, they are also an effective fighting tool.

Flashlights

For map-reading at night, a flashlight with a red lens is preferred, since the red light does not destroy night vision. However, only a few leaders will need these map-reading lights. The majority of the fighters will need flashlights with blue lenses, for finding their way at night, or for use under a poncho to inspect themselves for ticks, leeches, thorns and scratches. Blue light is much less visible at a distance than are either red or white light. A blue light, used to find one's way along a path in the dark, is much less likely to alert the enemy. Each fighter should have a small flashlight with a blue lens. If at all possible, these flashlights should use the same batteries as other equipment carried by the fighter (GPS, radio, electronic compass, etc.)

If at all possible, the flashlights used by both leaders and other fighters should use LEDs rather than regular flashlight bulbs. Batteries last much longer in LED flashlights than they do in regular flashlights. Since batteries are always a problem for troops in the field, and are likely to be even more so for Resistance fighters, anything that saves batteries is worth using, even if it is a bit more expensive at the outset.

Two other special-purpose light sources should be considered: chemical light sticks and electroluminescent lights.

Chemical light sticks contain chemicals that are activated by bending or shaking the stick. The chemical reaction then gives off light. The sticks come in various colors, and various levels of brightness (the brighter, the shorter the operating time). They are very useful for marking trails, for illumination inside tents or under ponchos, and other applications where a really bright light is not required. They have shelf lives of several years, and do not require batteries. However, once activated, they cannot be turned off.

Electroluminescent lights are made to replace chemical light sticks. They require batteries, but can be turned on and off. They come in various colors and serve much the same purposes as the chemical light sticks.

Non-Military Sources

One of the most important developments in recent years has been the increasing availability of military-equivalent personal equipment from commercial sources. Suppliers to various armies have found that campers, hunters, and outdoors enthusiasts are a ready market for the same kinds of personal equipment they sell to their military customers. A partial list of suppliers, with their web sites, is given at the end of the chapter. Some of their products are military surplus and can be obtained at low cost. Other products are expensive but of high quality. These latter may well be beyond the means of Resistance forces. However, they should be considered for specialized troops such as snipers and commandos.

References

Asprey, Robert B., *War in the Shadows: The Guerrilla in History*, New York, Morrow, 1994.

Kearney, Cresson H., *Jungle Snafus . . . And Remedies*, Cave Junction, OR, Oregon Institute of Science & Medicine, 1966.

Equipment Sources

ATS Tactical Gear
http://www.atstacticalgear.biz/cgi/commerce.cgi?display=home

Blackhawk   http://www.blackhawk.com/

Brigade Quartermasters   http://www.BrigadeQM.com

Campmor http://www.campmor.com/outdoor/gear/Home

http://www.cheaperthandirt.com   Cheaper than Dirt

http://www.dbtdefense.com/   http://www.DBTDEFENSE.com

Drop Zone Tactical   http://www.dropzonetactical.com/

Georgia-Outfitters.com   http://www.georgia-outfitters.com/index.html

Ranger Joe's   http://www.rangerjoe.com/

Shomer-Tec   http://www.shomertec.com/index.cfm

Tactical Gear Command
        http://www.tacticalgearcommand.com/

US Cavalry   http://www.uscav.com/

Chapter 9

Survival skills

Members of the armed wing of the Resistance will normally be living under much more austere conditions than they were used to prior to the war. Most will not know how to survive under austere conditions. Leadership of the Resistance must plan for their survival training, and may need to provide equipment and supplies.

Medicine and field sanitation

During the American Revolution, nearly nine times as many revolutionary soldiers died from disease as died from combat. The causes included poor diet, inadequate sanitation, and lack of proper medical care. Diseases such as dysentery, typhus, scurvy and smallpox decimated the ranks.[58] Smallpox has now been conquered, and we now know how to prevent scurvy. Moreover, we now know that germs cause disease, and know that simple sanitation can eliminate many causes of disease. Nevertheless, lack of proper medical care can result in unnecessary deaths of resistance troops. Any resistance movement must prepare for the medical requirements of armed resistance.

The Resistance forces must be trained in first aid. Lives can be saved by prompt action to stop bleeding, to seal sucking chest wounds, and avoid shock. The issues of hospital-level care and convalescent care will be addressed in Chapter 16. It is crucial that the Resistance forces be trained to provide the immediate care that will allow the wounded and injured to survive until they can reach treatment facilities. A good source is the Ranger Medical Handbook, available for download at http://www.ocdsterling.com/rangermedichandbook2007.pdf (Be prepared for a long download.)

---

[58] See the book by Reiss for historical details.

Cold Weather Problems

Fighters recruited from urban areas may not be used to working and surviving in the cold. Even rural recruits may be used to houses and barns. Living and fighting away from normal habitations may bring problems. Some of the most severe are as follows.

Wind Chill

Cold wind will drain heat from the body quickly. Even though the temperature may seem "reasonable," if there is much wind, the *effective* temperature can be much lower. That is, in the presence of wind, the body can lose heat at the rate it *would* lose heat at a much lower temperature in the absence of wind.

The fighter must protect against wind chill by wearing adequate clothing, including windproof outer clothing. Several layers are better than one heavier garment.

Frostbite

Frostbite involves actual freezing of the skin and underlying flesh. It can be avoided by adequate covering, including covering the face. Tight clothing that impedes circulation may lead to frostbite, however. If clothing becomes wet from water or sweat, it should be dried as soon as possible, as the water will drain heat from the body. The fighter should wear gloves, and should keep exercising the hands to avoid frostbite.

Feet are particularly prone to frostbite, since blood may have difficulty reaching the extremities, and the feet are in contact with cold ground and snow. Feet should be insulated with multiple layers of socks, and boots should be waterproof.

Water

Water presents two problems. One is crossing rivers or lakes. The other is drinking.

Crossing Icy Water

Wading or falling into water at or near the freezing point can be fatal. The sudden cold shock causes the body to curl up and to lose muscular control and begin violent shivering. Should this happen, the fighter must immediately take violent action to reach land or to get back into a boat. Once out of the water, the fighter must dry off as much as possible.

Drinking Water

Springs and small streams will be frozen over, making it difficult to obtain water for drinking. It is crucial that the Resistance fighters *not* eat crushed ice or snow. These rapidly drain heat from the body. Ice and snow must be melted over fire or some other source of heat such as a vehicle engine block.

Canteens should be insulated, to delay freezing as long as possible. Plastic canteens have some advantages over metal, but they cannot be warmed over a fire, and at a low enough temperature the plastic becomes brittle and may crack. For cold weather use, metal canteens are better than plastic.

Snow Glare

The sun's rays, reflected off snow, can cause snow blindness. Some form of eye protection is needed. Sunglasses will work satisfactorily. In their absence, however, a strip of bark or cloth with a narrow slit cut in it can serve as a substitute. The area below the eyes should be blackened with black camouflage makeup or charcoal.

Trench Foot

Trench foot results from the fighter's feet being wet for extended periods at temperatures just above freezing. The feet become cold and swollen, and may take on a waxy appearance. In extreme cases the foot or leg must be amputated. Prevention involves keeping the feet dry. In conditions conducive to trench foot, the fighter should carry extra socks in a waterproof container (even a sealable plastic bag will do), and change socks as needed. Wet socks must be dried out so they can be re-used.

Jungle Problems

Jungle regions typically have high temperatures and high humidity. In addition, they typically have pests such as insects and leeches, and thick vegetation including vines and thorns. Despite the high temperature, clothing should cover the entire body, to give as much protection as possible against insects and thorns. It should be light and loose fitting, however, to allow circulation of air.

It will be almost impossible to dry sweat-soaked clothing simply by hanging it up. It must be dried over heat. Clothing that remains soaked with perspiration will rot quickly, hence drying is important.

The combination of high humidity and high temperature means that the fighter will lose a great deal of water through perspiration. Thus a supply of drinking water is essential. Fortunately, in jungle areas it may rain almost daily (dry season) to raining almost continuously (rainy season). While water is thus plentiful, it must be purified, since bacteria of all kinds thrive in jungle waterholes.

Arid Region Problems

The primary survival problems in arid regions are water and temperature variations. Sandstorms are also a problem.

Water

By definition, arid regions are short of water. Resistance forces operating in arid regions must depend on springs, wells, and oases. Provisions must be made to supply the individual fighters with at least two liters (half a gallon) of water daily from these sources. If there are no such sources in a particular region, Resistance forces probably will not be operating in that region anyway. Government forces, with a logistics tail, will be able to operate in regions too arid for the Resistance.

Temperature Variations

The temperatures in arid regions can range from well below zero to well above body temperature. At the lower end of the temperature range, Resistance fighters must observe the same precautions against wind chill and frostbite as they would in cold regions. At the upper end of the temperature range, Resistance fighters must avoid dehydration, avoid sunburn, and avoid thorns and insect bites. In high temperatures, clothing should be light and loose fitting, but should cover the entire body in order to avoid sunburn. Note that ground surface temperature may be even higher than air temperature during the daytime. This means that the fighter's feet may be exposed to much higher temperature than the rest of the body.

Sandstorms

The soil tends to be loose in arid regions, even if it is not actually sand. Even light winds will cause sand and dust to blow around. High winds can produce thick clouds of sand that completely blot out vision. During such sandstorms it is essential to wear goggles and to cover the nose and mouth with cloth.

Summary

Depending on the nature of the country, the Resistance fighter may have to operate in extreme conditions. Surviving and remaining in condition to fight effectively depend on properly adapting to the existing conditions. Training and proper clothing and equipment will allow the Resistance to be an effective fighting force.

References
Medical Care

Benson, Ragnar, *The Survival Nurse*, Boulder, CO, Paladin Press, 2000. (Care of patients *after* doctors have patched them up.)

Coffee, Hugh L., *Ditch Medicine*, Boulder, CO, Paladin Press, 1993.

Dickson, Murray, *Where There Is No Dentist*, Palo Alto, CA, Hesperian Foundation, 1996.

Duke, James A., *The Green Pharmacy*, New York, St. Martin's, 1998.

DVD: "Gunshot Wound First Aid," available from Cheaper than Dirt

DVD: "Blunt Force Trauma First Aid," available from Cheaper than Dirt

Reiss, Oscar, M.D., *Medicine and the American Revolution*, Jefferson, NC, McFarland, 1998, ISBN 0-7864-0338-1.

Steele, Peter, M.D., *Backcountry Medical Guide*, Seattle, WA, The Mountaineers Books.

United States Army Institute for Military Assistance, *US Army Special Forces Medical Handbook, ST 31-91B*, 1982.

Werner, David, *Where There Is No Doctor*, Palo Alto, CA, Hesperian Foundation, 1996.

Wilderness Survival

Department of the Army, *U.S. Army Survival Manual, FM 21-76*, 1994.

The Survival Library on CD, 98 Military Manuals on CD, including many on survival, available from http://www.muddywaterpress.com/cd.html, $20 as of this writing.

United States Rescue and Special Operations Group, *Six Ways In & Twelve Ways Out* (out of print; may be available from online or used book sellers. Excellent, though. Get it if you can.)

Wiseman, John, *The SAS Survival Handbook*, New York, Harper Collins, 1986.

Web sites

http://outlands.tripod.com/survival/cache.htm

http://www.cheaperthandirt.com

http://www.usrsog.org/ Information on survival

Chapter 10

Land Navigation

Troops in the field need to be able to find their way from one location to another. In particular, they need to be able to find their way to an ambush site, to a rally point, to a rest camp, or other specific location. Ability to do this is critical to Resistance forces.

Map Reading

A map is essentially a picture of the Earth as seen from overhead. However, it is a very specialized picture, an abstraction. It does not show the Earth as it actually looks, but instead presents only those features important to the map user. A road map will show roads and towns, and possibly rivers, bridges, railroad crossings, and other features important to the motorist. A hydrographic map, instead, will show things of interest to the mariner, such as water depth, location of reefs and wrecks, lighthouses, and location of shipping channels. An airways map will show airports, beacons, surface elevations, air routes, and other features of importance to a pilot. That is, these different maps emphasize those features important to the user, and suppress all the rest. Regardless of the type of map, however, it is still a picture of the Earth, as the user would see it from the appropriate altitude, with only the important features marked.

One point must be kept in mind about maps. The Earth is (approximately) a sphere. Maps are flat. It is impossible to portray the spherical Earth accurately on a flat map. Every map is in some way a compromise, designed to represent a region as accurately as possible. On the Earth, lines of longitude converge at the poles. On the commonly used Mercator map projection, however, the lines of longitude are parallel. Near the equator, this isn't a serious problem. Near the poles, however, there is serious distortion, with features stretched in an east-west direction.[59] While the Mercator projection

---

[59] Compare the relatively large size of Greenland as portrayed on a Mercator flat map (apparently larger than the United States) and the apparently much smaller

distorts regions near the poles, it has the significant advantage that a compass course crosses all the meridians at the same angle (a so-called "rhumb line" course). For small distances, the deviation from a true "great circle" or minimum-distance course is not significant, and plotting a rhumb-line course on a Mercator map is much easier than plotting a true great circle course.

From the standpoint of the Resistance fighter, there are three kinds of maps that will be important. For urban operations, a street map is required. For rural operations, a topographic map is required. Each one, it its own way, presents those features the user is interested in, and suppresses all the rest. For instance, on a street map, color may be used to indicate the size or importance of the street, rather than the actual color of the paving. Parks, reservoirs, public buildings, and other urban features may be shown, but not in their true color. In addition, the Resistance fighter may use aerial or satellite photos.

For the typical operations of a Resistance unit, the problem of representing a spherical Earth on a flat map is not significant. City street maps and topographic maps are adequate for the purposes to which they will be put.

Topographic Maps

An example of a topographic map is shown in Figure 10-1. This map is a section of West Virginia. A topographic map shows roads, towns, railroads, political subdivisions, rivers and lakes. It also shows a scale of distances. What makes it a topographic map is that it shows elevations as contour lines. Each contour line is noted as to its height above a reference. In the case of this map, the reference is sea level. Contour lines provide important information about the "lay of the land." If they are close together, the land is steep. If far apart, the land is gently sloping or level. If closed, they indicate a hill (or a hollow). V-shaped contours indicate a valley. Topographic maps can be helpful in identifying suitable locations for ambushes and similar activities.

---

size portrayed on a globe. This illustrates the distortion of the Mercator projection near the Poles.

Figure 10-1. Example of Topographic Map (U.S. Geological Survey)

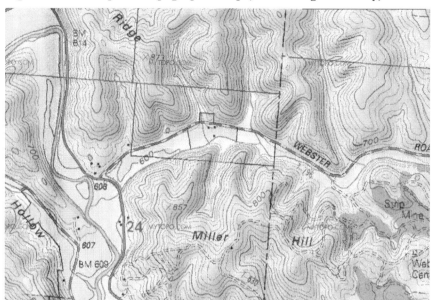

Street Maps

An example of a street map is shown in Figure 10-2.[60] The map shows streets, important buildings, parks, and other urban features. Street maps may or may not have a distance scale. Almost always, however, they will have grid markings like those shown at the edge of the map. These allow the user to find some feature in an index, then locate it on the map using the grid references. For instance, a high school is shown in Grid Square M-10.

---

[60] This map is a section of Dayton, Ohio.

Figure 10-2. Example of Street Map (Dayton, OH)

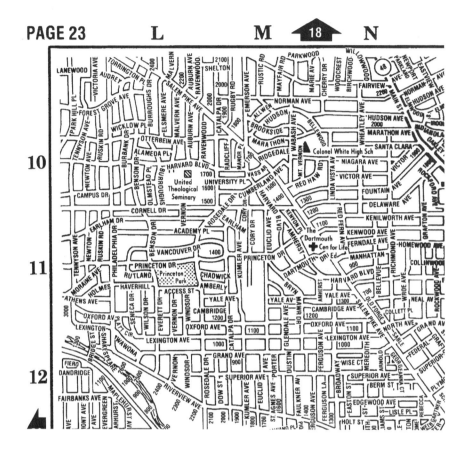

Aerial & Satellite Photos

An example of a satellite photo is shown in Figure 10-3. This is an image of Chicago, IL, obtained from Google Earth. Satellite photos vary in the resolution available, depending on the source. Those from NASA are usually of fairly low resolution. Those from commercial sources may have resolutions as good as half a meter. High resolution photos, up-to-date, can be expensive. However, for many purposes those available from sources such as Google Earth may be satisfactory. The Resistance should plan to make use of available satellite imagery in planning raids, ambushes, and similar activities.

Figure 10-3. Satellite Image of Chicago (Google Earth)

Using Maps for Navigating

There are two questions you may need to answer regarding land navigation. The first is "Where am I?" That is, can I locate my present position on the map? The second is, "How do I get to where I want to be?" Note that this second question does not require that you know where you are. It only requires that you know how to get to a specific place. As will be shown later, it is possible to navigate from a known starting point to a known destination without knowing where you are at every step of the way.

Global Positioning System (GPS)

GPS is a satellite-based navigation system. It uses twenty-four satellites orbiting the Earth in six different planes at an altitude of 20,200 km. The satellites have a twelve-hour period. The Coarse Acquisition (C/A) mode signal of GPS is at 1575.42 MHz. It provides an accuracy of 75 – 100 meters. The Precision-code (P-code) signal is at 1227.6 MHz. It has an accuracy of 16 meters. When augmented by Differential GPS, the GPS accuracy can be a few inches. GPS provides 2-D and 3-D coverage throughout the world.

P-code is encrypted by the US government to deny it to enemy nations. C/A can be degraded in wartime to deny precise targeting information to an enemy.

GPS is not the only satellite navigation system in existence. Russian GLONASS and European Galileo may also be available. However, receivers for these systems are not as readily available as are receivers for GPS.

Keep in mind that GPS may not be available to the Resistance. It may be degraded severely or turned off completely, if the U.S. government is involved in fighting elsewhere, or for other reasons that have nothing to do with your fight against your government. Other means of navigation may be required. So long as GPS is available, it is the best navigation aid. Because it may not be available, however, it is important for the Resistance fighter to know other means of navigation.

Compass and Map Navigation
    A magnetic compass points to the North magnetic pole, which is located in northern Canada, south of the true North Pole. The difference between magnetic north and true north is called "declination." There are maps that give the declination for specific areas on the Earth. The book by Seiden contains an example. Since most maps are based on true north, it will be necessary for the Resistance fighter to correct for declination when using a magnetic compass.

Compass Types
    There are two types likely to be of interest to the Resistance fighter: the baseplate compass and the lensatic compass.

Baseplate Compass

A baseplate compass is shown in Figure 10-4. The rotating dial can be used to offset the compass to account for declination. If at your location the declination is West (that is, the compass needle points west of true north), the rotating dial should be rotated *clockwise* a number of degrees equal to the declination. Conversely, if declination is East, the rotating dial should be rotated *counterclockwise*. Then when the needle is contained within the outline on the baseplate (and in the right orientation), the numbers on the rotating dial read degrees from true north.

Figure 10-4. Baseplate Compass

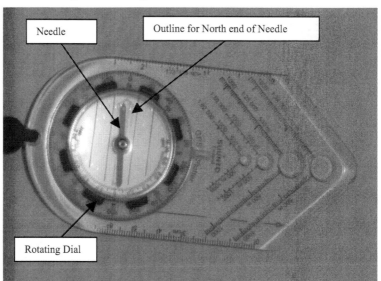

Needle

Outline for North end of Needle

Rotating Dial

Lensatic Compass

A Lensatic compass is shown in Figure 10-5. The essential features are a sighting wire and a sighting notch. In use, the compass is held near eye level. The user sights on a landmark by looking through the notch and lining up the sighting wire with the landmark. The lens then allows the user to read the bearing to the landmark.[61] The lensatic compass can be used to orient a map, however it is not as convenient to do this as it is with a baseplate compass.

---

[61] The baseplate compass can also be used to "shoot a bearing," but it is much more difficult to use in that way than is a lensatic compass.

Figure 10-5. Lensatic Compass (from FM 21-6)

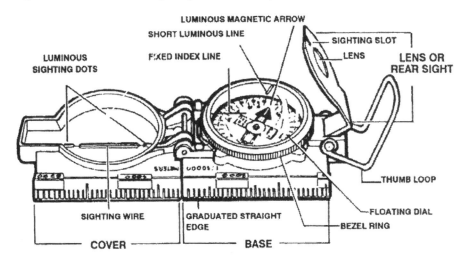

Some Lensatic compasses do not have an adjustment for magnetic declination. If so, then some arithmetic is required. If the declination is West (or minus), *add* the amount of the declination to the measured bearing. If the declination is East (or plus), *subtract* the declination from the measured bearing. This will give the true bearing, which can be plotted on a map.

Using Compass and Map

The baseplate compass is intended to be used with a map. The map is placed on a level, flat surface. The compass is corrected for declination. The edge of the compass is aligned with true north on the map. The map is then rotated until the compass needle is within the outline. Once this is done, the map is oriented to true north. The numbers on the rotating dial of the compass then correspond to bearings on the map.

With the baseplate compass, it is assumed you know where you are and can locate that point on the map, but you need to know the direction to get to your destination, which is also on the map. Orienting the map to true north will allow you to determine the bearing to follow to get to your destination.

The lensatic compass can conveniently be used to locate yourself on a map, by a process known as "resection." This is shown in Figure 10-6 (taken from FM 21-25). The idea is to "shoot a bearing" from your position to at least two prominent landmarks that can be located on the map (hills, towers, smokestacks, etc.) That is, you get the bearing from your (unknown) position to the landmark. You then draw on the map a line from the landmark back to you, at the "back azimuth" from the landmark. The back azimuth is computed as follows. If the direct bearing (including correction for declination) is less than 180 degrees, back azimuth is the direct bearing *plus* 180 degrees. If the direct azimuth is greater than 180 degrees, the back azimuth is the direct azimuth *minus* 180 degrees. Plot back azimuths from at least two landmarks on the map. You are at the intersection of the back azimuths. Ideally the landmarks should be about 90 degrees apart as seen from your location, to provide the greatest accuracy.

Figure 10-6. Locating yourself by resection.

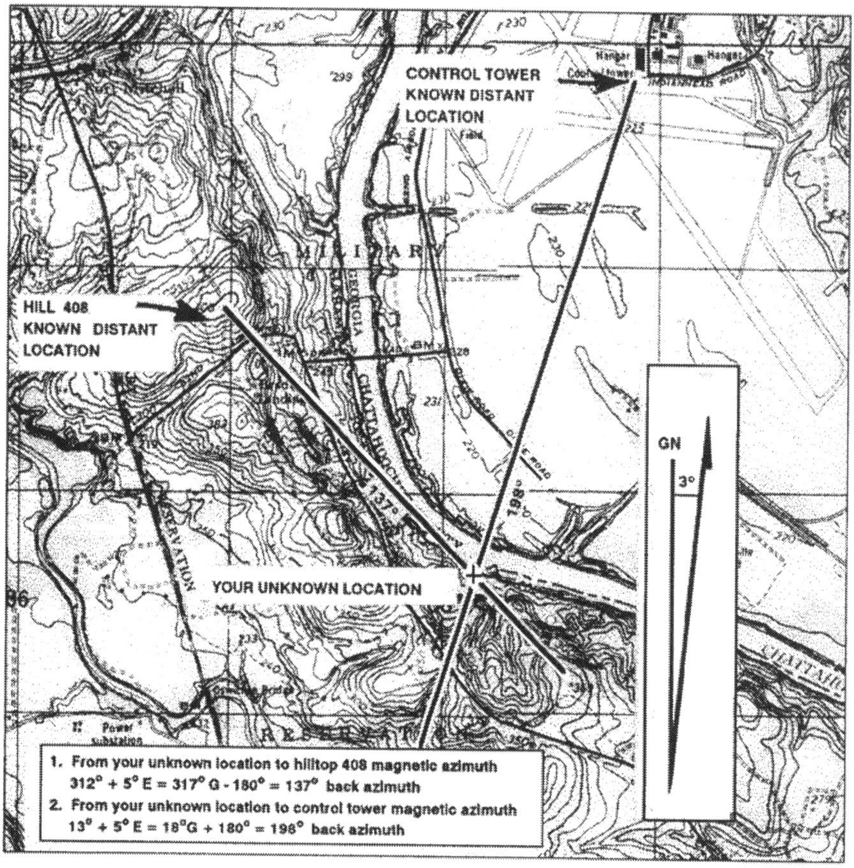
CONTROL TOWER
KNOWN DISTANT
LOCATION
HILL 408
KNOWN DISTANT
LOCATION
YOUR UNKNOWN LOCATION
137°
198°
GN
3°
1. From your unknown location to hilltop 408 magnetic azimuth
312° + 5° E = 317° G - 180° = 137° back azimuth
2. From your unknown location to control tower magnetic azimuth
13° + 5° E = 18°G + 180° = 198° back azimuth

Following a Bearing

Regardless of which method you use to locate yourself on the map, you then need to follow a bearing to reach your destination. The best method is to locate some landmark (hill, prominent tree, building) that is right on the bearing you want to follow. Simply head for that landmark. Even if you have to deviate from your course because of minor obstacles, when you reach the landmark you are on course, and can then repeat the process.

If there is no prominent landmark in the direction in which you want to go, but you are at some prominent landmark, you can reverse the process. From time to time, shoot a bearing back to your starting point. The back azimuth from that point will be the bearing you want to follow. If the back azimuth you measure is wrong, you know you have deviated from your desired course. You can then correct your course by moving sideways until you get the correct back azimuth.

If there are no landmarks available, one option is to send one member of your party ahead, using radio or hand signals to keep them on the correct bearing. Once they have gone far enough, have them wait while the rest of the party catches up.

Bearing and Distance Navigation

Navigating using compass and map allows you to know where you are all the time. You know the direction you must follow to reach your destination.

However, there is an alternative. Historically it has been known as *ded* (from *deduced*) reckoning. It amounts to keeping track of the distance and direction you travel on each leg of a multi-leg journey, especially if you have to deviate from the direct course to your destination to avoid obstacles or for other reasons.

Assume you are to reach a destination that is 600 yards away from your starting point, at a bearing of 40 degrees. From the starting point, take the compass bearing on which you intend to travel, which may be different from 40 degrees, because you want to avoid some obstacles. As you move, measure distance or time on that bearing. When you change direction, repeat the process. If on foot, count paces, or clock minutes and multiply by your rate of march. In a vehicle, use the odometer. The results can be recorded in a table such as that in Table 10-1.

Table 10-1. Record of bearings and distances.

Bearing degrees	Start	Stop	Elapsed Time/Distance
0			100 yds
15			150 yds
40			75 yds
70			100 yds
0			100 yds

(Use Start and Stop columns for starting and stopping times)

The bearings and distances can obviously be plotted on a map. At the end of each leg, you will know where you are relative to your destination. However, a map is not needed. Figure 10-7 shows the bearings and distances plotted on graph paper. The direct distance to the destination is shown as a dashed arrow. The legs from the Table are shown as solid arrows. At the end of the fifth leg, with a protractor and ruler you can read off directly the bearing and distance to the destination: 200 yards at 82 degrees. However, while graph paper is convenient, it is not needed. The path can also be drawn on plain paper. It can even be scratched in the dirt. So long as it is *drawn to scale*, a plot of bearings and distances is sufficient to navigate from a starting point to a point at a known distance and bearing, or to navigate back to the starting point, regardless of deviations from a direct path.

Figure 10-7. Plot of bearings and distances

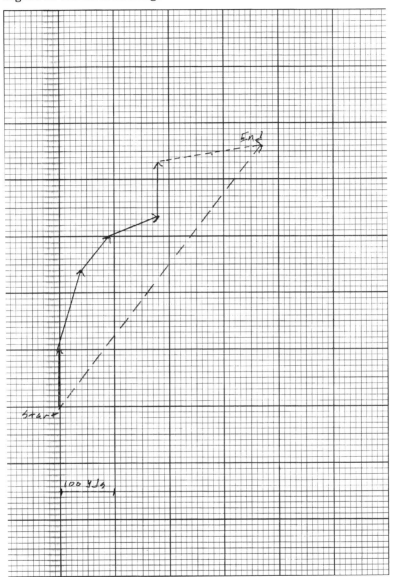

Urban Navigation

The map and compass navigation used in rural or open area is of little value in urban areas. Travel in cities is via streets and alleys. A street map is more valuable than a compass. Electronic street maps of many cities are available for GPS units. These maps

149

can be downloaded into the GPS, which then provides the user with his present position in the city in terms of street location rather than latitude and longitude. Even GPS may be of little help, however, since tall buildings block the satellite signals. Street signs may be far more useful than either a compass or a GPS in cities. Resistance fighters operating in cities must be able to use street maps to navigate from where they are to where they are needed.

Aerial and satellite photos are also useful, but they lack street names. However, street names can be marked on the photos prior to an operation, and they will give a more accurate representation of the actual physical layout of the city than even the best-drawn map.

Summary

Resistance forces will need to navigate from one point to another. If GPS is available, it is the best method to use. In the absence of GPS, Resistance force members should be trained to use map, compass, and ded reckoning.

References

http://www.armystudyguide.com/content/army_board_study_guide_topics/land_navigation_map_reading/index.shtml

Department of the Army, *Map Reading and Land Navigation, FM 21-26*, 1987.

Gallagher, James J., *Combat Leader's Field Guide*, Chapter 13, Mechanicsburg, PA, Stackpole Books, 1994, ISBN 0-8117-2425-5.

Hotchkiss, Noel J., *A Comprehensive Guide to Land Navigation with GPS*, Herndon, VA, Alexis Press, 1994, ISBN 0-9641273-2-6.

Paul, Don, *The Green Beret's Compass Course*, Woodland, CA, Path Finder Publications, 1991. (Instructions on ded reckoning.)

Seidman, David, *The Essential Wilderness Navigator*, New York, McGraw-Hill, 1995. (Essentially a map-and-compass instruction book.)

http://www.monsterguide.net/how-to-use-a-lensatic-compass.shtml, a web site that gives instruction on use of a lensatic compass.

Appendix To Chapter 10

As shown in the main text, you can navigate using bearings and distances, making a scale drawing of your path "made good." However, with the use of some mathematics, even a drawing can be eliminated.

In the example, the object was to reach a destination 600 yards away, at a bearing of 0 degrees. You could do this by moving 459 yards due north and then 385 yards due east. These are calculated, using sine and cosine functions as:[62]

Distance north = 600*cos(40)=459

Distance east = 600*sin(40)=385

Thus we can set up a table similar to the one in the main text (omitting the unused "time" columns), where "Northing" is the distance made good to the north, and "Easting" is the distance made good to the East. Northing is calculated as the leg length multiplied by the cosine of the bearing angle for that leg; Easting is calculated as the leg length multiplied by the sine of the bearing angle. If the travel is to the south or to the west, the sine and cosine functions will automatically attach the proper negative signs.

---

[62] Note that if your calculator or spreadsheet uses angles in radians instead of degrees (as Microsoft Excel does), divide the degrees by 57.3.

Table 10A-1. Calculated distances and bearings

Bearing (deg)	Distance		Northing	Easting
0	100		100	0
15	150		145	39
40	75		57	48
70	100		34	94
0	100		100	0
	Distances made good		437	181
	Distances intended		459	385
	Distances remaining		23	205
	83 degrees		206 yards	

The first five rows show the distance made good to the north and the east on each leg. These are calculated as the leg distance multiplied by the cosine and the sine of the bearing angle for that leg, respectively. The total distances made good north and east are shown in the seventh row. The intended distance is shown in the eighth row, and the distance remaining in both north and east directions, that is, distance desired minus distance made good, is shown in the ninth row. Bearing and remaining distance are shown in the tenth row. These are calculated as:[63]

Bearing = arctangent(Easting remaining/Northing remaining) (Note that the desired angle is measured from North)

Distance = Easting remaining/sine(Bearing). (Note that sums may not equal detail because of rounding.)

This exact calculation should be compared with the graphical calculation. The two are within the accuracy of the graphical calculation. For many practical navigation problems, the graphical ded reckoning method is "good enough," provided sufficient care is taken to make the drawing to scale. However, the mathematical

---

[63] Remember to convert between degrees and radians, if necessary.

calculation is more accurate and avoids the need to make a drawing.[64]

The mathematical calculation can be done on a laptop with a spreadsheet, if this is available. The calculation can be done more conveniently in the field using a PDA (Personal Digital Assistant) such as a Palm Pilot or similar device. The calculations can even be done, if less conveniently, by using a calculator with trigonometric functions, and recording each separate result in a table like Table 10A-1

---

[64] The mathematical calculation may amount to "over-refinement," since the errors in pace counting or shooting a compass bearing may come to several percent of the true value.

Chapter 11

Camouflage & Concealment

Resistance fighters must be able to blend in with their environment, if they are to survive. This applies not only to the fighters themselves, but to fighting positions, base camps, clinics, and other installations.

Personal Camouflage

The key words are Shape, Shine, Silhouette, Sound and Smell.

Shape

The human outline must be broken up. This is the reason for camouflage patterns in uniforms (woodland, desert, snow & ice, etc.) These irregular patterns not only help to match the terrain, they tend to disguise the human shape. Further disguise of the shape can come from vegetation (real or artificial) attached to the fighter's clothing, and head nets.

Face paint also helps to break up the outline of the human shape. The key to applying face paint is to reverse the usual light-and-dark appearance of the face. Portions that are expected to be dark (under the chin, under the nose, under the eyes) should be given a lighter color. Portions that are expected to be light (forehead, nose, chin) should be given a darker color. Moreover, the painting should not be symmetrical. The two sides of the face should look different. The painted pattern should cut across nose lines, cheekbones, and jaw lines. Any other exposed skin (ungloved hands, wrists above gloves, etc.) should likewise be painted to blend with the background.

Shine

Anything reflective or shiny should be either removed or covered. This would include watch crystals, mess kits, eyeglasses (thin mesh eyeglass coverings are sold for use by hunters), buttons, buckles, rings, bracelets, rifle 'scopes and other optics (use sun shades), goggles (keep them down, not on top of the head), and anything else reflective. These will stand out in moonlight and starlight, not just in daylight. At night, they are easy to pick up with night vision devices. Optics can also be detected by lasers, as they reflect the laser beam.

At night, lights of any kind give away the fighter's location. A cigarette, a flashlight, even a glowstick, can be seen at considerable distance. Glow-in-the-dark watches or tritium gunsights are visible at considerable range at night, and are readily picked up by night vision devices.

Silhoutte

The watchword here is "skyline." Fighters should never let themselves be seen on a skyline, silhouetted against the sky. Stay below the crest of hills. Stay in shadows to the maximum extent possible.

Movement catches the eye. In moving, try to stay behind bushes, shrubs, trees and hummocks. These help break up the silhouette

Beware of contrasting backgrounds. Not just the sky, but background of a color different from the fighter's clothing, or of a different shade (light against dark, or vice versa).

Sound

Sounds of movement, such as crackling brush, the rustle of clothing, the rattle of equipment, even the slosh of water in a canteen, can give the fighter's location away to the enemy. Stumbling over loose stones can likewise make noise. Fighters must beware of any such sounds as they move. Talking should be avoided if at all possible. Hand signals should be used instead.

Smell

Smell can be another giveaway. Scented soap, scented aftershave, and other cosmetics can alert the enemy to the fighter's presence. Even something as utilitarian as insect repellent can betray the fighter's presence. The Resistance should make every effort to supply the fighters with unscented soaps and other necessary products such as insect repellents and boot grease.

Camouflaging Movement

Resistance fighters must avoid detection while on the move, and disguise the fact that they have moved through a particular area.

On the move, stay in shadows as much as possible. Move through trees and brush. Crawl through tall grass. Avoid open areas such as fields and roads. Stay below hillcrests and ridgelines.

Just as important as not attracting attention while moving is not leaving a trail behind you that the enemy can follow. Avoid breaking brush as you move though it. Designate the last fighter in the group to "repair the damage" of passage: straighten out branches, brush out footprints, etc. Do not leave scraps of paper or other debris to lead the enemy to you. If you have to cross a stream, try to avoid having bubbles and debris float downstream, as these are signs that someone has crossed upstream.

Camps

Permanent or semi-permanent camps are almost essential to the Resistance. They are needed as places for fighters to rest and re-fit, as sites for hospitals, armories, and repair shops. More will be said about them in Chapter 17. Here the issue is hiding them.

Placing camps under trees is a good way to make them less visible. Even so, many of the same considerations apply to camps as to individual camouflage. Lights, sounds, and smells (fires, cooking) are clues to the presence of the camp. At low sun angles, buildings or tents under trees may cast long shadows; hence "shape" must be disguised as well. This can be done by use of nets and natural materials such as tree branches.[65]

---

[65] As an example of what can be done, *Ohio Outdoor News* for January 10, 2001, carried a description of a marijuana farm in a woods in central Ohio. "The whole operation was so artfully disguised with brushy barricade that it was virtually undetectable from just a few feet away." The "camp" included a tent and cooking facilities.

No matter how well a camp is camouflaged, trails and tracks leading to it may reveal its location. If defensive positions are dug around the camp, the "spoil" (earth removed from the positions) must be disposed of so that it doesn't give away the location of the camp. The same holds true for garbage pits and toilet pits. Stoves or fires, even if concealed, may still be detected by infrared equipment. Camouflaging them means not only hiding them, but making efforts to disperse flue gases as well. Camouflaging a camp means not only hiding it from observers on the ground, but from aerial and satellite observation as well.

Urban Camouflage

Resistance activities in urban areas need a different type of camouflage. People should dress to blend in with the other people in the area. Trucks and other vehicles may need fake signs, either copying real businesses, or nonexistent businesses. Fake or misleading signs on buildings can help disguise the activities within. If materials are sent through the mail, fake return addresses (e.g., a nonexistent business) will help disguise the communications. The key point is that urban activities should be made to look like something innocuous, something that doesn't attract attention.

Summary

The Resistance fighter must make every effort to become "invisible" to government forces. In rural areas, this means blending in with the surrounding terrain. In urban area, this means blending in with the people and the normal activities going on there.

References

Department of the Army, *Camouflage, FM 5-20*, Cornville, AZ, Desert Publications, 1968.

Idriess, Ion L., *The Australian Guerilla: Sniping*, Boulder, CO, Paladin Press, 1978. (While the book covers sniping, a great deal of emphasis is placed on camouflage.)

Long, Duncan, *Modern Camouflage*, Sharon Center, OH, Alpha Publications, 1992, ISBN 0-939427-65-6.

Chapter 12

Boobytraps

Although the name became popular in World War II, boobytraps have long played a role in warfare. They range from traps laid for the individual soldier who unsuspectingly moves a tripwire or picks up an innocent-looking object, to explosive devices large enough to disable vehicles up to and including tanks. The distinctive feature of boobytraps, as opposed to mines and other manufactured objects, is their expedient or improvised nature. They may utilize explosive sheets or blocks, hand grenades, artillery shells, aerial bombs, etc., but in a manner different from their original purpose. In some way the explosive material is "rigged" to go off when someone inadvertently trips it.

The Resistance should be very careful about using boobytraps. They should not be used in ways that might injure members of the population the Resistance is purportedly liberating from tyranny. Killing innocent bystanders is not a way to gain the support of the general population.

Essentials of Boobytraps

A boobytrap will involve a main explosive charge, possibly a booster charge (depending on the nature of the main charge), and a detonator such as a blasting cap. If the detonator is triggered electrically, a battery and switch will be required. If the detonator is triggered mechanically, a percussion cap and some spring-loaded mechanism for firing the cap will be required.

If a grenade, shell, or similar device is used as the explosive charge, the detonator, booster (if any), and main charge are already built in. All that is needed is some form of trigger. Normally the fuse is removed from the bomb or shell and replaced with some sort of detonator that will be activated electrically or by trip-wire. If the boobytrap is built "from scratch," each of the components must be provided.

159

Effectiveness of a boobytrap can be increased by surrounding the main explosive charge with shrapnel such as nails, screws, ball bearings, and similar material.

Triggering Devices

Since boobytraps are traditionally expedient or improvised devices, triggering mechanisms are open to the creativity of the person laying the trap. The following ideas are intended to stimulate thought, not to be an exhaustive list.

- Spring-type clothespins that close an electrical circuit when a tripwire pulls out a wedge;
- Mousetraps that close an electrical circuit when a tripwire activates the trigger;
- Tripwires attached to doors or windows that activate a detonator when the door or window is opened;
- Pendulum devices, such as a bolt suspended by a wire, that close an electrical circuit when the object containing them is picked up or tilted;

Delay Devices

- Wind-up clock with string wrapped around winding stem;
- Wrist watch: Mechanical, use minute or hour hand as electrical contact: Digital, use alarm circuit.
- Slow-burning fuse (improvise by soaking string in solution of potassium nitrate, then braiding three strands together)

Boobytraps as Obstacles

Resistance forces will not normally attempt to hold ground. Their goal is to carry out some kind of action, then "disappear." Boobytraps can be effective in slowing pursuit by government forces when Resistance forces are withdrawing from a raid or some other action. An obstacle, such as a tree-trunk dropped across a road, might be boobytrapped to delay its removal. Innocent-looking objects along a road or trail may be boobytrapped. Boobytraps themselves might be boobytrapped, so that an attempt to disarm one triggers another.

Boobytrapping a withdrawal route can increase the risk to the civilian population, if the pursuing government forces do not find and disarm all the boobytraps. This possibility must be taken into account before the decision is made to boobytrap a withdrawal route.

Post-Raid Boobytraps

Following a raid on some government installation, it may be desirable to leave boobytraps behind. These will cause delays in returning the installation to full operation. In addition, new people entering the installation, who are not familiar with what was there before the raid, are more likely than the regular occupants to trip boobytraps.

Desks, filing cabinets, and anything with drawers that are pulled open are candidates for boobytrapping. Likewise anything electrical, from coffee-pots to computers, radio and TV sets, ceiling lights, and desk lamps, is a candidate for boobytrapping. It will be important to rig these boobytraps carefully so that they are not obvious to government personnel returning to the installation.

Delayed-action bombs are also useful as post-raid devices. These are not strictly boobytraps, since they are activated by timers rather than by inadvertent actions of government forces returning to the installation. Like boobytraps, at the very least the possible presence of delayed-action bombs will delay the return to operation of the building or installation. Searching for and attempting to disarm delayed-action bombs will further delay the installation's return to service. If the bombs are not located and disarmed, they cause further casualties among government forces.

If post-raid boobytraps are to be employed, they must be brought by the raiding party. It is up to the commander to determine whether all members of the party should carry materials for boobytraps, or whether this task should be assigned to specially-designated members. For instance, if explosive breaching of the government installation is required to gain entry, this would ordinarily be done by specially-trained engineer personnel. These same personnel would already be familiar with explosives, and would be natural candidates for bringing and setting boobytraps. However, with proper training, all members of a raiding party might be designated to bring the necessary materials with them, and to set boobytraps on their way out of the installation.

Non-explosive boobytraps

While boobytraps tend to be associated with explosives of one kind or another, the Resistance should not overlook nonexplosive ones. Deadfalls, punji stakes, caltrops, and similar devices are almost as old as warfare itself. They particularly lend themselves to manufacture by the auxiliaries to the Resistance armed wing, since they are labor-intensive but do not require much in the way of tools or skill. Instructional materials on how to prepare these can be distributed to the non-fighting supporters of the Resistance.

Summary

Boobytraps are dangerous. Laying them can itself be hazardous. They can also injure or kill innocent bystanders. However, when properly employed, they can be very useful in harassing and delaying government forces, and denying immediate use of government facilities.

References

Department of the Army, *Boobytraps, FM 5-31*, September 1965.

Newman, Bob, *Guerillas in the Mist*, Boulder, CO, Paladin Press, 1997.

Chapter 13

Weapons Caching

Why Cache Weapons?

Before you shove that spade in the soil and start to dig a hole to hide your guns, ask yourself this question: why are you doing this? The purpose of burying guns is to preserve them until it's time to use them. Will there ever be a better time to use those guns than right now? If it's time to bury them, it's past time to dig them up! As Rabbi Hillel wrote in a somewhat different context, "If not now, when?" Remember the words of Winston Churchill:

> If you will not fight for right when you can easily win without blood shed; if you will not fight when your victory is sure and not too costly; you may come to the moment when you will have to fight with all the odds against you and only a precarious chance of survival. There may even be a worse case. You may have to fight when there is no hope of victory, because it is better to perish than to live as slaves.

Is burying your guns really surrender to tyranny on your part? If you don't have some plan for when to dig them up, you may as well let them be confiscated. Burying them is at best an interim measure, gaining time for something else. Have you decided under what circumstances you will dig them up again? Better make that decision before you dig that hole.

There are three situations under which it would be appropriate to cache (some of) your weapons:

- 1. The political trend is bad, but you can still obtain guns legally, and the government hasn't yet crossed the line justifying armed resistance. In this case, you are preparing for resistance while it's still relatively easy.
- 2. Gun confiscation looms on the horizon, and this is your last chance to hide your guns before the government goons come banging on your door.

- 3. Resistance has already begun, and guns must be stored safely between tactical operations.

In each of these cases, you have determined when you will dig your guns up again. Caching is simply a means of assuring that your guns will be available when the right time comes. However, each of these cases, the requirements for caching are quite different.

Preparing while it's still legal

In this case, you have reason to believe that armed resistance will be necessary in the future, but the time hasn't come yet. You are preparing for that eventuality, but you have no idea when it will become a reality. This means you must prepare for long-term storage of weapons and ammunition. The weapons may have to survive years of storage.

An effective means of long-term storage is putting the guns in an ABS or PVC pipe, of the kind commonly used for plumbing, and burying this vertically in the soil. Glue a permanent cap on the lower end.[66] On the upper end, use a threaded cleanout adaptor with a plug the same size as the pipe. Seal the threads of the plug with Teflon tape or with toilet bowl wax (used to seal around the base of the toilet bowl). If you use wax, put it on both male and female threads. Whether with tape or wax, start the plug by hand. Finish tightening it with pliers or a wrench. This will allow you to remove the upper seal and extract the guns without having to dig up the whole pipe. In this case, be sure to tie strings to the magazines, ammunition, and other small parts that will fall to the bottom of the pipe, or put them in a bag and tie a string to it. Secure the loose ends of the strings at the top of the pipe with something that won't come loose, such as the sight of a rifle standing vertically in the pipe. That way you can readily retrieve the small items without digging up the pipe.

An alternative "high-tech" storage method uses a plastic bag that has multiple layers of waterproof and vapor-proof aluminized plastic, and Tyvek™ for tear resistance. One commercially available

---

[66] Do not use silicone sealer. The acetic acid it gives off can damage metal items stored in the tube.

product involves a bag that is hermetically sealable using a clothes iron. The bag can be buried by itself, or better yet, enclosed in something that will provide mechanical resistance against tearing or attack by rodents or bugs.

Before sealing a gun into a container, it is important to clean it thoroughly. Use a good gun cleaner to remove all powder residue and lead and copper fouling. Clean the exterior and wear gloves when handling the cleaned gun.[67] Grease the interior of the barrel and all moving parts. It is especially important to remove all rust, since rust will encourage further corrosion. Look especially at sharp corners on stampings and the grooves of lettering or engraving, since the process by which these are produced induces stresses in the metal that encourage corrosion. Clean off the rust and grease the spot, to discourage further rust formation. Also, if a rifle has a sling mounted on it, remove the sling, clean any rust off the sling swivels or studs, and grease both the swivels/studs and the attachments on the sling.

Even if you store guns in an airtight container, you need something to protect them against residual moisture and oxygen. In the presence of moisture and oxygen, common metals corrode in the following order (from strongest to weakest oxidation): calcium, magnesium, aluminum, titanium, manganese, chromium, iron, cobalt, nickel, copper. Moisture and oxygen will preferentially attack metals early in the list. Thus to protect iron or steel, place some filings or chips of magnesium or aluminum in the container before sealing it. If possible, also place in the container a cloth bag filled with a desiccant of the type often found in bottles of pills and in sealed electronic equipment. You will, of course, need much more than the amount found in a pill bottle, since it must provide protection for a much larger volume.[68]

When you dig a cache, save the topsoil and put it back on top. An infrared scanner can tell the difference between the

---

[67] Fingerprints on the gun will be a starting point for corrosion. In addition, if the cache is found by the police, they will identify you as having touched the guns at least once.

[68] Silica Gel desiccant can be purchased in bulk from www.CheaperThanDirt.com.

neighboring topsoil and underlying soil. An improperly covered cache will stand out like a sore thumb on an infrared scan. The best time to cache something is in the autumn. If it is near trees the falling leaves will provide initial coverage, and the winter snows and rains will help blend the soil over the cache with the surrounding soil.

Where you place the cache is as important as how you prepare the guns for storage. First, you want the place to be unobvious. You don't want it to be the first place the government goons think to look. Second, you want it unconnected with you. If it is found through some mischance, you don't want it to point to you. Thus it should be somewhere away from your home, but close enough that you can get to it when the time comes. It should also be some place where you can retrieve the stored guns without being seen by neighbors or passers-by. Not only must the site itself be camouflaged, but also it must provide concealment for anyone going to it.

Any government agents searching for hidden guns will probably do so with electronic metal detectors. In an urban area, it may be possible to spoof the metal detectors by burying metal scraps in the general area of the cache. Bottle caps, sections of reinforcing bar, nails, and so on, will trigger the detector, and each must be unearthed to determine what it is. A series of false alarms may discourage the searchers and cause them to give up. A large area must be "salted" with these for the ruse to be effective. If you simply bury some bottle caps within a few feet of the cache, you might as well put up a sign pointing to it. This attempt at spoofing will be ineffective if the cache is in a remote area. A small area salted with nails, in the midst of a woods or a pasture, will be a dead giveaway that something important is buried there.

Don't think only of caching guns. You will also need ammunition, gun cleaning supplies, and spare parts such as springs and screws. Caching them is just as important as caching the guns themselves. A gun without ammunition, or with a broken recoil spring, or rusted out for lack of cleaning, is simply a club. It is no more effective than a baseball bat or a golf club.

Wherever you place your cache, it is critical that you be able to find it again. This means defining precisely where the container was buried:

- A specified distance along a specified bearing (either a compass course or a sight line to some permanent object) starting from a specified point (some permanent object such as a road culvert, a roadside mile marker, a corner of a building, etc.);
- The intersection of two sight lines from specified starting points;
- Directly under or next to some permanent object.

The cache site must be described in a report (which must itself be protected adequately) so that other members of the Resistance can find the site if the person burying it is under surveillance by the government. The report should state the method of caching, the type of container, the contents, and the details of the location. A photograph of the site, showing landmarks, is also helpful. The details of the location at the cache site (markers and sight lines) should not be on the same piece of paper as the directions to the cache site. Those directions should be kept on a separate sheet from the details of the site. Any government agents finding only one will be unable to use it to locate the cache.

It is important to sterilize the cache site after it is emplaced, to minimize the chances of its being discovered by the wrong people. It is equally important that the site be sterilized after the cache is emptied. You don't want the police to be wondering why there is suddenly a hole in the flower garden in the city park, and asking who was seen going to or from the park. The persons planning to retrieve the cached items must be prepared to fill the hole and restore the surroundings to their undisturbed condition. The hole may be filled with rocks or sticks. If there are no suitable materials at the site for refilling the hole, the retrieval team may need to bring with them something to fill the hole up again. This may be a container similar to the one being retrieved (one more reason for knowing what is in the cache and what the container is).

Last-minute preparations

This situation is different from the contingency storage described above. Gun confiscation will begin shortly, and armed resistance is therefore justified. The concern in this situation is to get the guns hidden before the house-to-house searches begin.[69] In this case you may not have the luxury of choosing the season or the ideal place for a cache.

Protection against rust and corrosion will still be important in this comparatively short-term storage. You don't want to dig up your guns two weeks after burying them, only to find that a heavy rain or a high water table has infiltrated your storage container. Hence the container must be just as watertight and airtight as in the case of long-term storage. However, there will be less need for sacrificial metals or desiccants. Instead of heavily greasing the weapons, a coating of oil may suffice. Cleaning, however, is still important. Any moisture on the gun can cause rust within a day or less.

As with the long-term storage, the cache must be located so it doesn't implicate you if it's found, and it must provide concealment for those who retrieve the guns when the time comes for that. Since finding such a place at the last minute might be difficult, it would be a good idea to identify the site for a cache ahead of time, even if you plan to delay using it until the situation becomes critical. In the same vein, acquiring the pipes or other containers in advance is important. They may not be available at the last minute.

Since caching may become necessary at any season, a good site for burying the gun container is one where the soil is already disturbed, such as a flowerbed or vegetable garden. A construction site may also provide a suitable caching site, if you are confident the actual hiding place will not be dug up as part of the construction activity.

---

[69] It might be asked, though, what are you waiting for? There are more houses, and more gun owners, than there will be searchers. The time to stop the searches is when they start, by organized armed resistance against the searchers. Don't let them pick you off one by one.

In this last-minute situation, another issue becomes critical. If you are known to be a gun owner, caching all your guns will be a mistake. When they come to your door, if you are not planning to shoot them, you must have a gun or two to sacrifice. Moreover, the sacrificial gun cannot be a junk gun. This will immediately arouse suspicion. You will be arrested, and "they have ways" to get the truth out of you. You had better be ready to sacrifice a good-quality gun, to allay suspicion that you have hidden some other good-quality guns somewhere else.

Temporary tactical storage

Once armed resistance has begun, it may still be necessary to cache guns and ammunition between tactical uses. This will be especially true for urban Resistance fighters in cities controlled by government forces. In this case, the cache must still provide protection against rust and corrosion, but must be readily accessible. The guns should be thoroughly cleaned and lightly oiled, but heavier protection is not needed.

Instead of burying the guns, they may be stored in concealed hiding places in buildings. The book by Robinson gives considerable information on false bottoms to drawers, hollow spaces in walls, dead spaces behind cabinets or under stairs, heating and cooling vents, and lots of other places you might not think of for yourself. These are suitable places for hiding guns between raids or ambushes.

Note that the scent of gun cleaning solvents may be a giveaway, even if the gun is hidden behind a wall. The gun should be cleaned away from the building in which it is stored, and it should be stored in something reasonably airtight, such as a Ziploc™ bag. In addition, it may be advisable to mask the solvent scent with incense, air freshener, or some other means.

Cache Security

The government may have located your cache. You should put telltales in the cache that can alert you to the fact that it has been disturbed and even replaced: a pebble, a bit of thread, or something else that is unlikely to be noticed by someone disturbing the cache, but that will alert you to the fact that it has been compromised.

The government may have located your cache but not disturbed it, in the hope of catching someone who comes to retrieve it. When it comes time to retrieve the cache, be alert for observers, or for electronic devices that may have been set up to "watch" the site. A new "utility box" may be the cover for a camera. Government forces may be planning to trace the people retrieving the cache back to their base.

Protecting Your Equipment

Guns, ammunition, gun-cleaning supplies, explosives, radios, batteries, code books, and many other items must be secured against government detection. Caching these items can protect them against loss to the government, and keep them ready for use. Regardless of how long the cache is expected to be in use, the cache itself must be well hidden. The items in it must be protected against moisture and animals. The cache itself must be accessible when needed. Proper planning ahead of time can make the difference between an appropriate and an inappropriate cache. It must be remembered that the purpose of burying a gun is to be able to dig it up again, in good condition and ready for use.

Seasonal issues

In some climates, the ground will be frozen hard during the winter. This may make it impossible either to bury a cache, or to retrieve one. This possibility should be taken into account when deciding the means of creating a cache. If freezing is a consideration, some method other than burial underground may be appropriate. This may mean hiding the cache inside a building, through some of the methods described in the book by Luger.

References
Books

Benson, Ragnar, *Modern Weapons Caching*, Boulder, CO, Paladin Press, 1990.

Connor, Michael, *How to Hide Anything*, Boulder, CO, Paladin Press, 1984.

"Eddie the Wire" (pseud.) *How to Bury Your Goods*, Port Townsend, WA, Breakout Productions, 1999.

Luger, Jack, *The Big Book of Secret Hiding Places*, Port Townsend, WA, Breakout Productions, 1999.

Robinson, Charles, *The Construction of Secret Hiding Places*, El Dorado, AR, Desert Publications, 71731, 1991.

RyanJcus, http://thesurvivalistblog.blogspot.com/2009/06/construction-of-pvc-pipe-cache.html. This video shows the construction of a PVC pipe cache.

Soldier of Fortune magazine, "Weapons Caching" (Reprint available from SOF Back Issues, PO Box 693, Boulder, CO 80306)

U.S. Army Special Warfare Center, *U.S. Army Special Forces Caching Techniques TC 31-29-A*, El Dorado, AR, Desert Publications, no date (also reprinted by *Soldier of Fortune* Magazine).

Wood, Charles, "Bury a Gun and Ammo for 15 Years," *Backwoods Home Magazine*, January/February 2009, pp. 71 – 73. (This article describes caching a gun in a PVC tube in the early 1990s, then digging it up 15 years later to find it in excellent condition.) Also available at http://www.backwoodshome.com/articles2/wood115.html

Web Sites

http://www.captaindaves.com/guide/cache.htm

http://cacheopedia.com/wiki/Cache_Containers

Chapter 14

Logistics

As someone has remarked, amateur warriors study tactics; professional warriors study logistics. Napoleon's maxim that an army travels on its stomach emphasizes the importance of logistics to successful warfare. This is just as true of a resistance movement as it is of a regular army. Guerrillas may get by with less in the way of "consumables" than does a regular army, but they cannot totally do without supplies. The resistance movement therefore requires an organization to support and supply the actual fighters.

Secure camps and safe houses are needed to permit the fighters to train, rest and refit, and if necessary to receive medical treatment. They are an important part of logistics. These will, however, be discussed in later chapters. This chapter will be devoted to supplies needed by both the overt and covert branches of the resistance movement.

Personal Equipment

A previous chapter describes the personal equipment the individual resistance fighter should plan to provide for himself. However, that initial supply will not last for the duration of the war. Boots and clothing wear out. Individual items rust, break, or are lost. It will be necessary to resupply the fighters with personal equipment. The Resistance must have an organization set up to do this.

Weapons

The most foolish mistake we could possibly make would be to allow the subject races to possess arms. History shows that all conquerors who have allowed their subject races to carry arms have prepared their own downfall by so doing. Indeed, I would go so far as to say that the supply of arms to the underdogs is a sine qua non for the overthrow of any sovereignty. So let's not have any native militia or native police. German troops will bear the sole responsibility for the maintenance of law and order throughout the occupied Russian territories, and a system of military strong-points must be evolved to cover the entire occupied country. – Adolph Hitler.[70]

One of the most important tasks of the logistics department of the Resistance, then, is the procurement or manufacture of weapons. While individual Resistance members may have been able to secure weapons prior to the start of armed resistance, there will still be a need for procurement of weapons, ammunition, repair parts (firing pins, springs, etc. for small arms) and cleaning supplies by the Resistance forces.

The government itself must not be overlooked as a potential source of supply. Raids on government armories and police stations are a traditional source of supply for Resistance forces. Likewise weapons and ammunition taken from captured or killed government forces are an important source for the Resistance. Finally, bribery should not be overlooked. Bribery of corrupt supply officers can be a fairly large-scale source of weapons and ammunition (these officers are not likely to be shot at by the Resistance, so they don't care). On a smaller scale, bribery of individual soldiers who are short-sighted enough to take cash in hand and overlook the risk of being shot at with their own ammunition can be a source of supply. Jim Morris describes seeing a grenade that a Cambodian Resistance fighter claimed to have purchased from an invading Vietnamese Communist soldier.[71]

Heavier weapons, such as mortars, machine guns, anti-tank and anti-aircraft missiles, and similar weapons will almost certainly have to be obtained from an external source, or through capture from the government. However, it is possible to manufacture pistols, rifles, submachine guns, light mortars, rockets, and similar items, in fairly simple shops. The Engineering Department of the Irish

---

[70] From *Hitler's Secret Conversations*, Cameron & Stevens, translators, Signet, 1961.
[71] P. 172.

Republican Army successfully manufactured mortars. Haganah, the Jewish defense force established in Palestine in the 1920s, initially smuggled small arms, but later began manufacturing them. The Viet Cong manufactured hand grenades, mines and similar ordnance.[72] Jim Morris describes a grenade launcher captured by Lebanese forces that was stamped "Made by Fateh," an armed element of the Palestinian Liberation Organization.[73] Hamas, the Palestinian organization fighting Israel, has developed and manufactures the Kassam series of unguided rockets. According to Israeli sources, the Kassam-2 was developed by Hamas, with technology it received from Iran. According to the Israeli Defense Forces, the 1.2-meter (5 feet) long missile has a range of 10-12 kilometers (6-7 miles) and can carry a 4-6 kilogram (8.8-13.2 pound) warhead. "Hybrid" rockets (solid fuel, and either gaseous or liquid oxidizer) are being built by high school and college students, as student projects.[74] The point is, weapons manufacture can be undertaken by a Resistance organization, if the raw materials can be obtained.[75] The references at the end of the chapter describe some of this manufacturing. The book by "Urbano" has a chapter on improvised weapons.

Guns are useless without ammunition. "Handloading" or "reloading" of ammunition is widely practiced, and can be a source

---

[72] When I was in Vietnam in 1962, I was informed that Viet Cong armorers had become sophisticated enough that they were stamping dates on the grenades they manufactured.

[73] P. 88.

[74] Some of these rockets have thrusts of up to 4000 pounds, and as sounding rockets, have achieved altitudes of over a mile. Rockets with ranges of 10 to 20 miles, are clearly within the capability of modest manufacturing shops. Moreover, with modern electronics, the rockets could be guided accurately. (*Aerospace America*, December 2008, p. 73 for information on these school-built hybrid rockets.)

[75] At one time, building inertial guidance systems was an expensive proposition, with gyroscopes and accelerometers costing in the thousands of dollars. As with much else in electronics, the cost has come down. Inertial measurement units with accuracy adequate for short-range missiles (a few tens of miles) are available for under $300 in 1000-unit lots. These still require additional electronics, including some computer capability, but a complete inertial guidance system for a short-range missile could be built for less than $1000. Considerable engineering skill would be required for the design, but manufacture would be comparatively simple. See the article by Tuite for more information.

of ammunition for the Resistance. Components (i.e., cartridge cases, primers, powder, bullets) are needed. The cartridge cases can often be scavenged from the ground after a battle. Bullets can be cast from lead (typemetal, wheel weights, etc.) (See the article by Venturino). Powder and primers may be more difficult to obtain, but with some effort and difficulty they can be manufactured. The Resistance should plan to supplement its other supplies of ammunition by reloading.

Explosives

The issue of explosives manufacture is too complex to even begin discussing it here. There are books in the reference section that give detailed instructions. The most important thing that can be said is that these instructions must be followed *in detail*. Failure to follow the instructions will lead to unintended and premature explosions. The only significant exceptions to this rule are black powder and ANFO (ammonium nitrate/fuel oil). These can be made and used in relative safety, as compared with explosives like nitroglycerine. Even so, the instructions should be followed *to the letter*.[76]

Explosives manufacture should be undertaken in sparsely-inhabited areas. Manufacturing explosives in the middle of a city, among the people the Resistance is trying to liberate from a tyrannical government, endangers the very people the Resistance is presumably fighting for. If discovered, it gives the Resistance a bad name among people who should be its supporters.

Zorpette gives a description of an explosives manufacturing facility found in Iraq:

---

[76] Manufacture of commercial black powder involves grinding the sulfur, charcoal, and potassium (or sodium) nitrate together. This is very risky for home-brew explosives manufacture. The CIA document in the References describes a much safer process for small-scale manufacture. The sulfur and charcoal are ground together. They are then mixed into a strong solution of potassium nitrate. The resulting slurry is poured into a container of rubbing alcohol. The gunpowder precipitates out. It can then be filtered through a cloth, dried, crushed, and sieved through window-screen, or while still moist, put through a kitchen potato ricer to make small grains. It is suitable for blasting, or for use in black powder firearms.

U.S. soldiers from the 101st Airborne Division, along with Navy EOD [Explosive Ordnance Disposal] techs, crept toward a cluster of buildings and tents believed to be a camp of al-Qaeda in Iraq, the main foreign insurgent group . . . Two of the first three buildings the raiders came upon had been used as a place to mix ammonium nitrate fertilizer with diesel fuel or urea to make bulk explosives and also to dry the resulting product. The third building was an IED-production house [Improvised Explosive Device]. . . Spotters on helicopters found a footpath near the third building leading through some tall grass to a living and cooking area that included several tents.[77] . . Over the next few days the EOD and other specialists uncovered a network of underground bunkers and tunnels underneath the tent area, including an al-Qaeda command-and-control center and another underground chamber that had been booby-trapped with a grenade. They found enough raw materials to make 4000 kg of home-made explosive and, in a nearby house, 1500 kg. of finished product. . . The investigators also found weapons and armaments, electronics training manuals in Arabic, $10,800 in $100 bills, some Sudanese money, and lots of ball bearings, which insurgents pack around an IED's main charge to maximize death and destruction. There were also personal computers and simple video-production facilities to make and mass-produce grisly propaganda video discs, which the team found stacked by the thousands in one of the underground chambers.

Obtaining the raw materials for explosives manufacture will be an important logistical task. Most of these raw materials are industrial chemicals of one kind or another. The Resistance will

---

[77] As explained in Chapter 11 on Camouflage, footpaths are a dead giveaway to the location of permanent camps. Efforts must be made to keep them from being formed, or to conceal them.

have to find ways to purchase them clandestinely, or to divert them from legitimate users.

Electronic Equipment

The Resistance will have need of electronic equipment of various kinds, including radios, computers, GPS receivers, night vision equipment, and telephones. The Logistics organization will need to procure or manufacture these items.

Radios

Radio communications can be useful to the Resistance, despite the fact that the government can use radio direction finders to locate transmitters. The Resistance will need to obtain radios of whatever type are decided upon as appropriate, but should be prepared to repair them, and even to manufacture radios if necessary

Batteries

As mentioned several times in this book, once the shooting starts, batteries for equipment such as radios, range finders, night vision devices, etc. may be hard to get. Rechargeable batteries should be used whenever possible. These can be charged in base camps where electricity is available. They can also be charged in the field using solar panels. The article by Pease describes solar-power circuits that the Resistance's engineering department can make, and which can be used by individual fighters to recharge the batteries in their equipment. The Resistance's Logistics organization should be prepared to purchase or manufacture these circuits.

Medical Supplies

The establishment of hospitals will be discussed in the chapter on Secure Camps. However, medical supplies are an important logistical need for Resistance forces, and must be acquired by the Resistance's logistical element.

If the Resistance forces have sources of supply external to their country, medicines and medical equipment will be among the important items to be brought in. While weapons have to be imported clandestinely ("smuggled"), it may be possible to import medical supplies "legitimately." That is, "front" firms may be established to import medical supplies legitimately, then divert them to the Resistance. In a similar manner, medical supplies may be diverted from legitimate importing firms, either directly or through domestic "front" firms.

It may also be possible for the Resistance to make use of existing "black market" arrangements to obtain medical supplies. The Viet Cong were able to obtain medical supplies through the extensive black markets that existed in Vietnam (Hawk, 2002). Similar arrangements may be possible in other situations.

Fund-raising

The Resistance will need money for purchasing a great variety of things: arms, food, medical supplies, clothing, and equipment of all kinds. Some of the funds can be raised from domestic sources, but foreign funds should be raised if at all possible. Sympathetic governments may provide funds, but these usually come with strings attached. It would be much better if the Resistance can avoid depending on funds from foreign governments. Privately-raised funds, although scarcer, are less likely to limit the actions of the Resistance, or to tempt the leaders handling the funds to embezzle them.

Domestically, it may be possible to raise funds openly by front groups that appear to have charitable or humanitarian purposes. Islamic terrorists created a vast network of "charities," which provided cover for both gathering and laundering funds for their activities.[78] Likewise the Irish Republican Army was successful in raising funds through allegedly charitable organizations in the United States.

Funds can be raised from people sympathetic with the Resistance by clandestine means. The Viet Cong were quite successful at this, although many of the contributions were less than

---

[78] Bodansky, pp. 367 – 395. *Terrorist Hunter* is essentially about tracking down the Islamic charities and their fund-raising.

fully voluntary. Nevertheless, if the Resistance has popular support, people will be willing to contribute money to the cause.

Foreign supporters may be reluctant to supply the Resistance with weapons, but be more willing to supply "humanitarian aid" such as medical supplies. It may even be possible to gather funds for this purpose openly in the foreign country, while funds for purchase of weapons cannot be gathered openly. As noted earlier, several Islamic organizations were successful in operating "charities" in the US that collected money for Palestinian forces fighting Israel, and the Irish Republican Army collected money in the US allegedly for "relief" purposes ("Noraid") in Northern Ireland. In these latter two cases, however, some or all of the money was allegedly diverted to weapons procurement.

Smuggling is another possible source of funds for the Resistance. Items scarce in the country, particularly imported or heavily-taxed items, may be smuggled in and sold to raise funds. Hezbollah supporters in the U.S. raised funds by smuggling cigarettes from low-tax states to high-tax states. The Resistance may be tempted to smuggle drugs. These can be very lucrative, as the FARC in Colombia has found. The so-called Kosovo Liberation Army was essentially a drug smuggling organization. However, this is in most cases a very bad idea. At best, it gives a bad name internationally to the Resistance. At worst, it adds to the corruption in the nation, making it harder to achieve a just peace after the victory of the Resistance.

Once cash is raised, it must be used in ways that are not traceable to the Resistance or to individual members. Cash itself is very hard for a government to track. However, as pointed out in the chapter on Government Response, exchange of old currency for new may hamper the Resistance's use of large amounts of cash.

An alternative to use of cash, especially in small amounts, is use of prepaid or "stored value" cards. These are purchased with a certain cash value recorded on them. They can be used anonymously, with the stored value being decreased as purchases are made, or cash withdrawn from ATMs. Even though the transaction is recorded in some central database, the user of the card is not identified. These should be purchased in advance of the need for their use. The initial value of the cards should be kept low, since if the government suspects that a card has once been used by the Resistance, the card may be canceled. The value of the card should be low enough that its loss is not serious. See the article by Vardi for more discussion of anonymous transactions.

Counterfeit Identification

Both the overt and the covert wings of the Resistance movement will need identification cards that will allow them to travel, make purchases, and respond to "Your papers, please." They may also need ration cards, passes permitting them to enter certain areas, cards certifying membership in trade or professional organizations, and social insurance cards. All these must be produced by the resistance organization.

Despite the attempts of governments to make their documents proof against counterfeiting, the technology for producing counterfeit documents manages to keep pace. The availability of computers, digital cameras, laminating machines, etc., make it easier and easier to produce fake ID cards, fake ration cards, fake restricted area passes, and similar documents. It will be important for the resistance movement to obtain the means for producing these documents in adequate numbers. If possible, the necessary equipment and supplies should be stockpiled in advance of the need for active resistance.

The reference books listed below give detailed information on how to produce counterfeit documents. They go into much more detail than is possible here. The point is simply that detailed instructions on producing counterfeit documents are available. The resistance movement should be prepared with the equipment and supplies that will be needed for this purpose, and have some people develop the skills needed to produce counterfeit documents of adequate quality. This preparation must be completed before it is needed. Moreover, as the technology of identification cards improves, the technology of forging must keep pace. Forging methods even a few years old may be obsolete in the face of advances in identification technology.

References

Explosives Manufacture & Use

Anonymous, *Black Book Companion*, Boulder, CO, Paladin Press, 1990.

Anonymous, *CIA Field Expedient Preparation of Black Powders*, Cornville, AZ, Desert Publications, undated.

Anonymous, "Explosively Formed Projectiles," *Soldier of Fortune*, February 2006, pp. 66 – 68.

Anonymous, *Two Component High Explosive Mixtures*, El Dorado, AR, Desert Publications, 1982.

Benson, Ragnar, *New and Improved C-4*, Boulder, CO, Paladin Press, 1995.

Benson, Ragnar, *Ragnar's Guide to Home and Recreational Use of High Explosives*, Boulder, CO, Paladin Press, 1988.

Benson, Ragnar, *Ragnar's Homemade Detonators*, Boulder, CO, Paladin Press, 1993.

Central Intelligence Agency, *Field Expedient Methods for Explosives Preparations*, El Dorado, AR, Desert Publications, 1977.

Davis, Tenney L., *The Chemistry of Powder & Explosives*, Hollywood, CA, Angriff Press, 1943.

Department of the Army, *Improvised Munitions Handbook, TM 31-210*, 1969.

Frankford Arsenal, *Improvised Munitions Black Book, vols. 1, 2, 3*, El Dorado, AR, Desert Publications, 1978.

Harber, David, *Guerilla's Arsenal*, Boulder, CO, Paladin Press, 1994. (Describes manufacture of various explosives, detonators, timers, and other useful items)

Galt, John, *The Big Bang: Improvised PETN & Mercury Fulminate*, Boulder, CO, Paladin Press, 1987.

Grupp, Larry, *Claymore Mines*, Boulder, CO, Paladin Press, 1993.

Lecker, Seymour, *Deadly Brew*, Boulder, CO, Paladin Press, 1987.

Lecker, Seymour, *Homemade SEMTEX*, Boulder, CO, Paladin Press, 1991.

Lecker, Seymour, *Improvised Explosives*, Boulder, CO, Paladin Press, 1985.

Lecker, Seymour, *Poor Man's TNT: Improvised Guncotton*, Boulder, CO, Paladin Press, 1995.

Lewis, Tim, *Kitchen Improvised Fertilizer Explosives*, Odessa, TX, Information Publishing Co., 1985.

McLean, Don, *Medicine Chest Explosives*, Boulder, CO, Paladin Press, 1995.

Mordecai, Thomas, *Professional Standards for Preparing, Handling, and Using Explosives*, Boulder, CO, Paladin Press, 1995.

Urbano (pseudonym), *Fighting in the Streets*, Miami, FL, J. Flores Publications, 1991. (Includes a chapter on manufacture of explosives using commonly-available chemicals and improvised equipment.)

Wallace, William, *The Revised Black Book*, Boulder, CO, Paladin Press, 1995.

War Department, *Explosives, TM 9-2900*, Randle, WA, Bohica Concepts, 1940.

Forged Identification

Benson, Ragnar, *Acquiring New ID*, Boulder, CO, Paladin Press, 1996.

Charrett, Sheldon, *Secrets of a Back-Alley ID Man*, Boulder, CO, Paladin Press, 2001.

French, Scott, *Who Are You*, Mt. Shasta, CA, Intelligence Here, 2000. Available from Paladin Press.

Sands, Trent, *Reborn in the USA, 3rd Edition*, Port Townsend, WA, Breakout Productions, 1998.

Fund Raising

Anonymous, *Terrorist Hunter*, New York, Ecco, 2003.

Bodansky, Yossef, *Target the West*, New York, Shapolsky Publishers, 1993.

Vardi, Nathan, "Cash is King," *Forbes*, April 27, 2008, pp. 36 – 38.

Medical Supplies

Hawk, Alan, "Jungle Medicine: Treating the VC Wounded," *Vietnam*, June 2002, pp. 42 – 48, 64.

Personal Equipment

Kearney, Cresson H., *Jungle Snafus . . . And Remedies*, Oregon Institute of Science & Medicine, Cave Junction, OR, 1996. This book is an incredible source of information on what works and doesn't work in terms of personal equipment for the individual warrior.

Pease, Bob, "What's All This Battery-Charging Stuff, Anyhow?" *Electronic Design*, February 5, 2001, pp. 122 - 130.

Weapons Manufacture & Supply

Anonymous, *How to Make a Silencer for a Mini-14*, Boulder, CO, Paladin Press, 1997

Anonymous, *Improvised Rocket Motors*, El Dorado, AR, Desert Publications, 1980.

Benson, Ragnar, *Breath of the Dragon: Homebuilt Flamethrowers*, Boulder, CO, Paladin Press, 1990.

Benson, Ragnar, *Guerrilla Gunsmithing*, Boulder, CO, Paladin Press, 2000.

Benson, Ragnar, *Home-Built Claymore Mines*, Boulder, CO, Paladin Press, 1993.

Benson, Ragnar, *Ragnar's Big Book of Homemade Weapons*, Boulder, CO, Paladin Press, 1992.

Benwood, Raymond, *A Guide to the Drilling, Reaming, and Broaching a Bolt Action Receiver at Home*, http://www.jpfo.org/boltaction.htm

Camper, Franklin J., *Mercenary Operations Manual*, El Dorado, AR, Desert Publications, 1986.

Dmitrieff, G., *Expedient Hand Grenades*, El Dorado, AR, Desert Publications, 1984.

Dmitrieff, G., *The Poor Man's Primer Manual*, El Dorado, AR, Desert Publications, 2001. (This book deals with manufacture of primers for rifle and pistol cartridges. It gives complete details of the chemistry of their manufacture.)

Dmitrieff, G., *The Poor Man's RPG*, El Dorado, AR, Desert Publications, 1996. (Note that this book describes how to build the rocket part, but does not deal with warheads. It describes "look-alike" weapons for re-enactors. For warheads, see the books on explosives.)

Farrell, Bic, *Backyard Rocketry*, Boulder, CO, Paladin Press, 1992.

Feuer, Eugene, *Undetectable Hand Grenades*, El Dorado, AR, Desert Publications, 1995.

Folgarelli, Mike, *The Butane Lighter Hand Grenade*, El Dorado, AR, Desert Publications, 1995. (Note that the butane in the lighter is not used. Only the case and the striker are used. Hence an empty lighter can be utilized for this purpose.)

Gunn, David, *The Poor Man's Ray Gun*, El Dorado, AR, Desert Publications, 1996. (How to convert a microwave oven into a dangerous microwave beam.)

Hogdon Reloading Center, www.hogdon.com. Reloading data for Hogdon, Winchester and IMR powders

Holmes, Bill, *Home Workshop Guns: The .22 Machine Pistol*, Boulder, CO, Paladin Press, 1995.

Holmes, Bill, *Home Workshop Guns: The Handgun*, Boulder, CO, Paladin Press, 1979.

Holmes, Bill, *Home Workshop Guns: The Submachine Gun*, Boulder, CO, Paladin Press, 1977.

Holmes, Bill, *Home Workshop Prototype Firearms*, Boulder, CO, Paladin Press, 1994.

Holmes, Bill, *The .50-caliber Rifle Construction Manual*, Boulder, CO, Paladin Press, 2002 (complete machining instructions for a single-shot rifle).

Lewis, Anthony, *Bazooka: How to Build Your Own*, Boulder, CO, Paladin Press, 1993. (Actually not a rocket launcher, but a shoulder-fired launcher for a tennis ball. The basic ideas (propellant, igniter, etc.) can be adapted to more useful projectiles.)

Long, Duncan, *Homemade Ammo*, Boulder, CO, Paladin Press,

Luty, P. A., *Expedient Homemade Firearms: The 9mm Submachine Gun*, Boulder, CO, Paladin Press, 1998.

Luty, P. A., *Expedient Homemade Firearms, Vol. II*, available as download from http://www.thehomegunsmith.com/. Price £10 as of this writing)

Metral, Gerard, *A Do-it-yourself Submachine Gun*, Boulder, CO, Paladin Press, 1995.

Morris, Jim, *The Devil's Secret Name*, Canton, Ohio, Daring Books, 1989,

O'Leary, Nero, a one-shot flamethrower, http://www.doingfreedom.com/gen/1202/squirt.html

Petty, Charles E., "Barrel Magic & Machine Work," *American Handgunner*, July/August 2007, pp. 48 – 49, 104.

Pugliese, Michael A., *Primer Cookbook*, M&M Engineering, Arlington, VT, 1998.

Simpson, Layne, "All About Barrels," *Rifle Shooter*, January/February 2008, pp. 60 – 63. (An introduction to the art of rifle barrels.)

Sweeney, Patrick, "Loads of Reloads," *Guns & Ammo*, May 2007, pp. 63 – 68. (How to set up for large-scale handloading.)

Towsley, Bryce M., "Building Your Own AR Upper," *American Rifleman*, March 2007, pp. 58 – 59. (Assembly of purchased components, not machining from scratch.)

Towsley, Bryce M., "Build Your Own Custom Rifle," *American Rifleman*, August 2005, pp. 58 – 61, 87. (Assembly of purchased components.)

Towsley, Bryce M., "Reloading .223Rem/5.56x45 mm NATO Military Cartridge Cases," *The American Rifleman*, pp. 52 – 54, September, 2009.

Truby, J. David, *Zips, Pipes and Pens*, Boulder, CO, Paladin Press, 1993. (Describes weapons made inside prisons. If they can do it there, you can do it in a workshop.)

Tuite, Don, "Tri-Axis Inertial-Measurement Units Combine Performance and Low Cost," *Electronic Design*, 08/02/07, p. 22.

Urbano (pseudonym), *Fighting in the Streets*, Miami, J. Flores Publications, 1991, ISBN 0-918751-14-4.

Venturino, Mike "I've Always Shot Cast Bullets," *American Handgunner*, September/October 2009, pp. 52 – 55.

Venturino, Mike, "Molten Mysteries," *Guns Magazine*, November 2009, pp. 54 – 57. (Casting lead bullets)

Wieland, Terry, "Lead is not Dead, *Rifleshooter*, September/October 2009, pp. 48 – 59. (casting lead bullets)

Wood, J. B., *Survival Gunsmithing*, El Dorado, AR, Desert Publications, 1986.

Zorpette, Glenn, "Bomb Squad Diary," *IEEE Spectrum*, October 2008, pp. 40 – 47.

Web Sites

http://www.cyberstation.net/~dwpaul/bs-home.htm (building an AR-15)

http://www.roderuscustom.tzo.com/ (general gunsmithing)

http://www.learnaboutguns.com/2008/12/08/another-reason-gun-bans-will-never-work-illegal-arms-market-video-clip/ (Illegal arms market in Durra, Pakistan. Making guns with hand tools. If they can do it, you can too.)

http://www.thehomegunsmith.com/ (information on making guns and ammunition with common tools)

http://www.ar15.com/forums/topic.html?b=1&f=5&t=90259 7 Casting lead bullets.

Chapter 15

Training

Resistance fighters can't just "grab a gun and head for the hills." To begin with, many Resistance recruits will have little or no experience with firearms. This will especially be true of urban recruits. Government restrictions on firearms will also reduce the experience level of recruits. Moreover, the Resistance fighter needs to know a great many things besides how to shoot. The armed wing of the Resistance must provide the training the recruits will need before they can become effective fighters.

It has been said that there is no such thing as a dangerous weapon; there are only dangerous people. The object of training is to convert the recruits into dangerous people. This chapter covers some of the things that should be included in training.

Weapons

It is impossible to be specific about weapons, since each Resistance situation is different. A Resistance force will have to fight with whatever weapons it can acquire. Even within a squad, no two fighters may be armed with the same weapons. Nevertheless, there are some things that apply in general.

Firearms

Marksmanship is of course an important matter. As pointed out in the chapter on sniping, American troops in Vietnam fired 200,000 small arms rounds for each enemy soldier killed. Resistance forces cannot afford that kind of extravagance. A Resistance force may be fortunate to have 200,000 rounds for the whole war, let alone to create one casualty among Government forces. Training in marksmanship then becomes critically important. Each shot must count. Unfortunately, there may not even be sufficient ammunition for much training. It may be necessary to use alternatives such as drilling recruits in use of sight picture and proper trigger management without actual firing.[79]

It is not sufficient just to train the fighters in marksmanship. They must also know how to keep their firearms operating under field conditions. They must know how to load *and unload* their firearms safely, how to field strip them, how to clean them properly, how to keep them clean in tactical environments, and how to clear jams. All of these things can be taught without actual shooting.

Firearms safety is another important part of training. On a conventional firing range, conventional troops are taught to keep the muzzle down-range, keep their weapons unloaded behind the firing line, and unload their weapons before leaving the range. Unfortunately, this is not realistic training for tactical conditions. Fighters must be taught how to live safely and be comfortable with loaded firearms. They must realize that the most important safety device is in their heads, not on the gun. They must constantly be conscious of muzzle direction, whether at rest or on the move; keep the mechanical safety on until ready to shoot; keep their finger out of the trigger guard until sights are on the target; keep the chamber empty and the bolt locked open when the firearm is put down; and place the gun so it won't fall over or get dirt in the mechanism when not being carried. These things must be ingrained to the point that they are instinctive. "Accidents" with loaded firearms are almost always the result of someone violating one of these rules. It might be argued that training on a "hot range," where weapons are always loaded, is unsafe. But if keeping weapons loaded isn't safe on the firing range, when will it be safe? If fighters are to be safe in combat conditions, they must learn to be safe with loaded weapons in training.

"Sighting in" is discussed in the chapter on sniping. However, it is not just for snipers. Every fighter must "zero" his rifle prior to combat, and re-zero it if conditions change or it has been

---

[79] There are laser devices intended for sighting in a rifle. However, they can also be used on an empty rifle to verify that the shooter is using proper trigger management, by noting whether the laser spot moves when the shooter pulls the trigger.

subjected to hard knocks. It is an important responsibility of Resistance leaders to insist on proper zeroing of his men's rifles.

Grenades

The hand grenade is a fairly close-in weapon. Its primary use is clearing enemy positions: trenches, foxholes, bunkers, rooms in buildings, etc. Fighters must be trained to throw a grenade accurately, and to judge safe distances when using grenades in the open.

The rifle grenade is fired from a rifle. This may involve using a blank cartridge to "boost" the grenade from the barrel of the gun, or may use what amounts to a shotgun shell to fire the grenade from a grenade launcher attached to the rifle. In either case, it is used at ranges greater than the hand grenade can be thrown. It is primarily used in the open, to attack enemy positions or groups. It may also be used to fire through openings (broken-out windows, etc.) in buildings. As with hand grenades, fighters must be trained to know when to use them, and to fire them accurately.

Mines

Mines are used primarily to delay enemy movement, or to deny territory to an enemy. Resistance forces use mines primarily in ambushes. However, they may also use mines to block use of trails by government forces, or to delay government forces that are pursuing them. Fighters must be trained to emplace mines properly and safely to themselves.

A critical point is that Resistance forces are fighting in their own country. They want to be able to live and prosper in their country after they win. This means that mines must be used sparingly. Contaminating your own country with mines that will continue to be deadly long after the war is over is bad strategy. Resistance fighters must be trained to remove the mines they have laid, if this becomes possible.

Battlefield Survival

A dead fighter is of no value to his cause. Resistance fighters must be trained to carry out their activities in ways that enhance the chances of their survival without compromising their chances of success. Some critical issues are camouflage, noise, litter and light discipline, and moving under fire.

Camouflage

This was discussed in detail in Chapter 11. The issue here is that Resistance fighters must be trained to think in terms of camouflage, of making themselves hard to see.

Camouflage is intended to let the fighter blend into the surroundings. Color and shape are the two most important considerations. Clothing colors should be chosen to blend with the background, rather than clashing with it. Resistance fighters must be trained to use camouflage paint properly on hands, face, and other exposed skin to help the fighter blend in. They must be trained to use natural materials (plants, leaves) or artificial materials (strips of properly-colored cloth) to break up the outline of the fighter's head and body, thus disguising the "human" shape.

The Resistance fighter must also remove anything that be highly reflective and thereby draw attention. Eyeglasses, watch crystals, shiny mess kits, and any other shiny items that would reflect sunlight, moonlight or starlight can destroy the effectiveness of camouflage. They must be trained to cover reflective items at all times.

Noise, light, litter discipline

Anything that "doesn't belong" can give away the position of the individual fighter or his unit.

Resistance fighters must be trained to exercise noise discipline whenever contact with the enemy is possible. Idle chatter must be eliminated. Noise of movement (crackling of brush, rustle of clothing, rattle of equipment, the *click* of taking off a safety, even the slosh of water in a canteen) may alert the enemy to the presence of the Resistance fighter or his unit. Fighters must be trained to tie equipment down, tape it, or whatever else is needed to prevent rattling.

At night, light from smoking, from flashlights, and even from glow sticks, can alert the enemy to the presence of the Resistance fighter. The Resistance fighters must be trained to avoid any lights, whether from carelessness or too frequent use of any kind of illumination.

There is a risk that litter may accumulate around camps, or around ambush sites during a long wait. Ration wrappers, cigarette butts, and other discarded items will be a dead giveaway of the location of Resistance forces. Fighters must be trained not to litter their surroundings. Even after a unit moves on, litter left behind will give the enemy information such as where the unit camped, how many fighters there were, what kind of supplies they had, and what routes they commonly take. It is crucial that Resistance forces not litter in the first place, and make sure any place where they stayed is left litter-free. This must be emphasized in training.

First Aid

The number one preventable cause of death in combat is bleeding, particularly arterial bleeding. Every fighter must be trained to administer first aid to stop the bleeding of a wounded comrade. There are several products on the market that cause rapid blood clotting. If at all possible, every fighter must be equipped with a packet of clotting agent, and be taught how to apply it. (The article by Yost discusses this in more detail.) With or without clotting material, the most important point is to apply pressure to the wound to reduce or stop bleeding.

Beyond immediate treatment for bleeding, Resistance fighters should be taught immediate treatment of wounds and injuries, prior to transporting the victim to a medical aid station.

The *Ranger Handbook* gives the following instructions regarding immediate first aid to a wounded or injured fighter:

- Open the airway and restore breathing
- Stop the bleeding and protect the wound
- Check and treat for shock

It's not enough that the Resistance fighter *know* this. He must be able to *do* it. Practice and rehearsal for first aid is just as important as any practice of any other skill. The *Soldiers Manual of Common Tasks* gives considerable detail on First Aid techniques, and a checklist of what the fighter must do to demonstrate his skill.

Reporting Intelligence Information

The Resistance fighter must be trained to report back what he has observed, and to this in a systematic fashion. The U.S. Army uses the acronym SALUTE to instruct troops regarding what they should observe and report. Resistance fighters can use the same system.

- Size. How many of the enemy? One group or several groups? How many in each?
- Activity. What are they doing? Resting? Moving? What direction? Digging fighting positions? Occupying buildings? Carrying out construction activities?
- Location. Where are they? Precise geographic location if possible (grid coordinates, or latitude and longitude), or direction and distance from prominent terrain (hill, river bend, tall building, etc.)
- Unit. Uniforms (army, marine, air force, police, etc.), unit patches, insignia. Distinctive signs or symbols. Identification numbers on vehicles.
- Time. When was the enemy observed?
- Equipment. What equipment was associated with the activity being reported (tanks, trucks, ambulances, other vehicles, artillery, aircraft, earth-moving machinery, etc.)?

The key point here is that training in what to observe and report gives the Resistance fighter a specific format for gathering and communicating useful intelligence data.

Unarmed Fighting

Given the disparity in armaments between the Resistance and the government forces, it is essential that Resistance fighters be trained in unarmed fighting. This can be especially important in the early phases of the Resistance, when arms may need to be captured from police or from military sentries. In addition, training in unarmed combat can help instill a "warrior mentality" in the Resistance fighters. They need to absorb the idea that *they* are the crucial element in combat, not their weapons.

Training methods

To begin with, Resistance fighters need "confidence building" training, just as regular troops do. This means things like obstacle courses, towers for rappelling, crawling under live fire, etc. They also need physical training to build up strength and endurance. Only when these basics are accomplished can more elaborate training be effective. Unfortunately, it will be hard for Resistance forces to find secure places for this training. Nevertheless, efforts must be made to achieve this training.

Resistance fighters must be trained in tactics as well as marksmanship. However, the tactics to be used by the Resistance will differ from those employed by conventional armies. Resistance fighters must be trained to conduct raids, ambushes, assassinations, and sabotage. Training must include small-unit tactics including use of multiple elements (assault, security, breaching, support, etc.)

To the extent possible, training should be carried out by practicing the skills needed. This includes not only marksmanship training, but also "hands-on" training with explosives, and practicing tactics such as eliminating sentries, "dynamic entry" of rooms, moving stealthily, and setting ambushes, and night operations.

Games such as "paintball" can provide realistic training in individual and small-unit tactics.[80] They allow people to recognize

---

[80] Jeffrey reports that the Islamic Lashkar-e-Taiba used paintballs, purchased in the US and shipped to Pakistan, as a training aid.

and correct their mistakes in a non-lethal environment, instead of in combat. Indoors, use of so-called "airsoft" guns, that fire small plastic pellets, can be very helpful in teaching room clearing, traversing stairways, etc., again in an environment that allows learning from mistakes. One thing must be guarded against, however: paintball and airsoft maneuvers may lead trainees to mistake "concealment" (hidden from the enemy) for "cover" (something that will stop bullets). This tendency must be guarded against by those in charge of the training.

Ultimately, however, "live fire" training is needed. The Resistance fighters must be familiar with the sights, sounds, and smells of combat.[81] This means they must train with the actual weapons, actual ammunition, etc. they will use in combat. Special care has to be taken in live fire training to avoid accidents, but trainers should remember that any reduction in realism, in the name of "safety," might prove costly in combat against real opponents who shoot back.

Jim Morris describes a training device for urban combat that he saw in use by Lebanese forces.[82] It consisted of stacks of auto tires, filled with dirt, and lined up to simulate alleys, streets, hallways, etc., with openings for rooms or doors. "Live fire" exercises could be conducted in this maze, since the tires and dirt would absorb grenade fragments and rounds from pistols or assault rifles (M-16, AK-47, etc.). Similar means might be used to simulate guard posts, police stations, and other kinds of targets. Resistance forces may have to use similar creativity to find ways of training their fighters in the kind of operations they will actually be conducting.

While live practice is the best training, it may not always be possible. Al Qaeda made use of videotapes and DVDs to teach its

---

[81] A police officer once told me of the experience of a fellow officer. That officer had always trained with .38 Special ammunition in his revolver, and had never fired the .357 Magnum ammunition he loaded with on duty. In his first raid, he fired one shot and thought his gun had blown up. He was not familiar with the sound and sight of his own gun when firing .357 Magnum ammunition.
[82] p. 80.

fighters how to clear a room, to conduct an assassination, to coordinate the elements of a raid, etc. Training videos like these can be distributed to elements of the Resistance who do not have the opportunity to conduct "hands on" training. They can be especially valuable before the Resistance begins actual combat operations, to improve the skill level of fighters, so their initial operations against unprepared government forces are more likely to be successful.

The North Vietnamese Army provided its troops in Vietnam with training manuals including drawings of the vulnerable points on helicopters. For each type of helicopter used by the US, the manuals provided silhouettes for recognition, and aiming points. The Resistance should provide similar manuals for its fighters: vulnerable points of helicopters and tanks, aiming points on unarmored vehicles, most effective places to position explosives, etc.

The Internet can also be used to distribute this information. Beichman describes use of an Islamist web site to instruct jihadists on how to assassinate a "Crusader." Waterman describes the use by Al Qaeda of web sites to provide training material to jihadists:

> [T]he latest bin Laden video was made available in five different versions, ranging from high-definition to a special format called 3GP that can be downloaded to mobile devices. The versions were downloadable at more than 20 different places on the Web, and most messages are also released on a CD-ROM format disc as well.

The Resistance can use the Internet to provide training and instruction to sympathizers with whom it does not have direct contact. The web site must be hosted in a sympathetic or neutral country, however, or it will quickly be brought down by government forces.

If possible, Resistance forces should make videos of ambushes and raids, so the videos can be used for training purposes. The videos should include the mistakes that were made, and the things that went wrong, as well as the successful aspects of the operation. Fighters viewing the videos will thus be better prepared to avoid those mistakes themselves.

Summary

Training is critical. Resistance fighters must have the skills they will need in combat, and must have confidence in their own ability to use those skills. The skills and the confidence can come only through training.

References

Beaver, William, *Practical Martial Arts for Special Forces*, Boulder, CO, Paladin Press, 1996.

Beichman, Arnold, "Chilling Killing Guide," *The St. Croix Review*, October 2006, pp. 16 – 19.

Cramer, Lenox, *War with Empty Hands*, Sharon Center, OH, Alpha Publications, 1986.

Department of the Army, *Guerilla Warfare and Special Forces Operations, FM 31-21*, September 1961.

Department of the Army, *Military Mountaineering*, September 1976.

Department of the Army, *Soldier's Manual of Common Tasks, STP 21-1-SMCT*, October 1994. (This manual provides very little training material as such. However, it provides excellent coverage of what the fighter should be trained to do, and checklists for evaluating whether the fighter has learned what he was taught.)

Department of the Army, *Special Forces Operational Techniques, FM 31-20*, no date.

Department of the Army Ranger Training Brigade, *Ranger Handbook SH 21-76*, July 1992.

Department of the Army, *Tactics in Counterinsurgency, FM 3-24.2*. April 2009. Available at http://smallwarsjournal.com/documents/cointacticsfm.pdf

Dolmatov, A. I., *KGB Alpha Team Training Manual*, Boulder, CO, Paladin Press, 1993. (Grabs, twists and throws you didn't even know there were to know.)

Fairbairn, Capt. W. E., & Capt. E. A. Sykes, *Shooting to Live*, Boulder, CO, Paladin Press, 1987.

Herbert, Anthony B., *Military Manual of Self Defense*, New York, Hippocrene Books, 1984.

Jeffrey, Terence, http://townhall.com/columnists/TerenceJeffrey/2008/12/03/from_pai ntball_to_mumbai?page=full&comments=true

Larsen, Christopher e., *Light Infantry Tactics for Small Teams*, Bloomington, IN, Authorhouse, ISBN 1-4184-7207-7 (available from online booksellers). (First section describes skills needed by light infantry.)

Martin, Tom, *Rappelling*, Mt. Sterling, KY, SEARCH, 1988.

Military Media, http://military-media.com/military/, a source of US Army training manuals and videos on CD-ROM and DVD.

Morris, Jim, *The Devil's Secret Name*, Canton, Ohio, Daring Books, 1989.

Newman, Bob, *Guerillas in the Mist*, Boulder, CO, Paladin Press, 1997.

Padgett, Allen, & Bruce Smith, *On Rope*, Huntsville, AL, National Speleological Society, 1987.

Rexer, Fred L., *Dead or Alive*, Houston, TX, IDHAC, 1977. (While ostensibly about the Colt .45 automatic, the focus is really on developing a warrior mentality.)

Specter Group, http://www.thespectergroup.com/MilitaryManualsDL.htm, 1000 military manuals for download or on DVD.

The Survival Library on CD, 98 Military Manuals on CD, including many on operation of specific weapons, available from http://www.muddywaterpress.com/cd.html, $20 as of this writing.

U.S. Army Marksmanship Unit, *Pistol Marksmanship Training Guide*, can be downloaded at http://www.giwera.pl/pliki/pmtg.pdf

Waterman, Shaun, "Al Qaeda tapes grow in number, expertise," *The Washington Times* national weekly edition, October 1, 2007, p. 24.

Yost, Mark, "Second Chance At Life," *The American Spectator*, February 2006, pp. 16 – 19.

Appendix To Chapter 15

This is a modified version of a training and equipment instruction published by an American militia group. It should be modified to fit your conditions, but can serve as a starting point.

Basic Training Guide

"Basic Training for XXXX_Militia members consists of formal monthly sessions at various locations throughout the state. To participate in any training event, each person must, at a minimum, complete a basic skill, gear and equipment certification. After completing requirements for membership the individual is authorized to wear the XXXX_Militia patch and is considered a rifleman candidate.

Each new rifleman candidate will have 120 days to complete the minimum skill based performance requirements. Each county leader within the group will serve as a guide to new members and help them negotiate the requirements. The Rifleman Candidate should spend more than the formal training time learning, practicing, and perfecting those skills required. Successful completion of Basic not only earns the new candidate respect among his peers, but allows him/her to have voting rights in XXXX_Militia put to the general membership by the Leaders Council (composed of the command function and all County leaders in the XXXX_Militia).

Basic Skill, Gear and Equipment Certification

To be certified, the following weapons, equipment and basic abilities must be possessed and knowledge of their use must be demonstrated.

Gear and Equipment

- Rifle   Military caliber capable; bolt or semi-automatic capable of engaging targets at a minimum of 250 meters.

- Ammunition – 100 rounds minimum and associated magazines, en bloc or stripper clips with appropriate bandoliers (as applicable) for carrying.
- Cleaning Kit – Appropriate to the rifle carried.
- LBE (Load Bearing Equipment) – Can be comprised of a harness ("Y" or "H") or a combat vest, web belt, and associated pouches for carrying required accouterments.
- Canteen or Hydration Bladder – Can be any 1 quart container (minimum); Camelbak type highly recommended; military type canteens will suffice as well.
- BDU Uniform – The XXXX_Militia dresses in BDU type uniforms. The pattern of camouflage on the uniform is left to the individual, however, for our AO, the Woodland pattern has become ubiquitous. Marpat and Multicam patterns are also acceptable. ACU pattern fatigues do not blend very well at all except in urban environments during limited visibility and are discouraged from use as are yellow desert colored boots (the idea behind camouflage is to make it difficult for an enemy to see you, not the opposite).
- Combat, Hunting, or Hiking Boots – They must be field capable, i.e., able to take a lot of abuse, provide ankle support, and basic comfort over long walks. Do not skimp on your boots! Many brands are available; just remember you get what you pay for. Don't become a liability to your group because you bought cheaply made boots!
- Individual 1st Aid Kit – Must contain: 1 battle dressing (compression type); 1 triangular bandage; 1 tube of Triple Anti-Biotic (such as Neosporin Plus) with or without pain reliever; 1 small roll of gauze; 1 4"X4" gauze pad; 5 band-aids (minimum); 1 pr latex gloves; either or – 1 additional battle dressing or 1 4X4 gauze pad. The kit can be held in a small plastic bag or in a USGI issue 1st aid kit. It must be on your person or LBE.
- Copy of the US Constitution and Declaration of Independence This can be had in a publication called, "The Citizen's Rule Book" and is small enough to carry in your shirt pocket. Get one. It should be on your person at all times when in the field, as the Constitution is the "supreme law of the land". [Note: This applies to the U.S. Your fighters

should carry whatever document contains the goals and objectives of your Resistance movement. Your fighters *must* be constantly aware of what they are fighting for!]

Skills

- Complete a 2 Mile Hike in 40 Minutes or Less – You must carry your rifle, LBE, ammunition, 1st Aid Kit while wearing your uniform and boots. You must complete your walk prior to performing your marksmanship demonstration. (You will be required to do this in 31 minutes to complete your "basic training"—the 40 minute requirement is just to make sure you're fit enough to begin your training!)
- Marksmanship Demonstration – You must shoot 10 rounds at a 6 inch tall AQT target at a distance of 100 yards. You must have 8 out of 10 within the border of the target to complete this demonstration. You will only have 3 attempts available. If, after 3 attempts, you cannot hit 8 out of 10, you must come back another time and again perform this demonstration.
- Weapon Field Stripping Demonstration – You must field strip your rifle into its major groups for cleaning, e.g., the barrel group and receiver group at a minimum. You must also put the rifle together and function check to ensure it works.

Initial Equipment

- Prior to beginning basic training, in addition to all equipment listed in the Basic Skill, Gear, and Equipment Certification, each Rifleman Candidate must have and be able to demonstrate:
- Poncho w/liner – It may be military or civilian, but must be colored so that it reasonably blends in if used as a shelter.
- Lensatic Compass – USGI highly recommended.
- Camouflage face paint – Enough for several applications
- Combat Knife or Bayonet – Fixed blade between 6 and 10 inches (blade length). If a bayonet is chosen, it must be mountable on the rifle carried.
- Personal flashlight with blue (or traffic light green) or red lens cover (colored cellophane can be used to rig a lens

cover). (Traffic light green is the least harmful color for night vision.)

- 100 Feet of 550 (parachute) cord – Minimum--200 feet is better.
- State Road Map – Can be obtained free at the State's Department of Transportation web site. [Note: this should be replaced by a map appropriate to your Resistance movement.]
- FRS (or FRS/GMRS) radio – Must have for communications. 20 plus mile range highly recommended; 10 mile range minimum acceptable.

Skills Demonstration

- Properly Bandage an Extremity – To a simulated one-sided wound to either an arm or leg. Demonstrate escalation of treatment from pressure to bandaging and then treat for shock.
- Camouflage self & equipment – You will have 30 minutes to paint self & use field expedient materials to camouflage your equipment.
- Construct a Poncho "Hootch" or Lean-To – Demonstrate the proper method for constructing an emergency shelter and be willing to spend the night in it.
- Complete a 3 mile walk with all listed equipment within 1 hour

Once these minimum equipment and skill requirements are demonstrated, the person wishing to join the XXXX_Militia is now a "Rifleman Candidate" and must complete "Basic Training" within 120 days of the day he starts the training. The evaluation may be conducted by the individual's county leader, the Training & Operations officer, or any NCO within the XXXX_Militia or a combination thereof. Evaluations may be done on days separate from group training, but must be witnessed/evaluated by at least two of the above named officers.

Completion of Basic Training

Rifleman Candidate: The following is what the RC must accomplish no later than 120 days after becoming a member. A general task listing is provided in addition to explanations that follow the task listing.

Skill or Task: Marksmanship

- Performance: Complete AQT Qualification IAW Course of Fire
  Standard: Score 120 pts or higher
  Time Requirement: Within 120 Days

Skill or Task: Equipment Check

- Performance: Demonstrate Required Gear/Equipment Possession
  Standard: IAW Equip Checklist
  Time Requirement: Within 60 Days

Skill or Task: Personal Camouflage

- Performance: Camouflage self & gear & not be discernable at 10 Meters
  Standard: IAW MW LP
  Time Requirement: Within 60 Days

Skill or Task: Physical Fitness Assessment

- Performance: Performed consecutively on the same day.
  20 Elevated Push Ups
  30 degree crunches (30 within 60 seconds)
  5 mile road march in under 80 minutes w/rifle, 3 day pack, & basic load of ammo/food/water
  Time Requirement: Within 120 Days

Skill or Task: Individual Movement

- Performance: Demonstrate
  High Crawl
  Low Crawl
  Monkey Crawl
  Rush
  Night Walk Technique
  Standard: IAW MW LP
  Time Requirement: Within 30 Days

Skill or Task: Team Security

- Performance: Demonstrate ability to set up a 'team triangle'
  Standard: IAW MW LP
  Time Requirement: Within 30 Days

Skill or Task: Land Navigation

- Performance: Demonstrate the ability to shoot a magnetic azimuth, back azimuth, convert mag to grid azimuth and grid to mag azimuth, plot 8 digit grid coord, and determine a correct pace count
  Standard: IAW MW LP
  Time Requirement: Within 120 Days

Additional Requirements

While the above performance requirements illustrate the minimum acceptable performance by RC's for membership in XXXX_Militia, the following information provides specifics on what additional knowledge and ability each RC should master as soon as possible.

Marksmanship

Without the ability to deliver aimed, accurate, deliberate deadly fire, the Minuteman's effectiveness is diminished almost to the length of his reach. To ensure the Minuteman can confidently engage at his weapon's maximum effective range when required, the following will be the standard for personal marksmanship.

Weapons Nomenclature.

The candidate must demonstrate the knowledge he or she possesses of the main battle rifle carried prior to completing the AQT. Skills required:

- Field strip into major groups and describe the purpose of the group in the weapon's function
- Describe the cycle of operation of the rifle
- Describe the common stoppages and malfunctions
- Describe required lubrication points & schedule as applicable to your rifle
- Describe how "mechanical zero" is obtained on your rifle

Demonstrate skill levels

- Rifleman Candidate: The candidate must be able to obtain the minimum qualifying score on a "Certification AQT" after shooting 20 rounds (120 pts).
- Rifleman: The candidate must be able to shoot 4 MOA @ 100 yards with his or her primary rifle (iron sights or low powered "scout" or CQB type scope). This ability will be measured by the "Fred's M14 Stocks" full AQT. The scoring window of "Marksman" must be achieved. Minimum Acceptable Score 140.
- Senior Rifleman: The candidate must be able to shoot 4 MOA @ 100 yards with his or her primary rifle (iron sights or low powered "scout" or CQB type scope). This ability will be measured by the "Fred's M14 Stocks" full AQT. The scoring window of "Expert" must be achieved. Minimum Score: 200 (160 if the course is conducted @ 100 yards with single 6" Fred's silhouettes).

Marksmanship clinics will be conducted quarterly so that tactical training can take place.

Camouflage

Camouflage self & equipment IAW applicable terrain features (rural or urban) in any of the following environments as directed.

- Rural:
    o Above ground
    o Below ground

- Urban
    o Among buildings, streets, cities & suburbs
    o Among populace

Physical Fitness assessment
Minimum Acceptable Fitness Level – must be performed consecutively on the same day started:

- 20 elevated pushups
- 30-degree crunches: 30 w/in 60 seconds
- Road March – 5 miles in 80 minutes or less with patrol pack (day, assault, or butt pack with all accouterments) & LBE w/primary weapon and basic load of ammo/water

Pushup and abdominal exercise technique will be demonstrated as necessary, usually before marksmanship clinics. Personal exercise by each person will be done on his or her own time. Road March practice may be conducted at any time during the training cycle with distances ranging from 2 to 10 statute miles. Annual 10 mile road marches with combat packs, basic load of ammunition, and primary weapon will be conducted with a 3 hours (about 18 minutes per mile) time limit over reasonably level ground regardless of weather conditions to demonstrate the physical abilities of the team, provide an opportunity to test out load balance, and build team spirit by shared performance of a rigorous training requirement. It is the personal responsibility of each member to keep himself within group fitness expectations.

Individual Movement.

In addition to the minimum requirements, each member will be trained in and evaluated on performance and knowledge of the following:

- Micro-terrain Appreciation and Employment
    - Micro-terrain definition: Terrain features that are comprised of natural and manmade features in the AO that provides cover and concealment to the individual, team, or squad of Minutemen. Micro-terrain has a significant impact on the probability of survival of the individual or team by how the cover and concealment it offers is employed. Examples of micro-terrain features: grasslands & swamps, gullies and rocks, depressions, road shoulders, water ditches, subsurface drains, sidewalk curb, small bushes, etc.

Harnessing the Senses
- Natural Night Vision

- Discovering signs of enemy presence: wilted foliage, fresh dirt, linear shapes, and subtle glint
- The importance of hearing
  - What to listen for: Marching, digging, artillery setup, sloshing canteen water, bayonet scabbard noise, coughing, footsteps, rifle report differences (AK vs. M16 vs. SAW etc.), gear noise, etc.
  - Sounds warning of danger: Grenade spoon "twang," absence of any background noise, dogs barking, flight of wild birds, even an agitated insect (what would make an insect mad enough to bother you?)

- Smell and technique: What to smell
  - Tobacco
  - Smoke
  - Urine
  - Feces
  - Chewing gum
  - Toothpaste
  - Hair tonic
  - Insect spray
  - Scented soap

- Touch (exposed skin works the best): What touch warns of:
  - Prongs of a mine
  - Wires
  - Any indicator of another human being
  - Differences in the medium being moved through (water, puff of air, etc.)
  - Residual heat from a prone body or shell casings
- Taste: An unexpected taste may be the only attack warning available in certain scenarios (chemical weapons)
- Sense Enhancement at the expense of others. All electronics surveillance devices have an inherent flaw: they must process everything they detect.
  - Heavy rain erases sound and virtually negates thermal imaging.

- Night Vision can easily be defeated by illumination behind a planned penetration point. In fact, any light source degrades the quality of NV.
- Observation techniques: How to look for the enemy
- Undiscovered movement: indiscernible movement toward an opponent
- Infiltration/Exfiltration: Getting in and out of enemy bases undiscovered.

Basic Knife, Tomahawk & Bayonet Techniques

- Sentry Removal
  - Aware of attack
  - Unaware of attack
- Silent Assault w/edged weapon of choice
  - 5 Angles of Attack
  - Roof Blocks
  - 5 Counters

Other Skills

- Fire Discipline: why, how, when
- Obstacle Breaching
- Land Navigation

Team Exercises

- Perimeter Defense
  - Fire team
  - Squad
  - Platoon

- Communications
- First Aid (Self & Others)
- Field fortifications
  - Rural
  - Urban
- Tactics
  - Withdrawal Under Fire
  - Envelopment
  - Flexible Defense

- o Delaying Actions
- o Ambush
- o Raid
- Reconnaissance
  - o External to the objective
  - o From within the objective
  - o Deception of electronic imagery
  - o Defeating NVG & Thermal imagery

Leadership

Leadership is critical to the success of any team in the field. Leaders must understand that each member of the team is vital and each sees things from a unique perspective that may hold the key to problems encountered. Once a team member has attained "basic" proficiency (Basic Training completed), the leader should solicit their opinions on exercise/training efficiency, field problems, and tactical workarounds for the "play book" without prejudice (accepting opinions without denigration). Additionally, at each level of expertise gained, all team members must complete the following:

Rifleman:

- Plan & execute a fire team strength (4 to 6 men) reconnaissance patrol with little or no assistance and complete the training mission without unit compromise
- Plan and conduct a one-hour block of instruction on any one of the following subjects during a scheduled training session:
  - o Night Vision Techniques
  - o Marksmanship Fundamentals
  - o Basic Patrolling
  - o Combat First Aid
  - o Field Fortifications
  - o Camouflage, Cover & Concealment
  - o Individual Movement Techniques
  - o Map Reading & Terrain Association
  - o The Lensatic Compass

Senior Rifleman

- Plan & execute a reinforced fire team strength (6 to 9 men) point ambush or security patrol with little or no assistance from higher command echelon and complete the training mission by exfiltration of the objective area without discovery
- Plan and conduct a two-hour block of intermediate level instruction on any one of the subjects above during a scheduled training session (the subject chosen may not be the one taught for Rifleman level)

Rifleman NCO

- Plan & execute a reinforced squad strength (13 to 19 men) raid mission including reconnaissance of the objective, infiltration of the squad, patrol base implementation and security, successful action at the objective, and exfiltration of the objective area without discovery or mission compromise
- Plan and conduct a four-hour block of advanced instruction on any one of the topics in the above list during a scheduled training session (the subject chosen may not be either of the subjects chosen at Rifleman or Senior Rifleman level). The instruction may include a formal written, verbal or performance evaluation.

NOTE: This is a basic Plan of Instruction and is only a foundation for group training and expertise! You should modify it to fit the conditions your Resistance movement faces.

Chapter 16

Secure Camps

Resistance forces will need locations where the following activities can be carried out:

- Fighters can rest and refit between actions;
- Wounded fighters can be treated;
- Resistance force commanders can meet with subordinate commanders to plan and coordinate activities;
- Subordinate elements can pass messages to higher command and to each other;
- Subordinate elements can obtain ammunition and supplies;
- Engineering and logistic elements can operate repair and manufacturing facilities;

To satisfy these needs, one or more secure base camps will be needed.

What is a secure camp?

To begin with, no camp is ever completely "secure." A camp is "secure" only so long as it is not known by government forces. Once the location of a camp is known, government forces can bomb it, or send ground troops to attack it.

In the early stages of the Resistance, no attempt should be made to "hold" base camps in the face of government attack. In fact, while the Resistance is still weak, any attempt to hold a camp in the face of attack will likely result not only in loss of the camp but annihilation of the forces in the camp. Survival of the Resistance force is more important than defense of physical facilities.

As the strength of the Resistance grows, and it begins to displace the government in regions of the country or sections of a city, a "trial of strength" may be more appropriate. At that stage, holding a fortified camp may serve to demonstrate that the

Resistance is able to match the government forces on an equal basis. Even then, however, it must be remembered that survival of the force is more important than holding a physical facility.

In either case, whether a camp is to be abandoned because the Resistance is yet too weak to hold it, or is to be held despite attack, the government forces should be made to pay a high price for attacking it. The *Special Forces "A" Camp Manual* provides a great deal of information on how to organize a camp for defense.

Types of Camps

There are three basic types of camps that Resistance forces may establish: the concealed camp, the disguised camp, and the underground camp.

The Concealed Camp

This type of camp is usually located in remote, wooded or jungle areas, where overhead foliage provides concealment for the camp. The key to security for this type of camp is concealment from government observation. This means there must be nothing to suggest to casual observers that a camp exists under the trees. The following factors must be taken into account in preserving concealment:

- All lights must be inside buildings with blacked-out windows, and fires should all be under cover;
- Buildings and tents must have their outlines broken up by some means so that at low sun angles their shadows don't appear as straight lines between the trees;
- Smoke from cooking fires should be dispersed by some means rather than allowing it to appear above the trees;
- Smells, such as food being cooked, or exhaust fumes from diesel or gasoline generators, should be minimized;
- Visible signs such as trails from frequent passage, or trees being stripped of dead branches for firewood, must be avoided;
- Garbage and waste from sanitary facilities should be given deep burial;

- Especially in cold weather, the temperature in camp buildings should be kept low, to prevent the government forces from using infrared detectors to locate the camp.

Concealed camps are almost of necessity located in remote areas. This aids in concealment, but may reduce their utility by lengthening the time needed for couriers or fighters to reach them.

The Disguised Camp

This type of camp achieves security by looking like something legitimate: a farming village, a marketplace, or simply a crossroads with a gas station and general store. Resistance forces may mingle clandestinely with the legitimate activity there, or may conduct bogus activity to simulate legitimate activity. In either case, to the casual observer, the camp must appear to be something completely legitimate.

While legitimate activity in a disguised camp serves as a screen for the activities of the Resistance, it also serves as a screen for government infiltrators. The Resistance's security forces must be alert for people who don't belong among the "regulars" at the site.

The government may suspect that the legitimate activity is a front for a disguised Resistance activity. The police or other security agencies may attempt to suborn some of the "regulars," either by rewards or threats. The Resistance's security forces must be alert to this possibility. Any change in the behavior of one of the "regulars" should be a cause for suspicion.

The "regulars" may come to suspect that some form of Resistance activity is being carried out at the disguised camp. They may talk to friends or neighbors. Persons not sympathetic to the Resistance may even report their suspicions to the police. It is imperative that the Resistance activities be made to look entirely legitimate.

The disguised camp is almost indefensible, especially if it relies on mingling with unrelated legitimate activity. An attack by government forces will kill or injure many among the legitimate "regulars" who have no connection with whatever Resistance activity was being carried out. The Resistance should plan to abandon a disguised camp that includes legitimate activity, rather than defend it against attack.

The Underground Camp

There are two types of underground camp, the natural cave and the constructed tunnel. Each has advantages and disadvantages.

Natural Caves

Natural caves were used by Afghans against both the Russians and the Americans. They do not require any construction, they can be occupied on short notice, they are fairly easy to defend, and they provide good concealment. However, they are usually located in remote and unpopulated areas, meaning that food and other supplies must be brought in from a distance, usually over fairly rugged terrain. If they do exist in areas where the Resistance is operating, their advantages and disadvantages must be weighed carefully.

Tunnels

The Viet Cong used tunnels very effectively against the Americans and the Republic of Vietnam. However, they were not the first to use tunnels as bases. Nearly twenty centuries ago, in the Cappadocia area of what is present-day Turkey, people carved out entire cities underground, to protect themselves against raiders. Early Christians in Rome dug catacombs under the city, as burial places and refuges. These underground installations in Vietnam, Turkey and Rome still exist, and are now tourist attractions.

The Viet Cong tunnels existed only in areas where the soil was suitable for the purpose. Likewise the underground developments in Cappadocia were dug in compacted volcanic ash, and the Roman catacombs were dug in compacted silt. The key point is that the soil in each case was self-supporting. Timbers and other supports were not required.

The Resistance probably will not have machinery for digging tunnels, even where the soil is suitable. Thus tunnels are labor-intensive, involving essentially pick and shovel work. This means they can be constructed only in populated areas, where there is a labor force to draw upon. Moreover, they take time to construct. The Resistance must hide the construction activity, and must dispose of the earth removed from the tunnels in a way that doesn't draw attention to the tunnels. The Resistance must also be assured of the loyalty of the workers who help build the tunnels. It takes only one disloyal or disgruntled worker to tip off the government about the location of the tunnels.

Tunnels are out of sight, but entrances must be concealed. Emissions, such as smoke, generator exhaust, cooking smells, and so on must be dispersed so they don't give away the location of the tunnels.

Tunnels must be designed to be defended. This may include multiple exits, boobytraps that are marked by symbols known to the Resistance forces using the tunnels, right-angled turns and U-turns to minimize the effectiveness of explosions in the tunnels, and methods to seal off tunnel sections that attackers flood with toxic gases. The book by Newman includes information on tunnel design and defense.

While the Viet Cong successfully used tunnels, new technology has made tunnel detection easier. For the past decade or so, archeologists have been successfully using ground-penetrating radar to locate and map ancient cities that are now buried under sand or earth. To protect against ground-penetrating radar, tunnels should be constructed under forests or under villages. The surface objects will then make it more difficult to use the radar against tunnels.

Despite the problems of constructing and defending tunnels, they have numerous advantages. They can be built where they are needed from a tactical standpoint. They provide a way for Resistance forces to "disappear" when being pursued. They provide a permanent "home" for the Resistance, especially the higher command levels. In areas where the soil is suitable and sufficient labor available, the Resistance should consider using tunnels for base camps.

Hospitals

The importance of medical care for wounded Resistance fighters cannot be overestimated. Medical care must start with the wounded fighter on the battlefield. Ultimately those with sufficiently severe wounds must be brought to a hospital. Ordinarily, Resistance hospitals will be located at secure camps, preferably in remote areas.

The term "hospital" need not mean an elaborate building. The article by Hawk describes Viet Cong "hospitals" that were essentially platforms under trees, where the medical personnel might be standing in knee-deep water. The Resistance hospital, even one in a cave, a tunnel, or a tent in a concealed camp, will be stripped down to bare essentials. The services of the trained physicians will have to be extended with partially-trained people. Physicians will be used only for situations requiring a high level of medical knowledge or skills. Success of American "Green Berets" demonstrates that non-physicians can be trained to provide routine medical care. The Resistance must provide this training to supplement the few physicians it will have.

Summary

The Resistance will require secure base camps from which to operate. These camps may depend on either concealment or disguise for security. In either case, the Resistance forces must keep them secret from the government for as long as possible. Once they have been discovered, the decision to abandon them after a brief fight, or to defend them heavily, will depend on the level of capability the Resistance forces have achieved vis-à-vis the government.

References

Anonymous, *Special Forces "A" Camp Manual*, Boulder, CO, Paladin Press, 1994.

Hawk, Alan, "Jungle Medicine: Treating the VC Wounded," *Vietnam*, June 2002, pp. 42 – 48, 64.

Newman, Bob, *Guerrillas in the Mist*, Boulder, CO, Paladin Press, 1997, ISBN 978-0-87364-944-5.

United States Army, *ST 31-91B, Army Special Forces Medical Handbook*, Boulder, CO, Paladin Press, 1988.

Werner, David, *Where There Is No Doctor*, The Hesperian Foundation, P.O. Box 1692, Palo Alto, CA 94302. (Available from the publisher and from Bohica Concepts)

Chapter 17

Safe Houses And Secure Areas

What is a safe house?

A safe house is not safe because you say it is. A safe house is safe only so long as the opposition doesn't know about it. As Jefferson Mack writes,

> "What makes a safe house safe? High walls? Strong locks on the door? An electronic security system? Electronic countersurveillance equipment? Well-armed guards? No. A safe house is safe because it appears to the enemy to be a place used by ordinary people for ordinary purposes . . . The only universal requirement is that any stranger who makes contact with those . . . inside the safe house will find no reason to suspect that the place is anything but what it appears to be."

In short, a safe house is a place the government does not suspect is being used by the Resistance for subversive purposes, because it looks so obviously harmless.

Why the resistance needs safe houses

There are many activities the Resistance will engage in that must be kept hidden from the government. A partial list includes:

- Meeting with potential recruits to the Resistance;
- Meeting with agents who are gathering information for the Resistance;
- Writing and printing clandestine flyers, illegal newspapers, and handouts;
- Planning ambushes, assassinations, and raids;
- Storing weapons and supplies;
- Training those to be involved in covert actions;

- Hiding Resistance operatives following some action such as an ambush;
- Collecting and distributing funds for the Resistance;
- Providing a place for wounded fighters to recuperate, or to await transportation elsewhere.

Any activity that must be hidden from the government, but must be conducted "under the noses of" the government, requires a safe house. The Resistance will find many uses for safe houses, and must establish them as early as possible. If the situation appears to be deteriorating, even before the Resistance begins overt action, it would be wise to start establishing safe houses.

Establishing a Safe House

The ideal safe house is a residence that is occupied by a loyal supporter of the Resistance, who has lived there for a long time and is known to be a good citizen, but who is not known to be a supporter of the Resistance. However, since the safe house will frequently be visited by different people, some "cover story" must be created to explain why this family is suddenly receiving these visits.

A somewhat less desirable safe house is one newly rented for the purpose. In this case, since there is no history of "good behavior" associated with the house, the agent renting it must establish an air of innocence with the landlord, the rental agency, neighbors, utility employees, mail carriers, newspaper carriers, and anyone else who has reason to be there legitimately. In particular, this means the house or apartment must be occupied by someone who carries on what appears to be a normal life: working, shopping, going to church, etc.

Another good possibility for a safe house is a place of business that people routinely enter and leave. A restaurant with a back room for private meetings, a doctor's or dentist's office with multiple rooms for patients, a business office with a conference room, etc. In this case the owner or manager of the business must be willing to work with the Resistance.

A safe house should have easy access by public transportation. If people may arrive by auto, it should have ample parking. It should have hidden spaces to hold documents, supplies, and even people being hidden. It should be somewhat separated from neighboring houses, to reduce the chances of neighbors becoming curious about the activities there. It should provide a clear view of its surroundings. It should have multiple escape routes, in case government agents come to call. No location will be perfect, but these factors should be considered.

A safe house used as a refuge for the wounded, for fighters following some action, for debriefing agents, for planning some future action, for storing weapons or explosives, or some similar activity that does not immediately affect those outside the house, must *never* be used for actions such as interviewing potential recruits, training untested recruits, holding prisoners or hostages, or any other activity that will result in its cover being "blown" in the event the recruiting fails, or the hostage is released. Safe houses for the latter purposes are typically "one-shot" locations. They are used for a specific operation and never used again.

Telltale Signs of a Safe House

How do safe houses become "unsafe?" Unfortunately, there are many ways.

Someone involved in the safe house is either suborned by the police, or was threatened by the police, or was working for them all along. To reduce the chances of this happening, the number of people who know about the safe house must be kept to a minimum. The fewer who know, the fewer who can tell about it.

Someone going to the safe house was followed by the police. Anyone going to a safe house, or taking someone to a safe house, must take precautions to make sure they weren't followed, or that followers have been shaken off. The details of anti-surveillance methods are beyond the scope of this book. See the book *Countering Hostile Surveillance* in the References.

A neighbor may suspect that some illegal activity is going on (e.g., drug dealer), and tip off the police. They would be wrong about the nature of the activity, but ultimately right about the fact of it. To reduce the chances of this, every effort must be made to make the safe house and the activities surrounding it look as normal and harmless as possible. There should be plausible explanations for everything.

Failure to maintain an atmosphere of normality. For instance, German police identified an Al Qaeda safe house because someone had rented an apartment, but there was never any electricity use. That was a tip-off that something out of the ordinary was going on. A safe house must look occupied. The ostensible resident(s) must be seen entering and leaving. Mail delivery, newspaper delivery, garbage pickup, etc. must all look normal. Lights should go on and off at appropriate hours. Radio or television should be played at appropriate hours. Car(s) should be parked overnight. There must be visible signs that the activity going on is the type of activity expected of the house or place of business.

The Underground Railroad

The term "underground railroad" was first applied to means for helping slaves escaped from the American South to travel safely to Canada. This "railroad" amounted to a series of safe houses, approximately 25 miles apart (one day's travel in a wagon). Some information about the original underground railroad can be found in the book by Tobin & Dobard.

The Resistance will undoubtedly need an underground railroad for a variety of reasons. For instance, should one of the members of the overt Resistance become identified with the covert Resistance, they (and possibly their family as well) will have to be taken to safety. Wounded fighters who are able to travel will need to be transported to a base camp. Leaders of the covert Resistance traveling to a meeting will have to go by clandestine means. The book by Mack on establishing an underground railroad describes how it should be done in modern times. The exact methods will differ from one country to another, but the basic principles remain the same. They have not changed much from the mid-19th century to the 21st.

Summary

Safe houses are "safe" because they look normal, even though they are used for clandestine activities. The Resistance will have need of multiple safe houses for a variety of reasons. These should be established as early as possible.

References

ACM IV Security Services, *Countering Hostile Surveillance*, Boulder, CO, Paladin Press, ISBN 978-1-58160-636-2.

Mack, Jefferson, *The Safe House*, Boulder, CO, Paladin Press, 1998.

Mack, Jefferson, *Underground Railroad*, Boulder, CO, Paladin Press, ISBN 978-1-58160-106-0.

Tobin, Jacqueline L., & Raymond G. Dobard, *Hidden In Plain Sight*, New York, Doubleday, 1999. (A description of how slaves in the American South used quilts to communicate amongst themselves. It provides a description of the original underground railroad.)

Chapter 18

Communications

The Resistance, both overt and covert branches, will need clandestine means of communication. Codes and encryption will be discussed in the next chapter. This chapter will deal with methods of sending clandestine messages, without regard to whether they are encrypted. There are two criteria for clandestine communications. They must be carried out a) without the government knowing that communication is taking place, and b) in such a way that the sender and receiver are protected.

There are numerous ways of satisfying these criteria while sending information from one element of the Resistance to another. Some are described here.

Internet Chat rooms

Many Internet services make private chat rooms available. On AOL, for instance, click on People > Chat > Enter or Start Private Chat. If you are starting the chat room, give it a name. If you are entering a private chat room someone else has already started, enter the agreed-upon name. Some prior arrangement must be made about time and chat room name. The name should be changed for each use.

Once in the chat room, you may discuss things without others being aware of the conversation. Obviously AOL knows the chat is taking place, and can allow the government to listen in. However, the chat room will likely not attract the attention of government agents and does provide a clandestine means of communication. If the use is discovered, however, the identity of the chat room users will be known, since they are signed up with AOL.

AOL is of course not the only provider of chat rooms. A Google search on "chat room" will identify many providers. Choose one with the least possible requirements on registration. Those that require payment should be ignored, since payments are easy to trace.

Telephone

Using a residence or business phone is clearly not a good way to maintain security. In the US, pay phones were at one time popular means for clandestine communication. However, they are disappearing as cell phone popularity grows, and in many foreign countries, they never existed at all. Nevertheless, where it exists, the telephone system can provide a means of clandestine communication.

Disposable Cell Phones

Criminal and terrorist groups have made extensive use of disposable cell phones. These are now widely available at fairly low cost. They should be bought for cash, not by credit card. Only brands for which no registration is required should be used.

The secret to security is to use such a cell phone *once only*, whether to call or to receive a call. Once the message has been sent, both sending and receiving phones should be disposed of in a way that fingerprints and DNA cannot be retrieved from them. This way it doesn't matter if the police determine that a message was send from phone A to phone B. Those phones will never be used again, and cannot be found.

The exception to one-time use is during a raid or ambush, where all use takes place within a very short time. The disposable cell phones in the raiding party may be used several times, but must be discarded in a secure manner once the raid is over.

Prepaid Phone Card

Prepaid phone cards can be bought in many stores. There is no record made of the purchaser. They can be used to make phone calls without identifying the caller.

Cards should be purchased in small denominations, and discarded after the first use. They should be discarded in such a way that fingerprints and DNA cannot be retrieved from them.

Logistical Considerations

Prepaid cell phones and phone cards should not be purchased in large quantities. That is likely to be a tip-off to the government. The Logistical arm of the Resistance must arrange for many small purchases, spread out over many stores, so as not to attract attention. These phones or cards can then be issued to Resistance operatives as needed.

Postal drops

Post Office boxes usually require considerable information from the person renting them. They are not suitable for clandestine use. However, firms renting private mailboxes are often less demanding in terms of the information required. These boxes are usually indoors, are available twenty-four hours a day, and offer privacy to the user. The biggest security risk comes from payment. If the firm will accept cash payments, then the renter can get away with giving a fake name and address when signing up. Mail sent to these boxes provides a clandestine means of communication.

Dead Drops

A "dead drop" is a physical location where one person can leave a message, to be retrieved later by another person. If done right, the sender and receiver need not even see each other.

The book by Myers suggests a number of places: inside the telephone in a phone booth (unscrew the cap and insert a small message), inside the display newspaper in a newspaper vending machine, in a paper towel dispenser in a public rest room, in a potted plant in a restaurant or other place accessible to the public (remember the plant will be watered; place the message in a waterproof container). The book by Fiery suggests many more places, including many that are not at first obvious, such as under the stair mat of a hotel fire escape, the stepping stones in public parks, under a bench in a public park, traffic cones along highway construction sites, highway guard rails, and furniture in furniture stores. The key is to look for nooks, crannies, holes, spaces, inside or under something that serves some other purpose.

Whatever you select as a dead drop, it should be something that will remain there long enough for the pickup to take place. Avoid things like drainpipes and culverts that might be flooded by rain before a pickup can be made.

The dead drop must be in a "dead zone" where both the person leaving something, and the person retrieving it, have adequate privacy for the transaction. You don't want to attract the attention of passersby when either leaving or retrieving something.

Once a dead drop has been agreed upon by both parties to the transaction, the following measures need to be taken.

The person leaving something in the dead drop must signal that the drop needs to be *serviced*. This can be something like a chalk mark on a lamp-post, a bit of graffiti on a wall, a potted plant moved from one side of a door to another. Whatever it is, it should be something that does not convey any information to the casual observer.

The person retrieving something from the dead drop must then provide some signal that the drop has been serviced. Whatever this signal is, it should also be something that does not convey any information to the casual observer.

The book by Myers has considerable information on selecting and using dead drops.

Live Drops

A live drop is simply a person who accepts something from one person and turns it over to another. Both sender and recipient go to the place where the live drop operates. This is different from a courier, who travels from sender to recipient.

The live drop should be someone who works in a place where there is considerable public traffic, but where people tend to mind their own business. A barber, a bartender, a librarian, or a receptionist, for instance, are able to deal with people without attracting attention.

The live drop must be able to give a signal that he or she has been compromised and is under duress, so that persons planning to leave or retrieve something are warned off.

There are risks in using a live drop. The person acting as drop will know both sender and recipient. He or she is thus a very vulnerable link in the communication chain. This is especially true if the live drop is used by many pairs of senders and recipients. The advantages and risks of the live drop should be considered by the Resistance before employing this method.

Internet Telephone

There are services that provide the equivalent of telephone voice service over the Internet. These can be a clandestine means of communication.

Voice Over Internet Protocol (VOIP)

VOIP is a system for converting voice to digital form and sending it over the Internet. It is converted back to standard form at the destination, and uses conventional telephone handsets at both ends. The big advantage of VOIP, from the standpoint of clandestine communication, is that the message does not look like a telephone conversation. It is mixed in with the millions of packets of digital data going over the Internet. It does not attract attention in the same way that regular telephone calls do.

According to *Aviation Week & Space Technology*, January 21, 2008, p. 45:

> The Chinese are using VOIP, which causes big problems for the US, because there's no wireless signal transmitted that can be easily intercepted, say US intelligence officials. Hezbollah has adopted the same system for communications in southern Lebanon so they can't be intercepted by Lebanese or Israeli analysts. The command-and-control network is then invisible in the RF spectrum. The move was necessary because the Israel Defense Forces have become adept at tracking cellular traffic.

Despite these advantages of VOIP, users must sign up and pay a monthly or annual fee. Thus the fact that they are VOIP subscribers will be known to the government

SKYPE

Skype is a service similar to VOIP. It has the same advantages and disadvantages.

Anonymous E-mail

There are web sites that are "anonymizers." E-mail sent through them has the original identifying data stripped off, thus disguising the source. However, e-mail coming to the site can be identified, and the operators of the site can be forced to identify the source of e-mail. One site, http://anonymouse.org, provides anonymous browsing, anonymous messaging, and anonymous posting on newsgroups.

An alternative to anonymizer sites is TOR, described in more detail in the next chapter. For each e-mail, it sets up a temporary route through several servers, thus disguising the message.

Amateur Radio and similar services

The availability of amateur radio (Ham radio) differs from one country to another. Some countries limit it very strictly; others are very liberal. In addition to amateur radio, there may be other radio services similar to Citizens Band, Family Radio Service, and General Mobile Radio Service, which are available in the United States. You should determine what is available in your country.

Typically, amateur radio operators face at least the following restrictions:

- They must pass a test to obtain a license;
- On each transmission they must identify their government-provided call letters;
- Each transmission must be "in the clear," i.e., no codes or ciphers except the standard Ham "Q-codes;"
- Transmitter power levels are limited;

- They must operate within legally-specified frequency bands.

Clearly, in using amateur radio, the Resistance will violate *every one* of these requirements. Resistance use of amateur radio is effectively "pirate radio." There are two major problems with such operation.

First, as with any radio transmission, the signals can be detected by the government. Moreover, the transmitter can be located if it stays on the air long enough, and stays in one place. Thus use of radio is vulnerable to government direction finding

Second, such pirate use of amateur radio frequencies will antagonize legitimate Ham operators, not only in your country, but in other countries as well, especially if your operation exceeds legal transmitter power limits. This will counteract your attempts to gain support from your fellow countrymen as well as people elsewhere. This negative effect should be taken into account before deciding whether to use amateur radio frequencies for Resistance communications.

The book by Ingram provides information on selecting and using radio communications.

Nevertheless, if such pirate operation is kept limited in scope, and the transmitters are moved frequently, amateur radio, or any of the alternatives that might be available, provides a means of broadcasting information to various elements of the Resistance. In many countries, transmitters and receivers can be bought openly. A license is usually not required to *buy* the equipment, but only to *operate* it. If the equipment cannot be bought openly, there are numerous sources of information on how to construct amateur radio transmitters and receivers. Publications of the American Radio Relay League are a good source. Amateur radio magazines, published in many languages, often carry information on building transmitters and receivers. Parts can often be salvaged from old radios and TV sets. The Resistance can make use of radio communications if the benefits outweigh the risks.

Physical Form of the Communication

In the past, a form of clandestine communication used by spies involved photographic reduction of the size of the message. The use goes back to the Franco-Prussian War in 1870, when Paris was under siege. Messages were reduced photographically and carried out of the city by carrier pigeon. Far more messages could be transmitted this way than had the pigeon carried the original document. Between World War I and World War II, the technology had developed to the point that a written page could be reduced to the size of a period and glued over a period or over the dot above an i or j, then read under a microscope, or blown up to normal size, by the recipient. Such a *microdot* would likely be missed by a postal or customs inspector examining mail or other documents.

With the advent of digital cameras and scanners, many of the camera and film developing methods of Twentieth-Century spies are obsolete. However, the principles remain valid, and can be used effectively by Resistance forces equipped with computers, digital cameras and scanners, and reasonably high-quality ink-jet or laser printers.

Typed Page Size Reduction

You may be dealing with a document that you have prepared yourself, or have obtained from some other source. To make it easier to transmit this document, you should reduce it in size. Depending on the source of the document, and the equipment available, there are several possible methods.

Word Processor Generated Documents

To reduce the size of a page of text generated by a word processor, proceed as follows. These instructions are specific to Microsoft Word, but other word processors have similar capabilities.

First, click on File > Page Setup. Set the margins on the page at 1" top and bottom, and 1.25" left and right (this is the default setting). Type the page as you normally would within those margins, using a font such as 12 point Arial. (Arial is easier to read after being reduced than is Times New Roman).

Second, select the entire page using Ctrl-A (hold the control key down and depress the A key). Set the font size to 3 (you may have to type it in if the drop-down menu doesn't go that low).

Third, select the entire page again if it was de-selected. Click on File > Page Setup and set the right margin at 6". The written text now occupies a block in the upper left corner of the page. It is probably unreadable if the computer screen is set for normal width.

Fourth, print the page. The text is readable under a magnifying glass.

The text is still a lot larger than a microdot, but the portion of the page with text can be cut out and concealed in a number of ways. It is small enough, for instance, to be taped to the back of an ordinary business card. It can be concealed much more readily than a full-sized page.

Note that if the document includes graphics, trying to reduce it in a word processor may not work well. Reducing a graphic along with text takes more skill than is required simply to reduce font size.

Digital Camera

If a page of already-printed text has been obtained from some source, a digital camera can be used to reduce the size of the page, as follows. The camera should have a resolution of at least five megapixels, if the image is to survive shrinking and still be readable.

First, photograph the page using even lighting. Adjust the distance and the focal length to include only the document, with as little extension beyond the document as possible.[83] If the camera has the capability, set it to the type of lighting (incandescent, fluorescent, daylight, etc.) being used. Flash is undesirable, as it tends to wash out the center of the page. However, use flash if no better lighting is available.

---

[83] Be careful not to include the background in the photo. You don't want the tile pattern of your kitchen or bathroom showing up in the photo. Place a large sheet of white paper under the document, if necessary.

Second, remove the camera chip and plug it into a computer, or connect a cable from the camera to the computer.

Third, use a program such as PhotoShop to import the image from the camera or chip. Specify at least 300 dots per inch (dpi), and more dpi if possible.

Fourth, click Image > Resize> Image Size. Resize the image to 2.5" in the longest dimension.

Fifth, print the image if the program will do this. Otherwise crop the image to include only the text, copy the image to the clipboard, and paste it into a word processor page, which then can be printed. The result is about the same as that of a page reduced as in the previous section.

One of the advantages of using a camera is that graphics can be captured just as easily as text, and can be reduced along with text in programs such as PhotoShop.

Digital Scanner

If you are working from a document that has already been printed, a scanner can be used even more readily than a camera. Place the document in the scanner. Import the image into a program such as PhotoShop. Reduce and print as in the previous section.

Digital Transfer

Once a document is in digital form, either from a word processor or from camera or scanner, it may not be necessary to print it out. If the recipient has a computer and the proper software, the document can be read directly in digital form. A compact flash card, a thumb drive, or any similar device, can hold large numbers of documents, and is small enough to be hidden easily.

Secret Inks

One classical method of clandestine communication is use of "invisible ink." The idea is to write in the invisible ink on the back of an otherwise innocuous letter, or on something else that appears to be ordinary. Nothing is visible on the back, and whatever is on the front will arouse no suspicion. Most invisible inks are fairly easy to prepare, and the writing does not take very high-tech means to read. Heat or ultraviolet light are sufficient to "develop" the hidden writing of most invisible inks.

Invisible inks for clandestine communication may work against an unsophisticated government, but are not very secure against a government with a sophisticated counterintelligence service. Depending on your estimate of the capabilities of the government you are dealing with, this method may or may not be suitable.

The book by Rubin gives a good summary of what is known about such inks, including chemical formulas.

Summary

The Resistance will need to send messages between various elements. In many cases, such as communication between the overt and covert wings, it will be necessary to conceal the fact of communication, not just the content of the message. The methods described in this chapter can be used for clandestine communications.

References

American Radio Relay League, 225 Main St., Newington, CT, 06111-1494 USA. www.arrl.org

Fiery, Dennis, *How to Hide Things in Public Places*, Port Townsend, WA, 1996. (available from Paladin Press)

Ingram, Dave, *Guide to Emergency Survival Communications*, Columbus, OH, Universal Electronics, 1997. Available from Bohica Concepts, P.O. Box 546, Randle, WA 98377, and from online booksellers.

Luger, Jack, *How to Use Mail Drops for Privacy and Profit*, Port Townsend, WA, Loompanics, 1988. Available from online booksellers.

Myers, Lawrence W., *Spycomm*, Boulder, CO, Paladin Press, 1991.

Pease, Bob, "What's All This Battery-Charging Stuff, Anyhow?" *Electronic Design*, Feb 5, 2001, pp. 122 – 130.

Rubin, Samuel, *The Secret Science of Covert Inks*, Port Townsend, WA, Loompanics Unlimited, 1987. Available from online booksellers.

Tobin, Jacqueline L., & Raymond G. Dobard, *Hidden In Plain Sight*, New York, Doubleday, 1999.

Waterman, Shaun, "U.S. eyes software touted by Islamist terrorists for Internet activities," *The Washington Times, National Weekly Edition*, Feb 5, 2007, p. 17.

Chapter 19

Encryption And Codes

Codes and ciphers

Codes and ciphers are two different methods of concealing the content of a message, although they can be used together.

A *code* is an arbitrary set of characters, selected from a *codebook*, to represent a letter, a word, or an entire phrase. A codebook is like a bilingual dictionary. The sender looks up the letter, word or phrase to be sent. These are listed in some systematic way, such as alphabetical order. With each entry there is a code group that represents that entry. The code group is transmitted. The receiver uses the other half of the codebook, where the code groups are listed in some systematic way, such as alphabetical order. Corresponding to each code group is the corresponding *clear text* meaning. Thus so long as both sender and recipient have duplicate copies of the codebook, they can communicate. One shortcoming of codebooks is that if the word or phrase that you want is not included, you can't send it. Thus it is important that the codebook include code groups for letters and numbers. For frequently used words or letters, codebooks often have several alternative code groups. This helps defeat attempts to break the code by statistical analysis of code group frequencies.

In principle, someone without a codebook cannot read encoded messages. In practice, of course, codes can be broken. A good discussion of code breaking is given in the book by Budiansky.

An *enciphered* or *encrypted* message is one in which each character in the original message has been substituted by some other character, according to a particular scheme. Instead of using a codebook to decrypt the message, the recipient needs to reverse the original substitution scheme in order to read the message. The classic Caesar cipher, attributed to Julius Caesar, simply involves replacing each letter in the original text with a letter a fixed number of places later in the alphabet, with wraparound at the end. A three-shift Caesar cipher, for instance, would replace the letter "a" with the letter "d." A Caesar cipher is very easy to break, and provides essentially no security at all. There are numerous variations of the Caesar cipher, all of which amount to changing the shift from one character to the next. These are also readily broken by modern computer methods.

The Resistance will need encryption methods that are very difficult to break. Some are described below. The references at the end of this chapter give more details of the methods.

Book Cipher

The Book cipher requires that sender and receiver have duplicate copies of the same book. The sender selects the words to be used from the book. The encrypted message consists of page number, line number on the page, word number in the line, for each word in the message. The Book cipher is simple to use, but extremely difficult to break. However, it may be difficult to find a book that has all the words the users may want to transmit. This is simply a variant of the codebook problem. If the word you want isn't in the book, you can't send it. The method has a distinct advantage, however. Possession of a book does not arouse suspicion that the owner has been sending encrypted messages. The book appears to be harmless. Possession of a codebook definitely would arouse suspicion.

One-time Pad

The name comes from the way in which this encryption scheme has been implemented in the past. Sender and receiver each have a pad, each page of which has a randomly generated "key," that is, a set of letters and numbers. The top page of the pad is used to encrypt a message. That page is then torn off and destroyed by some method such as burning and stirring the ashes (i.e., "one-time pad"). The recipient uses the corresponding page from his copy of the pad to decrypt the message, then likewise destroys the page.

This is an example of how it can be done. Assume you wish to send the message: THE QUICK BROWN FOX. You have a sequence of numbers that was randomly generated, to use as a key. You could set up a table as follows:

T	H	E	Q	U	I	C	K	B	R	O	W	N	F	O	X
20	8	5	17	21	9	3	11	2	18	15	23	14	6	15	24
10	48	01	50	11	01	53	60	20	11	81	64	79	16	46	69
4	4	6	15	6	10	4	15	22	3	18	9	15	22	9	15
D	D	F	O	F	J	D	O	V	C	R	I	O	V	I	O

The first line is the "clear text" message. The second line is the order of the letters in the alphabet (T is the 20th, H is the 8th, etc.) The third line is the key. In this case, the key was obtained from a table of random numbers in the mathematical tables edited by Selby, in the References. The fourth line is obtained by adding line 3 to line 2, modulo 26. That is, if the sum of line 3 and line 2 is greater than 26; subtract 26 enough times to bring the sum to a value between 1 and 26 inclusive. Thus $10 + 20 = 30$. Subtract 26 to get the 4 in the first cell of line 4. $8 + 48$ is 56; subtract 26 twice to get the 4 in the second cell of line 4. The fifth line is the letters corresponding to the numbers in line 4. This is the encrypted message. You can equally well send line 4 as the message, instead of converting it into letters, since the two lines are completely equivalent. A further possibility is to send line 4 by disguising it as some kind of numerical data, thus not only encrypting the message but concealing that it is a message.

To decrypt the message, reverse the process, as in the following table.

D	D	F	O	F	J	D	O	V	C	R	I	O	V	I	O
4	4	6	15	6	10	4	15	22	3	18	9	15	22	9	15
10	48	1	50	11	1	53	60	20	11	81	64	79	16	46	69
20	8	5	17	21	9	3	11	2	18	15	23	14	6	15	24
T	H	E	Q	U	I	C	K	B	R	O	W	N	F	O	X

The first line is the encrypted message. The second line is the order of the letters of line one in the alphabet. The third line is the same key used to encrypt the message. The fourth line is obtained by *subtracting* line 4 from line 3, modulo 26. If the difference is greater than 26, keep subtracting 26 until the remainder is between 1 and 26 inclusive. If the difference is *negative*, add 26 enough times to bring the result to a value between 1 and 26. Thus 4 − 10 = -6. Add 26 to bring the result to the desired range. 4 − 48 = -44. Add 26 twice to bring the result to the desired range. The final row is the clear text after decryption.

Classical "one-time pads" were often made small enough to fit under a postage stamp. Thus the "key" could be hidden easily, and physically carried in a clandestine manner. However, once found, a one-time pad will arouse suspicion.

Two things are crucial with respect to one-time pads. First, each page (or key) must be used *one time only*. The history of cryptography is full of instances where a message was broken because someone re-used a key. Second, the letters/numbers in the key *must* be randomly generated. It has been mathematically proven (Shannon) that one-time pad messages *cannot* be broken provided each key is used only once, and the keys are generated *randomly*.

It is the randomness requirement that turns out to be a problem. Generating genuinely random numbers is very difficult. The pseudorandom numbers generated by most PCs are *not* random enough. The algorithms used to generate pseudorandom numbers always repeat after a long enough period. Encryption methods based on them can be broken if sufficient computer power is brought to bear. The book by Myers includes a program that is claimed to generate genuinely random numbers. It does this by using the computer's clock to generate a "seed" for the random number algorithm. This avoids having the sequence of numbers repeat itself eventually. The program is written in an early version of the BASIC language. However, any moderately skilled programmer should be able to rewrite it in a more modern language. Such a program could be used to generate keys for use in one-time pads.

One of the major problems with one-time pads is distributing the keys. Obviously the distribution must be secure, and the disposition of used keys must be secure. Other problems arise in keeping sender and receiver "in sync" on which key is being used.

Instead of distributing keys, it may be possible to use keys that are already available. The key used in the example above was taken from a published table of random numbers. However, if the government became aware that this particular table was being used as a source of keys, it would then be easy for government forces to crack any messages they recovered. Even so, if reference books of the right kind are readily available, they may be used as the source of keys, provided this fact can be kept secret.

The *Statistical Abstract of the United States* is an annual compilation of statistics on population, the economy, etc., in the U.S. Many other countries have similar statistical compilations, and the UN publishes annual compilations of international statistics. These compilations might be used as sources of keys.

As an example, the table for populations of the fifty states (not including District of Columbia) from the 2008 edition of the *Statistical Abstract* was used. The population of each state is given in thousands of people. The final digit in each population figure is the result of rounding, which may tend to destroy randomness, hence it was not used. The second-from-last and next-to-last digits were taken from each state's population figures. This gave a set of 50 two-digit numbers. If the numbers were completely random, we would expect there to be five in the single-digit group (0x in the table, where x is a single digit), five in the 'teens, five in the twenties, etc. A chi-squared test showed that the deviation from expected was not statistically significant. The pairs were also broken into single digits, giving a set of 100. We would expect ten 0's, ten 1's, etc. A chi-squared test showed that the deviation from expected was not statistically significant. Finally, the list of 50 two-digit pairs was subjected to an autocorrelation test. The autocorrelations were well within the two-standard-deviation limit, implying that the autocorrelation in the sequence was not statistically significant. This implics that tables of population, of income, etc., can be used as sources of keys for one-time pads, provided some care is taken to avoid rounded digits. Each sequence can be used only once, however. The recipient must be informed of the page, category, and the columns from which to take the digits. And as with tables of random numbers, the source of the keys must be kept secret from the government. If your country publishes annual statistical reports, these might be used as a source of random numbers.

Another possible source of random numbers is a telephone directory. To test for randomness, one hundred numbers were taken in alphabetical order by name from a single page of a telephone directory. The last two digits of each telephone number were taken as "random" numbers (digits from the left end of the numbers are not likely to be random, since they are "exchange" numbers). A chi-squared test of these numbers showed that the deviation from expected was small, and the numbers could be considered random. An autocorrelation test, out to lags of fifty, showed that the autocorrelations were well within the two standard deviation limit, indicating little autocorrelation. Thus telephone directories are a possible source of keys for one-time pads.

The use of government statistical tables or telephone directories as a source of random numbers has the advantages that these documents are widely available, and their possession does not generate suspicion. However, the Resistance will still be faced with the problems of transmitting the keys (page number, column number, etc.), and of keeping sender and receiver "in sync" as successive messages are sent and keys extracted from the books. Note also that if persons A and B are using a telephone directory as a source of keys, and persons C and D are using the same directory, the re-use of keys must be avoided. Each pair using the same book as a source of keys must be assigned a different block of pages. Note that stockpiling old directories or old statistical references ahead of time can provide the Resistance with additional sources of keys, since these things tend to change from year to year.

One problem with this approach is that if the government becomes aware of the source of the random numbers (e.g., telephone book for a certain city for a certain year), and if sufficient computer power can be brought to bear, the messages can be cracked by sheer brute force. All combinations of numbers taken from the source can be tried. However, that represents enormous effort, and it may not be possible to apply that much effort to *every* message.

CryptoUP is a one-time pad program. It uses a file of single-use keys, not a pad of characters. It can be obtained at: http://www.geocities.com/cryptoup/. The user must supply the keys. This still leaves the user with the problem of obtaining randomly-generated keys. However, it simplifies encryption and decryption.

Overall, one-time pads are useful for short messages. If the requirements of one-time use and randomly selected keys are adhered to, they are (in theory) impossible to break. Distribution of keys is a serious logistical problem, however.

Pretty Good Privacy (PGP)

PGP was developed by Philip Zimmerman, who decided that private individuals should have the same encryption capability as large organizations. It provides very strong encryption.

The one-time pad (and the AES, described below), are single-key encryption systems. The same key is used for both encryption and decryption. It is thus essential to protect the key. PGP belongs to the class of public/private key systems. It uses two keys, one "public," in the sense that you make it known to others, and one "private," in the sense that you keep it to yourself only.

The public key can be used by others to encrypt a message to you. That's why it's made public. That message cannot be decrypted with the public key, however. Only the private key is capable of decrypting the message. No one else needs to know your private key. It should therefore be kept completely secret. In normal civil society, your public key would be published in a directory, along with your e-mail address. For purposes of the Resistance, however, public keys should be distributed only on a "need to know" basis. That is, only someone who will have a need to communicate with a particular person should have that person's "public" key.

PGP is a bit more complex than simply using two keys. It also uses a third key, a randomly-generated "session" key.[84] The message itself is encrypted with a method that can be decrypted

---

[84] It's not clear just how "random" this session key really is.

fairly quickly, using the session key. The session key is included in the message, encrypted with the recipient's public key. Only the recipient can decrypt the session key using his private key. This session key is then used to decrypt the main message. PGP handles all this automatically, with no action by the user other than addressing the message.

PGP provides for a digital signature in a message, which proves it came from you (provided you have kept your secret key secret). This is done by generating an ID for the message based on characteristics of the message itself, and encrypting that with your private key. The recipient can then verify that the message came from you, and that the message has not been altered in transit. This capability, of an unforgeable signature, and guarantee that the message has not been tampered with, is very important to the Resistance. It reduces the possibility that the government can hinder Resistance actions by sending false messages to Resistance elements.

More information about PGP is available at http://www.philzimmermann.com/EN/findpgp/index.html

The program itself can be purchased from

http://www.pgp.com/?l=prz

Free versions can be obtained through: http://www.pgpi.org/, which refers you to other sites.

A free ("trialware") version can be downloaded at:

https://woext.pgp.com/cgi-bin/WebObjects/Trial.woa?accept=on. This version has limited capabilities, but is equivalent to previous Freeware versions.

GnuPG

GnuPG, or GPG, is a Gnu-based program intended to be similar in operation to PGP. Free downloads are available at www.GnuPG.org. Versions are available that run under Windows™.

Everything said about PGP above applies, with little change, to GPG. The book by Lucas provides information on using GPG.

Advanced Encryption Standard (AES)

This is the current standard approved by the (U.S.) National Institute of Standards & Technology. It is approved by the U.S. government for transmission of classified data, hence can be considered to be very secure.

The version available for download at the URL below is easy to use. At the opening screen, click on Encrypt. You must specify the file you want encrypted, the file to receive the encrypted material, and supply a "key." The key may be a file, or you may enter one. The program then performs the encryption and saves the encrypted file. The encrypted file can be sent as an e-mail attachment, or saved to some storage medium to be transported to a recipient.

Decryption is equally simple. At the opening screen, click on Decrypt. Enter the key used to encrypt the file, the file to be decrypted, and the file to hold the decrypted version.

Information on AES can be found at:
http://en.wikipedia.org/wiki/AES

The software can be downloaded at:

http://downloads.zdnet.com/thankyou.aspx?&kw=encrypton click&tag=nl.e530&docid=214982&view=214982

Other sources are listed in the Wikipedia article.

Encrypting Records

Encryption is most commonly thought of in terms of communications. However, records should also be encrypted. Records captured by the government can reveal a great deal about the Resistance. Letting the government have rosters, inventories, locations of safe houses, etc. would cripple the Resistance.

Laptops

Guerrilla and terrorist organizations have adopted laptops on a widespread basis. Keeping records on a laptop avoids storing and transporting paper files. Such records are more portable than paper files. However, should government forces capture a laptop, all those records are available.

In March of 2008, Colombian forces conducted a raid against a FARC base just across the border in Ecuador. Several guerrillas were killed, including FARC's number two leader. The big haul, though, was a laptop containing many FARC records. These showed that the Venezuelan government had supplied FARC with money and weapons, and had offered to share oil revenues with FARC, and to obtain supplies of uranium for FARC.

This example shows that it is crucial to encrypt records on laptops. Once the records are encrypted, even if the laptop is captured, the government may not be able to read the records.

The compression program WinZip™ allows automatic encryption of files, using AES (www.winzip.com). This is a simple way of encrypting files to keep them secret if they are captured.

Mike May describes "hidden watermarks" in digital multimedia objects. Adobe Photoshop allows inclusion of invisible watermarks. A freeware program called *Stego* also allows inclusion of invisible watermarks in files. For more information on watermarking, see
http://en.wikipedia.org/wiki/Digital_watermarking

Desktops

The Resistance will undoubtedly have desktop computers at major headquarters, for data such as rosters, inventories, etc. These records must be protected, since it should be expected that any semi-permanent camp will be raided eventually. Any records on the hard drives of desktop computers must be encrypted. The passwords must *not* be stored on the same hard drive, and especially must not be written down anywhere in the headquarters. To the extent possible, all data should be stored on external storage (hard drives, thumb drives, ZIP drives, etc.), which can be removed (or destroyed) in the event the headquarters must be evacuated quickly.

Disks, external drives, etc.

All data on these should be encrypted, to protect against their loss to government forces.

Steganography

The term "Steganography" means "hidden" or "covered" writing. It refers to methods for hiding a message in an apparently innocent "carrier."

An early example of hidden writing was related by Herodotus, who wrote that Histiaeus shaved the head of his most trusted slave and tattooed a message on it. After his hair had grown the message was hidden. The message was read when the recipient shaved the head of the slave. The purpose of the message was to instigate a revolt against the Persians.

A more recent method involves burying a message in an apparently innocent text. The recipient is to count lines and words to find the hidden message. Another version of the same idea is to use a template, with holes cut in it. The sender places the template over a sheet of paper, then writes the message, one word at a time, in the holes. The sender then fills in the rest of the page with sentences that incorporate the words of the true message. The recipient has an identical template. When this is placed over the page, the rest of the page is masked out, and only the true message appears at the holes in the template. Whether this method uses a template or simply involves counting lines and words, the problem is to construct an innocent-appearing missive that includes the words of the true message.

With the advent of digital files, steganography has become much more popular. A "byte" in an image or an audio file is simply a number. The idea is to alter selected bytes in a file, to convey a message to a recipient who knows which bytes to look at. The usual procedure is to alter the "least significant bits" (LSB) of the selected bytes. There are numerous programs available to carry out the

247

process of hiding a message, and retrieving it. A CD, StegoArchive, has a collection of freeware and shareware steganography programs. A commercial product, Invisible Secret, first encrypts the message using one or another of the encryption methods described above, then hides it in a carrier file. See the references for information on these programs.

While hiding messages in digital files has many advantages, code breakers are working on *steganalysis* to uncover these messages. The fact that a byte has been altered may make it different from nearby bytes in the carrier. As an obvious example, a black pixel in the middle of an image of a snowscape will stand out clearly. However, even less obvious alterations may be located by comparing pixels in an image with nearby pixels.

In using digital steganography, it is not sufficient to hide a message in an image or audio file. The file itself must not attract attention, or it will be subjected to steganalysis, and the fact of a hidden message may be detected. Even if the message is encrypted and cannot be read without the key, the fact that sender and receiver are engaging in clandestine correspondence will arouse suspicion. Posting an image on a web site such as Photobucket or tinypic, where there are already many images, may help divert attention. While the poster is known, the recipient, who knows which image to look at, will be simply one of many people who looked at the image.

The article by Lubacz et. al. describes a subtle method of concealing communications using VOIP. Messages sent over the Internet are broken into individual "packets." Different packets need not all take the same route to a destination, nor need they arrive in order. Each packet contains "header" information that allows the receiving software to reassemble the packets in order. VOIP, however, does not make use of this header information, since waiting for a delayed packet might mean a "break" in the conversation. Instead, packets that are "too late" are discarded. However, selected packets can be loaded with information that is to be "hidden," and deliberately delayed. Any regular VOIP software will discard them. However, special software can save these delayed packets and put together the information they carry. Anyone listening in using regular VOIP software will never detect the delayed packets. Only users with the required specials software will be able to read the hidden message.

Hiding your tracks on the Internet

Even when messages over the Internet are encrypted, it's a good idea to hide the fact that they are being sent. Even if the government cannot read your messages, traffic analysis (who talks to whom) can reveal a great deal of information about your Resistance organization.

TOR is an anonymizer that routes packets through multiple servers. It can help disguise your use of the Internet. It has been used by dissidents in China and in Iran to get messages to the outside world without alerting the government. It can be downloaded at:http://www.wikileaks.org/wiki/Tor It can also be downloaded at http://downloads.zdnet.com/abstract.aspx?scname=Encryption+Software+-+Security+-+Windows&licfilter=free&docid=367631&promo=100500

Tor works best with the Firefox browser, but can be used with others, including Internet Explorer. The program "Incognito" works with TOR. More information about Incognito can be found at http://www.browseanonymouslyanywhere.com/incognito.

Global Positioning System

As noted in the chapter on Land Navigation, the GPS is a good way for fighters to navigate. However, the receivers are not secure. They keep an unencrypted track of where the user has been.

Terrorists infiltrating Iraq from Syria used GPS receivers to follow known safe routes into Iraq. When the infiltrators and their GPS receivers were captured, the government forces were able to interdict the routes.

Commercially available GPS receivers are not designed to allow for encryption of waypoints and tracks. If a GPS receiver is in danger of being captured, physical destruction is essential. Resistance forces must be instructed to destroy their receivers if capture is imminent. GPS receivers must be stripped from dead Resistance members (along with ammunition and weapons, of course) if their bodies must be left on the battlefield. Routes, tracks and waypoints such as caches must be protected by denying government forces the data stored on GPS receivers.

References

Budianski, Stephen, *Battle of Wits*, New York, The Free Press, 2000. (Codebreaking during WW II.)

Chesbro, Michael, *Freeware Encryption*, Boulder, CO, Paladin Press, 2001.

Cobb, Chey, *Cryptography for Dummies*, Hoboken, Wiley, 2004, ISBN 0-7645-4188-9.

Garfinkel, Simpson, *PGP: Pretty Good Privacy*, Sebastopol, CA, O'Reilly & Associates, 1995.

Hardy, Darel W., Fred Richman, Carol L. Walker, *Applied Algebra*, Boca Raton, FL, 2009, ISBN 978-1-4200-7142-9. (Several chapters explain ciphers and modern encryption methods. Highly mathematical.)

Johnson, Alan, "Steganography for DOS Programmers," in *Dr. Dobb's Journal*, pp. 48 – 51, # 261, January, 1997.

Lowman, David D., *Magic*, Stanford, Athena Press, 2001. (Breaking the Japanese code in WW II)

Lubacz, Josef, Wojciech Mazurczyk, and Krzysztof Szczypiorski, "Vice Over IP," *IEEE Spectrum*, February 2010, pp. 42 – 47.

Lucas, Michael W., *PGP & GPG*, San Francisco, No Starch Press, 2006, ISBN 1-59327-071-2.

May, Mike, "Invisible Watermarks," *American Scientist*, v. 85, March-April 1997, pp. 124 - 125.

Mollin, Richard A., *An Introduction to Cryptography*, Boca Raton, FL, Chapman & Hall/CRC Press, 2001, ISBN 1-58488-127-5. (Note: this book is highly mathematical. It is intended for the professional cryptographer, or the mathematician who is pressed into service as a cryptographer for the Resistance.)

Rotolo, Don, "A Simple Encryption Program for MARS Use," *CQ*, April 2007, pp. 79 – 82. (This program is intended to keep out casual snoopers. It is not strong enough to withstand attack by a competent government or commercial intelligence service.)

Rotolo, Don, "D-STAR Digital Data, CryptoUP," *CQ*, April 2008, pp. 74 – 79.

Schneier, Bruce, *Applied Cryptography: Protocols, Algorithms, and Source Code in C*, New York, John Wiley & Sons, 1994.

Selby, Samuel M. (ed.), *Handbook of Mathematics, 3rd Edition*, Cleveland, The Chemical Rubber Company, 1967.

Shannon, Claude (1949). "Communication Theory of Secrecy Systems". *Bell System Technical Journal* **28** (4): 656–715.

Software

StegoArchive CD, available from http://home.comcast.net/~ebm.md/stego.html. Price $21.95 as of this writing.

http://www.invisiblesecrets.com/ver2/index.html This is the source for a steganography program that hides data in pictures and audio files. Older versions are downloadable free; the latest version is for sale ($39.95 as of this writing). There are claims on the Internet that it has been broken.

Web Sites

http://en.wikipedia.org/wiki/One_time_pad This site mentions the problem of using already-published sources of random numbers. Once the source is known, all messages using it can be broken.

Chapter 20

Getting Your Story Out

The importance of getting your story out

Samuel Adams said, "It does not take a majority to prevail, but rather an irate, tireless minority keen on setting brushfires of freedom in the minds of men."

In a similar vein, John Adams wrote, "As to the history of the [American] revolution, my ideas may be peculiar, perhaps singular. What do we mean by the Revolution? The war? That was no part of the revolution; it was only an effect and consequence of it. The revolution was in the minds of the people, and this was effected from 1760 - 1775, in the course of fifteen years, before a drop of blood was shed at Lexington."[85] John Adams also wrote, "What do we mean by the American Revolution? Do we mean the American war? The Revolution was effected before the war commenced. The Revolution was in the minds and hearts of the people; a change in their religious sentiments, of their duties and obligations... This radical change in the principles, opinions, sentiments, and affections of the people was the real American Revolution."[86] The book by Maier traces the steps from opposition to the Stamp Act, through the non-importation associations of the late 1760s, through the effective collapse of English government in the colonies by 1773, with colonial legislatures assuming independent powers, to the Declaration of Independence itself. The article by Wolverton describes the effectiveness of John Dickinson's pamphlets in creating the public mood that made the American Revolution possible.

As both Adamses understood, it's not enough to undertake armed resistance. Shooting the tyrant's police and soldiers isn't enough. Samuel Adams was right. You must gain the support of your fellow citizens and the world public, and undermine the morale of the troops opposing you. As John Adams said, that means getting

---

[85] Letter to Thomas Jefferson (1815-08-24), The Works of John Adams
[86] Letter to H. Niles (1818-02-13)

your story out. The Revolution comes in changing the minds of the people. The task of the Resistance is to set Samuel Adams's brushfires in the minds of your fellow citizens.

Consider the American Declaration of Independence.[87] It was primarily written as a justification for declaring the colonies independent of Great Britain. It actually reads like a legal brief.

The Declaration begins by stating its purpose: to explain why the American colonies are declaring independence. It then asserts that all humans have rights originating from their Creator, and that the purpose of governments is to protect these rights. It then presents a list of the grievances of the American colonies against the government of Great Britain. It summarizes the attempts made by the American colonies to have their grievances resolved peacefully. Finally, it states that having failed to resolve the grievances peacefully, the American colonies have no recourse but independence from Great Britain.

Like the American colonists, you need to get the word out about your cause. Why are you resisting? What are your legitimate grievances? What are your objectives? To gain the support of your fellow citizens, and the approval of world opinion, you need to make these things known.

The obstacles

But how do you get the word out? If you're genuinely fighting for individual rights, for the right to run your life as you see fit, to raise your children as you see fit, to start and run your own business as you see fit, getting your story out is going to be tough. The international news media are all too ready to glorify Marxists and collectivists like the Viet Cong, the Sandinistas, the Palestine Liberation Organization, or even rioters who burn down a city such as Los Angeles.[88] But they're not going to glorify you. You'll get the same treatment the Contras did in Nicaragua and the Nationalists did in China. The news media will be calling you a "death squad." The

---

[87] It can be read at http://www.ushistory.org/Declaration/document/index.htm
[88] When rioters burn down a city, their sympathizers will justify it as "rage." "I don't approve of their methods, but I sympathize with their goals."

UN won't be designating you as the "authentic representative" of your people.[89] Instead it will condemn you as a terrorist.

Possible techniques

Somehow you have to get around this roadblock on the information highway. Here are some of the techniques you can use.

Samizdat

In the former Soviet Union, one means of getting the word out was called "samizdat," a word meaning "self published." People would type something with multiple carbon copies and distribute them. Each recipient was expected to re-type the thing, again making multiple carbon copies, and pass them on.

Clearly this is doing it the hard way, and if copying machines or printers are available, they should be used instead. An oppressive government, however, is likely to put controls on copy machines. While under Communist rule, Rumania required that copying machines be licensed.[90] To a tyrant, copying machines, printing presses, and even computer printers are weapons of revolution, and must be denied to the oppressed population.

Distributing pamphlets, flyers, and similar things by "self publication" is one way to get the word out. The important thing is to find ways to make copies, ways that are simple and available widely throughout the population. Distributing flyers can be a very effective means of getting your story out. The "White Rose" group in Nazi Germany conducted a campaign of placing anti-Nazi literature in phone booths, train stations and other public places. The Nazis thought the White Rose group was sufficiently dangerous that they went on a major campaign to track them down. Most of the

---

[89] Since when is it up to the UN to decide who is or is not the "authentic representative" of a people, anyway?

[90] It is now known that to discourage counterfeiting, the U.S. government and several foreign governments have required makers of copying machines to insert a microscopic serial number on all copies made on that machine. While this is intended to allow the government to trace counterfeit money, if the same is done in your country, it would allow the government to trace any pamphlets, etc., to a specific copying machine. This may keep you from using commercial copy shops.

White Rose members were ultimately executed.[91] They are today remembered as examples of nonviolent resistance to tyranny.

If copying machines or something similar are not available or are designed to print a serial number on copies, it may be necessary to resort to older technology such as silkscreen or mimeograph. Directions for making silkscreen, mimeograph, or hectograph (gelatin) printing equipment can be found in U.S. Army Field Manual FM 31-20. These are cruder methods of making multiple copies, but people used them for many years before there were copying machines, and they did work. They can be put back into use if necessary.

During the 2009 protests in Iran, the protesters wrote protest slogans on paper money. People were advised that if caught, they should say they got the money from someone else, such as in change at a flea market.[92] This is one way of getting protest slogans circulated widely.

Audio and Video Tape

Before the Shah of Iran was overthrown, the Ayatollah Khomeini distributed his revolutionary messages throughout Iran on audiotapes. These could be smuggled into the country easily, passed from hand to hand, played on inexpensive cassette players, and duplicated readily. They were simply a higher-tech version of samizdat. If your country has widespread availability of cassette players, this is one very good way of getting your message out to your fellow countrymen.

Videotape, DVDs and digital storage cards for videos should not be overlooked either. For communicating with the general public, the message must be clear and brief. In the United States, the Rodney King tape, apparently showing the police brutalizing a suspect, had an enormous effect on the public. In the same way, videotapes of government wrongdoing can be an effective way of

---

[91] See the article by Jasper. Also see the web sites http://en.wikipedia.org/wiki/White_Rose and http://sophieschollmovie.com/
[92] Of course, this risks having the money confiscated. Therefore it should be limited to bills of small denominations, to keep the loss small.

mobilizing sentiment in your favor. However, if the TV stations and networks are under government control, or are sympathetic to the government, they are not going to play your videos of government wrongdoing. Duplicating the videos and spreading them around will be the only means you have of getting them out. Videotapes, DVDs and digital videos are likewise a high-tech form of samizdat, but are harder to duplicate than audiotapes are.

Videos that convey your message can be even more effective than audiotapes, since they allow the viewer to see the person speaking. A charismatic leader can be very effective on video. Osama bin Laden, leader of the Islamic group that destroyed the World Trade Towers, made extensive and very effective use of videotapes to communicate with his network of terrorists and the Islamic public. Videos can also be used to show the activities of your resistance units, and offset government propaganda labeling them as "terrorists."

With the advent of computers capable of creating CD-ROMs and DVD disks, there are alternatives to videotape. These are even more high-tech than videotapes, but they are lighter, are less expensive, and can be played on most computers. Moreover, many new computers have built-in capability to "burn" CD-ROMs and even DVDs. These may be an even easier way of distributing your message than audio or videotapes.

Yet another avenue is web sites like http://photobucket.com/ and tinypic.com, which allow you to post pictures and short videos. It is necessary to sign up for these services, but that doesn't mean you have to be truthful in providing sign-up information.

Video production

It may seem that making videos (either tape or DVD) is too difficult for a clandestine resistance group. However, technology has made enormous changes within recent years. Low-cost video cameras that shoot broadcast quality video are available for prices under $4000. Good quality "consumer" video cameras are available for under $1000. Editing software, such as Adobe Premier, is now available for under $1000. A laptop computer with sufficient memory to do video editing and the capability to "burn" DVDs can be had for under $2000. Adequate equipment can now be had for a tenth of what it would have cost only a few years ago. According to Rita Katz, of the SITE Intelligence Group, a US terrorism research center:

Peshawar: Producing propaganda videos for Al Sahab is a three-step process

The first is to shoot the video. The second step - the most time-consuming - is to edit and produce the material, a process which requires skilled technicians but can be done in a simple mud hut anywhere in Afghanistan or the rugged border area of Pakistan.

Once the material is ready, step three is transmitting through an internet cafe. "The Al Sahab man doesn't have to lug his computer on his back into the cafe," Katz said. "All he needs is a small USB stick and the high-speed internet connection."

Al Qaeda technicians have also become skilled at evading American detection techniques. Katz said they often use techniques such as "proxy servers" to disguise the point of origin. Documentaries are sent in multiple files to improve security.

"The Al Sahab people know and study technology, the latest law enforcement techniques," Katz said. "They know they can transfer files and they know not to transfer the entire file, to divide it into small pieces that eventually is stored in a single location."

Yousuf said Al Qaida maintains its own cyberspace library, storing material in a secret server or servers so that the Al Sahab members do not have to keep incriminating material on their own laptops.

"There is a plan to make Al Sahab very big," Yousuf said. "It is part of the strategy. There are two parts. One is the fighting and the other part of the war is the media. We should carry out the media war because it inspires our people to come and fight."

In short, equipment is no longer the limitation on producing a good video. Scripting and acting are still important, however. Even so, you must remember you are not producing a video to compete with commercial entertainment. You are producing a video to get your message out to a large audience, and you are using the medium of video (tape or DVD) to carry that message. Good quality is important, but is secondary to the message. That must come through clearly, but not in a heavy-handed fashion. For instance, a video of government brutality does not need a lot of commentary. The brutality speaks for itself.[93]

Distribution of the final product can be by either physical distribution of tapes or disks, or posting on a web site for downloading (see the discussion below). If audio or videotapes, audio CDs, or DVDs are distributed physically, some effort should be made to disguise the true contents. Open an audio CD or tape with some innocuous-sounding music before going to the speech or instructions that contain the real message. A video, either tape or DVD, should open with something apparently harmless (e.g., kittens or puppies playing, a shot of some scenery or a public monument, etc.; however there should be no people in the scene who might be recognized). Make the opening appear to be a "home movie" of no great significance. Place the real material after this opening.

The article by Metz gives some information about "independent" movie making.

On-The-Spot Video

With the availability of cell phones that can take photos and even short videos, there are further alternatives available to the Resistance. The Resistance's designated videographers cannot be "on the scene" for every strike, protest march, or other event. In particular, they cannot be on the scene for spontaneous anti-government events. The resistance should encourage, and make provisions for, those who are on the scene to record the event with their cell phones, and make the recording available to the

---

[93] As of this writing, there is an amateur video at http://www.youtube.com/watch?v=VYaL4mA-bSY, of Iranian police shooting into a crowd of protesters and killing one. This is an example of what can be done.

Resistance. Setting up web sites in protected locations, making use of services like Photobucket, YouTube, Facebook, Qik.com, tinypic.com, etc., will allow the ordinary citizen who observes something important to record it and make it available for use by the Resistance. This not only adds to the number of "eyes" watching the government, it provides the dissident citizen with an opportunity to "strike a blow" without taking an excessive risk.[94]

Songs

Songs can be a very effective means of getting your message across. Songs have long been used by dissidents and resistance groups as means of winning supporters and conveying their messages. Labor union organizers, strikers, those engaged in civil disobedience, and those actively fighting, have used songs to rally their own followers, to bring their message to others, and to counter government propaganda. The Estonians used traditional folk-singing festivals, as well as rock concerts, to keep their traditions alive during the Soviet occupation. Even though the Estonians had no hope of driving out the Soviets, by song festivals they maintained their historical culture rather than become absorbed into "Russia." A documentary, "The Singing Revolution," has since been made to honor this activity (see the articles by Grisolano and by Welch). Another example is the tone poem *Finlandia* by Jan Sibelius. Even though it had no words, it was an effective protest against oppression of Finland by the Russian Empire.

To be effective, a song must have a message, must have strong lyrics, and must have a tune that can be sung readily. When creating a "resistance" song, there is nothing wrong with borrowing a well-known tune. The American National Anthem, *The Star Spangled Banner*, is sung to the tune of a drinking song that was popular at the time Francis Scott Key wrote the lyrics. For Americans, putting new words to the *Battle Hymn of the Republic*, to well-known folk songs such as *Casey Jones* or *Wreck of the Old Ninety-Seven*, or even to currently popular songs, would be natural

---

[94] During the 2009 protests against Iranian election fraud, protesters took cell phone videos of police brutality and uploaded them to sites such as YouTube. One woman, named Neda Agha-Soltan, killed by a police sniper, became the world-wide image of Iranian government brutality.

choices. Lyricists in your country should select tunes known to your audiences, and create new lyrics that convey the message of the Resistance.

Here are some examples of "resistance" songs that have been used in the past.

- *Joe Hill*, a song about a labor union organizer allegedly murdered by mine owners.
- *The Rising of the Moon*, essentially the battle hymn of the Irish Republican Army.
- *We Shall Overcome*, the "theme song" of the American civil rights movement.
- *Harry Pollitt*, an organizing song of the British communists.

This latter song can serve as a good example of the possibilities in "resistance" songs. Pollitt was an English communist who left the Party. They wrote a song about him, as though he had died.[95] It had a catchy tune and humorous lyrics, which were larded with subtle anti-religious and anti-capitalist propaganda. Any religious person who objected to the song could be fobbed off with, "Can't you take a joke?" But that's the point. A tyrannical government can't take a joke.[96] Every laugh at its expense is subversive. A tyranny depends on fear to keep it in power. Songs are therefore powerful ways of spreading resistance to tyranny, especially when they mock that tyranny. The same can be said for jokes.

---

[95] For a biography of Pollitt, see http://www.communist-party.org.uk/ourhistory/people/harry_pollitt.html. For the song itself, see http://www.limeliters.net/harry_pollitt_lyrics.html
[96] In 1933, at Stalin's orders, several playwrights and satirists were exiled to Siberia for plays, poems and stories that ridiculed the Communist regime. Rudolph Herzog has compiled a book of jokes told during the Hitler years in Germany (apparently available only in German). He reports that several of the jokes led to people being executed for telling them.

Jokes

Humor is not limited to songs such as that about Harry Pollitt. The joke itself can be a form of rebellion. In a 1945 essay, "Funny, but not vulgar," George Orwell noted, "every joke is a tiny revolution." (quoted in Rose) Unfortunately, jokes may be largely pain relievers for those subject to totalitarian rule, unless they are coupled with some prospect of relief from that rule. Hence jokes can be part of an information campaign, but they cannot substitute for more direct measures.

Jokes to be circulated by the resistance organization must use humor to present the difference between the current situation, as experienced by the people, and some more desirable situation. The fact that an anti-government joke is even being circulated can help reassure opponents of the government that they are not alone; someone else has similar views. If possible, the jokes should reinforce the message themes being expressed in more formal resistance communications.

Ridicule

The idea of the joke leads to the idea of ridicule. Saul Alinski, author of *Rules for Radicals*, a "bible" for American radicals, presented a number of rules for dealing with "those in power." Rule #5 is *"Ridicule is man's most potent weapon. There is no defense. It's irrational. It's infuriating."* Making individuals in the government the objects of ridicule can be an important part of getting your story out. This is emphasized in Alinkski's Rule # 12: *"Pick a target, freeze it, personalize it, and polarize it.* Cut off the support network and isolate the target from sympathy. Go after people and not institutions; people hurt faster than institutions." That is, "picking off" individual officials through ridicule can be just as effective as shooting them. It makes them useless to the oppressive government.[97]

---

[97] I once saw a campaign involving stickers placed on the hand dryers in public restrooms. The stickers read: "Push button. Hear (name of town)'s leaders." These were well-done printed labels. Labels can now be printed with home computers.

Clandestine Radio

Clandestine radio transmitters have been used by resistance movements in many areas of the world. They provide a means of getting the word out to anyone who has a radio capable of receiving the signal.[98]

A segment of the FM or AM spectrum not in use in your country can be seized by the Resistance and used as their channel. However, such a channel is easily jammed. If possible, the resistance should choose a channel adjacent to one important to the government, so that jamming will interfere with the government channel as well.

The big disadvantage of a clandestine transmitter is that it is easily located by the government. Most successful "Resistance" transmitters have actually been located in foreign countries friendly to the resistance. Transmitters operated within the "target" country cannot have a permanent physical location. They must adopt some subterfuge such as recording the programming at a secure location, then rapidly setting up the transmitter, broadcasting the recording, and shutting down and relocating.[99] Alternatively, the studio can be set up at a secure location, and the programming "streamed" over the Internet to the transmitter.

Such measures can be more effective if the transmitter is located in mountainous or wooded terrain that the government's "direction finders" cannot move through easily. However, a low-power transmitter intended to broadcast only to a single city can be moved around from one building to another fairly easily.

If brief broadcasts followed by transmitter relocation are to be effective, the transmissions must adhere to a schedule known to

---

[98] The Taliban set up about 150 illegal FM radio stations in the Swat Valley of Pakistan to broadcast propaganda and threats. The US is reported to be attempting to jam these transmitters. (Dreazen & Gorman)

[99] Zbigniew and Sofia Romaszewski had been jailed for operating an "underground" radio station in Soviet-occupied Poland. Reed quotes them as saying "We could only broadcast eight to ten minutes a day before going to another place to stay ahead of the police." (p. 5)

the intended audience. This need not mean broadcasting at the same time every day. Each broadcast might close with an announcement of the time for the next broadcast. However, the schedule should rotate among several fixed times so that listeners who miss one broadcast can get "back in sync" while missing only a few broadcasts.

Security of the transmitter while it is on the air is paramount. This may include posting watchers for government direction-finding units, and outposts to warn of the approach of police or other government forces. The transmitter operators should be alert to the possibility that aircraft will be used for direction-finding purposes. It may be important to identify government organizations that have this capability, and to station watchers near the bases for their aircraft. When the observers see the launch of a direction-finding aircraft, they can give advanced warning to the transmitter operators.

The Internet

The Internet can be a powerful tool for getting your story out. There are several ways of making use of it:

- Appeals to your sympathizers
- Announcements of forthcoming demonstrations or strikes
- Reports of government wrong-doing
- Reports of successful anti-government actions
- Training materials

The key, however, is that the site on which your material is stored must be outside your country, where your government cannot reach it.[100] Therefore you must identify a country friendly to your cause, where you can post the information you want to disseminate. One possible site is http://www.wikileaks.org. This site specializes in "publishing" materials that governments and other organizations try to keep secret. They provide an "anonymizer" program that allows people to hide the path by which a "leak" is transmitted. The

---

[100] The government may still "hack" your site. Be prepared to put it back in order in a short time.

anonymizer program would be useful in hiding the source of the transmission. Another site is www.LiveLeak.com, to which you can upload both still photos and videos. You may also use "social networking" sites such as YouTube or Facebook to post your videos.[101] Videos posted on such sites need to be short, of the order of 10 minutes or less. The owners of the site may take your message down, either because they think it is inappropriate for their site, or under pressure from their government. Even so, the video may be available for enough time to be useful.

You may face another problem. Your government may censor the Internet, blocking any messages or other text that contains "seditious" material, or blocking access to Web sites that are considered seditious. For instance, the government of China has established very tight censorship of the Internet, to keep its citizens from acquiring "undesirable" information. However, there are ways around this censorship, all depending on "help" from people outside your country. Since the technology is rapidly changing, details will become obsolete quickly. However, the general ideas can be found in the article by Fowler. The article by Morais describes some of the approaches used by Chinese dissidents. The article by Parker points out the importance of letting people know they are not alone in their opposition to the government. The Global Internet Freedom Consortium (http://www.internetfreedom.org/) provides downloadable programs that can be used to circumvent government Internet censorship and firewalls. Their programs were very helpful to Iranian dissidents following the fraudulent elections of 2009.

Some of the uses to which the Internet can be put as follows.

Internet "Broadcasting"
Many radio stations in the US duplicate their programming by putting an audio signal on the Internet. The Resistance can adopt this same technique for broadcasting its messages. Speeches, songs, jokes, and slogans can be distributed in this manner. The web site must be located outside your country, if at all possible in a country

---

[101] The Muslim Brotherhood has posted videos on Facebook calling for strikes and demonstrations against the Egyptian government. Opposition groups in Croatia have used Facebook to call for demonstrations against their government.

sympathetic to the Resistance, or at worst neutral. That may make transmission of the broadcast material to the web site more difficult, but it overcomes the problems of maintaining transmitter security associated with over-the-air broadcasts.

"News" Services

Web sites can be used to spread news of government abuses, of actions by the Resistance that are censored from domestic news, and pleas for support. Publishing this material on a Web site that can be accessed by people in your own country, even if they have to go through some convolutions to do so, can be very helpful in gaining support of your fellow citizens. It can also be helpful in gaining foreign support, by making your cause known to those outside your country.

Your "news" web site may be hacked, it may be blocked, or it may be shut down if your government puts sufficient pressure on the government of the host country. However, such actions merely show how dangerous your government thinks your Resistance Web site is. That should be sufficient encouragement for you to try to keep one step ahead of the censors.

Recruiting and Fundraising

Abu Musab Zarqawi successfully used the Internet to recruit members and solicit funds for al Qaeda in Iraq. This use included posting audio messages, video clips and photographs on a web site. This was often done by e-mailing the material to a sympathizer outside Iraq, who then posted the material on a web site. These web sites were located in countries that favored Zarqawi's cause, or were at least neutral.

For several months a computer programmer using the pseudonym "Irhabi" ran a Web site that was very successful in recruiting people for Al Qaeda, in disseminating Al Qaeda propaganda, and in teaching on-line seminars on things like Web site hacking. His base of operations was in England, however, and he was eventually tracked down and arrested. This illustrates the importance of having the Web site hosted in a nation that is at worst neutral, and preferably one that is friendly to the cause of the Resistance.

FAX and E-mail

> "Fax transmission bypassed Chinese censorship in 1989, giving protesters in Tiananmen Square two-way access to the outside world; e-mail and the Internet were factors in organizing opposition to Serbian strongman Slobodan Milosevic in 1999, laying the foundation for Milosevic calling an election he mistakenly thought he would win. Fax and Internet access provide some channels in the Mideast, especially to more Westernized elites."[102]

The authorities in your country may have found ways to block FAX and e-mail. However, the point is that you should take advantage of whatever technology is available. Find innovative and creative ways to utilize what you have.

Countering Government Internet Censorship

Your government may try to block access to "undesirable" sites on the Internet. There are two software programs that can be used to get around these blocks.

One is "Freegate." It was developed to permit people in China to "get through" Chinese blocks to the Internet. Details can be found at http://en.wikipedia.org/wiki/Freegate. Copies can be downloaded at http://download.cnet.com/Freegate/3000-2085_4-10415391.html.

Another is UltraSurf. Information and free downloads can be obtained at http://www.ultrareach.com/.

These programs can be stored and run from flash drives. They never need appear on as computer's hard drive. They not only counter censorship, but provide encryption and "clean up" a computer after use.

---

[102] Wohlstetter, John C., "Info-war invades Iraq," *The American Spectator*, August-September 2003, p. 47.

Text Messaging

Cell phones and PDAs (Personal Digital Assistants) that have text messaging capability have been used to organize rallies, street demonstrations and even riots. The idea is to send messages to people asking them to meet at a specific place for a specific purpose, and ask them to forward the message to everyone in their address book. By this means, people can be gathered quickly, and the actions of large numbers of people coordinated.

This method has been used to generate "flash mobs" for humorous or otherwise benign purposes.[103] More importantly, it has been successfully used for political purposes, such as to organize street demonstrations in the Philippines, a get-out-the-vote campaign in Korea, and a riot in Nigeria (Rheingold).

Social networks such as Twitter and Facebook have been used for similar purposes. Protesters in Moldava used not only cell phones but Twitter to mobilize thousands of people to protest government policies.

> "This small group of militants did not expect tens of thousands of people to answer their call," said Oazu Nantoi, head of the Institute for Public Policy think tank and deputy leader of Moldova's Democratic Party.

> "There were no political leaders at the site, no loud speakers, no means of organising this mass of people," he said.[104]

Be alert to take advantage of the technology available to you and your target audience. And be prepared for success. Speakers, public address systems, flyers, pamphlets, etc. should be ready when the crowd arrives.

---

[103] See http://www.wired.com/news/culture/0,1284,59518,00.html for more details of flash mobs.

[104] Agence France-Press, http://tinyurl.com/cbz27n

267

Social Networks

Networking Internet sites such as Twitter and Facebook, and video or picture sites such as YouTube, Photobucket, and Flickr, can be effective means of getting your story out.

During the protests following a fraudulent 2009 election in Iran, the opponents of the government made use of these social networks to get their story out to the rest of the world, and to organize their sympathizers. This despite the Iranian government's attempts to block access to these sites.

Opponents of dictator Hugo Chavez, in Venezuela, in 2010, used Twitter to post pictures of police brutality and to organize protests.

The social networks can be powerful tools for getting your story out, especially when immediate delivery is required. You should be prepared to use these tools effectively.

Pickets, Marches, Protests

These are traditional means of communicating with the public at large. Whether you can use them depends on just how much force the government is willing to use against you. Against a government that is bad enough to justify armed resistance, these peaceful means may be impossible to use. However, they should always be considered a means of getting your story out.

These methods may be appropriate for use by the overt organizations, in conjunction with the more violent means used by the covert portion of the Resistance. In any case, the messages should support the overall strategy of the Resistance.

The book by Holcomb contains a great deal of information on how to organize and conduct protests, strikes, etc. The web site http://www.docstoc.com/docs/3447148/GUIDE-TO-PUBLIC-ORDER-SITUATIONS provides some useful information on how to frustrate the attempts of police to break up demonstrations. You should take advantage of this information, instead of starting from zero and learning the hard way.

Satellite

Al Qaeda has successfully used satellite broadcasting to get its message out to the world, and to recruit members, funds and support. Satellite dishes in your country can be used by your supporters, and by those who want to hear your story, to receive the information you broadcast. As with a web site, the transmitter to the satellite must be located in a country sympathetic with your cause, and the satellite must be owned by an agency that is, if not outright sympathetic, at least neutral. One of the advantages of satellite broadcasts is that they will be difficult for your government to block. Video, audio, data and graphics can be distributed via satellite.

The Liberation Tigers of Tamil Elam succeeded in hijacking an idle transponder on an Intelsat satellite to broadcast their propaganda messages to Sri Lanka. This amounts to "piracy," but is an exception to the rule that a satellite transmitter must be in a friendly foreign country, and must use a transponder legally. The Resistance can utilize a transmitter within a region it controls, if it can find an idle transponder to "take over." However, the act of piracy tends to discredit the legitimacy of the Resistance, and should be used only as a very last resort. It would be much better to establish a transmitter in a friendly or neutral country and lease a transponder.

Expatriates/Refugees

One of the effects of a tyrannical government is to drive out of the country people who oppose the government. Prominent dissidents, officials of banned political parties, people who took part in demonstrations or protests, may have left the country in search of safety. They can still play a significant role in getting your story out.

The article by Stecklow and Fassihi describes how Iranian refugees in Turkey and other countries continue to post articles on web sites that oppose the Iranian government. They post information they receive from inside Iran about arrests, interrogations, and jailings. The information is then distributed via Facebook, Twitter, and other social networking sites.

While refugees must take care not to violate the rules of their host country, they can play an effective role in getting your story out. They are not faced with the same restrictions on use of the Internet and other communications media as are people still within the totalitarian country.

Who are the targets?

Who is it that you need to reach with your information campaign? There are several target audiences. The importance of each audience will vary with the specific situation faced by the Resistance. Moreover, the type of information, and the means of delivering it, may vary from one audience to another. Here are some of the major audiences you should plan to reach.

Your fellow citizens

A captured Viet Cong document had this to say about getting the message to your countrymen[105]:

> The revolution pertains to the people. The people
> undertake the revolution only when they are
> assimilated with revolutionary thought. The
> propaganda and indoctrination task plays a very
> important role in this. It constitutes the most essential
> link and always leads the way in the revolutionary
> movement. The propaganda task also involves the
> political indoctrination and leadership of the people's
> ideology to crush the enemy propaganda which
> poisons people's minds.

While the source of this document was anything but pro-freedom, the idea is still sound. It is important for the Resistance to get information to its fellow citizens. This is often difficult, but has been done under various circumstances. (See also the article by Horton for more on Viet Cong propaganda.)

During World War II, the German occupation forces in Europe took over all prewar newspapers and converted them into

---

[105] Quoted in Veith, p. 1.

propaganda organs. Despite this, the French underground actually published many newspapers to provide French citizens with information about actions the Germans wanted to hide, and about how the war was going outside France (that information was obtained via broadcasts from England)(Breuer). These newspapers also encouraged their readers to join the Resistance, and to refuse to cooperate with the Germans. They were an important channel of communication between the Underground and fellow Frenchmen. These newspapers were published on clandestine presses or in small print shops despite German control of newsprint supplies. Thus despite very serious difficulties, the French Resistance managed to maintain this channel of communication with its fellow Frenchmen.

One of the problems people living under tyranny face is that they feel alone. The government controls all communications and education, and uses that control to squelch any voices of opposition. Opponents of the government come to feel that no one else agrees with them; that they are surrounded by government supporters; that they face doom if they voice their dissent. Dissidents in China have found a way around this. Witnesses to a particular government atrocity simply post the message "I know" on the Internet. That message allows others who "know" to recognize they aren't alone.

It is crucial that your efforts to get your story out overcome this feeling of isolation among those who agree with you. Even though they may not be able to take action immediately, they must be made aware that they are not alone; that others share their views.

Government military and police forces

One of the most important audiences you can try to reach is the military and police forces against whom you are fighting. They are, after all, the ones shooting at you.

One message you want to get across to the soldiers and police you're fighting is that they will have to face justice when you win. Warn them of retribution after the victory of the Resistance, and appeal to their humanity and sense of justice. In the latter regard, the following quotation from Adolph Hitler, about how to deal with guerrillas, is relevant:[106]

> What should [the police] do, if the pigs push women
> and children out in front? I went through that in
> Chemnitz, where the red pigs spit on us while
> holding their children in front of them. We were
> completely defenseless. God forbid, if we had
> touched those children! Fighting against [guerrillas]
> is the same situation. If they push women and
> children out in front of them, then the officer or non-
> commissioned officer has to have the option of
> shooting them, regardless . . . The person carrying the
> gun has to be guaranteed complete cover from the
> rear. We can give him general orders, but we have to
> cover his back as well, so the poor devil doesn't have
> to say to himself, "Afterwards, I will be held
> responsible."

But this is precisely the point. You want the individual government soldier or policeman to believe that he will be held responsible after your victory. Moreover, you want to appeal to his conscience, even if you don't think he has one. You want to convince those opposing you that they shouldn't commit atrocities, even when ordered to do so. The individual government soldier, then, is a legitimate and important target for your information campaign.

A second message to get across to the soldier or policeman is how corrupt the government is that he's defending. If your resistance is justified, there should be no problem in finding examples of corruption, malfeasance, dishonesty, and fraud in the government itself, and in the higher ranks of the military and police. Make the point that the soldier who is getting shot at is protecting people who don't deserve to be protected.

---

[106] Helmut Heiber & David M. Glantz (eds.), *Hitler and His Generals: Military Conferences 1942 – 1945*, Enigma Press.

A third approach is to generate doubt in the mind of the soldier and policeman about the effectiveness of their equipment. A good example is given in the article by Fulghum. During the fighting in Lebanon in 2006, Hezbollah was able to intercept cell phone calls among Israeli forces. They applied conventional traffic analysis (who talks to whom) to gain information about Israeli force dispositions and plans. However, they claimed they had penetrated the encryption systems used by the Israelis. This raised doubts in the minds of US troops in Iraq about the security of their encrypted systems, if Hezbollah should pass the information on to Al Qaeda. In reality, Hezbollah had not succeeded in reading encrypted signals, but only unencrypted cell phone calls. Unfortunately for Hezbollah, doubts among Israelis and Americans were quickly eliminated. This illustrates the importance of telling the truth. However, sowing doubt in the minds of the military and police about their equipment, their leaders, and your capabilities can be an effective way of weakening their resolve.

Government officials

The legitimacy of your government is your ultimate target. Legitimacy is always in the eye of the beholder. All governments, even dictatorships, rest on their subjects' assumption of their legitimacy. Once a government ceases to appear legitimate in the eyes of its subjects, and in the eyes of foreign publics, it can maintain power only through force. If it loses legitimacy in the eyes of its own officials, its ability to use force is significantly diminished.

The government of the Soviet Union was not defeated in combat. It simply lost the last remaining shreds of legitimacy. Although Fidel Castro rode in triumph into Havana, the city wasn't conquered in battle. The Batista government had lost its legitimacy. Likewise the Apartheid government of South Africa finally lost its legitimacy and collapsed. Successful combat by the Resistance may lead to loss of legitimacy, but ultimately the goal is to destroy the legitimacy of the government by whatever means works.

Government officials, then, are an important target audience for your information campaign. Your objective is to create doubts in their mind: doubts about the legitimacy of the government they serve; doubts about the policies of that government; doubts about the future survival of that government. You must make them aware of things that they will not learn from the official news media: demonstrations, protests, strikes, government malfeasance and fraud, government atrocities, and battles with the armed wing of the Resistance. Make it clear that "I was just obeying orders" will not be an acceptable excuse for continuing to serve that government.

It would be much better if your government collapses from its own self-doubt than with heavy loss of life in combat.

The foreign public

One of the most disheartening things to the victims of a tyrannical government is to see leaders of foreign countries, especially leaders of democratic countries, treating the tyrants with respect. Thus an important audience for your story is the citizens of foreign countries, especially democratic countries. Your objective is to gain support for your struggle for freedom. Ultimately, you want the foreign public, and foreign leaders, to deny the legitimacy of your tyrannical government; to make it a pariah government.

You cannot expect the foreign public to give open support to the armed wing of your Resistance. You can, however, gain support among the foreign public for the overt Resistance. You need to inform your target audience of the facts of your circumstances: oppression, false imprisonment, denial of rights, and any atrocities committed by your government.

You will most likely have to circumvent censorship imposed by your government. You may also find that the foreign news media will be more sympathetic with your government than with your Resistance movement. Thus you will need to find ways to get around not only your government's formal censorship, but also the informal censorship of the foreign press.[107] The Internet may be a means of getting your story out of your country; however your

---

[107] CNN withheld news of atrocities committed by the government of Saddam Hussein, in order to keep its reporters in Iraq. For details see http://www.truthorfiction.com/rumors/c/cnn-iraq.htm

government may attempt to censor it. Putting your story on digital media, which can be transported out of your country by sympathetic visitors, may be an effective means of making your story known. However you do it, it is important to recognize that the foreign public is one of your target audiences.

The Resistance Forces Themselves

There are several reasons why the Resistance must communicate with its own forces: to raise and maintain morale, to prevent abuses, and to provide instruction.

Maintaining Morale

Both the overt and covert Resistance members need reassurance that the Resistance is making progress toward its stated goals. Thus they become an important target audience.

Members of the covert Resistance, in particular, will be undergoing significant hardships. They need to be informed of victories, and given evidence of support from their fellow countrymen. They need to be assured that the hardships they are undergoing are not in vain. Since the government is likely to suppress any information about successes of the Resistance, this information must be distributed by the Resistance itself.

While the members of the overt Resistance will not be undergoing hardships comparable to those of the covert Resistance, they are still taking some degree of risk: loss of jobs, denial of higher education for their children, even imprisonment. They need to be assured that their efforts are not in vain. Thus the Resistance must take care to inform the members of the overt Resistance about successes, including things like strikes, demonstrations, foreign support, etc. that will not be conveyed by the government-controlled news media.

Preventing Abuses

As noted in Chapter 1, a major problem with guerrilla warfare and armed resistance is that it can lead to "settling scores," "overkill," and other abuses. The leadership of the Resistance must communicate regularly with the fighting forces to warn against abuses such as stealing property, extorting money, and physical abuse of fellow citizens. When such abuses occur, they must be punished, and the fact of punishment communicated to other elements of the Resistance forces, as well as to the population at large.

Providing Instruction

You may not have the luxury of training camps in "remote areas." Thus you need to provide instruction to members of both the overt and covert Resistance. For those joining or already in the covert Resistance, instruction should cover the operation of weapons, use of explosives, infantry tactics, and similar matters. For those in the overt resistance, instruction should cover things like organizing strikes and demonstrations, means of producing flyers and other literature, and effective use of photos and videos of government atrocities. In short, instruction should cover the things members of the Resistance, whether overt or covert, need to know to carry out their functions. This information must be distributed for individual study, because the Resistance may not be able to conduct formal instruction.

Have a story to tell

All the means of communicating your story discussed above are worthless if you don't have a story to tell. Ultimately you must give the various target audiences information that will lead them to be sympathetic to your cause. Since you are fighting a system based on lies, you must be committed to spreading the truth, the whole truth and nothing but the truth. You must endeavor always to send messages that will ring true in the ears of your countrymen, as well as those people in other countries whose support you want. There is an enormous amount of moral and ideological high ground that has been abandoned by your foes. Claim it and use it.

Conclusion

This chapter might have been titled "propaganda," but that could be misleading. The term "propaganda" is all too often taken to mean untruths. As Israeli leader Abba Eban said, "Propaganda is the art of persuading others of what you don't believe yourself."[108] If you're genuinely fighting an oppressor, you don't need lies. The truth is your best argument. You want to convince others of what you already believe.

Alexander Solzhenitsyn, in his 1970 Nobel Prize lecture, said, "one single truth is more powerful than all the weapons in the world." This is a very strong statement, coming from a man who had "done hard time" in the Gulag, who had been exiled from his homeland, and whose writings were seen in that homeland only on surreptitiously circulated, laboriously-typed sheets of flimsy tissue paper (*samizdat*). He was right. Ultimately it was truth, not guns, which brought the downfall of his tormentors. Guns are necessary. But by themselves, they are not enough. Truth is also necessary. In the long run it is even more important than guns. Ideas determine which way people point their guns. Part of the task of a resistance movement is to get the word out -- out to its fellow citizens, and out to the rest of the world.

References

Anonymous, *Clandestine Operations Manual for Central America*, Cornville, AZ, Desert Publications, 1985.

Breuer, William B., *Top Secret Tales of World War II*, New York, John Wiley, 2000.

Defense Science Board, "The Creation and Dissemination of All Forms of Information in Support of Psychological Operations (PSYOP) in Time of Military Conflict," Department of Defense, Washinton, DC, May 2000. (Available at http://www.cryptome.org/dsb-psyop.htm)

Department of the Army, *Psychological Operations, FM 33-1*, July 1987.

Department of the Army, *Special Forces Operational Techniques, FM 31-20* (available from Paladin Press)

---

[108] Quoted in *Forbes*, January 30, 2006, p. 136.

Dreazen, Yochi J., & Shiobhan Gorman, "Pentagon Jams Web, Radio Links of Taliban," *Wall Street Journal*, April 18, 2009, pp. A1 (A6).

Fowler, Geoffrey A., "Chinese Censors of Internet Face 'Hactivists' Abroad," *The Wall Street Journal*, February 13, 2006, p. A1 & A9.

Fulghum, David A., "Doubt as a Weapon," *Aviation Week & Space Technology*, November 27, 2006, pp. 26 – 27.

General Headquarters, Irish Republican Army, *Irish Republican Army Handbook*, (reprinted 1981) Cornville, AZ, Desert Publications, 1956.

Grisolano, Julie, "Songs of Freedom," *Salvo*, Autumn 2008, p. 73.

Horton, Bob, "Ho Chi Minh's Propaganda Machine," *Vietnam*, October 2005, pp. 18 – 25.

Jasper, William F., "Sophie Scholl: The Final Days," *The New American,* April 3, 2006, pp. 28 – 30 (a review of the movie of the same title, about the White Rose group)

Maier, Pauline, *From Resistance to Revolution*, New York, W. W. Norton, 1991, ISBN 978-0-393-30825-9.

Metz, Cade, "Making an Indie Film," *PC Magazine*, May 23, 2006, pp. 76 – 82.

Morais, Richard C., "Cracks in the Wall," *Forbes*, February 27, 2006, pp. 90 – 96.

Ney, Col. Virgil, *Notes on Guerrilla War: Principles and Practices*, Command Publications, Washington, D.C., 1961.

Parker, Emily, "I Know Who My Comrades Are," *The Wall Street Journal*, February 27, 2007, p. A8.

Reed, Lawrence W., "A Tribute to the Polish People," *The Freeman*, October 2009, pp. 4 – 5.

Rheingold, Howard, *Smart Mobs: The Next Social Revolution*, Boulder, CO, Perseus Publishing, 2002.

Rose, Alexander, "When Politics is a Laughing Matter," *Policy Review*, December 2001, pp. 59 – 71.

Stecklow, Steve and Farnaz Fassihi, "Thousands Flee Iran as Noose Tightens," *The Wall Street Journal*, Friday, December 11, 2009, p. A1 (cont. A18).

Veith, George J., *Code-Name Bright Light*, New York, Dell Publishing, 1998.

Welch, Matt, "Can you hear the people sing?" *Reason*, May 2008, p. 13

Woverton, Dr. Joe II, "Penman of the Revolution," *The New American*, July 26, 2004, pp. 35 – 38.

"Zeke Teflon" (pseudonym), *The Complete Manual of Pirate Radio*, Tucson, AZ, See Sharp Press, 1993. (Note: much of the technology described in this book is obsolete. However, the information on how to operate a clandestine transmitter is still valid.)

Chapter 21

Attack And Defense

The Resistance must carry out two functions: attack the government, and defend both itself and the citizenry against the government. This chapter will discuss both attack and defense.

Attack

The ultimate goal of the Resistance is to overthrow the government and replace it with a government that will satisfy the original reasons for undertaking armed resistance. This can be done only by attacking the government. Initially those attacks will be limited. Only as the Resistance gains strength, and the support of the population, can more extensive attacks be made. Thus initially, the Resistance must plan attacks so that the attacking force can withdraw and "disappear" before government forces can successfully counterattack.

Ambushes and raids will be discussed in more detail in subsequent chapters. They are the most important and most frequent form of attack used by Resistance forces. However, the ultimate goal is for the Resistance to grow to the point where large-scale attacks and sieges can be undertaken. Until that point is reached, the Resistance will be limited to ambushes and raids, attacking government forces where they are weak, or are not expecting an attack.

Ruses and Deceptions

Resistance forces, especially in the early phases of the Resistance, will be heavily dependent upon ruses and deceptions. These are deliberate measures to mislead government forces about Resistance intentions. Some purposes of ruses and deceptions are:

- Mislead government forces about the true objective or target of an attack;

- Mislead government forces about the true location of Resistance forces they are pursuing, in order to lead government forces into traps;
- Enable the secure withdrawal of Resistance forces after a raid or ambush, by misleading government forces about withdrawal routes;
- Mislead government forces about the true strength of a Resistance force (lure them into attacking what they mistakenly think is a weak force, or deter them from attacking what they mistakenly think is a strong force);
- Mislead government forces into thinking an attack is coming at one place, when the attack is coming at another place entirely;
- Draw a government force into an ambush by staging an attack on a small force, then ambushing the relief force.

The key issue is that deception is always aimed at the *mind* of the government force commander, and subordinate commanders. The purpose of deception is to cause the government force leaders to *do something* that helps the Resistance by causing them to misinterpret the situation they are facing. If deception fails to bring about *counterproductive* action on the part of government forces, it has failed its purpose.

The Resistance commanders must always be thinking in terms of ruses and deceptions. Doing what the government forces expect will almost always lead to defeat. It is especially important to avoid falling into patterns of behavior that the government forces can anticipate. Every action should incorporate ruses and deceptions that cause the government forces to misdirect their responses. These should be planned as an integral part of the operation.[109]

As in any plan, the Resistance commander starts by deciding what he wants to do. He then decides what false image he wants to create in the minds of the commanders of the government forces he will oppose. This false image must be *plausible*. It must be within the range of what the government commander is willing to believe

---

[109] The commander should not forget Plan B: what to do if the deception fails.

about Resistance actions. Moreover, the means of carrying out the deception must be plausible. If, for instance, the deception plan involves false radio traffic, that traffic must conform to the Resistance's usual patterns if it is to be believed.

Once the deception is selected, then the deception plan can be devised. The plan will then specify what actions will be taken to create the deception. Depending on the nature of the true action, the Resistance commander must then allow time for the deception plan to be carried out, especially if its purpose is to cause the government forces to deploy to a place away from the true target.

Chapter XV of the book by Callwell gives some historical examples of feints by military forces engaged in "small wars." These might be useful to the Resistance leaders both as cautionary tales of what the government forces might do, and as examples of how opponents can be misled.

Night Operations

Guerrillas have traditionally operated at night. The darkness helped cover movement. Darkness made surprise easier. Darkness made it harder for defending forces to see attackers. To some extent, night vision devices have reduced these advantages of night operations. However, the advantages have not been eliminated entirely. Thus Resistance forces should be trained to operate at night, and should make use of the advantages inherent in night operations.

One important element of training deals with seeing at night. Daylight vision involves elements of the eye called "cones." They are capable of distinguishing colors, and are located at the central point of vision. However, they are not very effective at night. Night vision involves elements of the eye called "rods." They are located around the cones. In the daytime, we look directly at something to see it. At night, it is necessary to look beside something (right or left, above or below), to allow the rods to operate. That is, we must use "off center" vision. Resistance fighters must be trained to do this; it doesn't come naturally.

Night movement should take maximum advantage of shadows. This is particularly true under a bright moon. Fighters must also take care not to step on anything that might make a sound to reveal their position. Twigs, loose rocks, and so on must be avoided. Again, the fighters need training in soundless night movement. In particular, all their equipment must be silenced so it doesn't rattle or make other noise such as water sloshing in a canteen.

While sight is hampered by darkness, sound and smell are still fully capable. Fighters moving at night must listen for enemy movement, and learn to detect enemy positions by smells such as cooking. Senses of hearing and smell can be improved by training and practice.

A unit moving at night must provide for communication. Hand signals cannot be seen. Chemlights, luminous tape, even the luminous dial of a compass, can be used effectively. Moving the source vertically, horizontally, in a circular motion, etc. can be used to convey different information (halt; proceed; enemy sighted; etc.).

Navigation at night is much more difficult than in the daytime, since landmarks cannot be seen. "Shooting a compass bearing" on a landmark may not be possible. If GPS is available, it should be used. Across open ground, fighters can follow a compass bearing by watching the compass. Terrain contours can also be used for navigation, but these must be planned in advance using a contour map ("follow this ridge, then turn right at the valley, and follow the stream").

Use of night vision devices certainly is not limited to government forces. Commercial NVDs are now available, with prices ranging from around $200 to around $3000. As with everything else, better costs more. Even so, Resistance forces may be able to obtain NVDs that allow them to operate effectively at night. Even night vision rifle sights are available at varying prices (and corresponding performance).

Even binoculars can help at night, if they have sufficient light-gathering objective lenses. Binoculars with 40-mm lenses give fairly good vision under a bright moon. While not as good as NVDs, they are a vast improvement over the naked eye. Resistance forces should obtain them if at all possible.

Jamming Electronics

Jamming, that is, broadcasting noise on a frequency the government forces are using, can be an effective means of disrupting government communications. The jamming transmitter advertises its presence, of course, and is therefore subject to counterattack. However, jamming can be a very effective means of attacking the government's communications at critical times. During a raid or ambush, for instance, jamming the communications of the target force can delay the government's response. For jamming to be effective, the frequencies used by the target government units must be known, including alternate and emergency frequencies. Resistance forces should be prepared to use jamming as an adjunct to other attacks.

Jamming is of course not restricted to government radios. There may be occasions when jamming aircraft radar, ground radar equipment, or aircraft navigation aids, is appropriate. For instance, government forces may be using some kind of precision aircraft navigation system as a means for "blind bombing" of Resistance forces. Jamming these systems can also be an effective measure. It is critical that the Resistance learn as much as possible about government radars, bombing aids, etc., so that proper jamming equipment can be built or otherwise obtained.

Computer Hacking

Tyrants don't need to depend on computers. Josef Stalin, known to some of the Old Bolsheviks as "Comrade Filecard," ran a pretty tight ship with nothing but pencil, paper and typewriter. Today, however, oppressive governments are using computers. That gives them some powerful tools. It also opens them to some new attacks, especially if the computers are connected to a public telephone system or the Internet. Any resistance movement should be prepared to attack the government's computers, as part of its overall strategy.

Hacking into government computers to gather information will be covered in a later chapter. Here, the issue is attacking government computers with the intention of disrupting their use: erasing files, altering data, sending bogus e-mails from government computers, identifying government informers, copying and making public any data that will embarrass the government or specific officials, and anything else that reduces the government's ability to use its computers to oppress the people. During an attack or raid, a "denial of service" attack on government computers can degrade the government's response to the Resistance's action.

The more the government depends on computers, the more important this kind of attack is. Specific techniques are beyond the scope of this book. There are books available that provide a good introduction to computer hacking. The book by Erickson gives a good introduction to computer hacking and insertion of malicious software. In addition, there is a great deal of information on the Internet about hacking. The important point here is that attacking the government's computers can be very fruitful for the Resistance, and appropriate attacks should be included in other plans.

Defense

Initially, the Resistance's only means of defense may be to "disappear" when attacked by government forces. It is critical that the Resistance not be "forted up" in places that can be surrounded and captured by the government. Only as the Resistance gains strength and the support of the people can it afford to defend fixed positions such as base camps. However, it should never defend a fixed position simply for the sake of "holding ground." It is far more important that the Resistance forces survive to fight again than that they hold a position "to the death."

Eventually the Resistance must be able to defend base camps. They must be fortified, and have bunkers and defenses capable of withstanding severe artillery or aerial bombardment. However, "defense" may involve bringing in reinforcements to threaten the attacking government forces, rather than depending entirely on concrete.

Reinforcements for camps under attack must be alert for ambushes by government forces while on their way to the battle. They must be alert for air attacks. Finally, they must stage from assembly areas near the battle, rather than going directly to the relief of the base camp. The relief effort must be organized, rather than simply a matter of throwing troops into the battle haphazardly. A well-organized and prompt counter-attack can be a very effective form of defense for base camps and other Resistance facilities.

Defense Against Chemical Attack

Use of chemicals to disable enemy troops is at least as old as the Classical Greeks. Poisoning wells, catapulting dead horses or corpses into a city under siege, and similar methods, have been used throughout history. However, the modern use of chemical warfare can be traced to the introduction of poison gas during World War I.

Once gas warfare started, a wide variety of agents was quickly introduced: choking gases, skin-penetrating chemicals, residual chemicals for denying territory, and so on. Developments since then have been largely ones of refinement. However, the level of refinement is well beyond that achieved during World War I.

Use of chemical warfare has been banned by international treaty. However, that has not stopped governments from using chemical warfare. The Italians used mustard gas against the Ethiopians prior to World War II. Iraq used nerve gas against the Iranians in the 1980s, and against its own people after the first Gulf War. The evidence is not conclusive, but there is good reason to believe that the communists used Russian-supplied mycotoxins ("yellow rain") against anti-communist forces in Laos.

Of course, no civilized government would ever use chemical warfare against its own citizens. Nevertheless, there are many examples of internal use of chemical warfare by government. Iraq used poison gas against rebellious Shi'ites. The U.S. government used CS, a chemical prohibited by international treaty for military (but not police) use, against the Branch Davidians at Waco, Texas.

Because of the possibility that resistance forces may be attacked with chemicals, those forces must be prepared to deal with chemical attacks. At a minimum, gas masks should be obtained by the Resistance if at all possible. Bunkers and tunnels in base camps must have means for shutting off incoming air, and have alternate means for ventilation.

The material in the references is intended to be a guide to further information about defense against chemical attack. One online bookseller lists nearly fifty books on chemical warfare. Details are well beyond the scope of this book. Resistance forces anticipating chemical attack by government forces should prepare ahead of time to defend against such attacks.

Defense Against Helicopters

Resistance forces must expect that the government will make extensive use of helicopters. The Soviets did in Afghanistan; Saddam Hussein did after the first Gulf War, in suppressing the Marsh Arabs. Helicopters allow government forces to bypass roadside ambushes. They also provide government forces with highly mobile firepower.

Because of the likelihood that the government will use helicopters, it is essential that the Resistance be prepared to counter them. Missiles are of course the preferred method of countering helicopters. They can sometimes be obtained on military "black markets."[110] However, they are not essential in the fight against helicopters. The Afghan Resistance used heavy machine guns (.50 caliber or greater) effectively against Soviet helicopters (Gusinov). The Resistance can set up machine gun ambushes at crash sites, at sites where road convoys have been ambushed, or any other place where helicopters may be used. The reference TC-23-44 provides useful information on defense against air attack. Essentially, the trick is to throw lots of bullets in the path of the helicopter, giving a

---

[110] See the article by Gusinov.

high probability that the vehicle will run into some of them. Since it takes time for the bullet to get there, lead the air vehicle: lead fixed-wing aircraft by the length of a football/soccer field; lead a helicopter by half the length of a football/soccer field. Since the bullet will drop in flight, aim above the flight path.

In addition, the Resistance should set up warning networks around government helicopter bases (see Chapter 28 on Tactical Intelligence for more on an observer corps).

Defense Against Aircraft

Defending against aircraft, particularly jets, is much more difficult than defending against helicopters. Putting a lot of lead in the sky ahead of the aircraft may work, but the chances of hitting are much poorer than with helicopters.

Aircraft, unlike helicopters, need long runways. This means that there are fewer places from which they can take off and land. These airports can be watched to determine when they take off. Resistance forces can get some degree of early warning of attack by aircraft.

Aircraft are vulnerable on the ground. Mortar fire can be very effective, especially if the aircraft are exposed on hardstands. If they are in revetments, destroying them with mortars is more difficult, but not impossible.

Sabotage may be the most effective means of destroying aircraft on the ground. Getting sappers into a guarded airfield will not be easy, but if it can be done, thermite grenades placed on the wings above the fuel tanks, or satchel charges in the cockpit, will disable the aircraft.

Aircraft need fuel and ammunition. While it may be difficult to attack aircraft directly, it may be easier to attack trucks bringing fuel and ammunition to airfields, or to damage pipelines leading to the airfields.[111] Ambushing supply convoys may be the most effective way of defending against the government's aircraft.

Defense Against Tanks

Even professional armies have difficulty defending against tanks. This doesn't mean, however, that a Resistance limited to small arms and improvised weapons is helpless against tanks.

In open country (desert, farmland), about the only effective defenses against tanks are anti-tank missiles. It is impossible to "sneak up" on a tank to use short-range weapons. In this case, the Resistance would be better advised to attack the tanks while they are parked. Mortars can be effective against parked tanks. In addition, tanks break down frequently, and frequently get stuck in soft ground. While the tank is being repaired or pulled out of the mud, the crew is outside and vulnerable. As a stationary target, the tank is also vulnerable to mortar fire.

In heavily wooded areas, tanks are confined to trails. Mines and similar devices can be placed along the path the tank(s) must follow. It is easier for defenders to approach tanks and use satchel charges against them. Benson describes the use of a shaped-charge flamethrower against tanks and other vehicles. This is a container of gelled fuel, with a "shaped charge" explosive behind it. It is a directional weapon, and completely covers the tank with burning fuel.

In cities, tanks are confined to streets, and only to fairly wide streets at that. This constraint on the paths tanks can take means that mines and shaped-charge flamethrowers can be emplaced ahead of time. Narrow streets, alleys, and basements mean that defenders can place themselves close to where tanks must pass, and can be *below* the lowest level to which the tanks guns can be depressed. Attacks with satchel charges, Molotov cocktails, and thermite bombs then become possible. Upper stories and rooftops, as well as bridges and overpasses, are also suitable locations for dropping Molotov

---

[111] Even buried pipelines need pumping stations and other above-ground facilities. Destroying these, or cutting off power, can temporarily disable the pipeline.

cocktails or thermite grenades on tanks. Even paint sprayed or splashed on vision blocks can immobilize a tank, and make it vulnerable to further attack. Note that one of the effects of a Molotov cocktail or flamethrower on the engine air inlets is to starve the tank's engine of oxygen, and temporarily bring it to a halt.

Likewise in cities, fighters on motorcycles can approach tanks quickly and attack with satchel charges or Molotov cocktails. Use of alleys and side streets can make it much easier for the motorcyclist to approach the tank without being seen, and may keep the motorcyclist below the level at which the tank's armament is effective.

Regardless of terrain, sniper fire can be effective against tanks. If the driver or commander is standing up and looking out the hatch, he is a perfect sniper target. If the tank is "buttoned up," then vision blocks become the preferred target for sniper fire. Troops accompanying tanks, who defend the tanks against close-in weapons such as satchel charges, are likewise good sniper targets, since it is impossible for them to take cover and still carry out their mission.

Base camps can be defended against tanks by command-detonated mines and by shaped-charge flamethrowers. These weapons become more effective if obstacles can be placed around the base camp that limit the avenues by which the tanks can approach the base camp.

Lasers can be effective for "blinding" the night vision and thermal imaging devices on tanks. However, any lasers that Resistance forces can obtain readily are likely to have only limited range. Nevertheless, they can be helpful as part of a coordinated attack with close-in weapons.

Urban Warfare

Much of the literature on guerrilla warfare is based on experience in countries where the population is primarily rural and where there are "remote" areas. In countries that have large urban populations, fighting conditions will be much different. In a rural area, it may take hours or days for government relief forces to arrive at the scene of a raid or ambush. In a city, it may take only minutes. In a rural area, there are many miles of road on which to place ambushes. In a city, there are many fewer choices of places to stage an ambush. On the positive side, in a city there are many more people for the Resistance fighters to blend in with, making it harder for the government to find them. In addition, in an urban environment it will be easier for the overt organization to support the covert (fighting) organization with demonstrations, strikes, and protests. Likewise, safe houses are easier to establish and disguise in cities. For people in a largely urban society who are trying to overthrow an oppressive government, the differences between rural and urban fighting must be taken into account.

If the Resistance either chooses to or is forced to fight in urban areas, some changes are needed in organization and planning. Instead of base camps, urban fighters will use safe houses. While the rural guerrilla must know trails and terrain intimately, the urban guerrilla must know streets, alleyways, basements, street markets, multiple entrances and interior stairs in large buildings, fire escapes, rooftops, utility tunnels, and even sewers. While the rural guerrilla must be able to navigate cross-country, the urban guerrilla must be able to find his way through side streets and alleys. Instead of building underground bunkers, the urban guerrilla must fortify the insides of buildings, using timber and sandbags, and create firing ports (loopholes). Instead of escape routes, the urban guerrilla must think in terms of escape tunnels and back doors. Urban ambushes may include fighters on rooftops or upper floors of buildings. Urban fighting must make effective use of the "man made terrain" of a city.

The book by Oltusski relates his experiences in the revolution that brought Fidel Castro to power in Cuba. He describes the Cuban revolution from the urban perspective, and how the middle class in the cities supported the revolution with strikes, propaganda, and fund-raising. However, there was little actual fighting in the cities.

References

Chemical Warfare

Carey, Christopher T., *U.S. Chemical and Biological Defense Respirators*, Schiffer publications Lt., 77 Lower Valley Rd., Route 372, Atglen, PA 19310.

Romano, James A. (ed.), *Chemical Warfare Agents: Chemistry, Pharmacology, Toxicology, and Therapeutics, Second Edition*, CRC Press, ISBN 1-4200-4661-6.

Staff Report, "Gas Masks, Inc.," *American Survival Guide*, July, 1998, pp. 40 – 41.

Combat Operations

Benson, Ragnar, *David's Took Kit: A Citizen's Guide to Taking Out Big Brother's Heavy Weapons*, Port Townsend, WA, Loompanics Unlimited, 1996. (Available from online booksellers.)

Burnett, C. (translator), *Night Movements*, Port Townsend, WA, Loompanics Unlimited, 1913. Available from online booksellers. Also available as free download at http://www.members.tripod.com/colla/physical/skills/nightmov.html

Callwell, Col. Charles E., *Small Wars: Their principles and Practice*, Lincoln, NB, Bison Editions, 1996, ISBN 0-8032-6366-X

Department of the Army, *Vietman Primer, Lessons Learned*, reprinted by Col. David Hackworth, 1997.

Department of the Army Air Defense School, *Small Arms Defense Against Air Attack, TC 23-44*, June 1975.

England, James W., *Long Range Patrol Operations*, Boulder, CO, Paladin Press, 1987.

Gallagher, CSM James J., *Combat Leader's Field Guide*, Mechanicsburg, PA, Stackpole Books, 1994.

Gusinov, Timothy, "Soviet Afghan war holds lessons for American pilots in Iraq," *The Washington Times Weekly Edition*, February 26, 2007, p. 19.

Larsen, Christopher E., *Light Infantry Tactics for Small Teams*, Bloomington, IN, Authorhouse, ISBN 1-4184-7207-7 (available from online booksellers). (Information on patrolling in disputed or enemy-held territory.)

Latimer, Jon, *Deception in War*, New York, Overlook Press, 2001.

Oltuski, Enrique, *Vida Clandestina: My Life in the Cuban Revolution*, San Francisco, Jossey-Bass, 2002.

Popp, Major Dennis J., *The Night Fighter's Handbook*, Boulder, CO, Paladin Press, 1986.

Poole, H. J., *The Last Hundred Yards*, Posterity Press, Emerald Isle, NC 2002, www.prosperitypress.com. (Thorough coverage of small unit tactics and leadership.) (The current edition is sold only to US active duty military and veterans. Older editions are available as used books from online booksellers. It may be possible to have an older edition shipped into your country.)

Scales, Robert H., *Firepower in Limited War*, Novato, CA, Presidio Press, 1995.

United States Marine Corps, *Professional Knowledge, NAVMC 2614*, Randle, WA, Bohica Concepts, 1967.

Computer Warfare

Merkle, Robert, *The Ultimate Internet Terrorist*, Boulder, CO, Paladin Press, 1998, ISBN 0-87364-970-2.

Newman, Bob, *Guerillas in the Mist*, Boulder, CO, Paladin Press, 1997.Electronic Warfare

Electronic Warfare

Anonymous, *The Electronic Warfare Handbook*, Boulder, CO, Paladin Press, 1990.

Myers, Lawrence W., *Improvised Radio Jamming Techniques*, Boulder, CO, Paladin Press, 1989.

Urban Warfare

Anonymous, *Urban Combat: A Guide to Combat in Built-Up Areas*, El Dorado, AR, Desert Publications, 1994.

Department of the Army, *An Infantryman's Guide to Combat in Built-Up Areas*, *FM 90-10-1*, Boulder, CO, Paladin Press, 1994.

Urbano (pseudonym), *Fighting in the Streets*, Miami, FL, J. Flores Publications, 1991. (Not only describes ambushes and raids, but has information on making explosives and weapons.)

Useful Web Sites

Israel Defense Forces: http://www.idf.il/English/Units/Homefront/main.htm.

Chapter 22

Ambushes

Ambushes are conducted as surprise attacks by a hidden ambushing force against a moving target. They can be very effective, but depend for success on delivering an overwhelming volume of fire in a short time. Ambushes generally do not last long. Once the target is destroyed, or other objectives achieved, the ambushing force withdraws as quickly as possible. Delay gives the target time to call for reinforcements, or for artillery or air support. Unless the objective is to capture weapons or other equipment, little is gained after the first few minutes of an ambush.

Composition of the Ambush Force

The ambush force will have three major elements: the command element, the assault element, and a security element. Each of these may be further subdivided into teams, depending on the objective of the ambush. For instance, if the purpose of the ambush includes capturing weapons, the assault element may include porters or bearers.

Command Element

The command element includes the ambush commander, communications personnel, medical team, and any observers or photographers. The commander is responsible for triggering or aborting the ambush, and for ordering withdrawal. The commander is also responsible for coordinating the actions of the security element. The communications team is responsible for messages to and from the other portions of the ambush party.[112] Other teams making up the command element perform specialized duties such as providing immediate medical care for wounded fighters, or recording or photographing the ambush.

---

[112] A discreet method of communicating within the ambush party is the "tug line." This is a rope or string laid between ambush party elements. For instance, a security team may signal the approach of the target by a tug on the line. Only very simple messages can be communicated by this means, but it is a very secure communications method which is unlikely to alert the target.

Assault Element

The assault element includes the teams that will fire on the target. In addition to small arms, this may include automatic weapons, rockets or RPGs, mines, and mortars. Mortars, if used, will be located more distant from the location of the target than will the small arms. The assault element may also include searchers, bearers and porters, if the objective of the ambush includes capturing equipment or documents.

In some cases the "assault element" is really a mine or other explosive emplaced near where the target will pass. There may not even be anyone from the ambush party near the mine, if some form of remote detonation is used.

Security Element

The biggest threat to an ambushing force is being outflanked. The security element is responsible for protecting the flanks of the ambushing force, and for providing rear guard security during the force's withdrawal. The security element may also signal the approach of the target force to the ambush site.

Pre-Ambush Intelligence

It takes time to emplace the ambushing force at a point where the target will pass. This demands intelligence in advance of the ambush. Specific items of information will include:

- Nature of the target (supply convoy, troop column, important official, or what)
- Makeup of the target (number and types of vehicles, defensive forces in the target, placement of armored vehicles in the target, presence of air cover)
- Route of the target (specific roads/streets the target will traverse, alternative routes, stopover points)
- Timing (time of departure of the target, time the target is expected to be at various intermediate points)
- Identity of the target commander (e.g., convoy commander, bodyguard of official, etc. This information may help predict the target's response to the ambush.)

In addition to the specific information about the target, intelligence about the doctrine, SOP (standard operating procedure), and training of counter-ambush forces can help the ambush commander predict the response of the target.

Information about supply convoys, troop columns, and similar targets must be obtained in "real time" as the target departs from a base, or returns from a mission. This may be a supplement to information that there is a weekly supply convoy to a particular base, or that troops at an outpost are relieved on a regular basis. Information about the routine operation must then be supplemented with information about "this week's" convoy.

If the target is a specific individual (high-ranking military officer, police chief, government official, etc.), information must be collected about his habits, including things like time of departure for work, time of return from work, time of customary activities such as attending church or taking walks, typical routes (including alternates), identity of vehicle(s) used (make, color, license plates, any special markings such as parking or restricted area passes), number and armament of bodyguards, and typical clothing. The ambushing force should have photographs of the target, to verify that the right individual has been identified. While the target may be able to take alternative routes to and from work, all trips must begin at home and end at work (vice versa for the return trip). Therefore the most suitable places for an ambush are near either of these locations.

Once an ambush site is selected, surveillance must be undertaken to assure that the government forces haven't anticipated the ambush. This must take place right up until the time of the ambush. However, extreme care must be taken not to tip off the government forces, or any nearby residents, that the site is under surveillance.

Intelligence is the most important factor in staging a successful ambush. It is necessary that the ambushing force know when and where the target will be passing, so that the ambushing force can be put in place ahead of time.

The Ambush Site

Once the route of the planned target is known, a site on that route must be selected for the ambush. There can be no "ideal" ambush site, and even if there were one, it would probably be in some country other than yours. The ambush site should have the following features:

- Terrain or structures that force the target into a specific channel
- Has good fields of fire for the ambushing force
- Allows the ambushing force to occupy it and set up positions with good concealment
- Has covered routes for withdrawal

Normally the ambushing force will take up position on one side only of the target's route, to avoid "fratricide." However, if the site has elevations on both sides of the route, allowing the ambushing force to fire downward at the target, both sides of the route may be occupied. [113] This is referred to as a "linear ambush." In some cases, the ambushing forces may use an "L-shaped" ambush. In this type, the ambushing forces take up two lines, more or less at right angles to each other. One line may simply be a blocking force across the route. If the ambush site involves a curve in the route, then the ambushing force may take up positions "around" the curve. If an L-shaped ambush is used, special care must be taken to avoid fratricide. Each ambusher must be given a field of fire that avoids the other leg of the L. Machine-gunners, in particular, should have aiming stakes that limit their field of fire.

Approach to the ambush site

The ambush site should be approached from "behind." That is, the ambushing force should never appear on the route to be

---

[113] Note that this may complicate the ambushing force's arrival and departure from the ambush site. However, it does put the target in a cross-fire.

traversed by the target. If it is necessary to cross the route of the target, the ambushing force should do so at a point well away from the selected ambush site, then move parallel to the route.

Depending on the amount of time available, the ambushing force may stop at one or more rally points before moving to the ambush site. Near the ambush site, a "layup point" should be established, where the ambushing force rests before taking up final positions. At the layup point, the ambushing force members should relieve themselves, take their last drinks of water, eat rations that don't require cooking, and make any other final preparations.

Flank security teams must be put in position before the rest of the ambush force occupies the site. Once the flanks are secure, the main force moves into the site, and the rear guard takes up position behind the force.

At the ambush site, each member of the ambushing force must be placed in a position that gives a good field of fire into the killing zone, and which is screened from the route of the target. Once the ambushers are in position, camouflage is essential. There must be nothing that could give the ambush position away by sight, sound, or smell. Upon taking their positions, the ambushers should clear away anything such as twigs or gravel that might make a sound as they shift position. Camouflage should be effective from both sides, from front and back, and from overhead. If the ambushers will be in place for several hours, care must be taken to replace any vegetation used as camouflage if the leaves start to wilt.

Prior to the ambush commander triggering the ambush, the ambushing force must have weapon safeties ON. This prevents accidents that might reveal the force's position, or worse yet, cause casualties among the ambushing force. In addition, the sound of safeties being taken off can alert the target of the ambush. Safeties should come off only *after* the ambush commander opens fire.

While ambushes are often thought of as taking place in rural areas, the considerations above apply equally well to urban ambushes. The ambushing force must get into position before the target arrives, must be camouflaged so it won't be detected, and must have good fields of fire into the killing zone.

Pre-Ambush Reconnaissance

The ambush commander must make a final reconnaissance of the ambush site while the ambushing force is back at the layup point. This is to determine where the ambushers must be positioned, whether there are any potential "dead zones" where the ambushers' fire cannot reach, where the security teams should be placed, and where the ends of the killing zone will be.

Executing the Ambush

The ambush commander decides *when* and *whether* to spring the ambush. If the target force is too big, so that at least ninety percent of it will not fit into the killing zone, there is too much risk that the target forces outside the killing zone will make flanking attacks on the ambushing force. If the target force is more heavily armed than expected, or has immediate air cover by armed helicopters, the ambushing force may be overwhelmed. In such cases, the commander should elect to abort the ambush.

If the commander decides to spring the ambush, he should allow any advanced guards to pass through, and wait for the main body of the target to fill the killing zone. The ambush should begin with weapon fire, not with any non-lethal signals that would alert the target force and give them an extra second or two to respond. Heavy weapons, including machine guns, RPGs, anti-tank missiles, etc., should be used immediately. Mortars, if used, should follow up once the ambush is sprung. Individual riflemen should aim at specific targets, especially troops disembarking from trucks or other vehicles.

If at all possible, the target should be immobilized by halting the leading and trailing elements. Command-detonated mines, fallen trees, anti-tank missiles, etc., may be used to halt or knock out these elements, keeping the remainder of the target from escaping. In an urban ambush, a truck or bus driven across the street can be effective in blocking forward movement of the target.

Withdrawal from the Ambush

The ambush commander must terminate the ambush while conditions are still favorable, i.e., "quit while you're ahead." If the target is destroyed, or the target forces are retreating, the ambush is over. If the ambush is unsuccessful for any reason, the commander must begin to extricate his forces before they are destroyed.

If the target has been destroyed or begins retreating, and part of the objective was to capture weapons and ammunition, security elements must cross the route and take up position on the other side, to guard against a counter-attack. The assault element, including porters and bearers, then searches through the target. Survivors among the target force must be spared *unless* they offer resistance. Only those survivors offering resistance should be killed. However, whether wounded or not, they must be disarmed. Only if it was part of the objective will the ambushing force take prisoners. An exception to this may be made if a particularly valuable prisoner is unexpectedly found among the survivors (high-ranking officer or official).

The commander orders a head-count to be taken among the ambushing force, and ammunition is redistributed if necessary. The flanking security teams remain in position while the assault force withdraws. The security teams then become part of the rear guard. It is the responsibility of the rear guard to delay or halt any pursuit of the ambushing force. However, the rear guard must not attempt to hold a fixed position in the face of pursuit. "Fire and fall back."

Withdrawal should take place over a different route from the approach to the ambush site. The ambush forces will normally break up into small teams, meeting again at rally points. The object is to deceive the government forces about the size of the ambushing force, and the withdrawal routes.

Post-Ambush Intelligence Gathering

If at all possible, the ambush force should search the vehicles, and the bodies of dead and wounded personnel among the target force, for documents, diaries, orders, maps, identification papers, and anything else that may have intelligence value. The opportunity to gather information about government plans, government force locations, troop morale, and identity of target force leaders, should not be missed.

Heavy Weapons Ambush

When a target is ambushed, and the firing includes small arms, it is obvious that there are troops involved in the ambush. The target commander may attempt to counterattack the ambushers. If the attack is limited to mortars, grenades, claymore mines, etc., the target may be fooled into thinking it is under artillery bombardment rather than caught in an ambush. In such a case, the logical response by the target is to move rather than counterattack. The ambush commander should consider whether this possibility is worth exploiting. If it is, the ambush team need be only a few fighters, who will command-detonate the ambush.

References

Balor, Paul, *Manual of the Mercenary Soldier*, Boulder, CO, Paladin Press, 1988.

Newman, Bob, *Guerillas in the Mist*, Boulder, CO, Paladin Press, 1997.

Stubblefield, Gary & Mark Monday, *Killing Zone*, Boulder, CO, Paladin Press, 1994.

Thompson, Leroy, "Be Counter-Ambush Conscious," *Combat Handguns*, November 2006, pp. 82 – 85. (This article is written from the standpoint of a professional bodyguard, and focuses on protecting against ambushes. However, it is a concise survey of the types of ambushes insurgents may utilize.)

Chapter 23

Sniping & Counter-Sniping

A common form of armed resistance is the use of snipers against government forces and targets. Just what is involved in "sniping," and how does one go about it?

What is a sniper?

Lanning defines a sniper as follows. ". . . someone who uses a special weapon to shoot at an individual from a protected area far from the target."

There are four important aspects of this definition: the weapon, the sniper's location, the target, and the sniper himself. In this chapter we'll take a look at each.

The sniper's target

For the most part, the sniper's target is the individual enemy soldier. In obtaining kills, the sniper is far more deadly than is the ordinary soldier. In World War II, American troops expended 25,000 small arms rounds (rifle, pistol, and submachine gun) for each enemy soldier killed by these means. In Korea, the number doubled to 50,000 rounds. In Vietnam, the arming of each soldier with a fully automatic rifle raised the number to 200,000 rounds (Lanning p. 2). This does not necessarily mean that American soldiers were poor shots. On the battlefield, it's often hard to find an individual target. Sometimes the soldier will empty an entire magazine into foliage he believes to be concealing an enemy soldier. That raises the number of rounds per kill very dramatically.

Nevertheless, by contrast, American snipers in Vietnam averaged between 1.3 and 1.7 rounds per kill (Lanning p. 2). Of course a big part of the difference is that the sniper fired only when he had an identified target in the open. This automatically made a big difference in the ratio of shots to kills. The contrast does indicate the effectiveness of aimed shots *when a target is visible*.

Sniping, then, primarily involves targets of opportunity on the battlefield. The sniper waits in hiding, like a deer hunter, for a target to present itself. The target generally does not know that he is being targeted until it's too late.

The most common victims of sniper fire will be ordinary soldiers who have let down their guard and exposed themselves in the open because they do not realize the sniper is present. However, at its most effective, sniper fire will be aimed at more than the low-level grunt. The sniper ought to be aiming for the chain of command. Most military forces have already learned to protect the chain of command. They use toned-down insignia of rank, abandon saluting in the combat area, apply camouflage to the antennas of man-packed radios, and take other measures to make it difficult for snipers to identify the chain of command. Nevertheless, the sniper should make an effort to pick out the leaders and eliminate them.

In addition to the chain of command, snipers should focus on high-value targets such as machine gunners, radio operators, close air support controllers, artillery observers, vehicle drivers, and enemy snipers. By focusing on these high-value targets snipers can do much more damage to government forces than simply picking off common soldiers.

The sniper's targets are not limited to personnel. A precision shot to a critical part can put a major system out of action: vision blocks on tanks, hydraulic lines on artillery, engines on parked aircraft, etc. By choosing an important system, and disabling it at a critical moment, the sniper can very reduce the effectiveness of an enemy force, at least until the damage can be repaired.

The sniper's weapon

As noted in the definition, the sniper's weapon is special, in the sense that it differs to some degree from the weapons issued to the rest of the force.

The sniper rifle

Sniping will of course be done with whatever weapon the shooter has available. Nevertheless, if there are several weapons available, choosing the best one can significantly enhance the ability of a sniper to hit the target.

The essence of a good sniper rifle and cartridge combination is consistency. Assume that a rifle is mounted in a rifle rest so that it cannot move, and several shots are fired at the same target. So long as all the shots go through what is essentially the same hole, the sights can always be adjusted so that the bullet will hit the point of aim. If the bullet holes are scattered, however, no amount of sight adjustment can compensate for the lack of consistency.

How much scatter can be tolerated? A typical requirement for a sniper rifle is that the shots deviate not more than one minute of arc from edge to edge of a three-shot "group." One minute of arc subtends one inch at one hundred yards.[114] If the test rifle, when mounted in a rest, keeps all its shots within a one-inch group when the target is one hundred yards away, it is of sniper quality. Individual rifles of the same manufacture will vary in their degree of consistency. Some will do even better than one minute of arc. Some rifles currently available are advertised by their manufacturers as capable of half-minute of arc accuracy. Of course, if the best rifle available is capable of only two minutes of arc accuracy, that is what the shooter will have to use. It is still good enough for eliminating enemy troops at ranges of four or five hundred yards. However, it is unlikely to be usable for precise hits on enemy equipment such as tank vision blocks.

How does one go about modifying a rifle, or making one in the first place, to achieve the consistency needed for a good sniper rifle?

The first requirement is that the rifle's action be "bedded" securely in the stock, so that it doesn't move from shot to shot. This is often accomplished by using a fiberglass bedding compound to hold the action in place. The articles by Stoppelman and Sundra each give step-by-step instructions on glass bedding a rifle.

---

[114] One minute of arc is actually 1.047 inches at 100 yards, but it's customary to round it to one inch.

An even more effective bedding technique is so-called "pillar bedding," in which aluminum or steel "pillars" are secured to the stock, and the action to the pillars. Either method provides a very secure base for the action.

Although the action must be firmly bedded to the stock, the barrel must be "floated" or free to move. Even the heaviest barrels vibrate and whip as the bullet passes through them. This vibration is invisible to the shooter, because the magnitude is of the order of thousandths of an inch. However, that can be enough to make the point of impact vary from one shot to the next. If the barrel does not vibrate exactly the same way from shot to shot, the rifle will lack consistency. This means that the barrel must not touch any part of the stock. It also means that changing anything between sighting in the rifle and deploying it, such as clamping a bipod on the barrel or hanging camouflage material directly on the barrel, will alter the barrel's vibration, and change the point of impact from what it was when the rifle was sighted in. Even sighting in the rifle with the bipod clamped to the barrel is no guarantee of consistency, since the properties of the ground under the bipod may differ. When the rifle is being used for sniping, the barrel must be free to vibrate in the same way as when it was sighted in.

As indicated above, the groove of the stock in which the barrel fits must allow room for the barrel to vibrate without touching the stock. This doesn't mean a great deal of open space, however. It should be possible to pass a strip of paper from breech to muzzle without snagging on anything, but no more space than that is needed.

The stock itself should be sturdy enough that it can absorb the recoil transmitted from the action without flexing. Moreover, it should not change shape or size with weather changes. In addition, it should not warp or change shape if the shooter tightens a sling on his arm. If at all possible, a composite or fiberglass stock should be chosen. These are rigid and unaffected by moisture. The stock should also provide for fastening a bipod to the rifle, without putting any pressure on the barrel. Typically, a bipod stud is mounted on the bottom of the forestock just on the muzzle side of the forward sling swivel.

The main point of this discussion is that even a mediocre rifle may be improved by bedding the action and inletting the stock around the barrel, or replacing the stock with a composite one. If the shooter can start off with a rifle having these features, that is so much the better, but if the only available rifle lacks them, it may be possible for a gunsmith to upgrade it. The book by Boone gives detailed instructions on how to upgrade a rifle to sniper quality, especially on bedding the action and inletting a wooden stock (fiberglass stocks should not need inletting). The article by Boddington gives some simple ways to upgrade a rifle's accuracy.

Some comment should also be made about the barrel. The interior should be free of rust and pits. Moreover, any damage to the rifling at the muzzle will reduce the shot-to-shot consistency of the barrel. For this reason, serious sniper rifles are "crowned." That is, the muzzle is cut so that a rim of metal surrounds the actual exit from the barrel. This helps to keep the rifling from getting "dinged" through the inevitable rough usage the rifle will see in combat. The article by Towsley has instructions on crowning a rifle.

Cleaning a rifle can damage the barrel, if it is not done correctly. Pushing a patch or brush through the barrel inevitably causes the cleaning rod to bow out and rub the interior of the barrel. If at all possible, the patch or brush should be *pulled* through the barrel, from the breech to the muzzle. Insert the cleaning rod from the muzzle, without a patch. Push it far enough through that it sticks out of the breech. Insert a patch and pull the cleaning rod back out of the muzzle.

Re-using a patch simply redistributes the dirt. Use a clean patch each time. The usual advice is to first run a "wet" patch (one with cleaning solvent on it) through the barrel, let it sit for a few minutes while it dissolves powder residue. There are now foam products that fill the barrel and dissolve residue. The gun should be allowed to sit while these do their work. After using either a wet patch or foam, run a brush through the barrel several times. Run the brush all the way through the barrel. *Never* alternate direction with the brush still in the barrel. That damages the brush wires. After brushing, alternate wet and dry patches until a dry patch comes out clean. Following cleaning, put a few drops of gun oil on a dry patch and run it through the barrel. Before the next use, run a dry patch through the barrel to remove the oil. Proper cleaning will remove powder and metal deposits, and preserve the inherent accuracy of the barrel.

Ammunition

After the rifle itself, a major factor influencing accuracy is the ammunition. Again, consistency is the key. So long as the cartridges shoot to the same place, the sights can be adjusted to make the point of aim coincide with the point of impact. If the sniper has the luxury of manufacturing his own ammunition, three things must be controlled. First is bullet weight. All the bullets should weigh the same, to within a tenth of a grain.[115] Second is powder charge. The amount of powder should be the same in each cartridge, again to within a tenth of a grain. Third is interior cartridge case volume. Differences in case volume will change the rate at which the powder burns, affecting muzzle velocity and therefore point of impact. Interior volume is somewhat difficult to measure. The usual practice is to weigh the case both empty and full of water. Knowing the density of water (one gram per cubic centimeter at 4 degrees Celsius), the volume can be calculated. However, there is a simpler way to deal with the problem. The exterior case dimensions are rigidly controlled, since the cartridge must fit precisely within the rifle's chamber. Hence weight of the case is a good proxy for interior volume. More weight means less volume than other cartridges of the same exterior dimensions, since it means wall thickness is greater.

Thus the sniper loading his own ammunition should select bullets weighing the same, match them to cases weighing the same, and fill them with the same weight of powder. In reality, however, the shooter will most likely have to use whatever ammunition is available in the caliber of his rifle. The best approach is to weigh

---

[115] For those used to metric measure, a grain is .065 grams.

each cartridge and segregate the cartridges into groups of approximately equal weight. The rifle should be sighted in with cartridges from the same group as will be used in combat. Re-sighting will be needed when the sniper switches to a different group of cartridges.

The most popular sniping cartridge today is the Winchester .308. It has a reasonably flat trajectory and fairly light recoil. Depending on the ammunition available, it can be effective against personnel out to about 1000 yards. The M82 military sniper bullet, a 169-grain boattail, goes subsonic at about 800 yards, and accuracy deteriorates beyond that range. The newer 175-grain M118 bullet retains supersonic velocity to beyond 1000 yards, and is accurate at least to that range. Several manufacturers offer match-grade ammunition in this caliber. If a rifle and ammunition in .308 are available, this would be a good choice. If this choice is not available, however, there are other cartridge-rifle combinations available that are effective for sniping. A heavy hunting cartridge such as the .300 Winchester Magnum or the .338 Lapua are also good choices if these are available. The 7.62x54R, the .260 Remington, the 6.5-284 Norma, and the 7mm Remington Magnum are also respectable choices. In reality, of course, the shooter will have to make do with whatever is available, both rifle and ammunition. In such cases, the would-be sniper should test the ammunition at various ranges, to determine its capabilities.

If the sniper is loading his own ammunition, Winchester provides a ballistic calculator at http://ballisticscalculator.winchester.com/ that can be used to calculate trajectories.

The Telescopic Sight

Although some excellent sniping has been done in the past with "iron sights," nowadays sniping is universally associated with telescopic sights on the rifle. In reality, the shooter will have to made do with whatever telescope is available. However, if choices are available, here are some things to consider.

First and foremost, the 'scope must "keep its zero." That is, when the 'scope and rifle are sighted in, the 'scope must stay sighted in. It must be rugged internally, and it must not rattle, wiggle, or move on the rifle. The scope rings must be tightened sufficiently that the 'scope does not slide in them from the recoil. Similarly, the 'scope mount must be firmly attached to the action. If there is any loose play in the mount, the scope will not hold its zero. The only way to know if a 'scope will keep its zero is to test it. Sight the rifle in, then shoot it under as realistic conditions as possible, then determine whether it needs sighting in again.

The optics should give the shooter a clear, sharp image of the target. Coated optics are universal today, but if the shooter is forced to use an "antique" 'scope, some light may be lost through internal reflection, resulting in a less clear image.

The shooter may have to use whatever is available in the way of rifle 'scopes. However, if there is some choice, the power or magnification should be given some consideration. The higher the power, the narrower the field of view at any given range. Some compromise between power and field of view is necessary. At least 8 power is needed to make precise shots against targets at 400 yards. However, there is little to be gained by going beyond 10 power, even at longer ranges, and the reduction in field of view makes finding the target more difficult. A zoom or variable power scope will allow the shooter to use higher magnification when it is needed, and to widen the field of view by reducing power when that becomes more important.

If at all possible the scope adjustments for windage and elevation should have discrete "clicks" rather than simply a friction hold on the scope adjustments. Discrete clicks make it easier to adjust the scope while lying prone, and make it easier to return to an earlier setting if that is desired. Quarter-minute-of-arc clicks are the most desirable, but if only half-minute or one-minute adjustments are available, the shooter will have to make do with them.[116]

---

[116] Some more expensive 'scopes now have eighth-minute-of-arc clicks.

The reticle or crosshair in the scope is another consideration. Again, the shooter may have to make do with whatever is available. However, if choices are available, here are some considerations. The simplest reticle is the plain crosshair, as in Figure 23-1. Unfortunately, a compromise is required in the thickness of the hairlines. They must not be so wide they obscure the target, but they must be wide enough that they can still be seen in low light or against a dark background. An improvement is the duplex reticle, as in Figure 23-2. This has wide hairlines near the edges of the scope, with thin ones at the center. The eye is drawn naturally to the center, but the outer ends of the lines are heavy enough to stand out even in low light or against a dark background. A further improvement over the duplex is the mil-dot reticle, as in Figure 23-3. In this reticle, the narrow portions of the hairlines have small dots superimposed on them. These are used for estimating range, which will be discussed later (in some 'scopes these marks are straight lines instead of dots).

Figure 23-1. Simple Crosshairs

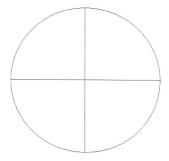

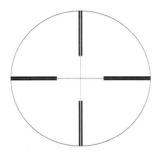

Figure 23-2. Duplex Reticle

Figure 23-3. Mil-Dot Reticle

Some 'scopes do not have crosshairs but have other types of markers. Russian-made 'scopes, in particular, use upward-pointing chevrons. The same considerations apply to them as to 'scopes with crosshairs.

There are now many 'scopes on the market that have "range-finding" reticles, which allow the user to estimate range by placing a pair of lines on a target of known size. Other 'scopes have multiple reticles. Once sighted in at a specific range, there are other horizontal lines that correspond to different ranges. This allows the shooter to "hold over" more precisely at long ranges, beyond that at which the rifle is sighted in. One such 'scope is described in the article by Gottfredson on Zeiss 'scopes.

Some 'scopes have so-called Bullet Drop Compensators (BDC) on them. These are adjustments like the click adjustments for elevation and windage, but they are calibrated for a specific cartridge. Once you have determined target range, you can "dial in" the range on the BDC, and the scope is sighted in for that range (it must, of course, be sighted in correctly at some range such as 100 yards before the BDC can be used at other ranges).

The bigger the objective lens (the one towards the target), the more light-gathering power the 'scope will have. Other things being equal, a bigger objective lens will allow sniping longer after sundown and sooner before sunup. However, the bigger the objective lens, the higher the 'scope must be mounted above the action. This can cause discomfort for the shooter, or even ruin consistency if the shooter does not get his cheek on the stock at the same place for each shot. Forty-millimeter objective lenses are standard today, but of course the shooter may not have any choice.

A useful addition to a telescopic sight is a leveling bubble, as in a carpenter's level. If the rifle is "canted" to left or right, even very slightly, this will throw the shot off. Some sights have internal bubbles, but external bubbles can be added if the telescope does not have an internal one. Either kind can help the shooter avoid canting the rifle, by keeping the bubble centered.

While a big objective lens is helpful at dawn and dusk, the crosshairs still may not be visible if there is not sufficient light. Some 'scopes have battery-operated illumination for the crosshairs. This can be very helpful at dawn and dusk, but batteries have the habit of failing just when you need them. If the shooter's 'scope needs batteries, the time to stock up is before the shooting starts. Even after the batteries fail, of course, the crosshairs are still useful in brighter conditions.

Two further items need mention: lens caps and lens hoods. When the rifle is not actually in use, some form of cap should be placed over both objective lens and eyepiece. This is to keep dust off the lenses, and help prevent them from being scratched. It also protects the crosshairs from being damaged if the objective lens faces the sun. The sunlight will be focused directly on the crosshairs and may melt them or burn them. A lens hood is simply a long tube that fits over the telescope at the objective end. It is intended to keep the sun from reflecting off the objective lens and thereby giving away the sniper's position. The hood should be at least as long as the diameter of the objective lens. Even with a hood, however, *if the sun is visible through the telescope, the sun will reflect off the objective lens and the reflection will be visible from the location of the target.* As soon as the sniper takes up his position, the lens caps should be removed, and a lens hood installed.

One further consideration is "eye relief." This is the maximum distance the shooter's eye can be behind the telescope and still see the entire image. Eye relief is important because the rifle will recoil when fired. If the shooter's head is too close to the 'scope, recoil will cause the 'scope to bang into the shooter's head. A cut on the forehead, or even damage to the eyeball, is possible. Eye relief of 3 inches is typical of good rifle 'scopes. When the 'scope is mounted on the rifle, it should be placed so that the shooter's eye is far enough back to take advantage of the full eye relief available from the 'scope.

Mounting the 'scope on the rifle so that it doesn't move or change zero is important. The article by van Zwoll has some practical advice on 'scope mounting. One trick target shooters find useful is to put rubber cement on the inside of the 'scope rings and let it become tacky before placing the 'scope in the rings. The screws should then be tightened down, but not so much that they distort the 'scope. An inch-pound torque wrench is useful in getting the right tension on the mounting screws.

Spotting 'Scopes

In addition to the 'scope on the rifle, the sniper needs another 'scope for spotting targets. The rifle 'scope is not suited for locating targets. The field of view is too narrow. Searching for a target would be like looking through a soda straw. A spotting 'scope is needed for target spotting. Most spotting 'scopes have variable power. The lower the power, the wider the field of view. Once a possible target is located, the power can be increased to make positive identification. If the sniper is being assisted by a spotter, the spotter then guides the sniper to the target by identifying landmarks near the target that the sniper can see through the rifle 'scope. The article by Gottfredson gives information about spotting 'scopes. The caveats about lens caps and lens hoods apply just as much to spotting 'scopes as to rifle 'scopes.

Mirage

The atmosphere is rarely still and uniform. If the air is being warmed by the sun, its density may vary. This causes the light rays coming from the target to bend, causing the target image to be displaced from the true location.[117] The bullet, not being affected by mirage, will go where aimed, at the phantom target instead of the real one. If the wind is blowing from the side, the phantom target will be displaced downwind. If the wind is from behind the shooter, the phantom target will be displaced above the true one. In a turbulent wind, the target may appear to dance about, even when the gun is held still. A skilled shooter can use the mirage, as seen through the 'scope, to estimate wind direction and velocity. The article by Gottfredson on optical illusions explains mirage.

Range

If a .308 rifle using match ammunition (Federal 168-grain boat-tail hollow-point (BTHP)) is sighted in at 100 yards, the bullet will have dropped nearly 16 inches below the point of aim at a range of 300 yards, and will be 105 inches low at 600 yards. This emphasizes the importance of knowing the range to the target.

The best way of determining range to the target is use of a laser rangefinder. This operates like an optical radar. The instrument sends an infrared pulse to the target and measures the "out and back" time of the pulse. This can be directly converted into distance,

---

[117] This is responsible for the apparent appearance of water puddles, or "mirages," on roads on warm days. The atmosphere nearest the road is less dense than the atmosphere just a few inches higher, causing light from the sky to bend.

which is then displayed on a digital readout. Ranges out to 1500 yards are readable, depending on the instrument. Most laser rangefinders are advertised as being accurate to within one meter. The big drawback to a laser rangefinder is that unless the shooter obtains one "while the getting is good," it will not be available when the shooting starts. A lesser drawback is that they do require batteries to operate, and these may not be available when needed. Again, a reason for stockpiling in advance.

Next best after a laser rangefinder is the optical "split image" rangefinder. This is essentially a pair of telescopes mounted on some kind of base. The two images, one from each telescope, are presented to the shooter's eye. They are not lined up, because each telescope is "looking" from a slightly different position. The shooter turns a dial that adjusts a mirror until the two images are aligned. A scale then gives range to the target. These devices are easy to use, and don't require batteries. Some high-precision ones are good out to 1000 yards. Others, lighter and of lesser precision, are good to lesser distances. You need to know the capabilities of the unit you are using.

Neither the laser rangefinder nor the split-image rangefinder require the shooter to know anything about the target. They measure distance directly. Many telescopic sights include scales on the reticle that allow the shooter to estimate the range to a target of known size.

The most common of these scales is the "mil dot" reticle mentioned above, shown in Figure 23-3. A mil is a measure of angle. An object one yard in length at a range of 1000 yards subtends an angle of one mil. A six-foot-tall man standing straight subtends 2 mils at 1000 yards and 4 mils at 500 yards.

In a typical mil-dot 'scope, the mil dots are ¾ mils wide and their centers are one mil apart. The shooter can use this information to estimate the range to a target of known size. For instance, if a man known to be six feet tall subtends an angle of 4 mils, he is 500 yards away. The mil dots can thus be used as a scale to estimate range to a target of known size. Even if the target is of unknown size, some nearby object (truck, tank, rifle) of known size can be used to estimate the range to the target.

If the target dimension is known, and the number of mils the target subtends is known from the 'scope reticle, range to the target can be calculated as:

$$\text{Range in yards} = \frac{\text{Target dimension (inches)} \times 1000}{\text{Target size (mils)} \times 36}$$

A calculator can be used to solve this equation readily, once the two unknowns (target dimension and target size) are known.[118] However, a slide-rule type of device, the "Mildot Master," simplifies the task. The sniper simply aligns the target size in inches with the number of mil-dots the target subtends in the 'scope, and reads off the range.[119]

If a duplex reticle is all that is available, even this can be used to estimate range. The thin portions of the crosshairs (right to left or top to bottom) on a Leupold Duplex telescope are ten minutes of arc wide when magnification is set to ten power. This corresponds to ten inches at 100 yards, twenty inches at 200 yards, etc. If an object you estimate to be ten inches wide just fills the space between the thicker sections of the crosshairs, you know it is 100 yards away. Other telescopic sights, at other powers, may be different. However, you can determine the angular separation on your telescope by sighting on an object of known width (or height) at a known distance. Once you know the angular separation of the thick portions of the crosshairs, you can quickly estimate the range of any object of known size.

If your sight has no reticle marks (simple crosshair, for instance), it is still possible to estimate range. Picture football (or soccer) fields laid end to end between you and the target. The range

---

[118] A useful practice is to prepare a "cheat sheet" of common objects, such as truck tire rims, enemy rifle lengths, etc., and the number of mils they subtend at different ranges. This should be laminated and carried with the rifle.
[119] More information about mil-dots can be found in the article by Fortier.

estimate will be crude, but it will be better than nothing. Another method is to use a map, especially a topographic map. Identify your location and the target's location on the map, and measure the distance between the two. Locate the target with reference to landmarks you can identify on the map, such as hills or other landforms, bends in rivers, etc. A topographic map is best for this purpose, since the landforms are clearly shown. (For more on topographic maps see the chapter on Land Navigation.)

Uphill/Downhill shooting

Whether the shooter uses a BDC, ballistic tables, or some other means of adjusting the 'scope for range, all the computations are based on the assumption that the target is on the same level as the shooter. In shooting uphill or downhill, a correction factor is needed. The amount by which a bullet drops depends only on the *horizontal* distance to the target. If the target is above or below the shooter, the *slant range* to the target, as measured by the range finder, is greater than the horizontal distance. The measured or estimated slant range must be reduced to the actual horizontal range, and that used as the basis for adjusting the scope. It does not matter whether the target is uphill or downhill, the same adjustment factor is used. The following table was originally published by the National Rifle Association in *The American Rifleman*. It was reprinted in *Shooting Times* for February 2002, p. 76.

Uphill/Downhill Slant Multipliers	
Slope Angle (Degrees)	Slant Range Multiplier
5	.99
10	.98
15	.96
20	.94
25	.91
30	.87
35	.82
40	.77
45	.70

If the slant range to the target is 200 yards, and the target is uphill (or downhill) at a slope of 20 degrees, the range used for setting the sights would be 0.94 x 200 = 188 yards. If the rifle-cartridge combination is fairly flat shooting, and the slope is not very steep, this correction can be ignored for shooting at enemy troops. For precision shooting at something like a tank vision block, however, this correction is essential.

Note that the Mil-dot Master, mentioned above as an aid to range-finding, includes a separate scale for correcting the range when the uphill or downhill slope is known. It also incorporates a scale, to be used with a weighted string, to estimate the uphill or downhill slope in degrees.

Laser rangefinders are available that incorporate compensation for angle. However, these may not be available where you are, and in any case are more expensive than rangefinders that lack this capability. If one is available, however, it can greatly simplify getting the range to target right.

Wind

A crosswind can significantly affect the flight of the bullet. A crosswind of 10 miles per hour will cause a .308 bullet to drift nearly 14 inches to the side by the time it reaches a target 400 yards away. This is a moderate wind, and as military sniping ranges go, not a very long range shot. Nevertheless, the drift is enough to cause a bullet aimed at the center of a soldier's chest to drift completely off the target. Thus obtaining wind speed is very important.

Various hand-held instruments are available for measuring wind speed. However, they measure wind at the sniper's location. If the sniper is hidden below a ridge or in the midst of some trees, the wind there might not be representative of the wind nearer the target. Most important is the wind between the sniper and the target. Next most important is the wind at the target. Wind at the sniper's location is least important unless it is representative of the wind between the sniper and the target.

Wind speed can be estimated by observing its effect on objects. At 2 to 5 mph, grass is agitated. At 3 mph wind can be felt on the face. At 5 to 8 mph, leaves are agitated continuously. At 8 to 12 mph, loose paper blows around. At 12 to 15 mph, small trees sway. By observing the wind's effects near the target and in the intervening distance, the shooter is better able to determine the wind speed.

Note that it is the crosswind that blows a bullet off course. A headwind or tailwind will have virtually no effect on the bullet. A wind at an angle to the line of sight to the target will have its effect reduced accordingly. For instance, a wind at forty-five degrees to the line of sight has only seventy percent of the effect of a wind at ninety degrees (full crosswind). Thus wind direction as well as wind speed must be determined, and the angle between wind and bullet direction taken into account. Tables for determining wind effect can be found in the book by Plaster. The shooter should copy onto a card the table for the specific ammunition he is using and carry the card with him. Note that in calculating wind drift, the actual *slant range* should be used, if shooting uphill or downhill, rather than the horizontal range used for calculating bullet drop. This is because the bullet actually travels that slant range distance, giving the wind that much opportunity to work on it.

Since a headwind or tailwind will not significantly affect the bullet, one possibility for the sniper may be to move to a location from which he is shooting upwind or downwind. If this is possible, it may be better than trying to estimate wind angle and the crosswind component of the wind. Even a move that reduces the crosswind component will help. If moving is not possible, then the sniper will have to factor in the effects of wind as well as effects of range.

More information about the effects of wind, including the effects of "mirage" on displacing the apparent position of the target, can be found in the CD-ROM "Winning In The Wind."

The sniper should not depend on calculating the effects of range and wind in the field. Too much can go wrong. The sniper should prepare a small card with the trajectory characteristics of the ammunition being used, and the precision of the 'scope adjustments. For instance, if the rifle is sighted in at 100 yards, the card should give the number of "clicks" up required at various greater ranges.

Cards computed for specific ammunition are available commercially. One such is the Ballisticard™ shown in Figure 23-4.

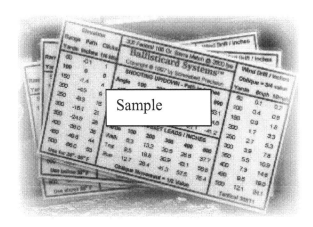

Figure 23-4. Ballisticard for a specific ammunition and rifle barrel length combination. Set of three for different temperatures. (From the Ballisticard web site.)

Sighting in

Sighting in is the process of adjusting the sights so that the point of aim coincides with the point of impact. Ultimately, this can be done only by actual firing. However, there are some ways to cut down the amount of shooting needed.

At what range should the rifle be sighted? In principle, the sniper should sight in his rifle at approximately the same range at which he expects to engage targets. However, this may not always be possible. The firing range available for sighting in may not have the length needed between firing point and target. Thus it may be necessary to sight in at a shorter range, and adjust the 'scope for known bullet drop at other ranges.

If possible, the shooter should get the rifle nearly sighted in before firing. There are several ways to do this.

Boresighting involves removing the bolt from the rifle and mounting the rifle firmly on some rest. Even a sandbag is good enough for this. Sight through the barrel at some small object at least 100 yards away. Then, without allowing the rifle to move, adjust the windage and elevation knobs on the telescope so that the crosshairs appear right on the object. At worst, the point of impact will be only a few inches off the point of aim when live rounds are fired.

Laser boresighters are now available to simplify sighting in. Some fit into the rifle's chamber, while others mount on a stud that is fitted into the muzzle. In either case, the laser projects a dot on the target. The windage and elevation knobs are adjusted until the crosshairs fall on the projected dot.

Once the rifle has been boresighted, the next step is firing shots at a target. Here it helps to have the assistance of a spotter. However, the shooter can do this alone if necessary. A spotting telescope is almost essential for this task. However, the procedure is simple. The crosshairs are placed on the target's aimpoint and a shot is fired. Note that a round "bullseye" is not the best choice of aimpoint. Much better is a colored square of at least one minute of angle size (e.g., a one-inch square at 100 yards). The crosshairs should be placed on one corner of the square, so that the square fits neatly into one of the quadrants formed by the crosshairs. Alternatively, the aimpoint may be diamond-shaped. The crosshairs should then be positioned to go through the "corners" of the diamond. If possible, the target should have a one-inch grid to allow ready measurement of the error.

If the shooter is being assisted by a spotter, the spotter should tell the direction and magnitude of the error (e.g., the shot was three inches low and two inches to the right). The windage and elevation knobs should then be adjusted to correct for the error. That is, if the shot was three inches low at 100 yards, the elevation should be brought up three minutes of angle (e.g., 12 quarter-minute clicks, 6 half-minute clicks, etc.) Once the adjustments are made, another shot is fired. This process is kept up until the point of aim coincides with the point of impact. [120]

Note that if the shooter doesn't have anyone to act as a spotter, he can make his own observations using a spotting 'scope. If the shooter doesn't have a spotting 'scope, there is no alternative but to walk down to the target after each shot and determine the error. The rifle 'scope is probably not adequate for observing the error. At a maximum power of ten, there is not enough magnification to get a good measure of the error at 100 yards. The spotting scope should be at least 30-power, and 50-power is better.

Once point of aim consistently equals point of impact, or the group is centered on point of aim, the rifle is sighted in at that distance. To use it at other distances, adjustments must be made. If the 'scope has a Bullet Drop Compensator, the adjustments are easy. Otherwise the shooter must "crank in" the appropriate corrections, based on knowledge of the bullet's trajectory, that is, of how much it drops or rises at distances other than the distance at which it was

---

[120] A device call the "AccuScope" can be helpful in this process. It amounts to a slide rule in which the shooter sets the range of the target and the miss distance in inches. The user then reads directly the number of "clicks" to move the 'scope. The device can be had for 'scopes with 1/8", ¼" or ½" clicks. It simplifies the calculations for the shooter.

sighted in (the bullet will be "high" at shorter distances, and "low" at longer distances).

The rifle should be sighted in again any time there is a significant change in conditions. A major change in temperature might justify re-sighting. Changing to a different lot of ammunition almost certainly will require re-sighting. The sniper can have confidence in his rifle only when he knows that it has been sighted in properly, and nothing significant has changed since then.

Software
Several manufacturers sell software that can be used with a Personal Digital Assistant (PDA), to calculate sight adjustments for range, wind, temperature, etc. Horus (www.horusvision.com) sells software that comes on an SD chip that can be plugged directly into the handheld device. It isn't necessary to upload or install the software. Horus sells three grades of software -- Sporting, Professional, and Advanced -- at differing prices. If the proper PDA is available to you, and you can obtain the software, sight corrections "in the field" can be made rapidly.

Fifty-Caliber Rifles
The recent availability of 50-caliber rifles has added to the sniper's capability. Targets can now include even lightly-armored vehicles. The "bullet-proof car" of a ruler or a wealthy individual is no longer proof against the sniper armed with one of these weapons. The 50-caliber rifle also extends the range at which the sniper can engage a target. If other conditions permit, a sniper can stand off at 2 kilometers or more and still make an effective shot. If one of these weapons can be obtained, it would be an important contribution to the sniper's armory.

The sniper's location
One of Murphy's Laws of Combat is, "If the enemy is in range, so are you." For the sniper, that is revised to, "If the target is in line of sight, so are you." That is, if the sniper can see the target, the target can (in principle) see the sniper. That is why the sniper must operate from concealment.

The chapter on Camouflage has more to say on this, but some points should be considered. The sniper should be dressed to blend in with the surroundings. To the extent possible, the sniper should be in a "hide" of some sort (in a "spider hole," behind a barrier, etc.) that provides concealment from the direction of the target. It is even better if the concealment also provides cover, i.e., is capable of stopping return fire.

The sniper hide should be located so that there is an adequate view of the entire area to be covered (e.g., no foliage masking part of the area, etc.). The hide should be located so that the sniper has a concealed line of retreat, since after his first shot he may become a target for enemy snipers or even enemy artillery. Since the sniper may occupy the hide for a considerable time, it should avoid things that would make it very uncomfortable, such as soggy ground or anthills. In urban areas, the sniper should beware of hot tar on roofs, of stones or broken glass on roofs, and of snow and ice. If at all possible, the sniper should put a tarpaulin or something similar down in front of the hide, to keep muzzle blast from kicking up dust that would give away his position. However, the ground cloth itself must be chosen so that it blends in with the surroundings. Otherwise the appearance of a patch of cloth of the wrong color will give away the sniper's position. The book by Idriess goes into great detail on the need for sniper camouflage.

Cords, rubber bands, strips of inner tube, double-sided hook-and-loop tape, and so on can be used to hold vegetation on the sniper's weapon (*never on the barrel*), clothing, pack, headgear, etc. Vegetation used should match that at the site where the sniper is hiding. However, it should not be picked from that site. That will denude the site and give away the sniper's location. The vegetation should be picked as the sniper approaches the hide or site, and brought in.

The sniper himself
The most important quality of a sniper is that he must be a predator. Being accurate on the firing range is a necessary but not sufficient condition. He must be willing to wait patiently, for hours if necessary, without growing bored or letting his attention wander.

He must not be in too great a hurry for a kill, but must patiently stalk his target.

The sniper's work is different from that of other soldiers. The sniper must have the courage to be alone, perhaps with only a team-mate, instead of having the moral support of comrades around him. He must be willing to put up with hardships, including but not limited to having insects crawl over him, the sun bake him, the rain soak him, and having no place to urinate or defecate except his own hiding-place, and maybe his own trousers.

The sniper must not hate the enemy but respect him as a quarry, just as a deer hunter respects rather than hates his quarry. Hate or revenge will warp his judgment, which must remain calm so his actions can be deliberate. The sniper must take the attitude that he is doing an important job, and saving the lives of his comrades who are somewhere else.

Finally, the sniper must be psychologically capable of shooting "up close and personal," even though the target is really hundreds of yards away. As one sniper put it, "when you look through a scope, the first thing you see is the eyes. There is a lot of difference between shooting at a shadow, shooting at an outline, and shooting at a pair of eyes. It is amazing that when you put the scope on somebody, the first thing that pops out at you is the eyes. Many men can't do it at that point." (quoted in Latimer, p. 45).

Sniper tactics

As noted above, the sniper's target may be a random enemy soldier who comes within view. However, to be most effective, the sniper should be seeking high-value targets such as the enemy's chain of command, or critical pieces of equipment. Exact tactics will depend on the circumstances. Key to all sniper tactics, however, is the idea that the sniper *must* operate at long distance from enemy forces. The sniper's rifle has much more range than the typical assault rifles or submachine guns utilized by the enemy's main forces. The sniper, then, should remain *out of range* of these weapons, while employing his own rifle to shoot enemy soldiers.

Ambushes

The most frequent operation of resistance forces will probably be ambushes. The main body of ambush troops will be firing at close range. It is a waste of sniper capability to place the sniper with the assault force in the ambush site. Instead, the sniper should be used to isolate the ambush zone by watching for and firing on enemy reaction forces, to fire at enemy troops fleeing the ambush kill zone, and to provide flank security for the ambush force. Once the ambush force begins to withdraw, the sniper should provide covering fire to slow down any enemy forces pursuing the ambush force. In this operation, the sniper(s) must be *part of* the ambush force, but not be *located* with it.

Raids

As in ambushes, the sniper(s) will not take part in the raid itself. They will instead be positioned to isolate the target by slowing down enemy reaction forces, and to provide covering fire for the retreating raiding party. Again, the snipers must be part of the raiding party, but not take part in attacking the raid objective itself.

River crossings

Snipers can be very effective in providing cover for river crossing operations. They stay behind while the main force crosses the river. Once a secure position is held on the opposite bank, the snipers can cross. However, if this is the only use of snipers in the whole operation, their special skills may be wasted.

Independent operations

Very few snipers are truly "independent."[121] Sniping must fit into some overall tactical scheme. The sniper, even when not

---

[121] Historically, there are exceptions. Jack Hinson conducted a one-man sniping war against Union forces during the American Civil War. For months he hid in a forest and sniped at Union riverboats passing on the Tennessee River. While he achieved well over one hundred kills, and occupied the efforts of up to nine regiments that hunted for him, his efforts had no effect on the flow of Union ship traffic on the Tennessee. Moreover, because he had no contact with Confederate forces, he could not provide them with what he learned about the timing and nature of Union ship movements. See the book by McKenney.

operating with a larger unit, will have been assigned some objective to be achieved. The most common forms of these independent operations are the sniper ambush, the sniper raid, and harassment.

In the sniper ambush, the sniper team is the entire ambush force. The team locates its hide a suitable distance from a route that enemy forces are expected to follow, or from some natural feature that will attract them (water hole, river crossing, etc.). If the sniper team sets itself up at 500 to 600 yards from a route the enemy is expected to use, it will be out of range of assault rifles and submachine guns. It can then fire at the first suitable enemy unit passing by. If the action is taking place in an area where water is scarce, a "water hole" might be a suitable natural feature to attract enemy forces, and thereby provide the snipers with targets. As with any ambush, however, once it is sprung the ambushing force must depart or it will be overwhelmed by enemy reaction forces.

In the sniper raid, the snipers position themselves outside the perimeter of some enemy installation and fire on either enemy personnel, preferably of high rank, or on enemy equipment that can be disabled by a few shots, such as aircraft engines or helicopter turbines. Once the objective is achieved, the snipers must withdraw before enemy reaction forces can pin them down.

In a harassing action, a sniper team will "shadow" an enemy unit that is making a sweep. The sniper team will stay completely out of range most of the time, but once or twice a day will approach within sniping range of the enemy unit, shoot one enemy soldier, then withdraw again. The key issue here is that the unit being shadowed must not be allowed to overwhelm the sniper team. The object is to slow down the unit, lower the troops' morale, and hinder the enemy unit in accomplishing its mission.

Intelligence gathering

By virtue of its operation, whether in an overwatch mode when accompanying a larger unit, or when operating independently, the sniper team is in an excellent position to gather information about the enemy units within its field of view. Numbers, equipment, direction of movement, and other details can be observed and reported to higher command either immediately or when the sniper team's mission is completed. This intelligence gathering activity is *always* part of the sniper team's mission, regardless of what other objectives it has been assigned. The resistance forces must plan for and be prepared to use this information promptly.

Sniper Training

Some successful snipers have succeeded without formal training. Vasily Zaitsev, the famous Russian sniper at Stalingrad, was a skilled hunter before being drafted into the Soviet Army. However, he essentially trained himself in tactical sniping skills after his arrival in Stalingrad. Nevertheless, formal training gives the sniper a better chance of surviving and being effective than does learning the hard way.

Pre-Resistance Training

Prior to initiating armed resistance, potential snipers can be encouraged to join gun clubs, hunting clubs, and marksmanship teams, to the extent that these organizations are legal. These activities provide familiarization with firearms. This can be particularly important for urban dwellers. They also give the sniper trainee the chance to receive instruction from experts, and to practice with his firearm. This training must include not only marksmanship (sight picture, trigger management, "doping the wind," reading mirage, etc.) but camouflage, target selection, and target stalking.

Post-Resistance Training

Once resistance has begun, the opportunity to use civilian gun clubs and marksmanship teams may no longer exist. Officers in the Resistance organization must be prepared to select recruits who appear to be better-than-average shots and put them through sniper training. This selection may be possible only after the fighter has demonstrated his capabilities in actual combat.

The exigencies of combat may preclude long training courses. Therefore the training must be intensive. The "washout" rate may necessarily be high. Nevertheless, efforts must be made to select potential snipers, withdraw them from regular activities, and put them through sniper training. At least it will not be necessary to disguise the training, as it would be if the trainees were pretending be sport shooters and hunters.

Clandestine Training

If the Resistance does not control any "liberated" territory in which training can take place, or if civilian marksmanship activities are illegal, it will be necessary to conduct clandestine training for snipers under the noses of the authorities. This will be particularly true if the Resistance is operating primarily in urban areas (see below).

Many marksmanship skills (sighting, trigger management, breathing) can be practiced using airsoft rifles, BB-guns, and pellet rifles. These skills transfer to sniper rifles fairly easily. Moreover, they can be practiced quietly in basements, garages, warehouses, etc. Other skills, such as range estimation and "doping the wind" can be practiced without a rifle. Camouflage and preparing sniper "hides" can likewise be practiced without a rifle. Even stalking a target can be practiced without a rifle.[122] There are also "first-person shooter" games that offer the player the opportunity to learn sniper tactics. However, these skills must be "confirmed" occasionally by actual live firing if the sniper is to have confidence in his own ability to hide, hit a target, and escape.

The important point is that even if sniper training must be conducted clandestinely, there are ways to do it.

Urban Sniping

Most discussion of sniping occurs in the context of a conventional battlefield, with snipers taking long-distance shots. However, with the increasing urbanization of the world, more and more combat is taking place in urban areas. From Stalingrad through Sarajevo, Grozny, and Baghdad, urban sniping is becoming more and more important. It differs from battlefield sniping in several important respects.

---

[122] Use a camera to simulate taking a shot.

The Urban Sniper Rifle

In a built-up area, the opportunity for a long-distance shot is very rare. Thus there is less need for an intrinsically accurate rifle. A rifle that would be inadequate for battlefield sniping at 500 yards might well be "good enough" at 100 yards. This fact greatly increases the number of rifles that can be considered suitable for urban sniping.

Another consideration is that the rifle to be used for urban sniping must lend itself to concealment while it is being transported to the sniper's hide. Collapsible or folding stock, shorter barrel, or even "take-down" capability are features that become important.

The Sniper Hide

Instead of a spider hole or similar type of hide, the urban sniper will be firing from inside an apartment, from a rooftop, or from some elevated site such as a tower. Concealment means staying out of sight. In an apartment, for instance, the sniper will darken the room, stay well back from the window through which he is shooting, and perhaps even drape a fine mesh fabric across the room. The sniper can see through it, but it blocks the view of anyone from outside. Choosing an apartment or office in a large building, with many windows, will make it more difficult for counter-snipers to locate the actual room used by the sniper.

Instead of using an apartment as a site, the urban sniper may instead use a car, van or truck that has been fitted as a mobile sniper's hide: windows obscured, a firing port in the back, interior lined with mattresses to deaden the sound of the shot, etc. The vehicle is simply one among many on the street, and provides a ready means of escape once the shot has been taken.

Flash Hiders & Sound Suppressors

When a sniper takes a long-range shot on an open battlefield, muzzle flash and the sound of firing are of little significance. In urban sniping, however, they become critical. Muzzle flash and sound will give away the sniper's position. It becomes very important to suppress these giveaways. In many countries, owning sound suppressors (so-called "silencers") is either illegal or highly restricted. The Resistance will have to manufacture them for its urban snipers. Some of the references give instructions on making them. Any well-equipped machine shop or automotive repair shop should be capable of turning them out.

Camouflage

The urban sniper doesn't depend on ghillie suits and similar camouflage while in his hide. He depends on camouflage while going to and from the site from which he takes his shot. While proceeding to the site, and while escaping afterwards, he must blend in with the other people on the street. He wants to look like part of the crowd, despite the fact he may be carrying a concealed rifle.[123] Moreover, he will want to have his face obscured by a billed cap, sunglasses, or some other means. The sniper must look perfectly ordinary on his way to and from the site for the shot.

Forensics/Counter-Forensics

On the battlefield, countering a sniper means using spotters and counter-snipers to watch for snipers. Once the sniper is located, a counter-sniper may take a shot, or artillery or air support may be called in to eliminate the sniper. A key difference between urban sniping and battlefield sniping is that the urban sniper attempts to hide among the people in the city where he plies his trade, rather than returning to territory controlled by his forces.

Countering the urban sniper calls for entirely different tactics. The government forces must use what are essentially crime-detection methods. Instead of countering the sniper immediately, they must find ways of identifying the sniper afterwards, and linking him to the shooting.

In the aftermath of a sniping, the police will question bystanders about what they heard, whom they saw, and whether they saw anything out of the ordinary. The police will also use whatever they can obtain from surveillance cameras that may be near the site (ATMs, store parking lots, etc.). Seeing the same person leaving the

---

[123] Or alternatively, the rifle might be carried by a bearer who will deliver it to the site, so the sniper himself isn't carrying it.

site of several sniping incidents will help the police identify the sniper. In addition, the police will look for patterns in sniping incidents: same type of hide, same type of gun, same type of bullet, etc. This will help them anticipate future incidents.

When someone fires a gun, they are enveloped in a cloud of gun-shot residue: fine particles of unburned powder, metallic residue from the primer, etc. This residue will stick to clothing, hands, face, and hair, and will penetrate ears and nose. A sophisticated police force will be capable of detecting this residue on a suspected sniper. The urban sniper must counter this with proper cover. A ski mask over the head, a nylon stocking over the head, gloves, a raincoat, and similar covering will help reduce the residue on the body. Nose and ears must be washed out after shooting. Ideally, outer clothing should be burned after taking a shot. Otherwise, all clothing must be washed *by hand (not machine; residue will be trapped in the filters)*, and the washwater disposed of where the police cannot locate it (dump in a canal, pour down a storm drain well away from the sniper's home, etc.).

Police will attempt to match the bullet recovered from the victim to a rifle. Thus the sniper's rifle must be stored where it has no connection with the sniper. In addition, after use the rifle must be wiped down to remove fingerprints, skin fragments (DNA), and any clothing fibers that might link the rifle to the sniper. Even if the police find the rifle, then, it must be made difficult for them to connect it to a specific individual. The article by Vaughan describes additional forensic techniques (DNA on cigarette butts and water bottles, fingerprints) being used to identify bomb-makers in Iraq. Some of these same techniques can be used equally effectively against urban snipers.

The urban sniper, like the battlefield sniper, does not work alone. He is part of an organization that supplies him with ammunition, selects targets, provides information on when and where the target will be, provides transportation and other logistics, and generally provides support. The police will attempt to penetrate this organization. This can be countered only by cell-type organization, with strict need-to-know about the identity of the sniper(s). Even that, of course, is not a complete guarantee of safety for the sniper, but the fewer who know who he is, the better.

In short, just as battlefield sniping involves a great deal more than marksmanship, urban sniping does as well. The differences must be taken into account by a Resistance organization that conducts activities in urban areas.

Summary

Sniping is a difficult and challenging task. However, it can play an important role in the operations of the Resistance. Sniping operations can be more effective if the Resistance leadership plans for and takes advantage of the special capabilities of snipers.

References

Books

Anderson, Keith, *How to Build Practical Firearm Suppressors*, El Dorado, AR, Desert Publications, 1994.

Anderson, Keith, *How to Build Military Grade Suppressors*, El Dorado, AR, Desert Publications, 2000.

Anonymous, *How to Make a Silencer for a .45*, Boulder, CO, Paladin Press, 1995.

Avery, Ralph, *Combat Loads for the Sniper Rifle*, El Dorado, AR, Desert Publications, 1981 (much of the information on powders and bullets is dated, but the information on cartridge manufacture is still pertinent).

Balor, Paul, *Manual of the Mercenary Soldier*, Boulder, CO, Paladin Press, 1988.

Boone, Dan, *The Poor Man's Sniper Rifle*, El Dorado, AR, Desert Publications, 1995.

Department of the Army, *Sniper Training and Employment*, *TC 23-14*, June 1989.

Flores, J., *How To Make Disposable Silencers*, El Dorado, AR, Desert Publications, 1985.

Frankford Arsenal, *Silencers: Principles and Evaluations*, Report R-1896, 1968.

Gilbert, Adrian, *Stalk and Kill*, New York, St. Martin's, 1997.

Halberstadt, Hans, *Trigger Men*, New York, St. Martin's, ISBN 978-0-312-34572-5. (Covers sniper training, use of snipers, and includes essays by snipers regarding their experiences.)

Hayduke, George, *The Hayduke Silencer Book*, Boulder, CO, Paladin Press, 1989.

Hollenback, George M., *Workbench Silencers*, Boulder, CO, Paladin Press, 1996, ISBN 978-0-87364-895-0.

Hollenback, George M., *More Workbench Silencers*, Boulder, CO, Paladin Press, 1998, ISBN 978-0-86354-994-0.

Idriess, Ion L., *The Australian Guerilla: Sniping*, Boulder, CO, Paladin Press, 1978.

James, Anthony & Gabriel Suarez, *Guerrilla Sniper*, Prescott, AZ, Infidel Media Group, 2008, ISBN 978-0-9802036-3-9.

Lanning, Michael Lee, *Inside the Crosshairs: Snipers in Vietnam*, New York, Ivy Books, 1998.

LeBleu, Joe, *Long Rifle*, Guilford, CT, Lyons Press, ISBN 978-1-5921-440-5. (Memoirs of a sniper in Iraq.)

McBride, H. W., *A Rifleman Went to War*, Mt. Ida, AR, Lancer Militaria, 1987. (Snipers in WW I)

McKenney, Tom C., *Jack Hinson's One-Man War*, Gretna, LA, Pelican, 2009, ISBN 978-1-58980-640-5

Noblitt, Tony M. and Warren Gabrilska, *Dead On*, Boulder, CO, Paladin Press, 1998.

Nye, R. D., *The Handy Dandy Super Duper Junkyard Silencer Book*, Phoenix, AZ, Firing Pin Enterprises, 1992.

Paul, Don, *The Rifle Rules*, available from Paladin Press.

Pegler, Martin, *Out of Nowhere: A History of the Military Sniper*, New York, Osprey Publishing, 2006, ISBN 1-86403-140-0.

Plaster, Major John L., *The Ultimate Sniper*, Boulder, CO, Paladin Press, 1993.

Senich, Peter R., *The Long-Range War*, Boulder, CO, Paladin Press, 1994.

Shore, Captain C., *With British snipers to the Reich*, El Dorado, AZ, Desert Publications, 1988.

Sutkus, Bruno, *Sniper Ace*, London, Frontline Books, 2009, ISBN 978-1-84832-548-7. (The autobiography of a German sniper in WW II.)

U.S. Marine Corps, *Sniping*, El Dorado, AZ, Desert Publications, 1991.

U.S. Marine Corps, *Sniping, FMF1-3B*, Mt. Ida, AR, Lancer Militaria.

West, John, *Fry The Brain*, Countryside, VA, SSI, 2008, ISBN 978-0-9714133-9-9 (History of urban sniping)

Zaitsev, Vasily, (transl. David Givens, Peter Kornakov, Konstantin Kornakov) *Notes of a Sniper*, Los Angeles: 2826 Press Inc., ISBN 0615121489 (Zaitsev was a Russian sniper at Stalingrad. Some of the exploits reported in this book may have been exaggerated for Soviet propaganda purposes.)

Articles

Boddington, Craig, "Seven Steps to Accuracy," *Guns & Ammo*, September 2006, pp. 56 – 59.

Boddington, Craig, "The Essentials of Eye Relief," *Guns & Ammo*, September, 2003, pp. 46 – 48.

Fortier, David M., "Demystifying the Mil-Dot," *Guns & Ammo*, December 2005, pp. 39 – 45.

Fortier, David M., "Tactical Titans," *Rifleshooter*, May-June 2009, pp. 36 – 40. (A review of cartridges suitable for sniper use.)

Gottfredson, Jacob, "Can You See It?" *Guns & Ammo*, December, 2009, pp. 28 – 29.

Gottfredson, Jacob, "Optical Illusions," *Guns & Ammo*, October 2009, pp. 12 – 13.

Gottfredson, Jacob, "Optics – Zeiss Hits the Mark," *Guns Magazine*, September, 2008, pp. 22 – 24.

Jones, Allan, "The Reloader and the Ammo Factory," *Shooting Times*, April 2009, pp. 8 – 11. (Information on how to prepare and reload ammunition for consistency.)

Latimer, Jon, "Sniping in Vietnam," *Vietnam*, April 2000, pp. 38 – 47.

Pearce, Lane, "Bulletseating Depth Can Affect Accuracy," *Shooting Times*, April 2009, pp. 18 – 21. (Information on handloading cartridges for accuracy.)

Roberts, Craig, "Marine Scout Sniper," *Soldier of Fortune*, August 2004, pp. 36 – 40, 75.

Roberts, Craig, "A Poor Man's Sniper Rifle," *Soldier of Fortune*, October 2006, pp. 28 – 30. (Describes upgrading an inexpensive rifle to sniper quality.)

Scarlata, Paul, "White Death," *Guns & Ammo*, November 2008, pp. 58 – 64. (The story of Simo Hayha, a Finnish sniper who killed numerous Russians during the "Winter War" of 1939 – 1940.)

Simpson, Layne, "To Bed a Rifle," *Shooting Times*, April 2009, pp. 44 – 49.

Stoppelman, Scott, "Glass Bedding Your Rifle," *Gun World*, May 2006, pp. 30 – 36.

Sundra, Jon R., "Rx for Rifles," *RifleShooter*, July/August 2008, pp. 34 – 38.

Sweeney, Patrick, "Is It Bed Time," *Guns & Ammo*, July 2007, pp. 50 – 53. (Glass bedding a rifle.)

Towsley, Bryce M., Glass Bedding a Rifle Stock, Part 1," *The American Rifleman*, June 2006, pp. 54 – 55. Part 2, *The American Rifleman*, July 2006, pp. 48 – 49.

Towsley, Bryce M., "How to Shorten and Crown a .22 LR Rifle Barrel," *American Rifleman*, September, 2006, p. 84 – 85.

Tubb, David, "Don't Be So Dense," *Rifleshooter*, September/October 2009, pp. 20 – 21. (Effects of density altitude on bullet trajectory)

Vaughan, Don, "CSI:Iraq," *Military Officer*, February, 2010, pp. 58 – 63.

Van Zwoll, Wayne, "Mount Up," *Rifle Shooter*, January/February 2008, pp. 24 – 25.

Van Zwoll, Wayne, "Scoped Out," *Guns & Ammo*, December 2008, pp. 46 – 50. (Information on how to mount a 'scope to a rifle.)

Van Zwoll, Wayne, "Shifting Viewpoints, *Rifleshooter*, September/October 2009, pp. 14 – 15. (Correcting a 'scope for parallax)

Videos

The Art of Camouflage. Documentary Recordings, P.O. Box 99788, San Diego, CA 92169, http://www.militaryrecordings.com The title is misleading. This video is actually about the construction of woodland ghillie suits for snipers. For that it's very good, but it doesn't cover other aspects of camouflage.

CD-ROMs

"Snipers," historical review of sniping. Available from International Historic Films (www.HistoricVideos.com).

"The German Sniper: The Invisible Enemy," copy of a 1944 German Army sniper training film, English subtitles. Available from International Historic Films (www.HistoricVideos.com).

Wigger, Lones & Lanny Gassham, "Winning in the Wind," available from www.askachampion.com. (The two "authors" are Olympic shooting champions.)

Equipment

AccuScope, available from several suppliers. www.accuscopeusa.com

Ballisticard Systems, available from Schwiebert Precision, PO Box 74, Atascadero, CA 93423, USA, http://www.ballisticard.com.

Web Sites

http://www.riflewarrior.com

http://www.snipercountry.com

http://demigodllc.com/articles/practical-long-range-rifle-shooting-equipment/

http://demigodllc.com/articles/practical-long-range-rifle-shooting-optics/

http://demigodllc.com/articles/practical-long-range-rifle-shooting-shooting/

Chapter 24

Assassination

What is assassination?

By assassination is meant the intentional targeting of a specific individual selected in advance. On the battlefield, a sniper targets a specific individual. However, that individual is a target of opportunity. The sniper did not come to the battle intending to target that particular individual. The assassin, by contrast, picks a target, then attempts to put himself in a position to kill that target.

Assassination has a long history as a revolutionary act. The assassination of the Archduke Ferdinand, which served as the trigger for World War I, was intended as a revolutionary action. Tsar Nicholas II was assassinated by a group of revolutionary anarchists. In numerous other cases, assassination has been considered an important part of revolution. Perhaps the classical example is the assassination of Julius Caesar by his colleague Brutus.

Justification for Assassinating a Leader

Is the mere fact of tyranny just cause? Jefferson wrote, "rebellion to tyrants is obedience to God." Unfortunately, very few people today would accept Jefferson as a moral arbiter, and Jefferson's own statement about "separation of church and state" has become a mantra for denying God's relevance to political affairs. John Adams wrote, "The right of a nation to kill a tyrant *in case of necessity* [emphasis added] can be no more doubted than to hang a robber, or kill a flea." Unfortunately, Adams' statement begs the question. What constitutes "necessity?"

Nevertheless, the issue seems clear enough. A tyrant who is responsible for crimes against the people cannot be brought to trial, and it seems absurd to deny the victims of the tyrant any recourse at all. Surely, one would argue, Adolph Hitler, Josef Stalin, Pol Pot, Idi Amin, Saddam Hussein, and a host of others, gave their subjects just cause for assassination. There can be just cause for assassinating a tyrant, but the decision cannot be taken lightly.

Assassinating the Leader

While assassination can be effective in reducing the power of a government, it may not be a very effective way of replacing a tyrannical government. In particular, it may not result in replacing the "Party of Tyranny" with anyone from the Resistance.

Some historical examples make the same point. One might argue that had Hitler been assassinated in the late 1930s, a great deal of grief would have been avoided. This is probably true, but it represents a special case. Hitler had already eliminated all potential Nazi rivals for his position. He had surrounded himself with weaklings who could not have carried on his policies.[124] Had he died or been assassinated, he would most likely have been replaced soon, not by another Nazi, but by one of the strong men from the opposition, who in fact did take power after 1945.

Had Lenin been assassinated before his actual death, probably the only effect would have been to hasten the rise to power of Stalin. While Stalin did eventually attempt to eliminate potential rivals among the "Old Bolsheviks," the fact is that his successors did attempt to continue his policies. The Gulags continued in operation, "wars of national liberation" flared up, and additional countries came under Communist rule. Stalin did not eliminate all the strong men around him. Indeed, Mikhail Gorbachev, the final Premier of the Soviet Union, is at this writing still a major player on the world scene, giving evidence of his own strength. Assassinating Stalin would only have hastened the rise to power of one of the Communists who in fact did succeed him.

Likewise, had Mao been assassinated before his actual death, he would have been replaced by one of the people who actually did ascend to power after Mao's death, and who continued Mao's policies of repression. The massacre at Tianenmen Square, for instance, was carried out under the orders of one of Mao's successors.

---

[124] Davidson describes the twenty-two top Nazis tried at Nuremberg. For the most part, they were not even just "ordinary" but incredibly dull people.

In short, assassination of the top tyrant is not only a difficult thing to carry out, it probably will not advance the strategic goals of the Resistance. Replacing one tyrant with another tyrant of the same stripe is not a very effective way of restoring freedom.

The Historical Record

The historical record is mixed: many successful assassinations, but little beneficial effect.

In Russia, the assassination of Alexander II had no significant effect on Russian policy. Alexander III simply took over. The Social Revolutionary Party, active in the first part of the 20th century, had a very successful record of assassinations of Russian government officials:

- 1903 – 3;
- 1904 – 2;
- 1905 – 54;
- 1906 – 82;
- 1907 – 71;
- 1908 – 3;
- 1909 – 2;
- 1910 – 1;
- 1911 – 1 (Peter Stolypin).

Creating this pile of corpses had no effect whatsoever on Russian policy, except for the crushing of the Social Revolutionary Party by the Tsarist government. Indeed, Alexander Solzhenitsyn argues (in his novel *August 1914*) that the assassination of Stolypin was a catastrophic mistake. Stolypin was making progress in reforming the Tsar's government, and his death opened the way for the Bolsheviks to take over.

By the same token, there have been four American presidents assassinated: Lincoln, Garfield, McKinley, and Kennedy. Their deaths had little or no effect on the US government. If anything, the effect of Lincoln's assassination was to make things worse for the South, since Lincoln was replaced by a Vice President too weak to stand up to those who sought vengeance on the South. We will never know if Kennedy would have gotten the US bogged down in a no-win war in Vietnam had he lived, but his death certainly did not improve things.

Despite this record of failure, Jones and Olken show that assassinations do have a tendency to democratize a tyrannical nation. Thus assassination of a leader may be a worthwhile project. It should not be undertaken, however, without careful thought.

The difficulty of assassination

Adolph Hitler represents perhaps the purest example of the potential benefits of assassination. Had he been assassinated in, say, 1935, subsequent history might have been a great deal better. He also illustrates the difficulty in carrying out a successful assassination.

In actuality, there were several German attempts to assassinate Hitler. As early as 1933, a group of communists plotted to assassinate Hitler when he spoke at a rally in Konigsberg, but the plot was discovered and the plotters arrested. In 1935, a group called the Right Wing Middle Class party infiltrated about 160 men into the SS, with the intention of getting close enough to assassinate him. Again, the plot was discovered and the plotters arrested. In 1938 a Swiss Catholic, Maurice Bauvaud, used a forged letter to get himself on a reviewing stand that Hitler would pass by. However, there were two rows of SS security troops between the stand and Hitler, and Bavaud concluded Hitler was out of range of the pistol he carried. Bavaud was captured as he attempted to return to Switzerland. In November 1939, Georg Elser succeeded in planting a bomb in the beer hall where Hitler had staged his "beer hall putsch" in 1923. A clock was timed to detonate the bomb while Hitler was making his annual speech there. Unfortunately Hitler cut his speech short and left before the bomb went off. The building was severely damaged and there were many casualties, but Hitler was not among them. Elser was captured as he tried to cross the border into Switzerland. The most famous assassination attempt, of course, is that of July 20, 1944, when a group of German officers delivered a bomb into a conference with Hitler and his staff. The bomb exploded, but Hitler survived. All the plotters were caught and executed. According to Moorhouse, at least forty attempts to assassinate Hitler have been documented. There may even have been more. All were unsuccessful.

In short, assassination doesn't seem to have a good record of success, in terms of accomplishing anything other than a few deaths. Assassinating top leaders does not seem to further any revolutionary goals. As Countess von Moltke, widow of one of the July 20 plotters, said of her husband's views, "It did not get rid of Hitler and it got rid of all the people who had worked against Hitler. That's what he thought would happen, and it did." (Quoted by Lawler.) (See also the article by Duke, about von Stauffenberg, one of the leaders of the assassination attempt.)

Assuming the revolutionaries have a just cause, and are genuinely intending to replace a tyranny with a just government, there is still the question of whether assassinating the tyrant is done to achieve a just peace, or instead is done out of vengeance. Replacing the tyrant with a just government might be easier if the tyrant were allowed to seek asylum in some other country. This is not an argument against assassinating a tyrant. It is an argument that the intention of the revolutionaries must be to make things better, and that the decision about whether or not to assassinate a tyrant must be based on the likely outcome.

Assassinating Lower-level Operatives

While it may be difficult and not very productive to chop off the "head" of the tyranny, it may be both easier and much more productive to chop off the "fingers." No government, whether tyrannical or free, can function without functionaries. There is allegedly a Chinese saying to the effect that you can conquer a country on horseback, but you can't rule it from horseback. The same applies to armored tanks. Eventually the tax collectors, the inspectors, the regulators, have to get out of their offices and mix with the people. When they do they are vulnerable.

Moreover, these bottom-level functionaries are not likely to have the same ideological motivation as do the top leaders. These functionaries are more concerned with their paychecks, their perks, and their pensions. It may be possible for the Resistance to achieve a tacit truce with these functionaries: "Ignore us and you can continue to enjoy your perks." To get to this point, however, it may be necessary to carry out a significant number of assassinations, to make it clear to the "fingers" that the threat is a real one.

The Decision to Assassinate

The decision to assassinate someone should not be that of one person. No one would argue that John Wilkes Booth and Lee Harvey Oswald were justified in taking it upon themselves to pass death sentences on Abraham Lincoln and John F. Kennedy respectively. In the case of Tsar Alexander II, the death sentence was passed by the revolutionary tribunal of the Narodnaya Volya (Will of the People). One may argue the extent to which they actually represented the Russian people, but at least the decision was not that of a single individual with a grudge or a delusion. It was the decision of an organized group that undertook deliberation before "passing sentence." A revolutionary group with any pretensions of justice should follow some kind of "due process" before making the decision to assassinate a public figure.[125] Several of the attempts to assassinate Hitler were the work of individuals, and failed to be the result of due process.

Possible Negative Consequences

As noted above, assassination of a leader may simply result in replacement by a leader as bad or worse. However, there may be other consequences such as reprisals. The Resistance should take this possibility into account.

An instructive example is the assassination of Reinhard Heydrich, Reichsprotektor of Bohemia, during World War II. The situation was very complex. The Czechoslovak government in exile, headed by Edouard Benes, was desperate to prove that it was still relevant. Heydrich was determined to prove that he could "Germanize" the Slavic Czechs, as a stepping-stone to bigger

---

[125] Moorhouse describes the system the Polish Underground used to select targets for assassination among German occupation forces and Polish collaborators.

appointments in conquered Russia. The Czech resistance, which had been well organized in 1940, had been crushed by the German occupation government.

Benes arranged with the British Special Operations Executive to have some refugee Czech soldiers parachuted into Bohemia, with the mission of assassinating Heydrich. Their contacts in the Czech underground opposed the assassination, on the grounds that it would result in severe reprisals. Despite the mission being badly botched, the parachutists carried it out anyway, and succeeded in blowing up Heydrich's car. Heydrich died in the hospital.

Hitler was determined to punish the Czechs for Heydrich's assassination. The village of Lidice was picked for destruction. One hundred ninety-nine men were executed, 195 women sent to prison camps, and 95 children simply disappeared, with only sixteen being traceable after the war. The houses in the village were burned to the ground, and the rubble bulldozed flat. During the summer of 1942, an additional 3188 Czechs were arrested, and 1357 condemned to death by special courts. In addition, 3000 Jews were deported "East," and 252 relatives of the parachutists were executed. The men were shot and the women and children sent to the gas chambers. The Orthodox Church throughout Bohemia-Moravia was dissolved and its property confiscated (some of the parachutists had hidden themselves in a church after the assassination). Four thousand people with relatives among the Czech exiles in England were rounded up and put in a special camp as hostages. All this was a horrible price to pay for the assassination of one man, who was replaced by his protégé, Karl Hermann Frank, who continued his policies. The only gain from all this blood was the decision of the Allies to demand that those responsible for atrocities like Lidice be tried for war crimes when the war was won. This didn't do anything to benefit the victims of the reprisals.

Innocent Bystanders

Even assuming that a tyrannical leader or an official of a tyrannical government is a legitimate target for assassination, his wife may not be, and his young children certainly are not. A discriminating attack against a tyrant must avoid targeting innocents, not only innocent members of his family, but innocent bystanders. For example, a bomb placed in a crowded courtroom, even in an otherwise legitimate attempt to eliminate a corrupt judge, would violate this criterion. The beer hall bomb targeted at Hitler may not have violated this criterion, since the hall was filled with Hitler's supporters from "way back." On the other hand, the bartender and the waitresses were not legitimate targets. Harming them may have done more damage to the anti-Hitler cause than the good of killing Hitler's Nazi colleagues did. The point here is that killing innocent bystanders may do more harm to the cause of the Resistance than the good accomplished by assassinating a legitimate target.

Prior to Conducting an Assassination

Given that the decision has been made to target an individual for assassination, the actual operation must be planned carefully. It must have the same care as the planning of any other military operation.

Background Intelligence

The Resistance must gather background information about the target, for planning purposes. The various types of information needed are as follows. These lists are intended to be suggestive, not inclusive. In particular cases, additional types of information may be needed.

Personal Information

This information should include, but not necessarily be limited to:

- Physical description
- Photograph(s)
- Typical wardrobes and clothing preferences
- Relatives and close associates

Behavioral Data

The target's practices and behavior must be studied and documented. This information should include, but not necessarily be limited to:

- Addresses of house(s), apartment(s), and other living quarters of the target
- Addresses of offices and other business locations utilized by the target
- Addresses of restaurants, theaters, gymnasiums, parks, and other places of recreation or entertainment regularly used by the target
- Tradesmen, professionals and others patronized by the target, to include doctors, dentists, barbers, tailors, lovers, brothels, and any others regularly visited
- Transportation, including cars, boats, aircraft or any other vehicles maintained or used by the target
- Regular times and places of visits to friends, family, tradesmen, places of entertainment, or others
- Habits or practices such as jogging, bicycling, regular lunches or dinners, hobbies
- Clubs, business or professional organizations regularly attended

Physical Target Data

For each possible location where assassination might be attempted, it will be necessary to gather physical data about the building, layout or site. This should include, but not necessarily be limited to:

- Location, floor plans or layout, structural details
- Neighboring buildings, including floor plans
- Nearby terrain, including topography, concealment (bushes, trees), and structures (manholes, culverts, overpasses, sewer openings, alleys)
- Security, including locks, fences, gates, alarm systems, guards, and details of badge and pass information

Mission Planning

On the basis of the background information developed regarding the target and the places where the target might be found, a specific mission plan must be developed. It should cover the following items:

- The specific location where the assassination attempt will take place
- The weapon(s) to be used (handgun, rifle, bomb, anti-tank grenade, poisoned needle, etc.)
- Badges, passes, uniforms, vehicle passes, or other items needed to gain access to the target site
- Location and time when the weapons and other items will be provided to the assassin(s)
- Transportation of the assassin(s) to the target site (if this is to be a stolen government vehicle, plans must be made for acquisition and hiding prior to the assassination attempt)
- Backup. If the assassination attempt fails, then what? A backup consisting of a second assassin (or team) on the site may be appropriate, depending on the circumstances.
- Escape route and transportation for the assassin(s) following the attempt
- Cleanup, including disposition of badges, uniforms, vehicles, etc. in a manner that does not provide information about the Resistance

Communications

The Resistance unit responsible for planning and carrying out the assassination of a specific target must arrange for communications with the assassin(s). At least three types of communications will be necessary.

- The "Execute" signal. The assassin(s) must be given a signal to execute the plans already developed and prepared for by the assassin(s). This signal must be delivered in a secure manner.
- The "Abort" signal. There may be some last-minute reason for calling off the assassination attempt (e.g., the mission has been compromised, or the target has changed plans). There must be a secure means for delivering this to the assassin(s) even if they have already begun to execute the plan.
- The "Outcome" signal. The Resistance must be informed immediately about the success or failure of the assassination attempt. Other plans, scheduled to be executed following the

assassination, will depend on knowing whether the attempt was successful.[126] Depending on circumstances, it may be more appropriate to have someone else on the scene to report the outcome, since police attention will be focused on the assassins themselves, not on anyone else on the site. If the assassination takes place at some public event, TV network coverage may be an effective means for learning the outcome. However, if the target is wounded but not killed, penetration of a hospital may be required to learn the degree of seriousness of the injury.

Summary

Assassination can be a useful tactic for the Resistance. However, the Resistance leadership should take into account the degree of difficulty in assassinating a particular target, the likelihood that the target will be replaced by someone who will continue the target's policies, and the likelihood and possible extent of reprisals.

Much of the planning needed for an assassination attempt is similar to the planning for a raid. More details regarding planning will be found in the chapter on raids.

References

Anderson, Keith, *How to Build Practical Firearm Suppressors*, El Dorado, AR, Desert Publications, 1994.

Anderson, Keith, *How to Build Military Grade Suppressors*, El Dorado, AR, Desert Publications, 2000.

Anonymous, *How to Make a Silencer for a .45*, Boulder, CO, Paladin Press, 1995.

Anonymous, *Selective Assassination as an Instrument of National Policy*, Boulder, CO, Paladin Press, 1990.

---

[126] The German Officers' attempt to assassinate Hitler was to be followed by actions elsewhere by Army officers who would seize Nazi headquarters and replace local Nazi leaders. Some officers began to execute these plans, not knowing that the assassination attempt had failed. They thus tipped their hand and were arrested and executed.

Anonymous, *Silencers .223*, Hurst, TX, Minuteman Publications, 1985.

Davidson, Eugene, *The Trial of the Germans*, U. Missouri Press, 1997 (paperback).

Duke, Selwyn, "Valkyrie: The Real von Stauffenberg," *The New American*, March 2, 2009, pp. 34 – 38.

Flores, J., *How To Make Disposable Silencers*, El Dorado, AR, Desert Publications, 1985.

Frankford Arsenal, *Silencers: Principles and Evaluations*, Report R-1896, 1968.

Hayduke, George, *The Hayduke Silencer Book*, Boulder, CO, Paladin Press, 1989.

Hollenback, George M., *Workbench Silencers*, Boulder, CO, Paladin Press, 1996, ISBN 978-0-87364-895-0.

Hollenback, George M., *More Workbench Silencers*, Boulder, CO, Paladin Press, 1998, ISBN 978-0-86354-994-0

Jones, Benjamin F. and Benjamin A. Olken, "Hit or Miss: The effect of assassinations on Institutions and War, Bureau for Research and Economic Analysis of Development," working paper # 150, May 2007, http://www.cid.harvard.edu/bread/abstracts/150.htm

Lawler, Justus George, "Hitler's Hammer, the Church's Anvil," *First Things*, November 2005, pp. 31 – 36.

McDonald, Callum, *The Killing of SS Obergruppen-Fuhrer Reinhard Heydrich*, New York, Macmillan, 1989.

Moorhouse, Roger, *Killing Hitler*, New York, Bantam, 2006.

Nye, R. D., *The Handy Dandy Super Duper Junkyard Silencer Book*, Phoenix, AZ, Firing Pin Enterprises, 1992.

Thomsett, Michael C., *The German Opposition to Hitler*, Jefferson, NC, McFarland & Co., 1997.

Chapter 25

Sabotage

What is sabotage?

Sabotage involves physical actions: blowing things up, burning things down, putting sand in the gears, putting sugar in gas tanks. However, it must not be allowed to degenerate into vandalism. Remember, your goal is to free your country from a tyrannical government. You don't want to ruin your country in the process.

Sabotage must be governed by the same "just war" rules as military combat: discrimination and proportion. Discrimination means sabotaging only those targets that hurt the government and aid in its overthrow. Proportion means that the good resulting from the sabotage must outweigh the damage done. In particular, sabotage that makes life more difficult for the general population is likely to decrease support for the Resistance. Likewise, sabotage that destroys infrastructure may make it more difficult for the country to recover after your victory.

Most sabotage actions will be independent of any other actions. This would include such things as damaging machinery in a government factory, spiking tires on government vehicles, cutting power lines to government installations, etc. They are carried out by individuals or small groups, on their own initiative. The only concern is that they satisfy discrimination and proportion.

Some sabotage, however, may be incorporated into other activities. If the Resistance intends to conduct a raid, blowing up the police radio tower to slow police response, or blowing up a bridge that government reinforcements must cross, might be part of the raid plans. These sabotage actions must be integrated into the raid plan in the same manner as other actions, described in Chapter 26.

In any case, sabotage must be part of an overall plan to weaken the government. The Resistance must inform its supporters about methods and suitable targets for sabotage. This is one more case where videos, simple instruction manuals, etc. should be prepared and distributed widely.

Selecting Targets for Sabotage

Military actions by the armed wing of the Resistance must support the overall strategy of the Resistance. Political actions by the overt branch of the Resistance (strikes, protests, pamphleteering, etc.) must support the overall strategy of the Resistance. This is also true of sabotage. The selection of targets for sabotage must also support the overall strategy of the Resistance. More importantly, targets that do not support the strategy of the Resistance, or whose destruction would hinder that strategy, should be avoided.

Military Targets

The government's military forces are obvious targets for sabotage. Arsenals, supply depots, vehicle parks, aircraft dispersal areas, vehicles and equipment can all be suitable targets for sabotage. However, the overall strategy of the Resistance may influence the choice of targets. For instance, if the Resistance hopes to gain either the support, or at least the neutrality, of the armed forces, sabotage that intentionally injures or kills members of the armed forces goes counter to that strategy.

Industry

Factories that produce goods directly for the government (munitions, military equipment) should be high on the priority list for sabotage. So should power lines supplying those factories, and the railroads and roads leading from them. If the government depends for a significant fraction of its income on exports, particularly of raw materials (petroleum, iron ore, lumber, etc.), sabotage of those industries is a way of directly attacking the government. If the government is receiving military supplies from a "friendly" government, sabotage of dock equipment (cranes, etc.) and of railroads and roads leading from seaports will harm the government. However, if this sabotage also shuts down important imports such as food, it may antagonize the population that the Resistance depends on for support.

Infrastructure

This includes roads, railroads, bridges, pipelines, electric transmission lines, water purification and sewage disposal plants, and other things that provide basic services to the population. Most of them are hard to guard, have many vulnerable points, and can be put out of operation for a long time by a well-planned attack. However, considerable thought should be given to whether any of these facilities should be targeted for sabotage. How much harm will it actually do to the government? Will the action support the strategy of the Resistance? Will it bring more harm to the cause of the Resistance than it will bring good? Random attacks on infrastructure may simply be vandalism rather than effective sabotage.

Communications

Communications are critical to a tyrannical government. Distributing propaganda to the public, sending instructions to government supporters (e.g., calls for marches or demonstrations), and keeping officials informed of government plans, all depend on communications. Striking at the government's means of getting its story out can be an effective tactic.

Explosives

There are references in Chapter 14 on manufacture of explosives. The caution offered there is worth repeating. *Follow the directions to the letter.* Some of the training manuals in the References explain how to use explosives. The same caution applies there: *follow the directions to the letter.* An old Navy saying is, "Ordnance rules are written in blood." Don't repeat the mistakes of those who didn't follow the rules.

Explosives are customarily divided into two types: high explosives and low explosives. High explosives have a rapid burning rate; low explosives have a low burning rate. The division between the two is somewhat arbitrary. Dynamite and TNT are considered high explosives; black powder is considered a low explosive.

From the standpoint of the user, the chief distinction between the two is that low explosives must be "tamped." That is, they must be in physical contact with the target, and must have a considerable mass surrounding them to confine the explosion and direct it at the target. While high explosives should be in physical contact with the target, tamping is desirable but not essential. For instance, a block of TNT placed against a railroad rail is more effective if tamped with a sandbag, but sufficient TNT will cut the rail even without tamping.

Explosives are most commonly used for "point" destruction: dropping bridge spans, cutting railroad rails, cutting pipelines, dropping electrical transmission and radio towers, and similar targets. Mines and roadside bombs are used against passing vehicles. The amount of explosives likely to be available to the Resistance will be insufficient for destroying large areas such as city blocks or large buildings.

The key to use of explosives is to attack those points in the target that bring about collapse or spread of the damage. Cutting a railroad rail, for instance, can cause derailment of a train. Dropping an electrical transmission tower can cut off power to an entire area. Blasting a bridge pier can case a span to fall.

If the Resistance is limited to low explosives such as black powder, the range of targets is more limited by the need for considerable tamping of the explosive charge. For instance, instead of cutting a rail directly, it may be more effective to dig under the railroad and place a large black powder mine, tamping the mine with earth put back in the hole. This obviously involves more time and more work than would using a high explosive charge. However, black powder mines have been used effectively in warfare. Their limitations must be taken into account.

In selecting targets for use of explosives, the Resistance will have to take into account the capabilities of the explosives available, and their quantity. The Resistance cannot afford to waste explosives by using insufficient amounts, or by not tamping low explosives adequately.

Incendiaries

Most incendiaries are more forgiving than are explosives. They are less likely to burn accidentally or prematurely. However, they must still be treated with caution.

For some purposes, incendiaries may be more effective than explosives. Thermite, for instance, may be more effective in destroying or damaging heavy machinery, armored vehicles, artillery pieces, etc., than explosives. A thermite grenade placed in the breech or the barrel of an artillery piece, or on the traversing and elevation mechanism, will put it out of action permanently. Likewise, factory machinery may be damaged beyond repair by use of thermite. Thermite is relatively easy to make and is safe to handle, but requires a high temperature to ignite. Magnesium ribbons, a mixture of sugar and potassium chlorate, or sparklers, will ignite thermite.[127]

For destroying wooden buildings, or buildings containing large amounts of combustible materials, an accelerant such as gasoline is needed. It is relatively safe to handle, and its vapors can be ignited readily. The incendiary should be placed where a natural draft will help spread the flames. Good places are in an inside corner, outside under an overhang, next to a window, or in an external "inside" corner. The manual by the Animal Liberation Front gives some useful directions in making effective use of gasoline-type incendiaries.

Regardless of the type of incendiary used, some kind of time delay mechanism will be needed. Several of the references describe delay devices for incendiaries.

Timers, Detonators, and other accessories

Explosives and incendiaries need to be activated at a time when the Resistance members who set them are safely away. Hence there is a need for timers and similar devices.

---

[127] Note that thermite gives off a great deal of ultraviolet light. The blaze should be viewed only through something like welders' goggles.

Timers

Digital watches and clocks can be used as timers. The voltage from the buzzer can be used to operate an electronic relay that in turn connects some device to a battery. Taliban sympathizers in Afghanistan used this method to launch rockets at US military bases. The watch could be used to connect the rocket launcher to a car battery. The delay could be set to give the attackers sufficient time to be well away from the area when the rocket took off.

Mechanical watches and clocks have long been used as timers. A wire can be placed through a hole bored in the watchglass. When a hand touches the wire, it closes an electrical circuit that triggers a bomb. Clocks can also be used in this way. Alternatively with a clock, the alarm-winding stem can be used. When the alarm goes off, the stem can be used to wind up a string that in turn triggers a bomb.

Chemical devices are commonly used as delayed-operation timers. A chemical is allowed to corrode through a container and activate an explosive or incendiary. Several devices of this type are described in the references.

Candles are sometimes used as delay devices. As the candle burns down, it either reaches a string or fuse, or its reduced weight allows something to tip over. Candles should be protected from wind if they are used as timers. Candles should *not* be used as timers for incendiaries containing volatile accelerants such as gasoline, as the fumes may produce a premature fire or detonation.

Remote Controls

In some cases an explosive charge must be detonated when a target is nearby. This means the target area must be under observation, and the explosive detonated by some remote control ("command-detonated"). A wide variety of means has been used for this purpose. A hard-wired detonator is the most secure, but the wire itself may be detected by the disturbance in the soil where it is buried. Other command detonation means include infrared controls such as TV remotes, and radio controls such as car door openers, RC model airplane controllers, garage door openers, pagers, and cell phones. Cell phones used for this purpose will have the ringer connected to the detonator (a relay and separate battery may be required). Cell phones can be used from anywhere in the world to call the cell phone connected to the bomb.

CB radios, Family Radio Service (FRS) radios, and ham radios can also be used for command detonation. The risk with these, however, is that the charge may be detonated prematurely by another signal on the same frequency. The risk of premature detonation can be reduced (but not completely eliminated) by making use of the "selective call" feature of some of these radios, whereby they will not respond unless a specific tone is first transmitted.

A more sophisticated method was developed by Iraqi terrorists. The explosive was placed beside the road, and was triggered when the target vehicle passed through an infrared beam. However, the device was not armed until an operator, at a more distant location, confirmed that a worthwhile target was approaching the site of the explosive. At that time the operator armed the device by radio, from a location outside the radius of any radio jamming devices on the target vehicle. See the article "Explosively Formed Projectiles" for more information.[128]

There are many devices in common use, such as garage door openers and cell phones, that can be adapted for use as remote detonators. The Resistance saboteurs will have to consider what is available to them and make use of it. In some cases, the aid of an electronics technician will be required. However, the techniques can be learned by even unskilled people who, in effect, carry them out by rote, without understanding the details.

Cyberwar

The discussions above have all dealt with physical destruction of something. Computer hacking involves either the alteration of bits within a computer, or shutting the computer down,

---

[128] Note that two cell phones can be used for this: one to arm the bomb when a worthwhile target approaches, the second for the actual detonation.

but not physically destroying it. For this to be done, the computer must be connected to the outside world in some way, either through a public network like the Internet, or a private network.

Hacking the Government's Computers

Hacking can serve two purposes, although usually not both at the same time. It can be used for sabotage, and it can be used for intelligence gathering. It will be discussed here in terms of sabotage, but resistance organizations shouldn't overlook the intelligence gathering applications. These are discussed at greater length in the chapters on Intelligence gathering.

Denial of Service Attack

This involves sending so many requests, or login attempts, to a computer that it cannot handle them. Typically, this is done by mobilizing thousands of computers to make requests of the target computer at the same time. In most cases this is done by surreptitiously placing a program (known as a "bot," short for robot) on the computers of thousands of unsuspecting owners. On call, or at a prescribed time, the bots begin the denial of service attack on the target computer. This practice should probably be avoided by the Resistance, as it means disrupting the computers of their fellow citizens, and will reflect badly on it. However, if supporters of the Resistance *outside* the country are willing to take part, it can be legitimate. Supporters *within* the country should not be used, as the presence of the bot on their computer will link them to the Resistance.

Reading and Alteration of Files

A skilled hacker can gain access to a computer by means such as stealing passwords, guessing passwords, or obtaining passwords by "social engineering." Once "in" the computer, the hacker can read files, alter files, and erase files. Reading files goes under the heading of "intelligence." This can be a very effective means of obtaining information about government actions and capabilities, background information on government officials, and even the identities of government agents. It may also be a way of learning how much the government knows about the Resistance. The intelligence value from reading government computer files will depend on how effective is the government's encryption or other means of disguising the information.

Sabotage involves altering or destroying files. A popular alteration is defacing a web site. Material on a government web site might be replaced by anti-government slogans. Beyond that, information about Resistance members might be altered or deleted. Information about government officials may be altered to direct suspicion at them. The range of possibilities is quite wide, and the action taken will depend upon what information the hacker can access, and what changes or deletions further the strategy of the Resistance.

Logic Bombs

Other forms of sabotage by hacking include altering a web site, collecting data from files (e.g., obtaining the names and addresses of government supporters), and corrupting government data bases. Logic bombs and similar programs are other possibilities. These are set to activate themselves at a particular time, and to do something like wiping out the computer's files. These things are much harder to do than is commonly supposed, but the techniques can be learned.

Cell Phones etc.

Hacking is no longer limited to computers. Cell phone networks, Blackberries™, iPhones™, and similar devices can be infected with viruses and Trojan horses. Release of such malware by the Resistance can cause it to lose the support of the population. However, if the malware can be restricted to government devices, this can be a very effective means of hampering government internal communications.

The Resistance should make every effort to train operatives in computer hacking, and use their services in conjunction with other activities such as ambushes or raids, and propaganda campaigns.

Cyberwar is becoming more and more important. The Resistance cannot afford to overlook it as a means of sabotaging the government. See the article by Fulghum.

Sand in the Gears

"Sand in the gears" can mean physically putting sand in some machine. However, it can also be interpreted figuratively. Simply disrupting the government's normal activities can be an effective sabotage measure. Flooding offices with paperwork, submitting requests for information, filling out forms incompletely so that they must be reviewed and filled out again, can all help slow down the bureaucracy.

Gumming Up the Data Base

Here's an example, taken from the Internet, of how one might go about gumming up a government database. This one has to do with Canadian gun registration, but the principles can be applied to many other things.

> Subject: GUERILLA TACTICS YOU SHOULD NEVER DO
>
> CILA / ICAL "Defending Canada's Heritage"
>
> GUERILLA TACTICS YOU SHOULD NEVER DO!
>
> December 4th, 1998 It appears some bright sparks have taken to writing "NEVER" across the firearms registration forms and sending them to (a politician). They didn't even need a stamp! (The politician) has them in a great big box in the middle of his office and is going to give them to Justice Minister (named) as a Christmas gift.
>
> Ho Ho Ho. Another practical joke being played by these very humorous folks is to take a whole stack of registration forms and register guns to their neighbors and other folks picked randomly out of a phone book. Sometimes these silly people even forget to include the money. They think it's really funny to have all

those people at the CFC phoning fictitious gun owners up to collect ten dollars on a gun that doesn't exist. They think it's really funny to have the costs of C-68 escalate through the roof!

Sometimes they even send the money. One of these jesters (I think his name was Simon) told me that he registered ten individual guns to ten non gun owners. AND HE INCLUDED THE MONEY. This zany guy said half the people that received registration cards would complain to the RCMP and they would spend A LOT OF MONEY trying to remove them from their great big "BRAINIAC" computer. But the really funny part was that half the people would simply throw the registration away like junk mail (since they didn't own a gun) and leave half the guns (and owners) in the system.

The knee slapper here is that these people and guns don't even exist. Now don't misunderstand. CILA would NEVER recommend these delinquents do such a thing. These baaad Canadians are trying to damage the Canadian Government's registration system. Even though measures like these will GRIND THE SYSTEM TO ITS KNEES in short order CILA thinks you should go "baa, baa" and blindly obey the rules.

Even though the Government of Canada has declared war on you, you should still obey.

PS: DON'T GIVE UP.

Almost any data base of a tyrannical government is worth gumming up. Entering false data, entering data for nonexistent people or organizations, and submitting incomplete data, are all good tactics for rendering the data base less useful for its intended purposes. This is not enough to overthrow the government, but it helps to weaken the government.

Summary

Sabotage can be an important element of the overall program of the Resistance. The targets selected for sabotage should be those that further the strategy of the Resistance. Efforts should be made to prevent sabotage from degenerating into vandalism that does not weaken the government but merely destroys things.

References

Computer Hacking

Fulghum, David A., "Cyberwar Is Official," *Aviation Week & Space Technology*, September 14, 2009, pp. 54 – 55.

Gorman, Siobhan, "Cyber Attacks on Georgia used Facebook, Twitter, Stolen IDs," *The Wall Street Journal*, August 17, 2009, p. A5.

Knightmare, The, *Secrets of a Super Hacker*, 1994, available from online booksellers.

Ludwig, Mark Allen, *The Little Black Book of E-Mail Viruses*, American Eagle Publications, Show Low, AZ 2002.

Meinel, Carolyn P., *The Happy Hacker*, Show Low, AZ, American Eagle Publications, 1998. (Much of the information on specific programs is out of date, but the principles remain valid.)

Meinel, Carolyn, P., *Überhacker!* Available from online booksellers.

Explosives and Blasting

Anonymous, *American Engineer Explosives in World War One*, El Dorado, AR, Desert Publications, 1990. (Covers a wide range of explosives, including handling precautions.)

Anonymous, "Explosively Formed Projectiles," *Soldier of Fortune*, February 2006, pp. 66 – 68.

Anonymous, *How To Destroy Bridges*, Boulder, CO, Paladin Press, 1988 (apparently extracted from an Army Field Manual)

Anonymous, *Improvised Shaped Charges*, Cornville, AZ, Desert Publications, 1982.

Anonymous, *CIA Field Expedient Preparation of Black Powders*, Cornville, AZ, Desert Publications, undated.

DeForest, M. J., *Principles of Improvised Explosive Devices*, Boulder, CO, Paladin Press, 1984.

Department of the Army, *Explosives and Demolitions, FM 5-25*, Randle, WA, Bohica Concepts, 1967.

Department of the Army, *Explosives and Demolitions, FM 5-250*, 1992.

Department of the Army, *Improvised Munitions Handbook, TM 31-210*.

Department of the Army, *Unconventional Warfare Devices and Techniques: References, TM 31-200-1*, Randle, WA, Bohica Concepts, 1966. (Also available from Gold Nugget Army Surplus.)

Harber, David, *Guerrilla's Arsenal*, Boulder, CO, Paladin Press, 1994. (Manufacture of explosives and time delay bombs)

Anonymous, *Instructor's Special Forces Demolitions Training Handbook*, available from Desert Publications.

Myers, Lawrence W., *Improvised Radio Detonation Techniques*, Boulder, CO, Paladin Press, 1988.

Myers, Lawrence W., *Smart Bombs*, Boulder, CO, Paladin Press, 1990.

Yates, Lyle D., *Home Brew*, Phoenix, AZ, Firing Pin Enterprizes (sic), 1996. (This book is primarily about tripwires and boobytraps.)

General Sabotage

Anonymous, "Earth First Death Manual," available from: http://www.mega.nu:8080/ampp/efdm/efdm.html (aimed at motorcycles, but lots of ideas for sabotaging vehicles)

Foreman, Dave and Bill Haywood, *Ecodefense*, Chico, CA, Abbzug Press, 2002. Lots of information on sabotaging machinery and vehicles.

Incendiary Devices

Animal Liberation Front, *Arson-Around With Auntie ALF*. This was once available as free download from the ALF web site. It has been removed. However, an Internet search will locate several sources. (Describes various incendiary devices)

Anonymous, *CIA Field Expedient Incendiary Manual*, available from Paladin Press. (Good discussion of delay devices)

Department of the Army, *Incendiaries, TM 31-201-1*, Randle, WA, Bohica Concepts, 1966. Also available from Gold Nugget Army Surplus.

Department of the Army, *Unconventional Warfare Devices and Techniques: References, TM 31-200-1.* Available from Gold Nugget Army Surplus.

Earth Liberation Front, *Setting Fires With Electrical Timers: An Earth Liberation Front Guide*, May, 2001. This was formerly available from the ELF web site. It has been removed from the site. However, an Internet search will locate several sources. (Describes electrical igniters for incendiaries)

Lumsden, Malvern, *Incendiary Weapons*, Stockholm, Sweden, SIPRI, 1975. (This book is about military incendiaries.

However, it has a great deal of information about incendiary mixtures and their effects.)

Whitney, Lyle, *Black Book of Arson*, El Dorado, AR, Desert Publications, 1987. (discusses the physics of fires, and how to set them effectively)

Sand in the Gears

Mack, Jefferson, *Secret Freedom Fighter*, Boulder, CO, Paladin Press, 1986. (The emphasis is on sabotage by people not involved in the armed resistance.)

Chapter 26

Raids

What is a raid?

A raid is a temporary invasion of some physical location, for a specific purpose, and for a limited time. Successful withdrawal is implied by the definition. In this chapter, "objective" will mean the reason for the raid; "target" will mean the physical location where the raid is to take place.

Raids may be carried out for a number of objectives, such as:

- Sabotage
- Facility destruction
- Prisoner snatch
- Rescue of captured Resistance fighters or hostages
- Seizure of documents or materiel
- Seizure of weapons

The Resistance leadership must clearly define the objective of any raid. Failure to define the objective is a guarantee of failure.

Once the objective is determined, the following steps must be undertaken: planning, preparation, coordination of separate forces involved, and execution, including withdrawal.

Planning the Raid

The raid must be planned in detail. The plan must spell out the tactical objectives of each element of the raiding party (entry team, blocking force, security elements, reinforcements, etc.), in support of the overall objective of the raid. The timing and positioning of each element of the raiding party must be described in the plan. The escape routes and rally points for each element must be described in the plan. If approach to the target takes place over several days, the safe houses and stopping points for each element of the party must be included in the plan.

If the purpose of the raid is to capture weapons, ammunition, or other equipment, the plan must describe how the captured materiel is to be transported, and where it is to be taken.

The raid commander should have a "timeline" showing what events are to take place, and which element(s) are involved in each event. The timeline is based, not on clock time, but on the sequence of events that is to take place (e.g., entry element cannot enter the target until the breaching element has broken in).

Communications

The communications plan must start with the question, who might need to talk to whom, and about what? If the only communication needed between two elements of the raiding party is "go or no-go," a simple communication system (one or two whistle blasts, one or two blinks of a flashlight, red or green flags, blasts on a vehicle horn) may be sufficient. Within an individual element of the raiding party, hand signals may be used. If more detailed information must be passed, greater "bandwidth" may be required, such as voice or graphics (photos or drawings), or (in extreme situations) live video. These latter inevitably demand a radio link.

The communications plan must specify what equipment will be available to each element of the raiding party, what types of information will be passed, what radio frequencies will be used (including alternatives), what colors of flares or flashlights or flags will be used, what code words will be used, who in each element is responsible for ordering the communication, and who in each element is responsible for sending and receiving communications.

Coordination

There will usually be several elements in the raiding party, each with a different role to play in achieving the objective of the raid. As part of the planning process, the role of each element must be described in detail, including what action each element will take in various contingencies. Planning must also include approach and escape routes, including alternatives.

Electronic Warfare

Depending on the nature of the raid, it may be necessary to intercept government communications during the raid, particularly any potential relief forces coming to the aid of the raid target. The raid plan should include whatever radio intercept operations are necessary, and include the intercept elements in the raid plan. The plan should also describe who should be informed of intercepted information.

Also depending on the nature of the raid, it may be necessary to jam government communications during the raid. The raid plan should include designation of the jamming element, and specify the frequencies that should be jammed, and the time for jamming to start and stop.

As with the other elements of the raiding force, the plan should include access routes, operating locations, and escape routes for the intercept and jamming elements.

Planning for Murphy

Things will go wrong during a raid. These must be expected and plans made to cope with them, rather than having them come as a surprise. Some of the possible failures are:

- Firearms malfunction
- Injuries or wounds among the raiding party, requiring casualty evacuation
- Radio failure
- Physical layout inside the target not as expected
- Opposition stronger than expected
- The target may be "empty"

Raiding party members must be trained to clear firearms malfunctions quickly, or to transition to a backup weapon immediately. Standing there trying to figure out what to do with a malfunctioning weapon is not acceptable.

If a raiding party member is injured or wounded, it is imperative that someone else in the party be prepared to step in and perform the functions of the disabled member. A location should have been designated as the collection point for the wounded. One or more members of the raiding party should have been designated as "medics" who are responsible for giving immediate care to wounded or injured members of the party. The raid must not lose momentum just because some members of the raiding party are disabled.

Radios may fail because batteries die, because the signals cannot penetrate the walls of a building, because the enemy has jammed the raiding party's frequencies, or for other reasons. Alternative signaling methods must have been planned for. Different methods may be required for different elements of the raiding force, e.g., verbal commands or whistles for those inside the target, flares or lights to communicate with blocking or covering forces, cell phones to communicate with higher headquarters.

Despite the best reconnaissance, the interior layout of the target may turn out to be different from what was expected and rehearsed. The important point is that this should not bring the raid to a halt. It is imperative that momentum be retained. This possibility must be taken into account, and the raiding party prepared to deal with it by means such as use of scouting parties to find alternative routes through the target, to allow the objective to be achieved. It is important that the raiding party be able to improvise on the spot, if things turn out to be different from expected. It is crucial that the team commanders on the spot be able to exercise initiative and modify plans when the original plan cannot be carried out.

Despite the reconnaissance undertaken prior to the raid, the opposition within the target may be much stronger than expected. The raid plans should include provision for this. If it is feasible to have reinforcements nearby, they should be on hand right from the start and should be prepared to support the raiding party. In most cases, however, unexpectedly strong opposition, or the discovery that the enemy is expecting the raid, will mean that the raid must be aborted. It is far more important to the Resistance to keep its strength intact than to achieve the objective of the raid at extremely high cost.

The object of the raid, e.g., an official to be snatched, a hostage to be rescued, documents to be seized, may no longer be present in the target. Government forces may have removed these, either in anticipation of a raid, or for other reasons. It is important that the raiding party be prepared to withdraw quickly if it is found that the target is empty. This fact must also be transmitted to higher headquarters as quickly as possible.

Preparing for the Raid
Preparing for the raid includes pre-raid reconnaissance, rehearsal, and assembly of the raiding force.

Pre-Raid Reconnaissance
It is essential that accurate and detailed information about the target be obtained prior to the raid.

Tom Ridge, former Homeland Security Secretary of the United States, described information obtained from the laptop of a captive al Qaeda operative as follows:

> There is no question about all the 40-page casing files found on the laptop computer of an al Qaeda operative. There is no question about the detailed surveillance carried out on the New York Stock Exchange, Prudential Financial, Citigroup, the IMF and the World Bank . . . Information on the types of uniforms worn by guards, potential escape routes, places where employees hang out – detail after detail down to the incline that exists on one of the underground parking garages – is shockingly black and white.

These al Qaeda operatives knew what they were doing. Their efforts illustrate the level of detail that pre-raid reconnaissance should collect. The key point, however, is that those in charge of the raid should specify the kinds of information that should be obtained by pre-raid reconnaissance (more about this in the chapter on Tactical Intelligence). The people doing the recon should not have to figure it out for themselves. They should, however, be alert to things that might affect the raid but that weren't asked for.

Pre-raid reconnaissance may include obtaining floor plans, maps, photographs (ground-level and aerial or satellite), measurements of height and construction of fences, locations of gates and locks, locations of doors and windows, counts of numbers of enemy personnel, descriptions of their equipment and uniforms, and verbal descriptions of the target, depending on the objective and the target. Photographs of fences and obstacles are particularly important.

If the objective of the raid is a prisoner snatch, or rescue of a Resistance member, photographs of the individual(s) must be obtained and provided to the raiding party, so they can recognize the person they are seeking. If the objective of the raid is to obtain documents or specific items, these must be described in detail so they can be recognized immediately. If enemy equipment is to be destroyed or sabotaged, information on vulnerable points and means of destruction should be provided. In short, the raiding party must have the information needed to recognize the objective and carry out the plan without hesitation.

Some of the material on physical layout of the target may be available from public documents and records. Some may have to be obtained by physical surveillance of the target. In the latter case, the persons carrying out the reconnaissance should disguise their data-gathering as innocent activities (jogging, walking a dog, entering a building for some apparently legitimate purpose). The people conducting the surveillance should blend in with whatever other people are normally near the target.

If the target is a government building, it may be necessary to carry out visits to various offices, on appropriate pretexts (obtaining copies of forms, inquiring about regulations, etc.), to obtain information about physical layout, numbers of guards, etc. For private or commercial buildings, the reconnaissance operatives may be real or bogus customers or clients. In any case, information about the interior of the target is important.

In some cases it may be desirable to obtain information about potential targets (police stations, radio & TV stations, government offices, power plants, etc.) in anticipation of future need. That is, the Resistance may maintain "target folders" on installations that may, at some time in the future, become "live" targets. It will probably be easier to obtain this information prior to initiating active resistance. If the Resistance organization anticipates "going active" in the near future, the opportunity should be taken to gather this information before the government is alerted to the Resistance's plans.

The information gathered from the various reconnaissance activities must be assembled in usable form. If at all possible, materials should be converted to electronic form. Digital camera photos can be directly stored. Documents might be scanned into computer files. This may be especially important for documents that can be reviewed in public facilities such as libraries or city engineers' offices but that cannot be taken out. Some documents, however, such as blueprints, cannot be readily reduced to a size suitable for scanning. These items must be retained in original form. Once reduced to electronic form, however, the documents *must not* be stored on a laptop or desktop computer. They must be stored on some removable medium and kept in a safe place. Duplicate copies should be kept in several places, if possible. Moreover, if they were processed on a computer, the hard drive must be overwritten completely. It is not sufficient to "erase" the files, since they remain on the drive until overwritten by other data, even if they are not in the file index.

Once the results of the pre-raid reconnaissance are compiled, the information should be broken down into packages appropriate for each of the elements of the raiding party. For instance, the blocking element need not have drawings of the target's interior. Each element of the raiding party should have maps of its own access route, rally point(s), and its primary and alternate escape routes. Compartmenting the information in this way serves two purposes. First, it reduces the amount of information each element of the raiding party must carry during the raid. Second, if a member of one element is captured, he will have no information about the other elements.

Rehearsal

The term "rehearsal" is fairly elastic. For a large and elaborate raid, rehearsal may involve a complete full-sized mockup of the target, in which the raiding party practices the entire raid, step by step. The rehearsal may even include "role players" representing the enemy forces expected to be in the target, the official to be taken prisoner, etc. At a lesser level, rehearsal may involve a sand table or equivalent, or simply maps and floor plans. In some cases, especially when the raid is based on time-sensitive intelligence, the "rehearsal" may simply be a pre-raid briefing. In the case of a briefing, it should cover the objective, a description of the target (including maps, exterior and interior pictures, floor plans), pictures of persons or descriptions of objects to be seized (if appropriate), and the roles of each of the elements of the party.

If the rehearsal is limited to a briefing, it is important that the elements of the raiding party have prior experience working together on raids. Staging an impromptu raid with inexperienced troops is a recipe for disaster. The more familiar the members of the raiding party are with what is to be done and what is expected of them, the greater the chances of success.

Assembly

Each element of the raiding party should have a specific assembly point. Members of that element assemble there prior to beginning the raid. On the approach to the assembly point, the members of each element should make use of cover, camouflage, indirect routes, etc., to hide the fact that a raid is in the offing. Blending in with normal activities along the route, and appearing to be engaged in harmless activities, are critical. This will obviously be difficult for those carrying weapons. Subterfuges may be needed (e.g., "homeless man" with his possessions in a shopping cart; woman with "baby carriage"). It may also be possible to preposition weapons and equipment at or near the assembly point(s) prior to the raid.[129] In any case, it is critical that the elements of the raiding party arrive at their assembly points without being recognized as a raiding party.

Once at the assembly points, the elements of the raiding party will execute their planned activities, usually after receipt of a "go" signal from the raiding party commander. The "go" signal may depend on a final reconnaissance to verify that the target is not "empty," or that the forces at the target appear to have no warning of the raid.

Coordination of Forces

Each element of the raiding party will initiate its planned activities on receipt of the "go" signal. For instance, the blocking force(s) will move to seal off the target, and notify the raid commander when this has been achieved. In most cases, the various actions will depend on prior actions by other elements of the raiding party. For instance, the entry element will not make its move until the blocking forces are in place. If explosive breaching of the target is required, the entry element will remain hidden until the breaching element has completed its work. Because of this dependence of one action on another one, it is critical that the communications plan include all the signals needed among the various elements of the raiding party. Some communications must be routed through the commander. For instance, only the commander should be authorized to give the "go" or the "abort" signal, hence any communications that would mean "okay so far" or "things have turned sour, call it off" must go through the commander. Other communications may go directly from one element to another. For instance, to save time, once the breaching element has completed its task, it may inform the entry element simultaneously with informing the commander.

Executing the Raid

The raid is executed when the commander is informed that all elements are in place, and the final reconnaissance (if needed)

---

[129] Weapons might be put in the trunk of a car or back of a truck that arrives at the raid site just before the raiding party gets there.

has verified that nothing has happened to change the plan. The commander issues the "go" signal. From that point on, each element must carry out its part of the raid plan, informing the commander (and other elements as appropriate) that a given step has succeeded, or that a problem has been encountered. The commander will track the "timeline" based on reports from the various elements of the raiding party.

It is crucial that the raid be prosecuted vigorously. Success in a raid depends upon hitting hard and moving fast. The raiding party must overwhelm the enemy forces in the target, achieve its objective, and then withdraw before enemy reinforcements arrive. Each step in the timeline must be carried out quickly, and each follow-on step begun immediately when the preceding step is complete.

It is important that the raid be planned in detail. It is equally important that the raiding party be able to deviate from the plan if it turns out that the actual situation is different from what was expected. Initiative on the part of the raid commander, and of the individual raid elements, will be critical when the plan turns out to be inappropriate.

Aftermath

After a raid, whether successful or unsuccessful, the Resistance must identify "lessons learned." What went well, what went wrong, what could have been done better? What equipment worked, what didn't work, and why? What additional information would have been important or useful? Every raid should be looked upon as an opportunity to improve the Resistance's capabilities. It should be remembered that the government forces will also be looking at "lessons learned." If there were any weaknesses in the raiding party's tactics that the target defenders failed to exploit, be sure that next time the government forces will be ready to exploit them. It is important to recognize and correct these weaknesses before the government takes advantage of them.

In some cases it may be appropriate for the Resistance to exploit the raid for public information purposes. Descriptions of torture by government agents, photos of torture equipment or torture chambers, captured documents that would embarrass the government, and even descriptions of the success of the raid itself, can be used to further the cause of the Resistance. The fact of a successful raid itself can encourage the rest of the citizenry by illustrating that the government is vulnerable. If it can be done without compromising important information, the Resistance should be prepared to exploit the raid through press releases, Web sites, "underground" newspapers, and any other means available.

As noted in the chapter on training, if at all possible, the raiding party should video the operation. The resulting tape or DVD can be used to train other raiding parties. It should also be used for critiques, to learn what went well and what went wrong.

Government Counter-Action

Many of the preparatory steps for the raid (intelligence gathering, pre-positioning weapons) must take place in the vicinity of the target. This gives the government intelligence-gathering agencies an opportunity to anticipate the raid by observing these preparatory steps. The Resistance must do everything possible to keep these preparatory steps from being recognized for what they are. To the extent that information can be obtained before the Resistance "goes active," the risk of being observed decreases. However, information several months old may no longer be valid. While preparation is important, the Resistance units must recognize that preparation also gives the government an opportunity to anticipate raids.

References

Balor, Paul, *Manual of the Mercenary Soldier*, Boulder, CO, Paladin Press, 1988.

Jalali, Ali Ahmed & Lester W. Grau, *Afghan Guerrilla Warfare*, MBI Publishing, St. Paul, MN, 2001. ISBN 0-7603-1322-9.

Lonsdale, Mark V., *Raids*, Los Angeles, CA, Specialized Tactical Training Unit, 1992.

Lung, Dr. Haha, *Knights of Darkness*, Boulder, CO, Paladin Press, 1998.

Naimark, Michael, "How to ZAP a Camera," http://www.naimark.net/projects/zap/howto.html

Ridge, Tom, A Nation on Alert," *The Wall Street Journal*, August 9, 2004, p. A12.

Chapter 27

Strategic Intelligence

Information on government activities and resources, i.e. "intelligence," is essential to success by the Resistance. George Washington had this to say about intelligence:

> The necessity of procuring good intelligence is apparent & need not be further urged – All that remains for me to add is, that you keep the whole matter as secret as possible. For upon Secrecy, Success depends in Most Enterprises of the kind, and for want of it, they are generally defeated, however well planned & promising a favourable (sic) issue.

While the secret inks and other methods used by Washington may be obsolete today, the need for intelligence remains as vital as it was in Washington's day. The Resistance must organize intelligence gathering and dissemination at least as well as Washington did. As Washington himself noted several times, timeliness is crucial, especially for tactical intelligence. It must be received, validated, and disseminated while it can still be acted on.

For our purposes, Strategic Intelligence is intelligence needed to formulate, update and modify the strategy of the Resistance. Ultimately, the goal of the Resistance is to replace the government with a better one. This may be done by defeating the government's forces in combat. However, that is not the only way. As discussed in an earlier chapter, destroying the legitimacy of the government can work just as well. Strategic intelligence will play a key role in either forceful or peaceful overthrow of a tyrannical government.

Who are the targets?

Determining who or what your intelligence targets are is the first step. Intelligence-gathering resources are limited. They must be focused on the most important targets. Targets include both organizations and people.

The following list is intended to be suggestive. Depending on your circumstances, you may not need to gather intelligence on all these possible targets, or there may be targets that are specific to your circumstances that are not listed here.

The government

No government is completely monolithic. All governments have factions that compete with one another. In some cases the competition is simply among individuals who wish to gain the favor of the top person. In other cases the competition is to impose certain views on the entire government, and then upon the nation. Both types of competition may exist in the same government. It is critical to identify the various factions in the government. These factions represent the "fault lines" in the government that the Resistance might be able to exploit.

The Army

Although the Army part of the government, it is listed separately because it is the part of the government that will be most strenuously opposing the Resistance. Considerable attention should be focused on gaining strategic intelligence about the Army. What is said about the Army applies as well to Navy and Air Force.

Government Auxiliaries

These are groups that are not part of the government, but act for the government. Historical examples include Hitler's Brownshirts, Mussolini's Black Shirts, Mao's Red Guard, Duvalier's *Tonton Macoutes*, and Ahmadinejad's *basiji*. Knowing how they will react to protests or other opposition to the government is important to the strategy of the Resistance.

Pro-Government Elites

This group includes think tanks, newspapers, TV networks, magazines of opinion, universities, and other individuals or groups that provide intellectual or economic support to the government. How much support will they give? Can they be persuaded to be critical of specific government actions or policies?

Pro-Government Mass Organizations

These are organizations that try to gain popular support for the government. Historical examples include the Hitler Youth, Stalin's Young Pioneers, Castro's Union of Communist Pioneers, and Mao's All-China Federation of Youth. How are they indoctrinating their members? What kinds of counter-information could be effective?

Pro-Government Political Parties

These are the political parties that support and take part in the government. What do they want? Why do they support the government? What are their differences with the government?

Large Businesses

One of the first steps of a totalitarian government is to take over large businesses, effectively incorporating them into the government. This is true whether the ideology of the government is socialist, communist, fascist, or some combination. It is important for the Resistance to know the extent to which managers of these companies are really sympathetic with the government.

Labor Unions

Large labor unions will be run by the government, or at least be co-opted by it. They will represent the interests of the government more than the interests of their members. For the most part, they will be sources of warm bodies for pro-government demonstrations, and for "heavies" to disrupt the activities of anti-government organizations. It will be important for the Resistance to know if there are union members who oppose government policies, or who want the unions to adopt more pro-worker stands.

Outside the Government

A totalitarian government tries to encompass all of society. As Benito Mussolini put it, "Everything within the state, nothing outside the state, nothing against the state." Nevertheless, even in totalitarian societies there may still be a shrunken and atrophied private sector, outside the state. These are some of the elements that might still exist outside the state.

Opposition political parties

Even though these are excluded from the government, they may still exist as organized bodies. They may even be allowed to run candidates who have no hope of winning. They may be able to provide moral support to the overt Resistance.

Churches

Even in China, "house churches" still exist outside the churches officially recognized (and controlled) by the Chinese government. Thus even in totalitarian societies, some churches may still operate independently of the government. Whether quietly or vigorously, these churches may speak against government policies they consider immoral.

Fraternal and Common-Interest organizations

These may be either religious or secular. They exist for purely private purposes, having little or no political relationships. Whether they exist for some form of mutual support, or for people sharing a common interest (hobby, sport, etc.), they may exist outside the government. The overt Resistance, by having its members join these organizations, may be able to contact like-minded people.

Small Businesses

These are typically "mom and pop" retail businesses, repair shops, restaurants, and craft workers. They are too small, and too many in number, to be easily incorporated into the State. It may be possible to mobilize them to protest government policies that harm them.

What do you need to know?

You need to gather information about organizations *as organizations*, and about the people in them.

Organizations

For each of the organizations you have decided to target, you need the following information.

Purpose

Why does the organization exist? What is its purpose or function? For government organizations, this is often spelled out in a law or directive that creates the organization and defines its purposes and powers. Private organizations instead may have a constitution, a charter, or some other document that defines their purposes and functions. These documents are the starting points for understanding an organization.

Structure

How is the organization structured? One national or regional level? National organization with local chapters? National organization with specialized branches, each nationwide? If it is only a local organization, from what region does it draw members? Understanding the organizational form is important to understanding how the organization works.

Membership

How do people become members? What are the responsibilities and benefits of members? Are there multiple levels of membership? If so, how do members "move up?" What provisions are there for ejecting members? This information is obviously important if the Resistance wishes to infiltrate an organization. It is also important in understanding how an organization is likely to respond to some external challenge or event.

Leadership

Who are the leaders, at each organizational level? How are leaders selected? Who has the authority to "unselect" a leader at any level? Knowing who the leaders are is important to understanding how an organization will respond to external events, or to internal challenges.

Sources of Funds

Organizations almost always need money to operate, even if for nothing more than to publish a newsletter and maintain a membership roster. How is the organization funded? Dues? Sales of items? External subsidies? It is unlikely that the Resistance will have sufficient funds to "buy" an organization, but knowing sources of funds may help in influencing an organization.

People

Organizations are not machines. It is the people in them who take action, and make them function. Knowing as much as possible about the people can help you formulate and refine your strategy for dealing with the organizations. Here are some of the things you need to know about the people who are your intelligence targets.

Place of Origin/Ethnic Affiliation

The importance of tribal or ethnic affiliation varies from one country to another. Even in countries where tribal or ethnic affiliation is "officially" unimportant, it may still be important to specific individuals. Knowing an individual's place or origin, or ethnic affiliation, may indicate the kind of biases the individual brings with him to his present position. What does he consider "normal" or "appropriate?" With whom is he likely to side in a dispute? For him, who is automatically "one of us?" Who is automatically "one of them?"

Education

Where did they go to school? What did they study? Who were their teachers? What was the general atmosphere of the school, that is, the things taught implicitly rather than formally? Who were their classmates? Who were their friends? What school organizations did they join? Did they hold any offices in class or school organizations? What caliber of student were they? School is one of the ways people in totalitarian governments enter the "old boy network" that runs the country.

Career History

What jobs or positions did they hold? Were specific individuals helpful or vital to them in gaining those jobs or positions? Who were their superiors? Who were their co-workers? Who were their subordinates? With whom did they deal in other organizations? How well were they regarded in those jobs or positions by others in the same organization? As with education, knowing these things helps you "connect the dots" of the "old boy network."

Spouse

Are they married? To whom? What is the spouse's background? To what extent does the spouse influence your target? Is the spouse a worthwhile intelligence target in his/her own right?

Neighbors, Friends, Associates

With whom do they associate apart from the official role that makes them your intelligence target? What is the nature of those associations? Are any of their associates also among your intelligence targets? Can any of their associates provide an entrée to the target, or provide information about the target's thinking?

Religion

Do they adhere to a religion? Which one? How strongly do they adhere to its doctrines, beliefs, and practices? Do they regularly attend a specific church, synagogue, temple, or mosque? Who else among your targets attends there? Do they take an active role, such as choir member, vestryman, etc.?

The purpose of this intelligence is to gain an understanding of the people who occupy important positions in the organizations you have decided are worthwhile targets. What are their connections with people in other organizations? What might their sympathies be? Can they be approached through someone else? What are their strengths, weaknesses, and vulnerabilities? Do they have any "buttons" that can be "pushed" by the Resistance? Answering these questions helps you determine what actions they may take, and how they may be countered.

How do you find out?

There are two classes of sources: open and clandestine. Open sources are those that are available to the general public. Clandestine sources are those that are kept secret from the public, but which you attempt to penetrate. You may have to use both for a specific target.

Open Sources

A common rule of thumb is that eighty percent of strategic intelligence can be obtained from open sources, without resorting to illegal or clandestine methods. This may be more true in open societies than for societies against which resistance is justified, but public sources are still worth exploiting.

Open sources include such things as:

- Newspaper and magazine articles about an individual;
- TV news and commentary programs that mention an individual;
- Mention in books about politics, industry, or other organizations;
- Directories, organization charts, phone books;
- "Who's Who" type publications;
- High school and college yearbooks;
- High school and college alumni publications;
- Articles, essays, books, college theses and speeches by the target individual;
- Internet searches on the individual's name;
- Public records, such as property ownership records, liens on property, property tax assessments, automobile registrations, voting registration, birth and marriage certificates, divorce records, court judgments;
- Membership directories of political organizations and organizations that attempt to influence government action or public opinion

Information from these sources can often be combined to provide a very complete picture of a target individual's background, beliefs, and habits.

Official pronouncements by government officials or by leaders of your target organizations also offer insight into their thinking, and possible future actions. Even if these pronouncements are intended to mislead the public, they provide useful information. The fact that they deny they are planning to do a certain thing means, at the least, that they were thinking about it.

Clandestine Sources

These are sources within the government, or in organizations outside the government. They become sources if they can be convinced to provide information to the Resistance. Levchenko gives the acronym MICE – Money, Ideology, Compromise, Ego as the four weaknesses of an intelligence target, which can be exploited to recruit them. The Resistance is unlikely to have much money for bribes. However, Ideology may be a way to gain the support of some people within an organization. That is, it may be possible to find people who secretly oppose the government, either in general or on specific policies, and who will provide information that helps the Resistance, either covert or overt, to work against those policies. Compromising people, by getting some information that could discredit them, bring shame or disgrace on them, get them fired, or bring retribution from the government, may be an effective means of gaining their cooperation. If there are factions or ethnic splits within an organization, appealing to Ego may be an effective means of getting individuals in one faction to provide information about individuals in another faction.

Regardless of how the Resistance recruits a source, the important thing is to find someone inside an organization who has access to the information desired. These need not be high-level people. People such as secretaries, typists, copy-machine operators, reports and publications clerks, mailroom clerks, document couriers, librarians, archivists, and organizational historians, all may have access to the information wanted by the Resistance. The object is to find the right person, and use one of the weaknesses to recruit him or her.

Tradecraft

Finding the person who has access to the desired information, and recruiting them, is only a small part of the effort. Enabling them to get the information out is just as important. Making an extra copy of a classified document is not sufficient. It is necessary to get the document out of the building despite provisions against such unauthorized removal, and get it into the hands of the Resistance.

Passing the information to the Resistance is often referred to as "tradecraft." There are a number of books in the **References** that deal with this issue. However, it is critical to understand that no book can teach tradecraft. First of all, the tricks keep changing. What worked five years ago may no longer be usable. Tricks such as the "brush pass," or swapping identical-looking briefcases, are by now well known to government counterintelligence agencies. The Resistance will have to develop its own means, drawing on the descriptions in the tradecraft books, but tailored to specific situations.

Part of tradecraft is means for physically removing documents from guarded places without being detected, and turning them over to the Resistance without the transfer being detected. Variations of the methods in the books will have to be devised to fit the specific circumstances of the person appropriating the document, the nature of the precautions against unauthorized removal of documents, and the degree to which the person delivering the document is under observation.

Documents need not always be removed as physical documents. If they are in electronic form, they can be transported on a disk, a thumb drive, or some other recording medium. If they are transported in this form, the same considerations apply as apply to the physical removal and transfer of documents. However, documents removed on disks or thumb drives may be uploaded to the Internet at an Internet Café, thus avoiding the need to physically transfer the document to someone. It may be possible to transmit documents out of controlled areas via the Internet. For instance, there are programs that capture keystrokes and transmit them via the Internet to a location where they are recorded. Copies of documents may be uploaded directly to the Internet. A document, carried out on the hard drive of a laptop computer, may be uploaded via Wi-Fi at an airport or other public place. A document may be photographed using a cell phone, e-mailed to someone, then deleted from the cell phone, all without physically removing anything from the premises. The book by Wallace deals with this type of intelligence removal.

Part of the value of the books in **References** is that they provide ideas you may not have considered. How to tell if you are being followed, how to use dead drops, how to send clandestine messages, etc. are not part of people's everyday thinking. Even if the specific methods in the books are by now too well known to be trusted, they will suggest alternatives that the Resistance can apply to specific cases. They should be read with this thought in mind.

Summary

As discussed in Chapter 4, you need a strategy. Strategic intelligence is intended to gather the information you need to create and refine the strategy by which you intend to replace your government with a better one. It is one of the most crucial activities of the Resistance, and should be given as much in the way of resources and effort as can be spared.

References

Anonymous, *Principles of Tradecraft*, Kansas City, MO, Militia Free Press, 1995.

Balor, Paul, *Manual of the Mercenary Soldier*, Boulder, CO, Paladin Press, 1988.

Dulles, Allen M., *The Craft of Intelligence*, The Lyons Press, 2006 (paperback reprint of hardcover edition)

George, Willis, *Surreptitious Entry*, Boulder, CO, Paladin Press. (available from online booksellers)

Harry, M., *The Muckracker's Manual*, Port Townsend, WA, Loopmanics Unlimited, 1984. (available from online booksellers) (Tells how to obtain information about organizations, mostly from public sources.)

Heidenrich, John G., *The State of Strategic Intelligence*, https://www.cia.gov/library/center-for-the-study-of-intelligence/csi-publications/csi-studies/studies/vol51no2/the-state-of-strategic-intelligence.html

Keegan, John, *Intelligence in War*, New York, Alfred A. Knopf, 2003.

Levchenko, Stanislav, *On the Wrong Side: My Life in the KGB*, McLean, VA, Pergamon-Brassey's, 1988.

Ludwig, Mark Allen, *The Little Black Book of E-Mail Viruses*, American Eagle Publications, Show Low, AZ 2002.

Mack, Jefferson, *Running a Ring of Spies*, Boulder, CO, Paladin Press, 1996.

Polmar, Norman and Thomas B. Allen, *Spy Book*, New York, Random House, 1997

Rapp, Burt, *Deep Cover*, Boulder, CO, Paladin Press, 1989.

School of the Americas, "Handling Sources," available through School of the Americas Watch, http://www.soaw.org/soam.html

VanCook, Jerry, *Going Undercover*, Boulder, CO, Paladin Press, 1996.

Chapter 28

Tactical Intelligence

For our purposes, tactical intelligence is information needed to win a battle, to avoid defeat in a battle, or to determine when a battle is propitious. In short, it is information related to tactical planning and tactical decisions.

What You Need to Know

What you need to know are the answers to the classical questions, Who, Where, What, When, and How. You might also like to know Why, but penetrating the mind of an opponent is difficult at best. You may be lucky enough to discern your opponent's reasons for doing something in advance, but you can't count on it.

Who are they?

In the case of government military forces, this is "order of battle" information. What units? What is the nature of the units: infantry, artillery, mechanized infantry, etc.? Who is in command? In the case of commanders, information on their strengths and weaknesses, gathered as part of strategic intelligence, becomes useful once they are identified as being part of a government unit of interest for tactical purposes.

For other types of units, such as police, building guards, or intelligence services, identity of individuals and the chain of command must be known.

Where are they?

When the Resistance is planning a raid, an ambush, or some other action, it is important to know where government forces are, both the intended targets and those that might intervene. This becomes even more important during a raid, an ambush, or similar action. Is the target really at the intended site of the raid, or moving toward the ambush? Where are possible relief forces? Are they on the move? Where are artillery or air units that might intervene?

What are they doing?

Are government forces moving? From where to where? Are they positioning themselves to defend something, or to attack a Resistance position? Checkpoints? Roadblocks? Cordons for searching an area? A sweep through an area where there is strong support for the Resistance? What is their objective?

When will they do it?

This becomes particularly important if the Resistance believes an attack by government forces is imminent. If the attack is overland, when will it be launched? If an air strike is launched, when will it arrive?

If instead the Resistance is planning some offensive action, information about the target is needed. If the target is a convoy, when will it depart from base? If the target is a specific individual, when will he leave home, office, or other location?

How will they do it?

What means will the government forces use? Movement along a single axis? Multiple columns? Paratroop drop? Helicopter insertion? Boats on a river or canal? Amphibious landing on a beach? Combination of these means? If the target is an individual, how is he traveling?

Obtaining Tactical Intelligence

There are a variety of ways of obtaining tactical intelligence. All means appropriate to a particular tactical situation must be used in conjunction with each other. Some of the possible ways are discussed below.

Scouting

General Nguyen Duc Huy attributed the North Vietnamese Army's successes against American troops to scouting. "We knew the battlefield. . . We knew the mountains; we knew the rivers; we knew so well the terrain. And . . . we watched the Americans very closely. (Adams, p. 39)

The Resistance should know the terrain better than the government forces know it. This includes both rural terrain and urban terrain.

Rural Terrain

This has been the traditional terrain for guerrilla operations. The Resistance forces should know intimately every valley, hill, trail, stream ford, spring, and cave in their area of operations. Detailed knowledge will allow the Resistance forces to conduct ambushes, evade pursuit, and hide from government forces.

Urban Terrain

Resistance forces operating in cities must know the urban terrain intimately. This includes not only streets but also alleys, the multiple exits from large buildings or markets, utility tunnels, sewers, basement entrances, fire escapes, and roofs. This knowledge is essential for preparing ambushes and surprise attacks, and for escape from pursuit.

Probing

Probing an enemy to gather information is not a new idea. For instance, during the Cold War, both US and Russian aircraft would regularly fly near the others' borders, to determine what radars would start transmitting, how long it would take for interceptors to be launched, what frequencies would be used for command and control, etc. All this information was intended for use should an attack ever take place.

Resistance forces can make use of the same idea. The following is a quote from *Soldier of Fortune*, regarding probing attacks made by Iraqi "insurgents."

> At the beginning, they would attack a convoy as a test of Americans reactions. It would look like a stupid attack, with no real meaning except killing Americans, but there was more to it. If you look at 150 times a day at a pattern, they would make hits on Americans in chosen places, to see the reaction of

where the helicopter would come, how much time it would take, how they would evacuate the wounded.

They watched closely how the Americans worked, and then they would compare that with different commanders on their computers. Now they know how to plan. They have first, second, and third attack patterns. They know which base the Americans are going to come out from, and they'll attack them on the way out, and on the way in. (June 2005, p. 53)

Another example is given by Zorpette, who accompanied a team of mine-clearing specialists on a route in Iraq:

After 40 minutes a spotter in one of the vehicles ahead of us sees something in the road and we all stop. It turns out to be a big metal box with two bricks in it and some wires attached – your basic fake IED [Improvised Explosive Device]. Word comes back over the radio and we wait while the Army specialists search for other devices.

Insurgents place dummy IEDs for any of several reasons: to videotape how a route-clearance team deals with an IED so they can refine their methods of attack, for example, or to halt the teams so they can fire rocket-propelled grenades at the vehicles.

A little while later we hear over the radio that just after we left, Iraqi Police stopped a car and detained the five men inside it. They had the standard trappings of IED emplacers: long-range cordless phones (used to trigger the bombs), AK-47 assault rifles, and a digital video camera. It's likely we had been videotaped.

Probes like the fake IED must be planned, and used to gather information about the government response. The Resistance must be creative in identifying the kinds of probes that will gain useful information. Once the information has been gathered, and it must be collated and distributed to the rest of the Resistance. When that is done, probes can be very effective in identifying patterns of governmental activity that can be exploited by the Resistance.

Electronic Intelligence

The Resistance can gather a great deal of information by monitoring government radio communications. Some of these communications may be encrypted, but even these can be provide useful information through "traffic analysis," that is, who talks to whom and when, and what happens afterwards.

When communications are not encrypted, even more information can be obtained. In that same interview with retired Viet Cong Brigadier General Bay Cao, he said:

> We studied your tactics, monitored your radios.
> Americans talked too much on radio. Too much.
> Give us much intelligence. We even knew when your
> B-52 bombing attacks would come. (Hackworth,
> "Why We Lost. . .")

During the Vietnam War, the Viet Cong (VC) and the North Vietnamese Army (NVA) developed signals intelligence to a high degree. Using captured American radio equipment and trained linguists, they "easily extracted intelligence on troop movements, artillery and air strikes, landing zones, perimeter defenses and transport of the wounded." (Zabecki, p. 42) In part, of course, this was possible because the American forces talked "in the clear," allowing the enemy to "read their mail."

In Iraq, Al Qaeda adapted satellite dishes and Internet video software to intercept the video downlinks from US unmanned aircraft (Gorman et. al). This allowed Al Qaeda to determine just what information the US was obtaining from the aircraft. Eventually US video downlinks will be encrypted. However, Resistance forces must be prepared to take advantage of any unencrypted signals used by the government they are opposing.

Whether government radio traffic is encrypted or not, the Resistance must make every effort to listen in and make use of the information gathered. Use of scanners, as described by Schrein, is one good way to intercept government communications, particularly police communications.

Part of tactical intelligence collecting, then, is identifying the frequencies used by various government agencies: military, police, fire, and other emergency services. Since the government military forces may be able to switch to frequencies used by other agencies, the Resistance should also identify frequencies used by highway maintenance, garbage collection, forestry, and any other municipal or regional services.

As with other types of intelligence, probing can be useful in collecting electronic intelligence. This may include things like calling in a fake bomb warning from a public phone, then scanning for frequencies used by government forces.

The Resistance should obtain not only frequencies, but things like unit names and call signs, names of unit commanders, vehicle numbers, and standard codes or "shorthand." This information can be used not only for early warning during operations, but also can be used to call in false information to mislead or misdirect government forces during operations.

Clandestine Information Gathering

In some cases the Resistance will need "inside" information about possible targets for raids or ambushes. This might include physical layout of bases, interior layout of buildings, notice when specific individuals are present in their offices, notice of departure of vehicles, or any other information not obvious from the "outside."

This information must be obtained from people who are legitimately "inside," but who will provide the needed information to the Resistance. They should be people who in a sense are "invisible" to the regular occupants, because they are not part of the regular organization that works there. Such informants would include cleaning people,[130] people servicing vending machines,

---

[130] Even "unclassified" trash can be useful in obtaining names of individuals in the organization, links to other organizations, telephone numbers, organizational codes and symbols, and other "routine" items.

people replacing light bulbs, people making repairs such as electricians and plumbers, utility workers, coffee shop or snack bar attendants, or anyone else who has reason to enter the base or building for some reason other than taking part in its operations. These people may be recruited to provide the information desired by the Resistance. In some cases they may be sympathetic with the Resistance, in which case they may be recruited by appeal to that sympathy. In other cases they may have to be misled as to the reason the information is being requested. The reason for the information should appear legitimate to the person being asked.

The Resistance may establish "front" organizations to provide services to government facilities. In this case the problem will not be recruiting people who are already "inside," but selling services to the government facilities.

However, it is done, this clandestine information gathering is essential for planning raids and ambushes. The Resistance must make plans to infiltrate those facilities where inside information is needed.

Prisoner Interrogation

For the most part the Resistance will not be taking large numbers of prisoners, and will not be holding them for lengthy periods. Most prisoners taken by the Resistance will be taken incidental to some other action. Interrogation will be brief at most, before the prisoners are released.[131] Interrogation should be realistic, in the sense that the questions asked are about things the prisoner should reasonably be expected to know. Identity of unit, names of immediate superiors, opinions of those superiors, where based, length of service, where trained, past operations, planned operations, status of training and morale, any problems with equipment or supply, complaints about equipment deficiencies, and any specific items that the Resistance leadership has determined are important.

---

[131] Killing prisoners is counter-productive. It provides government forces with an incentive to fight to the death, since capture means execution. In addition, it gives individuals among government forces an incentive to mistreat and kill captured members of the Resistance, regardless of what government policy might be regarding captured Resistance members.

The interrogation must be brief, and the interrogators must focus on specific information that the Resistance leadership wants to know. There will not be time for "breaking" a prisoner or gaining detailed information. The interrogation must be completed in time for the capturing Resistance unit to withdraw before it is counter-attacked. Prisoners will not normally be taken along by the withdrawing force. The presence of prisoners hinders the withdrawal, and risks revealing infiltration and exfiltration routes, as well as locations of base camps.

The exception to holding a prisoner for a lengthy period will be high-value individuals intentionally seized in raids. These will be held at a safe house, and may be subjected to lengthy interrogation. This interrogation will be much more detailed than that given ordinary prisoners. The specific nature of the interrogation will depend on the reason for seizing the individual in the first place. However, the methods will remain much the same: try to gain the trust of the prisoner; convince him "you might as well talk; we know it all already;" "prisoner X has already told us this, which makes you look bad; before we publicize it what is your side of the story;" etc. These methods are discussed in the several references on interrogation.

Captured Documents

Some raids are intentionally mounted for the purpose of capturing documents. In other cases documents will be found on prisoners captured during raids, ambushes, or other actions, on dead government soldiers, in vehicles damaged during an ambush or raid, or in fixed positions overrun during an action. The term "documents" is not limited to printed material. FM 34-52 describes captured enemy documents (CEDs) as:

> Any piece of recorded information, regardless of form, obtained from the enemy and that has subsequently come into the hands of a friendly force [in this case, the Resistance]. . . Types of CEDs are typed, handwritten, printed, painted, engraved or

drawn materials;[132] sound or voice recordings; imagery such as videotapes, movies, or photographs; computer storage media including, but not limited to floppy disks and reproductions of any of the items listed above.

Documents may be official or personal. Official documents are of government or military origin. FM 34-52 has a suggestive but not all-inclusive list of official documents:

Overlays, field orders, maps, codes, field manuals, identification cards, reports, sketches, photographs, log books, maintenance records, shipping and packing slips, war and field diaries, and written communications between commands.

Personal documents are described in FM 34-52 as:

Letters, personal diaries, newspapers, photographs, books, magazines, union dues payment books, and political party dues payment books.

Regardless of how they are obtained, captured documents must be processed properly. Nothing must be written on or added to them. They should be tagged with date and time of capture, place where captured, capturing unit, identity of the source (government unit from which captured, if known), and circumstances of capture (prisoner, government dead, damaged vehicle, building or other fixed position). This information should be written on a separate piece of paper attached to the CED. They must be transported to the appropriate intelligence processing unit. The information may be time-sensitive, hence rapid forwarding to intelligence analysts is important.

The "Observer Corps"

One of the strengths of a popular Resistance movement is that is has the support of a significant fraction of the populace. This strength can be capitalized upon by using the people as collectors of

---

[132] Military badges, patches, and other insignia might be engraved or drawn.

tactical intelligence. The idea is not a new one. Here are a few historical examples.

The "Flying Tigers" of WW II utilized Chinese observers to provide warning of Japanese aircraft taking off from airfields in China and approaching targets in Chinese-controlled territory. These observers simply radioed that Japanese aircraft were spotted, giving numbers and headings. This might not have been as good as radar, but it was a lot better than nothing, and allowed the Flying Tigers to be in the air instead of caught on the ground.

During WW II, "coast watchers" on islands in the South Pacific used amateur radio to inform Allied forces of Japanese ship and aircraft movements, and troop locations. These reports enabled Allied forces to anticipate Japanese attacks, and respond to them.[133]

The movie "Blackhawk Down," about an American operation in Mogadishu, Somalia, portrayed children making calls on cell phones, then holding the phones up to catch the sound of American helicopters flying overhead. The point is not whether this actually took place, but that use of cell phones is a practical means of gathering tactical intelligence and transmitting it to Resistance forces. Similar means can be employed to alert Resistance forces of the movement of government forces.

The following is a quotation from *Aviation Week & Space Technology*, Nov. 25, 2002, p. 56.

U.S. communications intelligence specialists . . . detect dozens of wireless telephone calls to Al Qaeda command groups every time an allied unit drives through a village . . . The village-based observer corps is a basic component of the Al Qaeda command and control system that manages a polyglot force that

---

[133] The amateur radio magazine QST, August 2009, p. 20, reported on the activities of one of these coast watchers, Paul Mason, who was awarded the Distinguished Service Cross by U.S. General Douglas MacArthur because of his important services. More information on the coast watchers at
http://www.arrl.org/search/?exp=1&q=VK4XH&x=9&y=12

usually stands well dispersed until they are ready to attack.

The commander that controlled Al Qaeda's reaction to Operation Anaconda [a U.S. attack on Al Qaeda forces in mountainous terrain] early this year [2002], which caused dozens of U.S. casualties, was a veteran of the fighting against the Soviet Union and simultaneously used at least five radio operators and communications channels, each involving one or more languages for each ethnic group involved (Arab, Pakistani, Uzbek, Afghan, etc.). The wireless telephones . . . tied the observer corps (some of whom also monitor aircraft flying out of allied bases) to the Al Qaeda and Taliban combat forces and the overall tactical commander. The system in Afghanistan is efficient enough that Special Operations members say Al Qaeda had a 48-hr. warning of Anaconda.

The validity of the estimate of 48-hour warning is beside the point. The important point is that Al Qaeda forces regularly gained advanced notice of U.S. troop movements through an "observer corps" that simply reported in by cell phone, satellite phone, or similar means when they spotted troops on the move or aircraft taking off.

The following item was reported in *Aviation Week* for May 12, 2003, p. 21.

In a widely reported encounter in Iraq, one Apache [helicopter] was lost to ground fire and almost all the formation were damaged . . . Army officials now believe the Apaches were hit so badly because Iraqi air defense operators knew the helos were coming. "Both the location of our attack aviation assembly areas and the fact that we were moving out of those assembly areas in the attack was announced to the enemy's air defense personnel by an Iraqi observer.". . . The reconnaissance is believed to have been provided by an Iraqi major general who alerted air defense operators using his cellular telephone.[134] In addition, in one town the lights were blinked off and on as the helicopters passed overhead, to alert Iraqi gunners.[135]

In the United States, cell phones and GPS units are being used to warn motorists of speed traps. The process involves signing up for a service that receives information from subscribers, then allows subscribers to download this information into their GPS, or to receive updated via an iPhone or cell phone.[136] However, the Resistance will have more important things to avoid than speed traps: check points, roadblocks, roving patrols, etc. Although the service claims to be worldwide, it may not be available in your country. Other approaches must be used. In any case, cell phones can be an important means of alerting people to these potential traps.

While cell phones can be a valuable tool for passing tactical intelligence, they can also lead the government to the users. Michael Gaddy, a veteran of several wars, gives the following advice:

> Counter measures are simple; never ever keep the phone on, or the battery in [when not using the phone]. Never store numbers in the phone, always use throwaway cell phones and change them often. Set up prearranged talk times, and always talk on the move.
> http://www.lewrockwell.com/gaddy/gaddy61.1.html

The "observer corps" can be especially important in urban operations. Snipers who attack checkpoints, ambush foot patrols, etc., need to know the patterns of operation. When do the patrols come by? When are the checkpoints relieved? Resistance supporters living near the checkpoints, on patrol routes, etc., can provide this information. The Resistance should take full advantage of the

---

[134] The event was also described in Newman, p. 61.

[135] Lumpkin, John J., "Under fire: Army defends choppers' combat role," *Dayton Daily News*, 8/1/04, p. A17.

[136] http://www.phantomalert.com/ for more information. A similar service is Porc411. Go to http://mail.ioerror.us/mailman/listinfo/porcupine-411.

information its urban supporters can provide on the behavior patterns of government forces.

While the means will differ according to circumstances, the Resistance should take advantage of its popular support by organizing and deploying an observer corps, instructing the members on what kinds of information are wanted, and how to report these.[137] It may be useful to distribute pictures of government tanks, trucks, aircraft, artillery, etc., so that the observers can accurately identify what they are seeing.[138] In any case, the observer corps members should report via cell phone, satellite phone, citizens band radio, amateur radio, taxi dispatch radio, e-mail, or whatever means are available, including courier.[139]

Satellite photos

At one time only national governments had access to satellite pictures. However, these are now commercially available. The news media frequently make use of these commercial photos for news reporting purposes.[140]

Satellite photography from commercial sources can be available to Resistance organizations as well as to the news media. Their prices may limit the extent to which the Resistance can obtain

---

[137] On May 23, 1862, General Thomas "Stonewall" Jackson's Confederate forces were approaching Front Royal, Virginia, at that time occupied by Federal forces. A young woman, a Confederate sympathizer, made her way out of the town and informed Jackson's aide, Lt. Henry Douglas, about the strength of the Federal forces. She identified a regiment of infantry, several artillery pieces, and several companies of cavalry. Knowing the exact strength of the Federal forces, Jackson and Ewell were able to capture the town. The key point here is that the young lady correctly identified the numbers and equipment of the defending forces. (Connelly, p. 40).

[138] Keep in mind that possession of these pictures may endanger the members of the observer corps, if the government forces take them as evidence that the holders are aiding the Resistance.

[139] In Afghanistan in the spring of 2008, villagers used cell phones to report to US and Afghan government forces the locations of Taliban safehouses and occupied villages. The same token, people friendly to the Resistance can warn of the approach of government forces.

[140] The article by Brown provides some examples.

them, but they can be a valuable source of information about government installations, for purposes such as planning raids.

In some cases it may be necessary for the Resistance to use "front" organizations outside the home country to purchase these photos, to disguise the fact that the Resistance is gathering information on specific targets, or to bypass restrictions placed on the distribution of these photos. Even if satellite photos can be obtained legally by organizations in the home country of the Resistance, care should be taken not to tip off the government that information is being collected about particular sites.

Google Earth™ and other services offer free or low-cost access to satellite data. These images are not always up-to-date, but for buildings and other fixed structures, this may not matter. The article by Weinberger discusses the use of these sources.

Unmanned Air Vehicles

Unmanned Air Vehicles (UAVs) have been used extensively by various national forces to observe enemy positions. These are essentially oversized model airplanes, with some kind of remote control link and a return link for data (images, etc.). UAVs fly high enough that they are usually invisible from the ground, and their motors are usually not audible from the ground. They can thus provide aerial reconnaissance without being detected.

There is no reason use of UAVs must be limited to government forces. The Resistance can develop and fly its own UAVs to scout targets before a raid, to track government convoys before ambushing them, and to provide additional security for base camps and other facilities.

The means for gathering data from a UAV may be as simple as incorporating a disposable camera in the vehicle,[141] all the way up to including a TV camera. Guidance may vary from remaining within sight of the control point, with visual contact with the UAV,

---

[141] At one time, radio-controlled model airplanes carrying disposable cameras were considered "arms" by the U.S. government and their export was forbidden. Magazine advertisements for them clearly stated the prohibition.

to including a GPS receiver that provides navigation and checkpoint information to the flight control system.

Building a remote control system and video link from a UAV is well within the capabilities of an electronics technician. An example of one such system is given in the article by Shvarzberg. Another one is described by Espinar and Wiese. Building one of these devices is not exactly trivial, but it can be done in a "hobby shop" or garage. The article by Raskin briefly describes how he took a model airplane kit, added a gyroscope for stability, video and still cameras, and a radio link, for under $10,000. The article by Schneider describes use of a commercially available kit for making a radio-controlled model airplane with a video camera. Remember, you don't need to build a UAV that can fly across the ocean. You need only something that can fly over a government installation, position, or convoy, at a distance of a few miles from you.

Network-Centric Warfare

The United States has pioneered in "network-centric warfare." The idea is to shorten the time "from sensor to shooter." Intelligence and reconnaissance data are made available to the lowest levels of the forces through radio links. Text, photos, even video, can be available to the lieutenant or sergeant on patrol via laptop and radio link. If the patrol encounters someone who looks suspicious, they can call up information about whether he has been interrogated before, whether he has been involved in anything before, etc. In short, all the information previously collected by the army can be immediately available to small units.

However, these techniques are not limited to the United States. Totalitarian governments will undoubtedly adopt them as well, for use by their internal security organizations. The cop on the beat will be able to call up photos and fingerprints of people suspected of being part of the Resistance. Security guards will have access to the "modus operandi" of raiders and attackers. Patrols and convoys will have information about ambush methods and tactics, including photos of previous ambush sites along the routes they are taking.

However, there is no reason the Resistance forces cannot adopt the same technology. Radio links, such as cell phones, may be monitored, and in any case give away the location of the user. However, data about a target, including photos, diagrams, GPS locations, etc. can be loaded into a laptop or even a Personal Digital Assistant for use by raid and ambush leaders. Keeping information in electronic form means it can be downloaded quickly to Resistance units undertaking a raid, an ambush, or other operation.

The Resistance should not only be aware of the use of network-centric warfare against it, but should take advantage of technology for its own use.

Information on Government tactics

Units engaged with government forces must collect information about how those forces were deployed, what tactics they used, what strengths and weaknesses were observed, and what counter-tactics were most effective. For instance, the Viet Cong were able to detect and use patterns of behavior of the American forces. In an interview with retired VC Brigadier General Bay Cao, he said:

> Our first step against the U.S. was to get experience (how the U.S. fought). Our second step was to develop tactics to counter your mobility and machines. . . We always knew your plans. You told us. First come your helicopters. Then your air strikes, and then your troops. Our aim was not to stand and fight, but to run away, unless we thought we could win tactically, or as in Tet, we could win a great psychological victory. (Hackworth, "Why We Lost. . .")

As this example indicates, information about the response times and tactics of government forces must be collected. One effective way of doing this is after-action reports. Each Resistance fighter in the action must be interviewed to determine what he saw and did.

Fusion

The term "fusion" is used among intelligence specialists to mean that "intelligence from all sources is brought together, correlated and cross-checked." (Budiansky, p. 55) Budiansky describes the activities of George Sharpe, an intelligence chief for the Union forces during the American Civil War (quoting a CIA document), as follows:

He "obtained, collated, analyzed, and provided reports based on scouting, spying behind enemy lines, interrogations, cavalry reconnaissance, balloon observation . . . flag signal and telegraph intercepts, captured Confederate documents and mail, southern newspapers, and intelligence reporting from subordinate military units."

While some of the sources used by Sharpe are obsolete, the principle remains the same. No matter what the source, the information must be brought together, evaluated, then promptly provided to the unit commanders who can make use of it.

A regular army, with a chain of command reaching from the individual soldier up to the chief executive of the country, may find it easier to set up a centralized agency to collect, process and distribute intelligence. Nevertheless, the Resistance, despite being less centralized, must find ways of collecting, processing and distributing intelligence. The key point is recognizing the need for this capability. Once the need is recognized, means can be devised that fit the specific circumstances of the Resistance.

Intelligence Processing

The information gathered by the means discussed above will be of little use if it doesn't get distributed throughout the Resistance. This shouldn't mean some centralized intelligence processing system, into which everything must pass before it goes out again. It does mean that some system must be set up to distribute intelligence, from whatever source, to all Resistance units that can make use of it. This system should be designed to be robust, so that it can't be damaged by an attack on a single point.

While the Resistance may not set up a central organization to receive and distribute intelligence, it must set up a central organization that receives all the tactical intelligence gathered by individual units. This central organization must examine the intelligence for consistency, for patterns, for behavior of individual government commanders, for exploitable weaknesses of government equipment, and anything else that can only be derived from looking at a large amount of data. The point is, information should go directly to those who can use it immediately, but it should *also* go to an element of the Resistance charged with collating information from multiple sources and identifying patterns of government behavior.

Summary

Tactical intelligence is critical to successful combat operations. Going into combat without it amounts to operating blindly. Good tactical intelligence comes from using all available sources, and combining the discrete bits of intelligence to discern patterns.

References

Adams, William L., "Conversations With the NVA," *Vietnam*, October 2005, pp. 37 – 40.

Alexander, Matthew, *How To Break A Terrorist*, New York, Free Press, 2008, ISBN 978-1-61523-244-4/

Anonymous, *Agents Handbook of Black Bag Operations*, El Dorado, AR, Desert Publications, 1991.

Anonymous, *Interrogation: Techniques and Tricks to Secure Evidence*, Boulder, CO, Paladin Press, 1991.

Benson, Ragnar, *Interviews, Investigations, and Interrogations*, Boulder, CO, Paladin Press, 2000.

Brown, Tim, "Open-Skies Image Analysis," *GeoIntelligence*, Nov/Dec 2003, pp. 40 – 42.

Budianski, Stephen, "America's Unknown Intelligence Czar," *American Heritage*, October 2004, pp. 55 – 63.

Central Intelligence Agency, *Interrogation*, ParaScope, Eugene, OR, 1999.

Connelly, Owen, *On War and Leadership*, Princeton, Princeton U. Press, 2002.

Department of the Army, *Infantry Scouting, Patrolling, and Sniping, FM 21-75, 1944.*

Department of the Army, *Intelligence Interrogation, FM 34-52*, September 1992 (available at http://www.globalsecurity.org/intell/library/policy/army/fm/fm34-52/) and http://www.fas.org/irp/doddir/army/fm34-52.pdf).

Eisenson, Henry L., *Scanners & Secret Frequencies*, San Diego, CA, INDEX, 1994.

Espinar, Vanessa, & Dana Wiese, "Guided to Gather: Toy Plane Upgraded with Telemetry," *GPS World*, February 2006, pp. 32 – 38.

Gorman, Sioghan, Yochi J. Dreanzen, & August Cole, "Insurgents Hack U.S. Drones," *The Wall Street Journal*, December 17, 2009, p. A1(A21)

Hackworth, David, "Why We Lost in 'Nam," *Soldier of Fortune*, December 2005, pp. 32 – 40.

Keegan, John, *Intelligence in War*, New York, Alfred A. Knopf, 2003.

Idriess, Ion L., *The Scout*, Boulder, CO, Paladin Press, 1982.0-375-40053-2

Mack, Jefferson, *Running a Ring of Spies*, Boulder, CO, Paladin Press, 1996.

McColman, John C., *Monitoring the Feds*, Lake Geneva, WI, Tiare Publications, 1996.

McDonald, Patrick, *Make 'Em Talk!*, Boulder, CO, Paladin Press, 1993.

Newman, Bob, *Guerillas in the Mist*, Boulder, CO, Paladin Press, 1997.

Newman, Richard J., "Ambush at Najaf," *Air Force Magazine*, October 2003, pp. 60 – 63.

Raskin, Jeff, "Toy planes can elude Star Wars shield," *Forbes ASAP*, March 25, 2002, p. 13.

Schneider, David, "DIY Eye in the Sky, *IEEE Spectrum*, February, 2010, pp. 20 – 22.

Schrein, Norm, *Emergency Radio*, San Diego, CA, INDEX, 1994.

Shvarzberg, Leonid, "Downlink Telemetry Module," *Circuit Cellar*, issue 185, December 2005, pp. 32 – 39. (See the article for Internet links to complete instructions.)

Von Schrader, Dirk, *Elementary Field Interrogation*, Delta, Ltd., no source given, 1978. (This is essentially a torture manual. Its primary value may be to warn Resistance members of what will be done to them to extract information.)

Weinberger, Sharon, "No Place to Hide," *Discover*, August 2008, pp. 30 – 37.

Zabecki, David T., "These guys are reading our mail," *Vietnam*, February 2009, p. 42.

Zorpette, Glenn, "Bomb Squad Diary," *IEEE Spectrum*, October 2008, pp. 40 – 47.

Chapter 29

Counterintelligence

Counterintelligence is intended to defeat the government's attempts to gather intelligence about the Resistance. It can be divided into three major activities: operational security, deception, and rear area protection.

Operational Security

Operational security means keeping the government from knowing what the Resistance plans to do. Both the overt and the covert organization need to be concerned with operational security. However, the problems in the two organizations are different.

Operational Security: The overt organization

There are four things the overt organization needs to protect or protect against.

The first is the link to the covert organization. This link absolutely must be protected. The government will undoubtedly believe that there is a link, despite the denials of the overt organization. However, the identity of the individuals who provide that link must be protected. Knowledge of their identity within the overt organization must be on a strict "need to know" basis. If a member of the overt organization can carry out his functions without knowing the identity of the link(s), or even that there are such link(s), then he has no need to know. Only those who must actually coordinate actions with the covert organization have a real need to know. No other members of the overt organization even need to know that there are such links.

The second is to assure that no members of the overt organization do anything illegal. That would bring the law down on the overt organization. This means careful education of all members regarding what is and is not consistent with the policies of the overt organization. Anyone who advocates doing anything illegal should be cut off from any further activity in the overt organization.

The third is to avoid actions by members (and especially leaders) that would bring discredit or disgrace on the overt organization. Embezzlement of funds, conduct involving moral turpitude, public statements contrary to organization policy, etc., must be prevented if possible, and corrective action taken if necessary. This means that the overt organization must have some internal controls that will help prevent these unpleasant surprises.

The fourth is protection of plans for actions such as strikes, protests, marches, leafleting campaigns, etc. These are legal, but will have their maximum impact if the government does not know about them ahead of time. However, in many cases it will still be possible to go ahead with them even if the government becomes aware of the plans for them. Hence operational security here is not as important as are the other three matters.

The overt organization is ostensibly a group of people who are not trying to overthrow the government, but only get the government to recognize their rights. In principle, it is open to everyone who shares its stated principles. However, this means the overt group runs the risk of being infiltrated by government agents. In the United States, the federal government makes a practice of infiltrating "anti-war" and other dissident groups.[142] The overt organization must assume that it is a target for infiltrators.

Infiltrators can be divided into three categories. First is the passive infiltrator. He attends meetings, collects literature, takes part in protests and marches, and tries to find out who is who in the organization, but does not take an active role. The second is the pretend activist, who appears to throw himself into the operations of the organization. This type of infiltrator may attempt to take a leadership role: treasurer, membership chairman, or some other position where he has insight into the entire organization. The third type is the *agent provocateur*. This type tries to trick people into making compromising statements, or he tries to talk people into undertaking action that is violent or illegal.

---

[142] More examples can be found at
http://security.resist.ca/personal/informants.shtml

The third type is dangerous, but is actually the easiest to spot. Anyone who starts advocating violence or illegal acts should automatically be banned, and the reasons made plain to the membership. Even if they're not an infiltrator, the organization cannot tolerate them.

The second type is the most dangerous, and is the most difficult to spot.[143] Background checks, as described at http://security.resist.ca/personal/informants2.shtml, can help uncover this type of infiltrator. However, the organization can wreck itself if people start suspecting the most hard-working members of being infiltrators. Hasty accusations should be avoided.

So long as the organization's literature, list of officers, etc., are known to the public, the first type cannot learn much that will hurt the organization. The major concern is that after people get used to them being around, they morph into type two or type three.

In short, the overt organization must protect its link(s) with the covert organization, must assure that its members don't do things to discredit it, and must guard against infiltrators wrecking it.

Operational Security: The covert organization

The covert organization is operating full time in the field, and faces operational security problems that differ from those of the overt organization. The following considerations must be taken into account in achieving operational security.

Infiltrators

The covert organization must guard against infiltrators, just as does the overt organization. However, everything said about infiltrators in the overt organization applies here as well and need not be repeated. The only significant difference is that the infiltrator into the covert organization must find some way to communicate with his superiors in the government, while remaining in the field

---

[143] http://original.antiwar.com/justin/2009/07/30/obamas-secret-police/

with the Resistance. Watching for such attempts at communication is an important way to detect such infiltrators.[144]

Cellular Structure

Depending on circumstances, use a cellular structure for the organization. This will be much easier for urban sabotage and espionage units. It will be virtually impossible for full-time fighting units.

The idea is that the organization consists of small groups. The members of each group know other members and their leader. They do not know any other members or leaders. The leader knows a leader at the next level up, but does not know anything about adjacent groups at the same level. The leader at the next level up may know only two or three group leaders. This structure limits the damage when the government penetrates one group. However, it becomes very unwieldy. The cellular structure should be used where it makes sense, but not be imposed where it doesn't.

Communications Security

There are two aspects to communications security. First, to prevent the government from knowing the contents of communications. Second, to hide the fact of communications. Radio messages can be encrypted, but the transmission itself gives away the location of the transmitter and the fact that a message was sent. The chapter on Communications covers this in more detail. At this point, suffice it to say that Counterintelligence includes using methods to conceal both the content of a message, and the fact that a message was sent.

Camouflage

The government will use various methods to search out the covert Resistance in the field. These may include satellite images, aerial photographs, infrared images, and radar. If one of these methods gives a hint, the government will follow up with human reconnaissance. The material in the chapter on Camouflage will be useful in helping conceal the presence of the covert Resistance.

---

[144] The fighter who needs to "take leave" to visit a sick wife may be an infiltrator.

Preparing Fighters to Resist Interrogation

It is inevitable that members of the Resistance will be captured. The government may use "aggressive" measures to extract information from these prisoners. However, the Resistance should make every effort to prepare its fighters to resist interrogation. Some of the measures for making government interrogation of prisoners less effective area as follows.

- Do not inform fighters of future operations;
- Do not inform fighters of the unit designations and leaders of other units;
- Use aliases for unit leaders where possible;
- Instruct fighters to remain silent for a given period of time after capture (e.g., one day), so whatever information they eventually give up will be out of date;
- Use plausible cover stories for information given to the fighters, so they cannot reveal the true situation;
- Publicize cases where captured Resistance fighters have been killed or mistreated by the government;
- Make use of a cellular structure to restrict knowledge of personnel and operations.

Deception

Deception has two main goals: to surprise the government, and to provide security for own forces.

Surprise

Surprise involves doing one thing when the government is expecting the Resistance to do something else, or not do anything at all. The action of the Resistance may come as a complete surprise, or the government may realize the true situation only when it is too late to react to it. Key to achieving surprise is concealing the location of Resistance units, not only in camp but when on the move toward some objective. This involves not only passive measures such as camouflage, but active measures to convince the government forces that the Resistance units are somewhere other than where they are, or have some objective other than the real one.

417

Security

Security involves keeping the government forces from knowing the location and identity of Resistance units. That means not only defeating the government's intelligence system by denying it true signals, but spoofing it by providing false signals.

Deception Operations

Whether for surprise or security, a deception operation starts with the commander's objective: "I want the government to think X," where X is something that will lead the government to doing something detrimental to its own objectives. The question then becomes, why should the government think that? The information reaching the government through its normal intelligence channels should be such as to cause them to think X. This means carefully deploying false signals to any of the government's means of gathering information. This might mean lighting apparent cooking fires at a false camp location; sending heavy radio traffic from one location while the true force elsewhere is observing radio silence; or leaking information through a known government informant. The key to a successful deception operation is that the false information must be *consistent* and *plausible*. Conflicting or implausible signals will lead the government intelligence agencies to recognize a deception operation.

Keep in mind that the government will be using not only technical means to gather intelligence on the Resistance, but human intelligence as well. Informants, whether voluntary or coerced, can provide the government with considerable information on the Resistance and its operations. Deception operations should take this into account.

Liberated Area Protection

The overall strategy of the Resistance may call for taking control of certain geographic areas, effectively replacing the government in those areas. Not every Resistance movement needs to do this. The Resistance may be operating in areas where government control never was very strong,[145] or in remote areas that are difficult for the government to reach. In many cases, however, it will be necessary to liberate some territory. This will give the Resistance a more secure base, while denying the government the taxes and supplies it formerly obtained from the area. Moreover, operating from a liberated area will enhance the credibility of the Resistance with potential foreign supporters.[146]

In liberated territory, the Resistance will have to conduct counterintelligence against three groups of people: stay-behind government sympathizers, infiltrators, and raiders.

Stay-Behind Sympathizers

Some of the people in the liberated territory may be sympathetic with the government. This group may include former government officials and their relatives, retirees from the government's military forces, and those with relatives in government-held territory. There may also be "fence-sitters," who wait to see whether the Resistance will be successful, and who can be convinced to take actions favoring the government or hindering the Resistance.

These sympathizers may provide intelligence to the government about the nature and activities of the Resistance, location of bases, identity of leaders, etc. They may even conduct sabotage. The task of the Resistance's counterintelligence activities, with regard to these people, is to identify them, isolate them, and neutralize them. Once they are identified, it may be desirable to provide them with false information as part of the Resistance's deception campaign. If possible, it may be desirable to "turn" them, so they willingly cooperate with a deception operation.

---

[145] An example is the North West Frontier in Pakistan, where the Taliban effectively set up their own government.

[146] During the American Revolution, the French would not provide aid to the Americans until they had demonstrated they could win battles against the British.

Infiltrators

These are people who enter the liberated area clandestinely, with the intent of harming the Resistance in some way (espionage, sabotage, spreading false rumors about the Resistance, etc.). They may be people who formerly lived in the area, and who therefore know the language, the territory, and the social structure, and who have relatives or friends who may cooperate with them. Counterintelligence should be alert for people who suddenly "return" from government territory. If they are legitimate refugees from the government, they may be useful sources of information. However, knowingly or unknowingly, they may be part of a government deception operation. Any information obtained from them should be considered as tentative, until confirmed by independent sources.

In any case, the Resistance's counterintelligence organization must be alert for people who infiltrate the liberated area. They may be genuine refugees, in which case their presence should be welcomed. However, they may be government agents, and this possibility should be investigated.

Raids

The government will undoubtedly attempt to retake liberated territory. However, the concern here is not with military offensives intended to recapture territory, but with temporary incursions by military forces. These raids may be intended to capture or kill Resistance leaders, to destroy important buildings, factories, supply depots and other facilities, or to terrorize the liberated population.

The key to blunting or forestalling such raids is the establishment of an "observer corps" within liberated territory, which can report any suspicious activity such as armed groups moving through, either occupied or abandoned campsites, or evidence of previous passage such as trails or discarded material. The participation of the liberated population is essential in protecting against raids.

Computer Security

The Resistance will inevitably make use of computers, both desktop and laptop. It is almost inevitable that some of these will be captured. Therefore it is essential that information on the hard drives be made secure. This means not only encrypting files you want to keep, but removing traces of internet activity, removing all traces of deleted files,[147] and removing traces of application, such as temporary files from word processors.[148]

Summary

Counterintelligence, to offset the government's intelligence operations, is as important as the Resistance's own intelligence operations. This means specific individuals must be responsible for counterintelligence. Moreover, counterintelligence activities such as deception operations must be integrated into the strategic and tactical plans of the Resistance. This means that the counterintelligence staff must work closely with the Resistance commanders.

References

Alexander, Matthew, *How to Break a Terrorist*, New York, Free Press, 2008, ISBN 978 –1-61523-244-4. (Autobiographical story of how American interrogators in Iraq worked their way up from low-level prisoners to the top man Al Zarqawi. The book will be useful in preparing Resistance members to resist the tricks of interrogators.)

Anonymous, *How To Spot Informants*, Kansas City, MO, Militia Free Press, 1995.

Anonymous, *Interrorgation: The CIA's Secret Manual on Coercive Questioning*, Eugene, OR, ParaScope. (Good information

---

[147] http://www.keepitprivate.com/1/default.aspx?rs2=4637 Commercial software $29.

[148] One program that claims to provide high security for hard drives can be found at http://security.resist.ca/personal/informants2.shtml. Other programs are also available.

on how interrogation is conducted, and can strengthen the defenses of those facing interrogation.)

Department of the Army, *Counterintellingence, FM 34-60,* October 1995. Available for download at http://www.fas.org/irp/doddir/army/fm34-60/.

George, Willis, *Surreptitious Entry,* Boulder, CO, Paladin Press, 1990.

Hinkle, Douglas P., *Mug Shots,* Boulder, CO, Paladin Press, 1990.

McColman, John C., *Monitoring the Feds,* Lake Geneva, WI, Tiare Publications, 1996.

Raimondo, Justin, "Obama's Secret Police," http://original.antiwar.com/justin/2009/07/30/obamas-secret-police/print/

School of the Americas, "Counterintelligence," available through School of the Americas Watch, http://www.soaw.org/article.php?id=58

Zaenglein, Norbert, *Secret Software,* Boulder, CO, Paladin Press, 2000.

Chapter 30

Lives, Fortunes, And Sacred Honor

You have only the rights you are willing to fight for. As Frederick Douglas put it in 1849:

> Power concedes nothing without a demand. It never did, and it never will. Find out just what the people will submit to and you have found out the exact amount of injustice and wrong which will be imposed upon them; and these will continue till they have resisted with either words or blows, or by both. The limits of tyrants are prescribed by the endurance of those whom they suppress."

If you are unwilling to fight for a particular right, you will sooner or later lose it, and probably sooner than later. Even in a free country, each generation must be prepared to fight for its rights all over again, if they hope to pass them on to their children.

This book has been a guide to how to fight for your rights, should it come to that. However, freedom is never free. Before you undertake to fight for your rights, you should contemplate what it might cost.

The signers of the Declaration of Independence pledged "our lives, our fortunes, and our sacred honor" to the cause of American freedom. How did they fare? What happened to them? What did the Revolution cost them? As it turned out, many lost their lives and most lost their fortunes.[149]

Carter Braxton of Virginia, a wealthy planter and trader, saw his ships swept from the seas by the British navy. He sold his home and properties to pay his debts, and died in poverty.

---

[149] Information taken from http://www.ushistory.org/declaration/signers

John Hart was driven from his home by the British shortly after the death of his wife, because of his activity with the Continental Congress. He had to hide out in nearby mountains. His home was looted by the British. He died of illness during the course of the Revolution.

Thomas Heyward, Jr. was captured by the British while commanding a force of militia at the siege of Charleston.

Arthur Middleton was captured by the British when Charleston was captured. He was held prisoner for over a year. Most of his fortune was destroyed.

Lewis Morris suffered the loss of all his property and most of his wealth during the Revolution.

Robert Morris raised funds for supplies for Washington's army, on the basis of his own wealth and credit. He lost 150 ships at sea, depleting most of his fortune and rendering his credit worthless. He died in poverty.

Edward Rutledge was captured during the third British invasion of South Carolina, and was imprisoned for over a year.

Richard Stockton was captured and imprisoned by the British. In prison, he was treated badly and was in poor health when finally released. He died in poverty.

George Walton, as a colonel of militia, was wounded and captured by the British. He was imprisoned for nearly a year until a prisoner exchange took place.

Vandals or British soldiers, or both, looted or burned the properties of Clymer, Ellery, Floyd, Gwinnett, Hall, Heyward, Middleton, Ruttledge, and Walton.

In all, five signers were captured by the British as traitors. Twelve had their homes ransacked and burned. Two lost their sons in the Revolutionary Army, another had two sons captured. Nine of the 56 fought and died from wounds or the hardships of the Revolutionary War.

The experiences of the signers of the Declaration of Independence should not come as a surprise. As Montaigne put it:

> Those who give the first shock to a state are naturally the first to be overwhelmed in its ruin. The fruits of public commotion are seldom enjoyed by the man who was the first to set it a-going; he only troubles the water for another's net.[150]

Despite all the signers suffered, not one defected to the British or went back on his signed pledge. All retained their sacred honor.

Those who contemplate armed resistance to an oppressive government should also contemplate the likely personal cost. However, as with the issue of proportion in Just War doctrine, they must also contemplate the cost of not resisting an oppressive government. The price of freedom is high. The cost of tyranny is even higher. It is worth repeating here the message Winston Churchill had for the British on the eve of World War II:

> "If you will not fight for right when you can easily win without bloodshed; if you will not fight when your victory will be sure and not too costly; you may come to the moment when you will have to fight with all odds against you and only a precarious chance of survival. There may be even a worse fate. You may have to fight when there is no hope of victory, because it is better to perish than to live as slaves."

James Madison spoke of the necessity of the Declaration of Independence as follows:

> "The freemen of America did not wait till usurped power had strengthened itself by exercise, and

---

[150] Edwards, Tryon, *The New Dictionary of Thoughts*, New York, Doubleday & Company, 1974, p. 575.

entangled the question in precedents. They saw all the consequences of the principle, and the avoided the consequences by denying the principle."

In other words, the freemen of America realized where the policies of King George would inevitably lead, and they denied where it would lead by forging the Declaration of Independence leading to the American Revolution and the establishment of the union of the several states.

You have been warned. Freedom is not free, but slavery exacts a far greater price. If the need arises, do not hesitate to take up arms in defense of freedom, even against your own government.

Appendix A

General references

The following books provide general information about the entire scope of armed resistance. They can be used as compact sources of information, but are not as detailed as the books referenced here in specific chapters.

Camper, Frank, *Live to Spend It*, El Dorado, AR, Desert Publications, 1993. (intended for mercenary soldiers, but much useful information)

Irish Republican Army, *Handbook for Volunteers of the Irish Republican Army*, Boulder, CO, Paladin Press, 1985.

Jones, Virgil Carrington, *Gray Ghosts and Rebel Raiders*, McLean, VA, EPM Publications, 1984.

Jones, Virgil Carrington, *Ranger Mosby*, McLean, VA, EPM Publications, 1944.

Keegan, John, *A History of Warfare*, New York, Vintage Books, 1993.

Keegan, John (ed), The *Book of War*, New York, Viking, 1999.

Koch, Thomas, *The Militia Battle Manual*, El Dorado, AR, Desert Publications, 1996.

Wilson, Nolan, *The Minuteman Handbook*, Bowling Green, MO, InfoTech Publications, 1995.

Von Dach, Major H., *Total Resistance*, Boulder, CO, Paladin Press, 1965.

Wade, Norman M., *The Operations and Training SMARTBook*, 2/e, Lakeland, FL, The Lightning Press, 1999. (This book provides a good overview of U.S. Army organization, tactics and doctrine.)

Appendix B

Patrick Henry's Famous Speech

"Mister President, it is natural to man to indulge in the illusions of hope. We are apt to shut our eyes against a painful truth. Is this the part of wise men, engaged in a great and arduous struggle for liberty? Are we disposed to be of the number of those, who, having eyes, see not, and having ears, hear not, the things which so nearly concern their temporal salvation?

"For my part, whatever anguish of spirit it may cost, I am willing to know the whole truth; to know the worst, and to provide for it. I have but one lamp by which my feet are guided; and that is the lamp of experience. I know of no way of judging the future but by the past. Let us not, I beseech you, sir, deceive ourselves longer.

"Sir, we have done everything that could be done to avert the storm which is now coming on. We have petitioned; we have remonstrated; we have supplicated; we have prostrated ourselves before the throne, and have implored its interposition to arrest the tyrannical hands of the ministry and Parliament.

"Our petitions have been slighted; our remonstrances have produced additional violence and insult; our supplications have been disregarded; and we have been spurned, with contempt, from the foot of the throne!

"In vain, after these things, may we indulge in the fond hope of peace and reconciliation. There is no longer any room for hope. If we wish to be free -- if we mean to preserve inviolate those inestimable privileges for which we have been so long contending -- if we mean not basely to abandon the noble struggle in which we have been so long engaged, and which we have pledged ourselves never to abandon, until the glorious object of our contest shall be obtained -- WE MUST FIGHT!

"I repeat it, sir, we must fight! An appeal to arms and to the God of hosts is all that is left us!

"They tell us, sir, that we are weak -- unable to cope with so formidable an adversary. But when shall we be stronger? Will it be the next week or the next year? Will it be when we are totally disarmed, and when a British guard shall be stationed in every house?

"Shall we gather strength by irresolution and inaction? Shall we acquire the means of effectual resistance by lying supinely on our backs and hugging the delusive phantom of hope, until our enemies shall have bound us hand and foot?

"Sir, we are not weak if we make a proper use of those means which the God of nature has placed in our power. Three millions of people armed in the holy cause of liberty, and in such a country as that which we possess, are invincible by any force which our enemy can send against us. Besides, sir, we shall not fight our battles alone. There is a just God who presides over the destinies of nations, and who will raise up friends to fight our battles for us.

"The battle, sir, is not to the strong alone; it is to the vigilant, the active, the brave. Besides, sir, we have no election. If we were base enough to desire it, it is now too late to retire from the contest. There is no retreat but in submission and slavery! Our chains are forged. Their clanking may be heard on the plains of Boston! The war is inevitable -- and let it come!

"I repeat it sir, let it come! It is vain, sir, to extenuate the matter.

"Gentlemen may cry 'peace, peace' -- but there is no peace! The war is actually begun! The next gale that sweeps from the north will bring to our ears the clash of resounding arms! Our brethren are already in the field! Why stand we here idle?

"What is it that gentlemen wish? What would they have? Is life so dear, or peace so sweet as to be purchased at the price of chains and slavery?

"Forbid it, Almighty God - I know not what course others may take; but as for me, give me liberty, or give me death!"

#

Patrick Henry then took his seat. No murmur of applause was heard. The effect was too deep. After the trance of a moment, several members started from their seats. The cry, "To arms!" seemed to quiver on every lip and gleam from every eye.

No written records of this speech exist. The words were so powerful that they were etched into the minds of every man present, who later assisted biographer William Wirt to bring words to paper.

Patrick Henry lived from 1736 to 1799. This speech was given before the Virginia Provincial Convention (assembled after Lord Dunsmore had suspended the Virginia Assembly) which was debating whether to send the militia under arms to defend the colony against the Crown's Government, an act of treason.

In arguments against the Stamp Act of 1765, he said, "If this be treason, let us make the most of it."

Made in the USA
Lexington, KY
03 January 2013